WOMEN
WILL VOTE

WINNING SUFFRAGE
IN NEW YORK STATE

SUSAN GOODIER AND
KAREN PASTORELLO

⌃ **THREE** HILLS

AN IMPRINT OF CORNELL UNIVERSITY PRESS

ITHACA AND LONDON

First published 2017 by Cornell University Press

Printed in the United States of America

Library of Congress Cataloging-in-Publication Data

Names: Goodier, Susan, author. | Pastorello, Karen, author.
Title: Women will vote : winning suffrage in New York State / Susan Goodier and Karen Pastorello.
Description: Ithaca : Cornell University Press, 2017. | Includes bibliographical references and index.
Identifiers: LCCN 2017012369 (print) | LCCN 2017015259 (ebook) | ISBN 9781501713200 (pdf) | ISBN 9781501713194 (ret) | ISBN 9781501705557 (cloth : alk. paper)
Subjects: LCSH: Women—Suffrage—New York (State)—History. | Feminism—New York (State)—History. | Women—Political activity—New York (State)—History.
Classification: LCC JK1911.N7 (ebook) | LCC JK1911.N7 G67 2017 (print) | DDC 324.6/2309747—dc23
LC record available at https://lccn.loc.gov/2017012369

Cornell University Press strives to use environmentally responsible suppliers and materials to the fullest extent possible in the publishing of its books. Such materials include vegetable-based, low-VOC inks and acid-free papers that are recycled, totally chlorine-free, or partly composed of nonwood fibers. For further information, visit our website at cornellpress.cornell.edu.

We dedicate this book to our granddaughters, Mercedes, Julia, Joslyn, Kaylin, Chloe, and Callie, with much love.

Contents

ACKNOWLEDGMENTS

We met because we are both members of the Upstate New York Women's History Organization. Its goal is to encourage and support scholarship and continuing education related to women and gender in upstate New York. We are historians of women's political and labor activism in the nineteenth and early twentieth centuries; much of our scholarship has focused on New York State. During the course of researching and writing *No Votes for Women: The New York State Anti-Suffrage Movement*, Susan began drafting another book on woman suffrage. Then Karen provided the impetus for this project when she suggested that we coauthor a book on the New York State movement. An early discussion with Michael McGandy of Cornell University Press encouraged us to pursue our idea of organizing the book with a focus on groups usually peripheral to the suffrage story. By also laying out the trajectory of the broader state movement, our book, we hope, will motivate the continuing recovery of stories of the many fascinating women (and men) from every hamlet, village, town, and city who devoted energy to the challenge of securing women's voting rights in the state.

Of the many women's historians who have inspired us, two in particular deserve special recognition: Sally Roesch Wagner and Judith Wellman. Generously opening her extensive research files to us, Sally motivates us with her unwavering commitment to women's and Native American history. She urges us to recognize not just the debt we owe to our activist foremothers, but to be aware of the racism and elitism that marred their movement. Similarly, we are greatly indebted to Judy for her research, writing, and mentorship. She and Ann Dexter Gordon presented at the September 2015 Upstate New York Women's History Organization conference in Seneca Falls. Although we were well along in our work by then, Judy profoundly affected us with her suggestions (might we use the word "demands"?) for continuing research into New York women's rights history. Her affirmation, prodding, and pleasure in our work mean a great deal to us. Scholars of women's history everywhere owe a great debt to both Sally and Judy.

Our work is, of course, further informed by those who have written on the suffrage and women's rights movements, as is clear from our bibliography.

But we owe special gratitude to David Kevin McDonald, whose 1987 dissertation informed our work in many important ways. Marguerite Buckman Kearns, the granddaughter of the suffragist Edna Buckman Kearns, welcomed Susan into her home to organize and read her extensive collection of papers documenting her grandmother's suffrage activism in Rockland. In the process, Marguerite has become a valued friend and colleague. In addition, the scholars Jean Baker, Paula Baker, Nancy Cott, Anne Derousie, Ellen Carol DuBois, Laura Free, Julie Gallagher, Susan Lewis, Linda Lumsden, Sandra Moats, Grey Osterud, Carolyn Ostrander, Elisabeth Israels Perry, Shannon Risk, Randi Storch, Rosalyn Terborg-Penn, Lisa Tetrault, and Nancy Unger all have had an influence on our thinking and writing.

As always, the Rochester United States History (RUSH) draft writing group has offered valuable expertise and advice. Alison Parker, who suggested the idea of a draft writing group several years ago, has unfailingly supported our writing and research within and outside the group. In addition, Michael Brown, Tamar Carroll, Jon-Paul Dyson, Peter Eisenstadt, Carol Faulkner, Jenny Lloyd, Rachel Remmell, Mark Rice, Nancy Rosenbloom, and Suzanne Schnittmann, especially, but also other members of the group at one time or another, have helped steer this project forward, chapter by chapter. They never shy away from challenging our ideas and arguments, but they do so in nurturing and energizing ways.

Throughout the writing process, papers presented at both Upstate New York Women's History Organization and Researching New York conferences have offered more opportunities to discuss New York State woman suffrage topics. Special thanks go to Carol Faulkner and Will Walker for their valuable comments on our papers. Our audiences' provocative questions when we have presented on various aspects of our research have inspired us. Talks supported by Humanities New York (formerly the New York Council of the Humanities) on woman suffrage, anti-suffrage, and black women's suffrage activism often elicited suggestions for additional places to look for answers. We both really appreciate the continuing work of members of the various chapters of the League of Women Voters, an organization descended from some of the very organizations we write about here. Right along, we have benefited from the burgeoning interest in woman suffrage on the part of many interested individuals across the state and beyond.

Colleagues and staff at our respective institutions have helped us both directly and indirectly. At Tompkins Cortland Community College, Lolly Carpenter, Bev Carey, Kathleen Boyd, John Conners, Carl Penziul, Rochelle Mike, Susan Cerretani, Kathy McDonough, Jeanne Cameron, Tina Stavenhagen-Helgren, Dave Flaten, and other members of the social sciences department often expressed interest in our work. Librarian Margaret Anderson consistently welcomed our most challenging research questions. She eagerly unearths the most obscure information! We also relied on the assistance of library staff members, including Barbara Kobritz, Lucy Yang, Morgan Howland, and Gregg Kiehl. Members of the History Department at SUNY Oneonta, including and especially the secretary, Dawn Tompkins, have assisted in various ways. Special thanks go Thomas Beal, Danny Noorlander, Bill Simons, and Matthew Henley. Bill Ashbaugh facilitated a much appreciated course reduction, and April Harper helped with obtaining our student research assistants, Amore Swann and Meagan Moore. Andrea Gerberg and her colleagues in the interlibrary loan department located unique sources for us. Brenda Sundall, also of the library, arranged for a large monitor in a library carrel to serve as our office for one vitally important year. We deeply appreciate being able to research, think, problem solve, and write in such supportive environments.

Funding for this project has come from a Margaret Storrs Grierson Scholar-in-Residence Fellowship at the Sophia Smith Collection, a SUNY Institute of Technology United University Professions Individual Development Award, a Bordin-Gillette Researcher Travel Fellowship at the Bentley Historical Library at the University of Michigan, a Jacob Rader Marcus Center fellowship at the American Jewish Archives, a fellowship at the New York Public Library, and a grant from the Gilder-Lehrman Institute of American History. A Library Research Award at the Rare Book and Manuscript Library of Columbia University came at a perfect time. The SUNY Oneonta History Department also provided multiple funding resources for this endeavor.

Judy Wellman and an anonymous reader offered important suggestions to improve our manuscript. Richard Hamm, Judy VanBuskirk, Nancy Dafoe, and especially Vivien Rose, who is tough to please but amazingly generous with her critique, all read a later draft and offered invaluable criticism. Julie Gallagher read the chapter on black women and offered astute comments and suggestions and then read the revised chapter. Jennifer Lemak and Ashley Hopkins-Benton at the New York State Museum asked for brief articles drawing on research we were already engaged in, helping us to think more deeply about those particular topics. Both of them have been very supportive throughout our research and writing process. Michael McGandy, Sara Ferguson, Bethany Wasik, and Julia Cook of Cornell University Press deserve special thanks for their assistance with this book project.

Lots of people in various archives at institutions of higher education have responded thoughtfully to our questions, provided the materials we needed, or shared their knowledge of suffrage sources with us. Amy Hague, Susan Barker, Karen Kukil, and other members of the staff at the Sophia Smith

Collection of Smith College, as always, supported this project. Thai Jones and Pamela Graham helped us with research logistics at Columbia University. At Swarthmore College, Chris Densmore, Pat O'Donnell, Susan Morikawa, and Celia Caust-Ellenbogen of the Friends Historical Library, and Wendy Chmielewski of the Peace Collection, all assisted us in various ways during our research stage. Over the years, Mary Huth and Lori Birrell at Rush Rhees Library at the University of Rochester helped with research there. The staff at the Carl A. Kroch Library, and Patrizia Sione and Barbara Morley at the Kheel Center for Labor-Management Documentation and Archives, both libraries of Cornell University, offered valuable research advice during our visits there.

Other amazing people have helped with this book in ways great and small. At the New York State Library, Nancy Haran, Allan Raney, and Doug O'Connor found the state documents we needed. Jennifer Byrnes of the Rochester Public Library gladly looked up hard-to-find sources for us late one Saturday afternoon and always came through when we called on her. Jim Dierks at the New York Museum of Transportation promptly responded to our questions about trolleys. Shari Gollnitz at the McClurg Museum in Chautauqua County; Sheila Gregoire at the New York State Grange Head-quarters; and Matthew Mac Vitte at the Seward House Museum in Auburn all accommodated our research needs at their respective institutions. Robin Nowell, the historian of the Rochester African Methodist Episcopal Church, shared her knowledge regarding Hester Jeffrey's connection to the commemorative stained glass windows in the church.

Christine Ridarsky and Michelle Finn at the Rochester City Historian's office helped with other questions about Rochester local history. David Ment worked with us at the New York City Municipal Archives; Rose-marie Tucker, the Groton Town Historian, helped with Tompkins County suffragists; and Mindy Leisenring and Tabitha Scofield at the Cortland County Historical Society enthusiastically opened their county suffrage records to us. We also appreciated the efforts of Rod Howe and Donna Eschenbrenner at the History Center; Carol Kammen, the Tompkins County historian; Nancy Assmann at the Cayuga County Historian's Office; Sarah Kozma at the Onondaga Historical Association; Tim Duerden at the Delaware County Historical Association; and Wendy Polhemus-Annibell at the Suffolk County Historical Society. We are as excited by the enthusiasm for suffrage research at the local level as they are.

Many people helped us in our efforts to illustrate the woman suffrage movement in New York State. First and foremost, Bob Kibbee graciously drew on his vast expertise as a cartographer to create two vital and original maps for this book. Ken Florey is always eager to help with identifying and suggesting images. Bob Cooney helped us locate the cover image. Others who assisted us deserve special mention, including Lea Kemp, Sarah LeCount, Kathryn Murano Santos at the Rochester Museum and Science Center; Michael Bloomfield at the National Archives and Records Administration; Amy Hague and Nichole Calero of the Sophia Smith Collection; Nanci Young of the Smith College Archives; Lynn Duchez Bycko, Donna Stewart, and Vern Munson at the Michael Schwartz Library, Cleveland State University; Mark Gaipa at the Modernist Journals Project; Angela Courtney at the Lilly Library of the University of Indiana at Bloomington; Laura Peimer at the Schlesinger Library on the History of Women in America; Kia Campbell, Chamisa Redmond, Tatiana Laracuente, and Tomeka Meon Myers of the Library of Congress; Andrea Felder at the New York Public Library; and Rachel Appel at Bryn Mawr. Kevin Franklin in Colonie sent us several photographs of parades in the Albany area, and Rose Gschwendtner gave us permission to reproduce one of the images in her collection. Patty Van de Bogart and Bob Yavitts at Tompkins Cortland Community College, and Diana Moseman at SUNY Oneonta, assisted with technical needs.

We thank our friends and families for their patience, understanding, unwavering support, and hospitality. We have no idea what we would have done without being able to stay with Alice Siegfried in Oneonta, who always had room for us both. Philione Fried welcomed us to her lovely New York apartment during our research trip to Columbia University. We are grateful to David, Dominique, Chris, Jamie, and Katy. Karen offers special thanks to Jimmy for keeping her grounded in the present despite her tendency to luxuriate in the past. Susan thanks Chris, who unfailingly supported our work, listening as we worked through some of our writing challenges, even when he preferred we engage in some outdoor adventure. Family members Jan, Karen, Dad, Jeremy, Jessica Anne, Jason, Jessica Renée, and Britt always offered their encouragement. And finally, we dedicate this book to our granddaughters, who inherit the promise of justice, equality, and civil and political rights that women activists demanded for all citizens of the United States.

TIMELINE

1827	New York State abolishes slavery
1836	Ernestine L. Rose and Paulina Wright petition New York legislature for women's rights
1846	Six women from Jefferson County petition delegates to the state constitutional convention demanding political rights
1846	New York State Constitutional Convention
1848	New York State bill securing rights of property for married women passes
1848	First local Woman's Rights Convention held in Seneca Falls
1848	Emily Collins founds Women's Equal Rights Club, South Bristol
1849	Emily Collins sends petition with sixty-two signatures asking for women's right to vote to Albany legislature
1851	Elizabeth Cady Stanton and Susan B. Anthony meet in Seneca Falls
1852	Third National Woman's Rights Convention held in Syracuse; Matilda Joslyn Gage and Susan B. Anthony enter movement
1860	Married Women's Property Act expanded
1861	Civil War begins
1863	Woman's National Loyal League founded to demand an end to slavery
1865	Civil War ends
1866	American Equal Rights Association founded to gain universal suffrage
1867	New York State Constitutional Convention adds the word "male" to the definition of a citizen
1868–73	Matilda Joslyn Gage and hundreds of other women vote or attempt to vote
1869	New York State Woman Suffrage Association founded
1869	National Woman Suffrage Association and American Woman Suffrage Association founded

1872	Victoria Woodhull runs for president of the United States on the Equal Rights Party ticket
1872	Susan B. Anthony arrested for voting
1874	Woman's Christian Temperance Union founded
1876	Matilda Joslyn Gage and Susan B. Anthony illegally present Declaration of Rights of Woman at Centennial Celebration in Philadelphia
1876	Woman's Christian Temperance Union endorses woman suffrage
1880	New York women win school suffrage
1881–87	Matilda Joslyn Gage, Elizabeth Cady Stanton, and Susan B. Anthony co-edit *History of Woman Suffrage*
1884, 1888	Belva Lockwood runs for president of the United States on third-party ticket
1886	Protest at the Statue of Liberty's unveiling
Late 1880s	Colored Woman's Equal Suffrage League of Brooklyn founded
1890	National Woman Suffrage Association and American Woman Suffrage Association merge to form the National American Woman Suffrage Association
1893	Gage adopted into the Wolf Clan of the Mohawk Nation, publishes *Woman, Church, and State*
1893	New York State bill giving mothers equal guardianship with the fathers of their children passes
1893	Grange and American Federation of Labor endorse woman suffrage in New York
1894	New York State Constitutional Convention
1895	Elizabeth Cady Stanton publishes *The Woman's Bible*
1895	New York State Association Opposed to Woman Suffrage founded
1901	Woman Taxpayers' Bill passes in New York
1903	Women's Trade Union League of New York organized
1907	Equality League of Self-Supporting Women founded (renamed Women's Political Union in 1910)
1907	College Equal Suffrage League founded
1908	Empire State Federation of Women's Clubs founded as the umbrella organization of New York State African American women's groups
1909	Woman Suffrage Party of New York City founded
1909	Voters' League of Woman Suffrage founded (more commonly known as the Men's League for Woman Suffrage)

1909	Political Equality Association founded
1910	Heterodoxy founded
1911	Wage Earners' League for Woman Suffrage founded
1913	Man-Suffrage Association Opposed to Woman Suffrage founded
1913	New York Wage-Earners' Anti-Suffrage League founded
1913–15	Empire State Campaign
1915	New York State Woman Suffrage Party founded
1915	New York State referendum for woman suffrage fails
1917	United States enters World War I
1917	New York State referendum passes, granting women full suffrage (excludes Native American women)
1917–19	Silent Sentinels, including more than fifty New York women, picket the White House; 168 women serve jail time
1918	House of Representatives passes the woman suffrage amendment
1919	Woman suffrage amendment passes the Senate
1919	Plans made for founding the League of Women Voters
1920	Nineteenth Amendment guaranteeing women the vote is signed into law

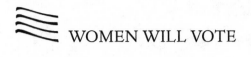 WOMEN WILL VOTE

Introduction
From Ridicule to Referendum

Lillie Devereux Blake of New York, like many other women, resented the exclusion of women from economic and political life but also feared joining the "abused and ridiculed movement" that was woman suffrage in the late 1860s. Despite her fear, she visited the office of the women's rights paper the *Revolution* at its headquarters in the Women's Bureau in Manhattan, where she met Elizabeth Cady Stanton.[1] In Blake's case, after she began lecturing for the woman suffrage movement, all of her relatives but her sister "refused to maintain contact with her" and many of her socially well-connected friends cut her off.[2] Blake's experience was not unique, but it can provide insight into the problems of social as well as political reform. Across the seven decades between 1846, when a few Jefferson County women publicly claimed the right to vote, and the passage of the New York State referendum in 1917, thousands of women—and some resolute men—engaged in the irrepressible fight for woman suffrage.[3] At the end of the campaign, Carrie Chapman Catt celebrated the dedication and sacrifice of countless New York women, both prominent and obscure, who made what she called the "very greatest victory" possible.[4]

The ebb and flow of the woman suffrage movement over those seven decades reflected the dynamic social, economic, and political changes taking place in the national context. The movement crossed class, race, ethnic, gender, and religious boundaries during periods of great upheaval in the United

States. At the same time, the movement itself caused social and political turmoil. With roots in revolutionary rhetoric, nurtured during the antebellum period and abolition, the woman suffrage movement endured throughout the course of westward expansion, the Civil War and Reconstruction, and culminated in the Progressive Era. Each of these historic epochs influenced the manifestation of the woman suffrage movement in New York State, often in dramatic ways. Over time, drawing from a political culture of their own, women suffragists learned to effect change in the greater society. Three generations of New York State women fought a complicated, sometimes frustrating, but ultimately rewarding battle to obtain the right to vote. In the process, women opened for themselves new opportunities in the social and political spheres.

New York, by 1900 the most densely populated state in the nation with 7,268,894 residents, led the United States politically, economically, and culturally.[5] In addition to its diverse and burgeoning population, New York City, with its five boroughs supporting six daily newspapers, ranked as the largest city in the country. Publishers easily disseminated suffrage literature broadly across the state and beyond. At the same time, suffragists collected materials from other state campaigns. With numerous suffrage organizations headquartered in New York City and elsewhere throughout the state, suffragists actively engaged audiences everywhere in their efforts to convince the electorate of women's right to vote. The "most intensively organized State in the Union" by 1915, New York was of particular importance to the final success of the national woman suffrage movement. When, with their vote in the 1917 woman suffrage referendum, the New York male electorate officially recognized the full voting rights of women in the state, the number of representatives in Congress who ostensibly supported a federal amendment increased substantially.[6]

In 1916, New York commanded forty-five electoral votes and forty-three seats in the House of Representatives.[7] It became the first state east of the Mississippi River to recognize women's right to full suffrage (not just presidential suffrage), and it did so by referendum, that is, by a vote of the people, not by a constitutional amendment. Historians of the national suffrage movement suggest that the New York passage marked a pivotal point in the struggle for women's votes because once New York enfranchised its female citizens, the emphasis of the movement shifted away from state-by-state campaigns to the federal campaign.[8] However, the story of the nearly seventy-year New York state-level movement has remained obscure. Most accounts of woman suffrage in New York concentrate on the origin years, leaving the fascinating history of the victory in the Empire State virtually untold.[9]

Exploring the attitudes and activities of women who risked public censure to advocate for suffrage under—as well as outside of—the auspices of the New York State Woman Suffrage Association allows for a more nuanced understanding of the radicalism inherent in women's demand for political rights, the shifting nature of the movement, resistance to women's rights, and the ultimate acceptance of women voting. Through the long decades of the suffrage campaign, New York women could celebrate legislative triumphs, including property rights for married women, shared child custody rights, rights to their own wages, a limited ability for taxpaying women to vote, and school suffrage. Women fought long and hard for each of these rights, and then had to fight to keep them, yet increasingly they met with legislative success. As women gained confidence in their achievements, they adjusted their arguments and tactics to win voting rights in New York. Seasoned activists then helped push the federal amendment through Congress, guaranteeing every woman citizen in the nation the right to vote.

This book highlights the struggles and issues surrounding the attainment of woman suffrage in New York State by diverse groups of women and men. It presents an original treatment of groups not previously considered to any extent by historians and focuses particular attention on upstate New York.[10] This study brings together activists belonging to five disparate groups—rural women, working-class immigrant women, black women, male suffragists, and radical women—all of whom, despite glaring differences, sought the same goal: votes for women. They did not form a single coalition but created a fluid, responsive movement of sometimes incongruent alliances. Occasionally one group made overtures to another for the purpose of collaboration. Yet several of the highlighted groups would have willingly excluded members of the other groups, if necessary, to win their own enfranchisement. Even though they did not formally work together, their concurrent activism was critical to the ultimate success of the woman suffrage movement. Consequently, these groups shaped the complex network that defined the mass movement for women's political rights in New York.

The first chapter details the development of a woman suffrage movement in New York State as it positions the state in the broad historical context of the national woman suffrage movement. Some rural upstate New Yorkers demanded social and political reforms for women well before the Civil War. As a result of controversy sparked by the Fifteenth Amendment, which granted African American men the right to vote, women founded two national organizations and the New York State Woman Suffrage Association. State leaders dominated the movement in terms of strategy and tactics, and several of them rose to national prominence. By the last decade of the nineteenth century, suffragists had come to recognize the importance of fluidity and pliability in addressing their appeals to the broadest possible audiences. The divergent groups advocating for women's enfranchisement disagreed with each other over specific strategies, tactics, and whom to include, but they unfailingly agreed that women needed the vote.

Until the early twentieth century, rural residents made up the majority of the state's population. Chapter 2 demonstrates how rural women in upstate villages and towns, often considered to be apolitical, actually embraced the suffrage spirit, causing a number of pro-suffrage hotbeds to emerge outside of New York City. Many suffrage leaders had deep roots in the towns, villages, and farms of the state. Suffrage discussions and debates sponsored by lyceums, granges, branches of the Woman's Christian Temperance Union, or political equality clubs became a form of entertainment for families, especially during the summer months. Taking advantage of opportunities to participate in the political culture shaped during the transition from an agrarian to a market economy, contingents of rural women helped lay the foundation for a broad-based state suffrage movement. With the broader base of rural women supporting the movement, rural activists could now appeal to husbands and fathers in these areas to garner electoral support. By 1910, leaders shifted campaign tactics from attempting to convince legislators to support suffrage to persuading the (male) electorate to secure a state referendum for women.

Working-class immigrant women, another important but often underestimated group, also contributed to the movement, and they are the central focus of chapter 3. Working-class women touted the vote as a viable solution to wage woes and threatening working conditions. They did not need elite suffragists to empower them; working-class women transferred the speaking and activist skills they had honed in the labor movement to disseminate their suffragist convictions. In addition, many of the women possessed some of the same qualities suffrage leaders valued in their workers; being young and single, they had the freedom to travel the state and the ability to appeal to broad, working-class audiences. They compensated for class tensions by appealing to multi-ethnic voters as Irish, German, Russian, Polish, Jewish, and Italian women joined the suffrage alliance. Chapter 3 illuminates a unique aspect of the coalition while revealing threads of class and ethnic tensions arising in the movement.

Similar to that of immigrant women, the story of black women in the New York State woman suffrage movement, covered in chapter 4, is marked by strained racial relations and exclusionary practices. Virtually every African American women's club in the state advocated for suffrage regardless of the ostensible purpose of the organization. Black women, like white women, saw the vote as a panacea, able to solve their specific problems relating to racial violence, education, employment, and workers' rights. Although white women seldom invited black women to join in their suffrage activities, black women found ways to advance the cause and participate in the movement. Pervasive racism complicated black women's suffrage activism, but it cannot diminish their contributions to mainstream suffragism. Rarely separating women's political rights from other fundamental rights, black women's suffrage activism showed creativity and ingenuity and did not always mirror white women's activist strategies. Black women's influence on black male voters helped secure women's political enfranchisement in New York State.

Chapter 5 shifts attention to men, the only empowered contingent of the suffrage movement. While some men had always voiced support for woman suffrage, no sustained men's organization existed in the state until 1908.[11] That year, Anna Howard Shaw, president of the National American Woman Suffrage Association, encouraged the founding of the Men's League for Woman Suffrage, which then served as an affiliate of the New York State Woman Suffrage Association. These elite white men, often raised or living in suffrage households, risked embarrassment and censure by publicly displaying their support for woman suffrage. As their participation became routine, the novelty of it wore off. These privileged male champions of woman suffrage inspired men of other classes—including urban immigrants and rural, upstate men—to reconsider their suffrage stance. This unique aspect of the suffrage coalition thereby played a lesser but crucial role in winning the vote for women.

Inspirational marketing and pageantry, accompanied by radicalism, helped to modernize and define the public image of the mainstream suffrage movement to attract women as well as men. Chapter 6 chronicles the ways that, following a period of deliberate self-assessment and revision between 1908 and 1910, a new generation of woman suffrage activists revitalized their cause, demonstrating the fluidity and responsiveness of the movement to modernity. As they challenged traditional notions of womanhood, "new woman" suffragists appropriated modern technology, harnessing the power of beauty and imagery to elevate the notion of woman suffrage. They redirected public opinion by making suffrage modern, fashionable, and commonplace. In effect, when radical women enhanced and transformed the popular perception of woman suffrage in the early twentieth century, they coalesced some of the distinctly different suffrage groups as they made the cause both exciting and impossible to ignore.

This cohesion was dramatically interrupted by the outbreak of war in Europe, the subject of chapter 7. Contradictions and upheaval related to the war marred the last three years of the suffrage campaign in New York. Most suffragists and anti-suffragists turned their attention from suffragism to patriotism, war preparedness, or pacifism between August 1914 and April 1917, when the United States entered the war. The movement, which previously faced divisions among members of its rank and file over tactics and strategies related to women's enfranchisement, now divided along new lines of patriotism and militarism. Sensitive to citizenship rights and responsibilities, most suffragists felt compelled to choose a position in response to the war. Nevertheless, they insisted on keeping their campaign before the public, most often linking suffrage with patriotism to highlight their worthiness for full citizenship.

The energies of women suffragists overcame the distractions of war to engage in legislative and political maneuvering in the crucial years between 1915 and 1917, the primary focus of chapter 8. While legislative activities are occasionally mentioned in preceding chapters, suffragists' interactions with elected officials receive more coverage here. Rural, immigrant, and black women rarely had the ability to lobby the state legislature directly. Mainstream suffragists, however, eventually fortified by male supporters, maintained their legislative lobbying efforts throughout the entire movement. Although the suffrage referendum failed in 1915, ever-resilient suffrage activists immediately rallied to analyze their shortcomings, draw on extensive experience, and systematically target male politicians and voters. After decades of disappointment on the part of suffragists, New York men finally acknowledged women's inherent right to the franchise with their own votes. In effect, chapter 8 challenges the prevalent idea that the right of women to vote came as a consequence of their war work, arguing instead that almost seventy years of women's tenacious efforts culminated in 1917 with the New York suffrage campaign victory.

This study places New York State at the forefront of the movement in the eastern United States. Its success had a profound effect on the national movement. Therefore this book concludes by exploring the ways that suffragists used their enfranchisement to push the Nineteenth Amendment forward. As seems usual for suffragists, there is no one path activists followed. Some women, radicalized by their efforts in New York State, joined the militant National Woman's Party and picketed the White House. Others took their organizing skills, including canvassing and lobbying, to campaigns in non-suffrage states. The activism of the disparate groups that comprised the successful state suffrage movement infused the national campaign for woman suffrage with newfound energy.

 CHAPTER 1

Tenuous Ties

Creating a Woman Suffrage Movement in New York State

In September 1852, at the Woman's Rights Convention in Syracuse, twenty-six-year-old Matilda Joslyn Gage clasped the hand of her five-year-old daughter and asked the chair's permission to speak. In her first public speech, Gage boldly articulated principles she would expound upon her entire life: "I do not know what all the women want, but I do know what I want myself, and that is, what men are most unwilling to grant; the right to vote. That includes all other rights. I want to go into the Legislative Hall, sit on the Judicial Bench, and fill the Executive Chair."[1] She made an indelible impression on both Susan B. Anthony and the chair of the meeting, Lucretia Mott. Her visionary ideas surely stirred her audience.

Gage was the daughter of reform-minded and progressive parents, and her Fayetteville home served as a station on the Underground Railroad. Gage's connection to the abolition movement, her patriotic commitment to the Civil War (1861–1865), and her membership in the American Equal Rights Association informed her commitment to citizenship rights for women, a relationship common to many early women's rights activists. The impetus for the founding of the New York State Woman Suffrage Association came directly from Gage. She and other New York suffragists pushed past women's traditional boundaries to try to block political candidates who refused to support women's rights, including the right to vote in school elections.[2] Women like Matilda Joslyn Gage inspired the building of a state-level movement for woman suffrage.

Women began agitating for rights long before the Civil War. Ernestine Rose, Paulina Wright (Davis), and Elizabeth Cady Stanton presented petitions to New York State legislative committees in the 1840s seeking to reform the legal status of married women.[3] In 1846, three groups of women, including six women from Depauville in Jefferson County, submitted petitions to delegates considering changes to the state constitution demanding "equal . . . civil and political rights with men."[4] Although the demand for suffrage fell flat, two years later, on April 7, 1848, the governor of New York signed the "Act for the More Effectual Protection of the Property of Married Women" into law.[5] Just one month earlier, forty-four married women in the western counties of Wyoming and Genesee had penned a caustic statement regarding their political rights to the New York State Assembly: "When women are allowed the privileges of rational and acceptable beings, it will be soon enough to expect from them the duties of such." The women maintained that they owed no allegiance to the government since that body deprived them of their political rights.[6] Despite these few isolated instances of women demanding their rights, state and local governing officials only reluctantly granted minor property rights to women.

Gathering Forces for the Suffrage Movement

A few select rights for married women did not satisfy female or male proponents of equal rights in New York State. In 1846, the Unitarian minister Samuel J. May of Syracuse, an abolitionist and friend of many early women's rights activists, asked why "half of the people have a right to govern the whole" and wove calls for equal rights into his sermons. By 1853, his tract "The Rights and Condition of Women" had been broadly disseminated by the nascent women's movement as part of its tract series.[7] John Fine, a judge and, later, a Democratic congressman from St. Lawrence County, argued that women and men had the right to property, voting, and office holding, as he informed his Ogdensburg lyceum audience in 1847.[8]

Meanwhile, five upstate New York women, including Elizabeth Cady Stanton and the Quakers Lucretia Mott, Martha Coffin Wright, Jane Hunt, and Mary Ann M'Clintock, decided to take matters into their own hands. They made plans to hold a women's rights convention in Seneca Falls on July 19 and 20, 1848. Stanton and M'Clintock penned a document based on the Declaration of Independence. The Declaration of Sentiments laid out women's restricted rights pertaining to marriage, guardianship of their children, divorce, wages earned, religion, politics, and taxation without representation. The women issued a call for the two-day convention in Seneca County newspapers and to African American anti-slavery activist Frederick Douglass's Rochester-based *North Star*.[9] The announcement called for women attendees only on the first day in order to afford them the comfort of speaking freely. Elizabeth Cady Stanton read the Declaration twice that first day. The resolutions sought to elevate women's position in legislation, industry, the church, and the public and private spheres. The second time Stanton read the Declaration, she included the eleven resolutions, eliciting discussion from the audience about ways to improve women's lives. Lucretia Mott also spoke on the first day, as did Mary Ann M'Clintock's daughter Elizabeth.[10]

Word about the convention spread, drawing an even larger crowd the second day. James Mott, the husband of Lucretia Mott, presided over the morning meeting as the secretary read the previous day's minutes. Stanton reread the Declaration of Sentiments, which the audience unanimously voted to adopt. The audience then voted separately on each of the resolutions. The lengthy list of "repeated injuries and usurpations on the part of man toward woman" culminated with the ultimatum "that it is the duty of women of this country to secure to themselves their sacred right to the elective franchise."[11] When Stanton introduced the demand for women's right to vote, controversy erupted. Frederick Douglass brilliantly defended Stanton, rescuing the resolution from near defeat. Stanton and others appreciated the irony of the only black man at the convention saving the suffrage plank. Sixty-eight women signed separately from the thirty-two men who affixed their signatures to the document.[12]

The historic resolutions passed at Seneca Falls sparked a series of women's rights conventions and meetings at the local, state, and national levels. Some of the people in attendance at Seneca Falls held a second convention at the Unitarian Church in Rochester the following month, with Abigail Bush presiding. Building on the momentum of the success of the first two conventions, Stanton wrote to the radical Quaker and abolitionist Amy Kirby Post in Rochester, posing the question: "How shall we get possession of what rightfully belongs to us?"[13] The prolonged discussion concerning women's rights and the 1854 petition campaign for increased property rights for women and woman suffrage influenced state-level legislation.[14] By 1860, the New York State legislature passed the Earnings Act, giving married women full rights of contract over their personal, financial, and real property. It also made them joint guardians of their children, with the same inheritance rights as a man if a spouse died intestate.[15] Clearly the men in power began to consider seriously the merit of women's citizenship rights. Women's rights conventions, most often held in New York State, took place annually until the Civil War.

A Divisive War

When war erupted in April 1861, patriotic women's rights activists set aside their personal goals for equality and enfranchisement to show their support for the Union cause. In May 1863, Stanton and Susan B. Anthony, who joined the women's rights movement in 1852, founded the Women's Loyal National League, headquartered at the Cooper Institute in New York City, to petition for hundreds of thousands of signatures and lobby for a constitutional amendment to abolish slavery.[16] Membership in the league offered women their valuable first opportunity to engage in congressional politicking. Their experiences in soldiers' aid and relief societies and in coordinating sanitary fairs during the war enhanced their administrative and collaborative talents.[17] The women honed many of the skills they would use later to win woman suffrage in New York State when they returned to their women's rights activism at the end of the war.[18]

When the Civil War ended in April 1865, legislators set the terms of Union victory with amendments to the Constitution. Discussions relating to a fourteenth amendment suggested adding the word "male" to the definition of a citizen, despite the efforts of women's rights activists. Articulating the sense of betrayal these women suffered, Stanton lamented that "as our constitution now exists, there is nothing to prevent women or Negroes from holding the ballot, but state legislation, but if that word 'male' be inserted as now proposed . . . it will take us a century at least to get it out again."[19] Wendell Phillips, orator, reformer, and a leader in the abolition movement, claimed reluctance to "mix the movements," as he wrote to Stanton in May 1865, because it "would lose for the negro far more than we should gain for the woman."[20] The public resisted recognizing the full citizenship rights of women, although northerners more readily accepted the notion of citizenship for African American men.[21]

The controversy related to a fourteenth amendment spilled over into the first postwar women's rights convention held at Steinway Hall, New York City, in May 1866. The attendees, drawn from the ranks of abolitionists and women's rights activists, prepared an address to Congress to express their interest in universal suffrage. To agitate more effectively toward that goal, Martha Coffin Wright proposed the establishment of a national American Equal Rights Association, with a "human rights platform" guaranteeing universal suffrage.[22] Members of the association also intended to set a precedent for state action at the 1867 constitutional convention in New York by convincing the delegates to strike from the state constitution the words "white male." This would enfranchise all New York State citizens over the age of twenty-one and "make the Empire State the first example of a true republican form of government."[23] Members of the association engaged in lobbying and petition efforts to "remove racial and sexual restrictions" and prevent the insertion of the word "male" into state constitutions as well as the fourteenth amendment.[24]

Women and men, black and white, joined the American Equal Rights Association. Members elected Lucretia Mott as president, and Elizabeth Cady Stanton, Frederick Douglass, and Henry Ward Beecher as vice presidents. Susan B. Anthony and Henry B. Blackwell served as secretaries. Black women who joined the association included the former New York slave Sojourner Truth, the author and social reformer Frances Ellen Watkins Harper, the civil rights and suffrage activist Harriet Forten Purvis, and Louisa Jacobs, the daughter of Harriet Jacobs, the author of *Incidents in the Life of a Slave Girl*.[25] Already, white activists disregarded black women's rights, as Truth asserted in an 1867 speech before the association: "There is a great stir about colored men getting their rights, but not a word about the colored women."[26] Her impassioned plea foreshadowed the shifting divide between black and white women throughout the suffrage movement. Meanwhile, the association's work failed to alter the wording of the Fourteenth Amendment, which the states ratified two years after the founding meeting. Turning its attention away from national debates for the time being, the Equal Rights Association continued state level agitation through lobbying and petitioning.[27]

Their labors did not pay off in New York, where white women as well as black women experienced legislative neglect. Members of the Equal Rights Association had canvassed the state in 1866, inundating members of the legislature and constitutional convention delegates with literature in their efforts to gain support for universal suffrage.[28] Although woman suffrage failed, the delegates did approve suffrage and the elimination of property requirements for black men in 1867. However, voters defeated the proposed change to the state constitution in 1869. In addition to retaining the word "male," thereby keeping women disenfranchised, the state constitution kept large numbers of African American men from voting by demanding stricter property and residency requirements for them.

It would necessitate the ratification of yet another amendment before black men obtained equal voting rights in New York State.[29] Outraged by the power of states to keep black men disenfranchised, Radical Republicans proposed a fifteenth amendment in late 1868. It asserted that voting rights would not be "denied or abridged" by "race, color, or previous condition of servitude."[30] While some suffrage supporters accepted the omission of the word "sex" for the promise of future Republican support for federal action on votes for women, Anthony and Stanton harshly criticized the proposed amendment for its intentional exclusion of women.[31] The passage of the amendment secured voting rights for black men at the federal level and sent women back to the states to argue for themselves. Essentially, the split in ideology between those who supported black men's rights and those who sought universal rights fractured the women's movement for more than two decades. And, with the greater national focus on voting rights, women's rights activists shifted their focus to the singular demand for woman suffrage.[32] The pivotal moment of opportunity failed in the United States, and these national discussions strongly influenced New York State-level legislation.

The historian Sally Roesch Wagner attributes much of the early suffragists' radical vision of women's rights to an "indelible native influence."[33] In addition to reading about Haudenosaunee activities in local papers, early suffragists had sometimes close associations with native women. The Quaker missionary Lucretia Mott traveled to the Seneca Falls Convention after visiting a Seneca settlement at Cattaraugus, where she had witnessed Seneca women's "political, spiritual, social, and economic power." Elizabeth Cady Stanton often encountered Oneida women when she visited her wealthy abolitionist cousin, Gerrit Smith, at his home in Peterboro. In 1893, the Mohawk Nation would adopt Matilda Joslyn Gage into the Wolf Clan, bestowing on her all the voting rights of native women.[34] Although rarely acknowledged in today's suffrage literature, the higher status of native women within their own culture offered an example of the possibilities of increased respect and equality for all women.

Legislative Exclusion Divides New York Suffragists

Women's rights advocates faced virtually insurmountable obstacles as they sought to alter the course male legislators promoted. The situation exploded during the third annual meeting of the American Equal Rights Association at Steinway Hall, New York City, in May 1869, as arguments erupted over the proposed fifteenth amendment. Chaired by Lucretia Mott, the convention hosted speakers who highlighted issues that would divide suffragists for the duration of the movement. Elizabeth Cady Stanton called for a determined effort on the part of the association to push for a sixteenth amendment to enfranchise women; Susan B. Anthony proposed a motion to refuse support for a fifteenth amendment without a sixteenth amendment enfranchising women. Following the defeat of Anthony's motion, Frederick Douglass, among others, promoted the immediate acceptance of black suffrage and a continuation of work for woman suffrage.[35] In spite of calls from the audience for women speakers, according to Anthony's biographer, men "wrested the control of the meeting from the hands of women and managed it to suit themselves."[36] Tempers flared, heated arguments ensued, and the membership as a whole could not find any resolution.

This rupture on Wednesday, May 12, 1869, also marks a major division in the ranks of women's rights activists. That evening, Stanton, Anthony, and representatives from nineteen states met at the offices of the Women's Bureau at 49 East 23rd Street. Elizabeth Stuart Phelps had purchased the building and rented space to women's societies and businesses. One of the few public meeting spaces open for women reform activists, it housed the *Revolution*, a weekly women's rights newspaper published by Stanton and Anthony from 1868 through 1870.[37] They established the National Woman Suffrage Association at the bureau. After a debate, they voted down a proposal to exclude men from the new organization.[38] The most outspoken New York women dominated the national association and worked to gain suffrage rights for women at the federal level. At odds with the national association's strategies, Lucy Stone and her husband, Henry Blackwell, established the Boston-based American Woman Suffrage Association at a convention held in Cleveland, Ohio, in November 1869.[39] The American Woman Suffrage Association supported black suffrage and sought enfranchisement for women on a state-by-state basis rather than at the national level. This lack of cohesion at the national level, lasting for another twenty years, allowed New York suffragists to dominate the national movement.[40]

Establishing the New York State Woman Suffrage Association

Even as they led the nascent but intense national-level suffrage activity, New York State women's rights activists also invested a great deal of effort at the local level. While the story of the national-level woman suffrage movement is one of repeated failure until its ultimate success in 1920, the story of the New York State Woman Suffrage Association, founded in 1869, is one of minor, but repeated, successes. The United States Supreme Court decision in *Minor v. Happersett* in 1875 made it clear that the granting of suffrage rights rested with the states while it denied the concept of national citizenship.[41] The New York women's rights activists Martha Coffin Wright, Matilda Joslyn Gage, and Lillie Devereux Blake always focused on gender issues much

broader than obtaining the right to vote. Women's access to higher education and the professions, property rights in marriage, and gender-based salary differences formed the subjects of their writing as much as did woman
suffrage.[42] New York women continued to expand their rights, building on
the property rights act of 1860, gaining custody rights to their children in the
same year and the right to vote in school board elections in 1880. They also
won the right to vote for, and run for, the office of school commissioner in
1892, the right of women property owners to vote on measures concerning
assessments and tax increases in 1901, the right to vote on tax propositions
in villages and towns in 1913, and the right to full suffrage in 1917.[43] The
state-level achievements made the existence of the New York State Woman
Suffrage Association critical to the strategies, and eventual success, of the
national organization.

Matilda Joslyn Gage called for a convention to establish the New York State
Woman Suffrage Association on July 13 and 14, 1869, at Congress Hall in the
resort town of Saratoga Springs. Prominent reformers such as Amy Post, Martha Coffin Wright, Eliza Wright Osborne, Lydia Strawbridge, Samuel J. May,
Susan B. Anthony, and Lillie Devereaux Blake joined more than one hundred
other interested women and men to discuss woman suffrage in the state.[44]
According to the *Revolution*, the convention to found the New York State association garnered broad attention and support.[45] The secretary recorded its
constitution in a brand new bound minutes book and laid out the directives of
the new organization. Members justified their existence as follows:

> Whereas the denial of the right of the ballot to woman is in direct
> opposition to the genius of our institutions and the Declaration of
> Independence, which says that "all just governments derive their
> power from the consent of the governed," and that taxation without
> representation is base injustice; therefore we the citizens of the State of
> New York, believing that the ballot is the legalized voice of the people
> [and] is the right of every law abiding citizen in the state, do associate
> ourselves together for the purpose of securing it to every woman of
> the state.[46]

By the close of the convention, the women had elected officers, staffed an
advisory council divided by district, gathered commitments from representatives of thirty-three counties, and drawn up a preliminary membership list.[47]
Following the convention, Gage visited central and western counties, including Wayne, Orleans, Niagara, Erie, Genesee, Chemung, Tioga, Tompkins,
and Broome, to help establish auxiliaries of the New York association and
encourage suffrage activism.[48]

Matilda Joslyn Gage founded the New York State Woman Suffrage Association in Saratoga Springs in 1869. One of the primary theorists of the woman's movement, Gage would write *Woman, Church, and State* in 1893 in one of the first attempts to show how organized religion exacerbates injustice and discrimination against women. Image courtesy of Sally Roesch Wagner and the Matilda Joslyn Gage Foundation, Fayetteville, NY.

The association relied on grassroots organization, urging a "county woman suffrage society, auxiliary to the state association; in each town or village a local society, auxiliary to the county."[49] Officers of the state association provided a simple constitution for even small groups of women in rural areas, encouraging them to organize and elect a chair and secretary. Any of the suffrage groups across New York could affiliate with the state association by paying dues of not less than five dollars for a year. They encouraged each group to set aside money for the purchase of books and tracts, which the New York State Woman Suffrage Association could readily supply. Representatives from each county in the state served the state association as vice-presidents.[50] Within a few short years of the founding of the New York State Woman Suffrage Association, nearly every county boasted suffrage groups—often called political equality clubs in the rural areas—as affiliates of the association.

The New York State Woman Suffrage Association held annual conventions at various locations across the state to broaden the appeal of suffrage (see appendix 1).[51] Eager women in the county organizations hosted state conventions and managed meeting logistics. Originally members held meetings in the summer, but in 1874, Matilda Joslyn Gage suggested that they hold them during the cooler weather in the autumn.[52] Although about 800 people attended the founding meeting, various sources reporting on the conventions indicate that annual conventions typically drew between 100 and 150 attendees until suffrage popularity increased after 1890.[53] Members welcomed men such as Samuel J. May at their conventions, but fewer men attended meetings as the century drew to a close.[54] Women came from farms, villages, towns, and cities across the state and met the women who led the movement they had joined. Attending these conventions strengthened networks between women, who took their enthusiasm home with them and shared it with members of their local clubs and communities.

New York suffragists elected Martha Coffin Pelham Wright, Lucretia Mott's younger sister, as their first president. Grace Greenwood, the first female journalist for the New York Times, described Martha Wright as "a woman of strong, constant character, and of rare intellectual culture." Despite a reputed "lifelong fear of public speaking," Wright had presided over anti-slavery and women's rights meetings since before the Civil War.[55] Susan B. Anthony and Matilda Joslyn Gage separately wrote to Wright requesting that she accept the office of president of the state association. For health reasons, she initially turned them down.[56] With continued pressure exerted by her friends, she eventually accepted the office. Disliking dissension of any kind, she consistently encouraged women to unify for "our cause."[57] At Wright's unexpected death on January 4, 1875, Matilda Joslyn Gage stepped in as president for the next year.

Under Gage's tenure, a women's committee formed to appeal to the New York State legislature to amend the state constitution to provide for women's voting rights. The judiciary committee reported adversely on the proposal. Women's rights advocates made similar but ultimately unsuccessful efforts every year thereafter, until 1894. Additionally, three of the state association presidents in the early years also served at the national level.

Their ideas influenced activities at both the state and national levels, often linking their initiatives. They participated in state legislative hearings and, in 1874, asked that women be released from paying taxes until they had the right to vote. Not surprisingly, that bill failed. Other state legislative activities included advocating for the right to vote for the United States president, vice-president, and state officers. Women from other states often attended New York State Woman Suffrage conventions, adding to the potential for broader influence on the part of New York activists.[58]

In 1876, as part of the Philadelphia celebration to commemorate the centennial of the founding of the United States, Gage and Anthony illegally presented the "Declaration of Rights of Woman." Prior to the event, Gage rented office space to prepare for the exposition. She drafted the declaration and procured five tickets for the event to be held in Independence Hall. A congressman from Michigan, Thomas W. Ferry, denied them permission to present the document during the ceremony. Nevertheless, Gage and Anthony interrupted the proceedings and defiantly handed a parchment copy of the declaration to the shocked chairman and left the building, scattering additional copies of the declaration amid the stunned audience. Then they appropriated an empty bandstand outside, and Anthony read the declaration aloud to a predominantly female audience, after which they adjourned to the First Unitarian Church for a five-hour meeting with speeches and music by members of the Hutchinson family of singers.[59]

The New York State Woman Suffrage Association benefited from the unique attributes of its respective leaders and remained stable during the nineteenth century. While the capable Susan B. Anthony functioned as president of the New York State association from 1876 until 1877, her national tours promoting woman suffrage often precluded her from presiding at the annual conventions or from being directly involved with work at the state level.[60] Between 1875 and 1878, Gage frequently represented the state association in Albany, addressing legislative committees, working for a wide variety of women's rights bills, and participating in rallies in New York City.[61] Gage, accompanied by Lillie Devereux Blake and Dr. Clemence S. Lozier, who founded the New York Medical College and Hospital for Women in 1863, the first for women in New York State, addressed the New York State legislature in 1876 on the woman suffrage question. According to the report given at the eighth annual National Woman Suffrage Association convention held in Washington that year, legislators "favorably received" the report, and the press extensively quoted its words.[62]

One of the most inspired examples of direct activism on the part of these women was their attempt to register and vote in various kinds of elections in towns and cities such as in Brooklyn, New York City, Buffalo, Albany, Ithaca, Ogdensburg, Utica, Poughkeepsie, Rochester, Freeville, Canastota, Randolph, and West Winfield.[63] In May 1868, Schenectady women had voted in a local election on the question of erecting waterworks.[64] Gage, like other women's rights activists, took every opportunity to challenge the political barriers women faced. In July 1871, she led nine property-holding women in an attempt to vote in an election to decide on a tax levy.[65] The following month, she justified her reasons for taking part in the action, contending that "it is simply impossible for any person to do as well for another person as that person will do for [herself]. There is no protection quite equal to self-protection."[66] When Rochester authorities arrested Anthony for voting in 1872, Gage heavily supported her, canvassing throughout the state and presenting her speech "The United States on Trial: *Not* Susan B. Anthony."[67] In 1873, the Rochester residents Amy Post and Sarah E. Owen attempted to register to vote in a state election. These experiences highlighted the necessity of a federal amendment to enfranchise women, for a right granted by a state could easily be rescinded.[68]

Winning the Vote in School Elections

From at least 1876, New York suffragists agitated for the right to vote in school elections. Like women of other northeastern states, they argued that women should vote on issues relating to children. In 1877, the state senator from Monroe County, William N. Emerson, proposed legislation that would allow any woman who met the same qualifications required of men to be elected to any office of school administration. Lillie Devereux Blake led a passionate campaign for the passage of this bill during several sessions of the New York State Assembly.[69] Despite an outpouring of support from across the state and in both houses of the legislature, Governor Lucius Robinson vetoed the bill, claiming that because under the Constitution women did not have the "right of suffrage," that deemed them ineligible for "all offices connected with the department of education."[70] Seething over Robinson's opposition to school suffrage, Blake and other members of the New York State Woman Suffrage Association responded to the governor's bid for reelection in 1878 by coordinating the efforts to oppose him. Suffragists wrote letters and published circulars, raised money, and organized a statewide speaking tour.[71] Their efforts may have had some effect, for Robinson's opponent, the suffragist-endorsed Republican candidate Alonzo B. Cornell, won the election. Blake herself won election as president of the New York State Woman Suffrage Association in 1879. Bold, exciting, and sometimes controversial activities characterized her eleven-year tenure.

Blake and other suffragists celebrated when the new governor signed the bill granting New York women the right to vote in school elections on February 15, 1880.[72] Women who met the property and citizenship requirements could vote for "school trustees, district clerk, tax collector and librarian, and . . . on questions of taxation and on all matters" put before the school meetings of the district where they resided. The officers of the New York State Woman Suffrage Association urged women to use this right, seeing it as a "long step toward the end of an old and vast wrong—the total disenfranchisement of a majority of the grown people of the Empire State."[73] Later that year, Matilda Joslyn Gage proudly led 102 women to the polls in Fayetteville, where they helped to elect an all-female school board.[74]

While many women across the state voted in school elections, "hundreds of women in this State were debarred by falsehood and intimidation." People heard "wild statements": the governor had recalled the bill, it did not apply to cities and villages, it had been repealed, or only rich women could vote. Some women faced threats of physical violence at the hands of their husbands if they voted, and men blew smoke in the faces of women who exercised their right in the dirty little room set aside for voting in Port Jervis. Men in Long Island City stoned a woman for encouraging other women to vote. The newspaper in New Brighton threatened women with jail if they attempted to vote.[75] It is a wonder that any women actually voted in school elections under these circumstances. Nevertheless, women realized that they did have some power to affect political decisions and elections.

Testing the Reach of Women's Political Power

Competition, rivalry, and personality conflicts plagued the woman suffrage movement, as they do all movements, in New York as elsewhere. In 1884, in order to cover the city of New York more effectively, Lillie Devereux Blake and Dr. Clemence Lozier created the New York City Woman Suffrage Party. Lozier served as president of a New York City suffrage organization from 1873 to 1886.[76] The existence of these multiple, sometimes competing organizations shows the internal power struggles that sometimes hampered the progression of the suffrage movement. Although Lozier presided for Anthony at the ninth annual meeting of the state association, held at Republican Hall in New York City, the state and city organizations often clashed on issues related to strategy. Blake's outspoken and confrontational tactics made many moderate upstate members uncomfortable.[77]

Religion represented one of the most controversial issues among women's rights activists at every level. Although most meetings opened and closed with prayer, not everyone agreed with the close connection to religious observance. In 1883, at the annual convention held at City Hall in Troy, Gage requested that she be "relieved from her connection" as vice president-at-large because her "actions in the future in relation to certain aspects of the movement might not be approved of by the association." Her colleagues refused to allow her to resign even though *Woman, Church, and State*, Gage's carefully researched *magnum opus* on the history of the oppression of women through the church, could offend some of the more conservative suffragists. When published in 1893, it indeed caused extensive controversy.[78] Gage's thinking aligned with that of Elizabeth Cady Stanton, similarly at work on her *Woman's Bible*, in which she asserts that women would remain oppressed as long as they acquiesced to the power of a secular state dominated by patriarchal theology and obeisant religious orthodoxy.[79]

Some more daring suffragists endeavored to draw attention to women's subservient position in the United States. On October 27, 1886, at a meeting of about sixty members of the New York State Woman Suffrage Association, Matilda Joslyn Gage "predicted that such was man's tyranny and perversity that blood would have to flow in torrents before women could secure their rights," exciting enthusiastic applause. She went on to declare that making "the Statue of Liberty a woman was simply setting up a gigantic lie in the gaze of the nations" and mocks "the dreadful and outrageous slavery" women everywhere endured.[80] The women wrote a resolution stating that the statue "points afresh to the cruelty of woman's present position, since it is proposed to represent Freedom as a majestic female form in a State where not one woman is free."[81]

The very next day, an aroused Lillie Devereux Blake staged a protest over the erection of the Statue of Liberty in New York Harbor. She rented the cheapest cattle barge she could find, which the owner had assured her would be scrubbed clean. The owner, however, did not clean the barge, and some of the women refused to board the boat. Those who did board suffered with the damp day and the general discomfort of the barge. Yet Blake persevered, and with "banners unfurled" they protested the symbolism of the statue and the exclusion of women from political life. Their demonstration drew the attention of reporters, thereby satisfying at least one of the goals of Blake and her supporters. One newspaper falsely reported that the women joined the steamers, tugs, police boats, yachts, and vessels of war to protest their exclusion from the ceremonies that day.[82]

Another effort by the New York State Woman Suffrage Association, to draw attention to the exclusion from official recognition of women's part in historical struggles, came in 1889, when the association held its convention close to ceremonies commemorating the centennial of George Washington's New York City inauguration. Members pointed out "the injustice which, while imposing on them [women] the burdens of sharing in the taxation which pays for the pomp of these ceremonials, denies to them any part in the public proceedings."[83] New York women struggled throughout the movement to enlighten a public that persistently denied them political, social, and economic equality. Many citizens became painfully aware of the hypocrisy of ceremonies celebrating nationalistic events and of the entrenched habit of oppression all women in the United States endured.

Right along, suffragists in New York paid close attention to the laws of their state as they pertained to women, frequently publishing tracts on the topic of women's rights.[84] Heavily involved in legislative work, they wrote forcefully on the "injustice with which [women] are treated by the State, where in point of numbers they are in excess of the men." They argued that women could not choose their rulers or hold civil office and that the state held them amenable to laws they did not help create, taxed them without consent, and treated those of the *femme de pave* class—prostitutes—more harshly than "their peers in vice." In marriage they did not have full legal control of their children, they could not inherit from their children, the husband had control of their common property, a husband could imprison his wife in their home, and a widow did not have the same rights of property a widower held.[85] Some suffragists agreed with Stanton that all issues that infringed on women's rights more broadly must be addressed at the same time as they agitated for the right to vote. Others agreed with Anthony that the suffrage movement should "stay aloof from other reforms."[86] Both ideologies continued to inform the woman suffrage movement.

Suffrage Forces Reunite and Refocus on State Campaigns

In 1887, negotiations between the leaders of the American Woman Suffrage Association and the National Woman Suffrage Association began as the groups sought unification of the suffrage forces that had split in 1869. The impetus for the negotiations came from Susan B. Anthony, who wished to increase membership numbers, and thereby the collective power, of a single national woman suffrage organization. Gage adamantly opposed the merger because it included a strong Woman's Christian Temperance Union contingent, but the vote took place while Gage was visiting her children in South Dakota.[87] She subsequently severed her connection to the new National American Woman Suffrage Association and founded the Woman's National Liberal Union, an organization focused on the continuing separation of church and state. Anthony mollified Elizabeth Cady Stanton, who also opposed the merger, when she requested that Stanton serve as president of the new association.[88]

At the twenty-second convention of the New York State Woman Suffrage Association, held at the Universalist Church in Rochester on December 16 and 17, 1890, members voted to become an auxiliary to the National American Woman Suffrage Association.[89] Following two days of lengthy discussions, members of the state association decided to adopt the constitution of the National American Woman Suffrage Association with only those changes necessary to meet the unique needs of the state association. Without a dissenting voice, members agreed to "abide by the proposed amendments at this session as the State work for the ensuing year really demands such a measure." Anthony presided in place of Blake.[90] As the scholar Eleanor Flexner points out, the joining of the National and American suffrage associations resulted in a focus on state campaigns rather than on the federal campaign the National Woman Suffrage Association had long advocated.[91]

Blake's tenure as president also ended in 1890, and Jean Brooks Greenleaf took the helm of the New York State Woman Suffrage Association. Greenleaf, like increasing numbers of women in the 1890s and beyond, saw the vote as a panacea. She believed, "when woman has the ballot [all] will be made right."[92] Blake continued to be involved at some level of the suffrage movement and in legislative work for women's rights until she became ill in 1906. Blake and Anthony had long disagreed over strategy and long-range goals; Anthony focused far more on obtaining the vote while Blake concerned herself more broadly with women's rights.[93] Blake's work on legislation caused Anthony consternation over the years, as she wrote in 1897 to Mariana W. Chapman during Chapman's tenure as New York State Woman Suffrage Association president. Anthony claimed that Blake "persisted in going before the committees to advocate concurrent resolution as a representative of the Suffrage Association, [although] you and the Legislative Committee would make a public protest against such action; that she was not placed upon the Legislative Committee because the Association did not wish her to represent that body." Furthermore, Anthony continued, "she has usurped authority to act for the State Assoc[iatio]n precisely as she usurped, in her report to the National on every possible question, our National Authority. She needs curb and bit, etc. mightily." Nevertheless, Anthony told Chapman, "I shall leave you who are at the helm to fight the state battle as best you can; I have quite enough to fight the national battle with her."[94]

The situation presented far more than a simple disagreement between women who stood contentedly in the shadows of their fathers, brothers, or husbands and women who wanted to stand beside men as enfranchised

Jean Brooks Greenleaf,
Pres. N. York State W.S.As'n,

Jean Brooks Greenleaf, president of the New York State Woman Suffrage Association from 1890 to 1896, followed the eleven-year presidency of the dynamic Lillie Devereux Blake. New York State held its 1894 Constitutional Convention during Greenleaf's tenure. Her presidency marked a shift to a more conservative state suffrage organization. Image from the Carrie Chapman Catt Papers, courtesy of the Special Collections Department, Bryn Mawr College Library.

equals. The historian Alan Grimes suggests, in his study of the Puritan ethic and woman suffrage, that the "prevailing social and political assumptions" would have to change if women acquired political status.[95] Religious assumptions would also have to adjust. Such drastic and pervasive changes meant a

radical shift in deciding who would hold power, and it took several generations to accept the idea that women might have even the slightest access to
men's power. Suffrage discussions did find audiences outside of Congress,
nationally and in New York State, mostly as a result of the ceaseless work of
state-level leaders, such as Matilda Joslyn Gage and Lillie Devereux Blake, and
other members of the state suffrage organizations. Nevertheless, in general,
the public did not take their ideas seriously; many people thought them pre-
posterous. An editor for *Harper's Weekly* pointed out that the remarks made
during a discussion of the "Woman Suffrage Bill" on the floor of the New
York State Assembly made it clear that the men thought the proposition was
"a mere joke even by many who support it." A commonly cited reason for
the lack of serious support remained the "opposition of women themselves."
The *Harper's* writer posited that nothing prevented women from voting if
they wanted to do so, concluding that women simply did not want to vote.
The article suggested that women themselves should be polled on the topic,
opining that the result would be very instructive.[96] Regardless of the results of
any polls of women, they would not be making the decision about whether or
not they would be franchised; that remained for the men to decide.

 CHAPTER 2

"Ruffling the Somewhat Calm Domain"

Rural Women and Suffrage

In 1914, a female farmer from Delaware County, New York, expressed her indignation when she watched her hired man leave for the polls on Election Day. She told the National American Woman Suffrage Association's County Chair, Jennie O. Curtis [Mrs. Henry White] Cannon: "I own my own farm, set up my own table, pay all the taxes, and my [hired] man goes and does the voting and I stay at home and he votes the way I don't want him to."[1] Many rural women felt similarly frustrated and tried to influence their menfolk as they headed into town for a day at the polls. Family members tended to rally around common causes and usually supported the same candidates. Yet, no matter how politically astute women prided themselves on being, the formal political process excluded nineteenth- and early twentieth-century farm women, as it did all women in New York State.[2] Rural women advocated for suffrage through three separate organizations between 1868 and 1917: granges, the Woman's Christian Temperance Union, and political equality clubs.

Agricultural work dominated and controlled the daily lives of nineteenth-century New Yorkers. Women belonged to families that obliged all their members to contribute to the family economy. Changes in education, crop production methods, communication, markets, transportation systems, and law all affected farming. Rural women bore and raised children, tended gardens, spun and wove wool and flax, made and mended clothes, knit socks and mittens, dipped candles and filled lamps, boiled soap, milked cows, fed and slaughtered animals, hauled water and wood, did laundry, and cleaned, cooked, and preserved foods to last over the winter months. Some bartered eggs or freshly churned butter for the necessities they lacked. Housewives bartered with local merchants, trading handmade items for dry goods, toiletries, and other products. Annual fall markets in rural centers offered customers homemade applesauce and sauerkraut and household wares such as straw brooms, feather pillows, and baskets—all surplus products of farm wives or daughters.[3] Even with long, hard days, women's labor was not as valued as their husbands' work because their efforts more rarely generated income.[4] Industrialization gradually eroded the long-established patterns of rural women's lives.

With the approach of the twentieth century, important transitions played out in farmhouses, small towns, the marketplace, and the wider economic world. Women in the northeast began to purchase soap, lamp kerosene, clothing, and food as merchants reached deep into the countryside. Singer sewing machine salesmen came calling even in the most remote areas.[5] Montgomery Ward and Sears and Roebuck mail order catalogues enticed women to own the latest novelties as they purchased household necessities.[6] The historian Grey Osterud, who studies the lives of upstate women in rural communities in the early twentieth century, maintains that the forces of change had roots in the dynamics of the relationship between countryside and city. As transportation improved, rural dwellers found it easier to make their way into town or to a nearby city to shop, to patronize nickelodeons or saloons, or to attend church.[7]

For most of the years between 1846 and 1920, a welcome respite from the labors of farm work came in church on Sundays, a place that also encouraged benevolent community engagement. Worship services fulfilled the need for religiosity; gatherings that followed provided the opportunities to socialize that so many rural women craved. Descendants of the Christian revivalists who came of age during the so-called "Burned-Over District" heyday of the early 1800s, upstate women formed the majority of membership in virtually every church.[8] By the mid-nineteenth century, New York women who had belonged to ladies' aid societies, attended literary clubs, and coordinated church missions began to graduate to more active reform associations, including abolition, temperance, and diet, dress, and moral reform.[9] Women voluntarily performed benevolent and charity work with remarkable zeal; their participation in the world outside their homes revealed the depths of their political and economic subordination. As the new century approached, women joined temperance societies, granges, and suffrage clubs as they attempted to affect legislation and policies related to women's rights.

Although New York State remained a predominately rural state until the first decades of the twentieth century, it harbored pockets of progressive and liberal-minded citizens, often suffrage supporters. For example, the abundance of resources in Chautauqua County in the southwest corner of the state facilitated its transition to modernity. This agricultural region boasts six lakes and miles of shoreline along Lake Erie. Steamers traveled up and down the waterways while trolleys offered an overland way to reach locations otherwise inaccessible. Railroads running through towns like Fredonia and Jamestown provided quick and easy transportation for farmers' crops and livestock and for travelers headed to points west. In addition to being a transportation hub, the county had become a prosperous dairy and grape-growing region. Adults eager to expand their intellectual and cultural horizons attended lectures sponsored by the renowned Chautauqua Institute. By the late 1880s, Chautauqua County emerged as a locus of rural reform activity, hosting the first grange in the country, the first chapter of the Woman's Christian Temperance Union, and the first formal political equality club.[10]

Rural women in Chautauqua and across upstate New York did not hesitate to articulate their dissatisfaction over their lack of political rights. In fact, a number of women who became prominent suffrage activists had deep rural roots. Born on farms, they spent their childhoods in bucolic communities, or kept house in the country as married women. In short, these daughters, wives, and mothers may have sensed their subordinate political status even as young girls. Some, like Elizabeth Cady Stanton and Susan B. Anthony, dedicated their lives to remedying this situation and became the vanguard of women's rights forces. Others with far less acclaim, like Chautauqua County granger Eliza Gifford and Ithaca Women's Club founder Louisa Riley, led unprecedented fights for social and political rights. Tracing the path of rural women's activism helps to explain the dispersion of suffrage sentiment throughout the state. As they confronted male resistance and social constraints, rural women formed a premier coalition vital to the overall state suffrage movement.

Rural People Talk Suffrage

Word of the suffrage movement spread to the hinterlands through lecturers who targeted upstate towns and villages before and after the Civil War. Susan B. Anthony's talk at Bemis Hall in Canandaigua in 1855 convinced schoolgirl Caroline Cowles Richards that "the world would never go right until the women had just as much right to vote and rule as the men."[11] After the war, in return for their stimulating lectures on the lyceum circuit, speakers expected an audience, fees, and travel expenses. James Redpath, a Boston newspaperman, founded a lecture circuit that attracted a number of women's rights notables, including the charismatic Elizabeth Cady Stanton, the flamboyant Anna Dickinson, and the lovely Lillie Devereux Blake.[12] Tired of women's rights conventions, Stanton, who recognized the circuit as a "great feature of American life," traversed the country for over a decade earning enough money to put two of her sons through Cornell University.[13] Stanton carefully crafted her popular "Our Girls" talk in 1876 around lyceum constraints. In her discussion of raising and socializing girls, Stanton challenged expectations about traditional gender roles, subtly alluding to women's rights but not overtly pushing for suffrage.[14]

Chautauqua Week became a standard early–twentieth-century feature of summer life in upstate towns and villages when Kent Vawler, a Chicago lyceum bureau manager, popularized traveling tent lectures on a variety of topics, including temperance and suffrage. Rural residents, who sometimes associated theater performances with "wickedness and abandon" and often found political rallies distasteful, did not hesitate to attend lectures, regardless of the topic.[15] In many places the lyceum circuit retraced the connections and networks forged by reformers prior to the Civil War. Before the circuit faded away in the 1920s, lecturers helped to win the acceptance of a number of progressive ideas in rural communities, ranging from penny school lunches to woman suffrage. In fact, the lyceum provided one of the earliest forums for suffrage activism.

Granges and Woman Suffrage

Many of the rural women who partook of lyceum lectures in the summer months belonged to granges. In the wake of the Civil War, the federal Commissioner of Agriculture, Oliver Hudson Kelley, founded the Order of Patrons of Husbandry, more commonly known as the Grange, to address farmers' problems, particularly in the devastated South. Kelley, a former Minnesota farmer, belonged to the Freemasons, so he envisioned the organization as a fraternal society with local, county, state, and national levels designed to bring farmers together for mutual support.[16] Kelley's niece Caroline Hull convinced Kelley that women should also play a part in the nascent organization. In 1867, while the Grange was still in the early stages of planning, Agriculture Department employee William Saunders traveled from Washington to Fredonia, New York. Fredonia farmers welcomed the opportunity to ally with an organization that would serve their interests. Chartered on April 16, 1868, Fredonia's Grange Number 1 became the first grange in the country.[17] As was the case in Fredonia, the majority of northeastern granges grew out of preexisting agricultural and horticultural clubs or societies.[18] Granges offered women the possibility of becoming politically active in a mixed organization. The connection between granges and woman suffrage strengthened over time. By 1914, a Delaware County farmer could remark that "most all the farmers' wives want the vote, and any one who says they don't just don't know anything about it."[19] The most ambitious women grangers hoped to advocate for their rights in the world outside their homes. Most granges welcomed women as members, yet the reception women received as well as the latitude they enjoyed within their local organizations depended on the attitude of male leaders and members.[20]

Very early in its history, the Grange became immersed in equal suffrage debates as a consequence of accepting women members and printing literature attesting to women's value to the organization. One of the Grange's first official documents in 1874 called for the "proper appreciation of the abilities and sphere of woman" but it did not specifically mention women's rights. Inclusion of women in grange activities also did not necessarily translate to endorsement of the women's rights movement.[21] Some grangers adhered to the view of married women whose vital civic responsibility lay within the home.[22] By the late nineteenth century, however, most rural residents instead focused on the common interests of women and men who shared the work of sustaining family farms and worked together in their communities, thus challenging the notion of separately defined gender roles.

More people, like the family of Newark Valley dairy farmer Ralph Young, believed that democracy required recognition of women's political voice and would benefit from their participation.[23] Although women shared work with men in farm families, grange members rarely elected women to leadership positions and often restricted them to women's work committees. For women members, nonetheless, the Grange represented an organization where they could voice their support for temperance and suffrage as well as alleviate the monotony of their daily lives, which many believed ruined women's physical and emotional health.[24] Granges did enable women to form bonds of solidarity with other women even as they pursued mutuality with men.[25] Some grange women eventually became outspoken activists.

Rural New Yorkers had been debating political questions concerning women for years when, in 1875, the Ladies' Committee issued a report on women's status in the Grange. The report contained a "guarded call" for equal suffrage that provoked a "flurry" of responses from male grangers opposed to woman suffrage. In one anti-suffrage letter printed in the *Husbandman*, the official organ of the Grange, a writer contended that women would get no benefit from voting. Ella Goodell from Canastota crafted her response by borrowing from the women's Grange initiation statement, which read that woman "was intended by her Creator to be neither the slave, the tyrant, nor the toy of man, but to be his helpmeet, his companion, his equal."[26] One of the Grange's most vocal proponents of women's rights, Goodell reasoned that women's voting rights would ensure the triumph of temperance and that, perhaps even more important, the power of the ballot would benefit overworked farm women. Goodell envisioned that the intrinsic value of suffrage would inspire rural women to read and think, which would in turn equip them to rise above their drudgery to a higher level of woman's sphere.[27]

Eliza Gifford echoed Goodell's propensity for women's rights, going on record as being in "favor of giving the ballot to woman and for prohibition of manufacture and sale of intoxicating liquor."[28] Raised on a farm in Ellicottville, Eliza Cornelia Robinson taught school for seven years prior to her marriage, in 1852, to Walter C. Gifford, a farmer. Eliza Gifford joined Jamestown Grange Number 244 in part because she believed that "the women of the family need the associations the Grange affords them more than the men." Her husband became Master of the New York State Grange in 1873 while Eliza rose to serve as Master of the Subordinate Grange and the Pomona Grange.[29] Eliza Gifford abhorred the double standard of morality as it applied to women. She read voraciously about women's rights but found that even those articles referred to women who protested as "strong-minded" or "Screechers." Gifford allied with suffragists who pushed for equal rights at home, in the church, and in the state. She believed that "humanity can never be capable of its greatest achievements until the wife and mother takes her proper place beside her husband, his co-equal and helpmate."[30]

Gifford, who would eventually serve as the first vice-president of the Jamestown Political Equality Club, emerged as one of New York State's leading woman suffrage advocates. In 1881, she persuaded the New York State Grange to endorse an equal suffrage resolution at its annual convention in Utica. According to one report, Gifford's resolution "was followed up every year by similar work in county, state, and subordinate Granges until it has come to be recognized throughout the state that the Grange is in favor of equality before the law without distinction of sex."[31] The state grange continued to support women's equality and cooperated with the Woman's Christian Temperance Union and the New York State Woman Suffrage Association's suffrage campaign throughout the 1890s. Despite the continued suffrage resolutions and the petitions the Grangers sent to the state legislature in Albany, anti-suffrage views among certain members persisted. In 1891, Eliza Gifford brought the issue to the attention of the national Grange.[32] Grange equal-suffrage advocates rejoiced when the national Grange finally endorsed a resolution supporting equal suffrage for women in 1893.

In 1900, Susan B. Anthony wrote to thank Gifford personally for the petition campaign that she had organized and that Anthony had forwarded to Washington, as well as for the Grange resolution voicing the organization's support for suffrage at the national level. Anthony praised Gifford's ongoing efforts on behalf of women's rights: "If all the men and women of all of the various organizations of the country would but express their opinions as strongly as did the Grangers, our Legislators would soon feel sure of themselves if they voted for Woman suffrage."[33] State suffrage association organizer Harriet May Mills presented the legislators with figures of suffrage supporters that included large numbers of grange members. Women grangers were instrumental throughout the suffrage campaign. In Delaware County, in 1914, for example, the New York State Woman Suffrage Association's Delaware County Chair, Jennie Curtis Cannon, recruited Mrs. Haddow of Arena, with eighteen years of experience as a grange lecturer, for county suffrage work.[34] The granges continued to collaborate with the New York State Woman Suffrage Association until women won the vote.[35]

Suffrage and the Woman's Christian Temperance Union

Like Anthony, many grangers and other rural women cut their suffrage teeth as temperance activists. For upstate women, the issue of temperance ran deep. Alcoholic fathers or husbands often mentally abused or physically harmed their wives and daughters.[36] Isolated rural residents watched as their neighbors or relatives endured harsh treatment at the hands of an addicted family member. Others lived in poverty on failing farms where men squandered money from the sale of crops on alcohol rather than on necessities. Most victims suffered in silence. Alcoholic behavior became especially problematic when men from remote areas drank in town and town residents blamed them for causing trouble.[37]

The most prominent anti-liquor organization, the Sons of Temperance, founded the Daughters of Temperance as an auxiliary in the 1840s. Yet, at their 1852 national convention in Syracuse male leaders instructed "the ladies . . . to listen, not to take part in the proceedings."[38] Resenting women's marginalization in the movement, Anthony led a small contingent of women to found the Woman's New York State Temperance Society, intended to press the legislature to regulate and limit the sale of liquor. Emily Clark of remote LeRoy, in Livingston County, delivered a petition with 28,000 signatures to the legislature in 1852. However, the legislators dismissed the document because women's names accounted for the majority of the signatures.[39] Following this latest rebuff, the temperance society president, Elizabeth Cady Stanton, contended that temperance legislation would become a reality only after men recognized women's right to the ballot. She pressured the group to name woman suffrage as its priority, a controversial mandate. Prompted by a decision to admit men to the society's convention as well as internal dissention over the stance on suffrage, Stanton and Anthony left the organization by 1854.[40]

The first Woman's Christian Temperance Union in the nation came into existence on December 15, 1873, a few days after the Protestant minister and circuit lecturer Dr. Diocletian Lewis delivered an inspirational lecture in Fredonia on his way to Ohio.[41] Lewis employed a strict agenda that attempted to use prayer and persuasion to ban the sale of liquor, close saloons, and stop men from drinking. Women officially organized as the Woman's Christian Temperance Union of Fredonia, with the first statewide convention held in Syracuse the following year. Delegates at the state convention planned to expand their reach to a national level.[42] Members elected Annie Wittenmyer as the first national president and established headquarters in Ohio. While the temperance crusaders' tactics experienced success in the Southern Tier and Finger Lakes regions of New York, some women expressed reluctance at joining an official organization that adhered to a narrow "gospel temperance" platform.[43]

Frances Willard, born in Churchville, near Rochester in Monroe County, had been a supporter of suffrage ever since she, "with a strong ache in [her] heart," and her sister had watched as her father and brother "drove away to vote," leaving the female members of the family behind.[44] After graduating from North Western Female College in Chicago, Willard began a career that eventually landed her a teaching job at Genesee College in upstate New York.[45] Willard joined the Woman's Christian Temperance Union in 1874 as an editor for its official publication, the *Union Signal*. She warned Wittenmyer, no supporter of woman suffrage, that she could not suppress her suffrage views much longer. With a magnetic appeal that approached the zealous evangelical preachers of the day, Willard articulated her commitment to the cause of woman suffrage to a group of Methodists at a temperance camp meeting in the summer of 1876. Her speech attracted the attention of Susan B. Anthony who wrote to offer "a word of cheer," urging Willard to "go forward . . . for Temperance and Virtue's Sake—for Woman's Sake."[46] With the support of her colleagues, Frances Willard began her ascension in the union.

Willard titled her talk to the fourth Woman's Congress in Philadelphia in October 1876 "Home Protection." She warned that in the face of the escalating "rum power," women's power of suffrage became necessary to counter the evils of alcohol.[47] Willard biographer Ruth Bordin asserts that "her message was loud and clear: 'We have carried ballots to men year after year, urging them to vote; but we have made up our minds that it is just as easy for us to vote ourselves.' "[48] The pro-suffrage faction of the Woman's Christian Temperance Union won a decisive victory with Willard's election to the presidency in 1879. Membership numbers burgeoned after Wittenmyer stepped down, and the union became the largest women's organization in the country.[49] The reform goals of temperance and women's rights—goals shaped by women and for women—began to appeal more broadly. Willard's advocacy for the vote as the only means to "ensure proper male behavior" contributed to the organization's growth as the organization contributed to the expansion of woman suffrage support.[50]

Temperance advocacy accompanied suffrage advocacy in rural areas across the state. In each town and village slated for "districting," women crusaders wearing white ribbons in their buttonholes traveled "from house to house, store to store, and office to office" touting the temperance message. Willard instructed the "white ribboners" to make a special effort to enlist the wives and daughters of state legislators. She created a committee to oversee the distribution of petitions and temperance literature throughout the state, targeting "every minister of every church, . . . the president of every temperance organization, and . . . every society in the state." She manipulated legislative lobbying strategies to secure a special committee on temperance rather than working through the Judiciary Committee in Albany where "progressive temperance measures usually die."[51] In 1881, Frances Willard adopted an all-inclusive social justice plank and labelled it the "Do-Everything" policy, thrusting the union further into political action with the creation of a new Suffrage Department.[52] The department conducted state and municipal campaigns for women's votes, often in conjunction with the state suffrage movement, although the New York State Woman's Christian Temperance Union did not formally endorse woman suffrage until 1885.[53]

Until the early 1880s, some national-level union members nominally favored the Republican Party, which generally supported temperance. However, when the Republican administration under James A. Garfield virtually ignored the Woman's Christian Temperance Union, its more progressive members reached out to the Prohibition Party to encourage political action. With a strong upstate presence, the party appealed to rural residents and was welcoming toward women—women served as convention delegates—and the party endorsed woman suffrage.[54] Willard sought support from the Populist Party but experienced rejection.[55] From that point forward, the union leadership shifted away from partisan involvement toward cooperation with suffrage forces to support the passage of a state suffrage amendment.[56] Their frustrating experiences with men encouraged women to work autonomously.

In the 1890s, the New York State Woman's Christian Temperance Union president, Ella Boole, advanced temperance tactics to a new level when she began to encourage workers to go beyond sending petitions to be read at legislative hearings and instead write directly to legislators.[57] She gained a reputation as a skilled lobbyist at hearings in Albany. Her concurrent national-level efforts to have liquor removed from military installations, Indian reservations, and government buildings met with success.[58] In addition to fighting for prohibition, Boole became a tireless advocate for woman suffrage.[59] She forged ties with the New York State Woman Suffrage Association by speaking at annual conventions in New York City, in 1891, and in Brooklyn, in 1893.[60] Temperance leaders initially considered the 1896 passage of the Raines Law—which granted regulation of liquor licenses to the state, placed an excise tax on spirits, wine, and beer, and gave local liquor boards the option to require high license fees, as well as to enact Dry Sundays—a victory.[61] Charlotte Baldridge, a member of the Geneva Political Equality Club, spoke on "Woman's Work in the Woman's Christian Temperance Union" in 1898, praising the organization for "the special link" connecting the two groups. According to Baldridge, the union made it possible for women to "hear the sound of their own voices in assemblies."[62]

Most important, the union managed to forge "a broadly based political movement," one that cast the concerns of women "in terms of a broad vision of the public good," and whose hierarchical structure, derived from Matilda Joslyn Gage's 1869 New York State Suffrage Association plan, became a model for reform.[63] Throughout the movement, the Woman's Christian Temperance Union continued to cooperate with organized suffragists. In December 1909, the New York State Woman Suffrage Association president, Ella Hawley Crossett, joined Boole and a representative from the Federation of Women's Clubs to meet with Governor Charles Evans Hughes in Albany to demand suffrage support, which he would not offer until 1916.[64] While the union advocated a balance of power between women and men based on morals associated with family values rather than on a vision of equality between the sexes, its overtures to men did little to advance the women's cause at this stage.[65]

Emergence of Political Equality Clubs

For the most part, during the last two decades of the nineteenth century, suffrage activism remained concentrated in the central and western counties of the state.[66] Disappointed by the uneven support from male grange members in the late 1880s, and frustrated by the Woman's Christian Temperance

Union's retreat from partisan politics in the late 1890s, rural suffragists organized clubs more intentionally for the purpose of political equality, usually under the auspices of the New York State Woman Suffrage Association.[67] Women's political clubs tended to be upstate, centered in small cities and large towns, but even some tiny villages and hamlets hosted vibrant clubs. Political equality clubs—otherwise referred to as political study clubs, equal suffrage clubs or leagues, or equal franchise leagues—agitated primarily for woman suffrage, but some simultaneously pursued morally-charged campaigns against vices such as alcohol or tobacco.[68] Political equality clubs promoted a variety of activities from collecting signatures for petitions to creating and coordinating bold public events. Rural women, working toward women's right to vote, pushed past conventional boundaries and relied on women-centered networks to become a crucial part of the coalition working to achieve political equality, rights, and autonomy.[69]

In the wake of an inspiring address by the New York State Woman Suffrage Association president, Lillie Devereux Blake, at the opera house in Jamestown, in Chautauqua County, women established one of the first formal political equality clubs in the state. Mary Seymour Hall gave the opening address to a thirteen person "assemblage" at the home of Mrs. Daniel Griswold in 1887. The local Jamestown Political Equality Club inspired the founding of clubs in surrounding communities, such as Kennedy, Mayville, Frewsburg, Ellington, Fredonia, Sinclairville, South Stockton, Gerry, Westfield, Harmony, Kiantone, and Dunkirk.[70] By 1888, these clubs, in conjunction with Pomona and Ross granges, formed the regional Chautauqua County Political Equality Club.[71] New York rural women replicated this pattern in counties across the state.

Innovative leaders, like Dunkirk's Elnora Babcock, helped the county club grow quickly; Babcock convinced the Chautauqua Institute's management to proclaim the one day a year that they devoted to discussions of political rights as Political Equality Day.[72] Suffragists from across the nation sent their leading advocates bearing banners representing their organizations to attend the first Political Equality Day on July 25, 1891. Welcomed by Chancellor John H. Vincent, Susan B. Anthony, Anna Howard Shaw, and Zerelda (called the "Deborah of Temperance," or Deborah, by her colleagues) Wallace each gave sensational addresses that reiterated the history of the movement and encouraged "hard work until women everywhere voted."[73] The crowd, adorned in yellow ribbons and numbering into the thousands, drew coverage by the *New York Times*. The Woman's Christian Temperance Union president, Frances Willard, wrote jubilantly to Anthony: "Dearest Susan, 'I could sing Hallelujah over you and our Anna Howard Shaw and Deborah Wallace.

It was the biggest day Chautauqua ever saw.' "[74] Political Equality Day earned a permanent place on the Institute's calendar.

1894 New York State Constitutional Convention

Political equality club members also sought to affect state legislation. For example, Eliza Gifford's activism in the Jamestown Political Equality Club and the Jamestown Grange provided her with an opportunity to enter politics and lead others. In 1893, while serving as chair of the legislative committee of the Chautauqua County Political Equality Club, she worked through the grange to secure rights for women in the upcoming New York State Constitutional Convention. Gifford and other suffragists encouraged the grange to ask its members to vote for convention delegates who favored equal suffrage. Gifford also petitioned the state legislature to enact a law empowering women to vote for delegates and to vote on an amended constitution. The state grange accepted Gifford's resolutions at its annual meeting, in Ithaca, in February 1893.[75] She led the Grange's Women's Work Committee in undertaking a massive campaign to contact all organizations known to be friendly to woman suffrage. The Republican assemblyman (later New York State attorney general), Egbert E. Woodbury, from Chautauqua, introduced the bill, and Republican James T. Edwards, representing Cattaraugus and Chautauqua, submitted it to the Senate. The bill passed in the Assembly by a vote of 72 to 27 but never made it out of committee in the Senate, so no further action was taken.[76]

Suffragists had high hopes for the approaching 1894 New York State Constitutional Convention. Both Governor David B. Hill (1885–1891) and Governor Roswell P. Flower (1892–1894) recommended that women be allowed to sit as delegates at the upcoming constitutional convention. However, voters nominated only one woman, Jean Brooks Greenleaf, president of the New York State Woman Suffrage Association and Rochester resident. In the meantime, suffragists embarked on a massive campaign to gather support for a suffrage amendment. Beginning in December 1893, a committee worked to distribute "thousands of letters, petition blanks, leaflets, and suffrage literature," and to collect statistics on the women taxpayers in almost 600 cities and towns who, according to suffragists, faced taxation without representation.[77] Locally and nationally prominent suffrage leaders traveled to all corners of the Empire State to speak at mass meetings. Seventy-four-year-old Susan B. Anthony spoke in all sixty counties.[78]

The New York State Constitutional Convention convened on May 8, 1894, to consider revisions to the state constitution. Gideon Tucker, a member of the Convention's suffrage committee, presented the resolution requesting that the word "male" be eliminated from Article II, Section 1 of the state constitution. By the time the sessions opened, woman suffrage workers from the state organization had gathered 5,000 petitions with 332,148 names (about half belonging to women). Approximately fifteen percent of state voters signed the woman suffrage petitions. Five percent of these voters came from the cities of New York, Brooklyn, and Buffalo, as compared to twenty-five percent of voters from upstate.[79] Other groups, including the Woman's Christian Temperance Union, the New York Conference of Friends, granges, labor unions, and multiple religious and secular organizations, as well as private individuals, also submitted petitions and memorials, bringing the total number of signatures to the 600,000 mark.[80] The suffragist and Woman's Christian Temperance Union member Isabel Howland, from Sherwood, south of Auburn, counted, labelled, bundled, and tied each volume of petitions with a wide yellow ribbon. County and organizational representatives dramatically presented their respective volumes to the convention president, the "lordly, aristocratic, wire-pulling" (as Anthony put it) Joseph A. Choate.[81] When Mary Burt, the president of the Woman's Christian Temperance Union, came forward with her voluminous petitions tied in white ribbons, a porter had to be employed to take them down the aisle in a wheelbarrow.[82]

President Choate appointed a committee on woman suffrage. Suffragists did not realize at the time that the majority of the members of this committee actually opposed women's enfranchisement.[83] After suffragists found out that the seventeen-member suffrage committee had been stacked against them, they armed themselves with powerful speeches to argue their position. Susan B. Anthony, president of the National American Woman Suffrage Association, and Jean Brooks Greenleaf spoke on May 24. Throughout the month of June, women representatives from each of the state's senatorial districts filled their five-minute timed allotments with compelling speeches. On June 7, at an evening rally, six women from Brooklyn, including Mariana Chapman and Mary Craigie, argued that although women paid taxes, they were the "political paupers" of the state.[84] At the conclusion of the hearings, the committee wrote a report opposing the removal of the word "male" from the constitution. The report galvanized suffragists to turn out in full force for the weeklong discussions that followed.

On August 15, 1894, Choate's ally, the stanch anti-suffragist Elihu Root, addressed the convention. Root argued that "suffrage would be a loss to women." After all, he continued, if suffrage "means anything, it means entering upon the field of political life[,] and politics is modified war." Root declared that "true government is in the family [where] woman is supreme and woman rules the world."[85] Root's address helped to propel him to the top ranks of the Republican Party hierarchy; eventually he would serve in the administrations of William McKinley and Theodore Roosevelt. As anticipated, the convention vote—98 opposed and 58 for—decided that the question would not be put before voters in a referendum.[86] Greenleaf, who had orchestrated suffrage activities throughout the entire convention, articulated the suffragists' perspective: "In this convention 98 men dared to say that the Freemen of the State should not be allowed to decide whether their wives, mothers, and daughters should be enfranchised or not. There were 58 men constituting a noble minority, who loved justice better than party power, and are willing to risk the latter to sustain the former." According to the suffrage leader, the disappointing loss meant that fewer than a hundred men at the convention had overruled the desire of over a half-million petitioners.[87] The determined president of the Wyoming County Political Equality Club, Ella Hawley Crossett, issued a call to all political equality clubs to "redouble their efforts to create suffrage sentiment." Crossett publicly recognized the work of Anthony and Greenleaf and all suffragists who represented "our cause in Albany" for conducting themselves with "rare dignity and grace."[88]

The 1894 Constitutional Convention stimulated the development of the New York State Association Opposed to Woman Suffrage. Small groups of women, in cities such as Albany, Utica, Brooklyn, and New York, had been meeting for a year to strategize about ways to prevent the removal of the word "male" from the constitution. They also collected signatures on petitions that they submitted to the convention. They argued that women had enough to do to take care of their families and homes, that forcing women to enter the world of politics would destroy the natural balance of gender relations critical to the efficacy of the State, that the ballot should be backed by the ability to serve in the military, and that most women did not want the burden of the vote. Although the groups disbanded immediately following the convention, they would establish the formal organization in 1895, with the wealthy philanthropist and day nursery founder Josephine Jewell Dodge as founding president, and thus continue to plague New York woman suffragists until 1917.[89]

Progress at the Local Level

At the turn of the century, the notion of enfranchising women seemed more popular upstate than downstate, which may have been due in part to the dynamism of the political equality clubs.[90] Upstate leaders dominated the New York State Woman Suffrage Association and they regarded New York

City as a "lost cause" because of its lack of suffrage organizational activity.[91] Political equality clubs expanded or contracted at different rates, or occasionally merged or dissolved, depending on the personalities of the leaders as well as the local political climate. Greenleaf operated as president of the New York State Woman Suffrage Association from 1890 to 1896, at the same time as she presided over meetings of its auxiliary, the Rochester Women's Political Club. In 1891, Crossett founded the Wyoming County Woman Suffrage Association and followed that by establishing a political equality club in the village of Warsaw.[92] Crossett, too, became president of the state association, serving from 1902 to 1910, years after she began working at the local level. Both women testified before Congress on behalf of suffrage during their respective tenures. These clubs and their leaders concentrated on bills of interest to those living upstate and in small towns.[93]

Lesser-known women who emerged as leaders in their respective communities made a difference as well. Elizabeth Smith Miller, the wife of a prominent banker, and her daughter Anne Fitzhugh Miller acted as stewards for the movement in Geneva, founding the Geneva Political Equality Club in 1897 and the Ontario County Political Equality Club in 1903. New York City–born Marion Sanger relocated to remote Ogdensburg upon her marriage to Julius Frank, taking her suffrage principles with her and leading the local political equality club in the North Country.[94] Building on a long tradition of organizing for women's reform activism, political clubs often evolved from established clubs, originally founded for a different purpose. Some women formed Susan B. Anthony political equality clubs, such as the one founded by the Rochester-area African American suffragist Hester Jeffrey, and the Susan B. Anthony Club, chartered in 1895 in Wellsville, Allegany County, which was eventually superseded by another political equality club.[95] Small town clubs even led the battle within the New York State Federation of Women's Clubs to endorse suffrage.[96] When New York City leaders blocked the submission of suffrage groups to the state federation, small town leaders formed the Western New York Federation of Women's Clubs.[97]

Rural in nature, these clubs often organized as auxiliaries of the New York State Woman Suffrage Association, and their diverse activities were similar to those of urban suffragists, ranging from recruiting new members to speaking before legislative hearings in Albany. Club members concentrated on publicizing the cause and gaining male support for a woman suffrage amendment to the state constitution. Political equality clubs and their participants coalesced around the goals of equal rights and full citizenship for women. Suffragists elsewhere aspired to follow the lead of Chautauqua County. Recognized as the most organized county in the state by 1900, under

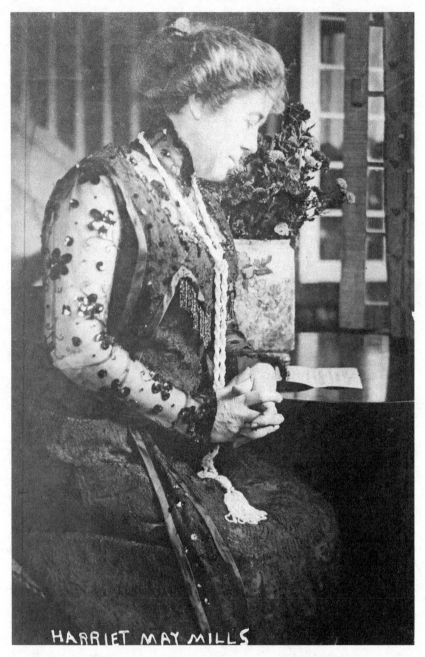

HARRIET MAY MILLS

Harriet May Mills of Syracuse began her career with the New York State Woman Suffrage Association as an organizer and lecturer, traveling extensively to help establish political equality clubs and promote woman suffrage across the state. She held various positions in the state suffrage association and served as president from 1910 to 1913. Image courtesy of the Prints and Photographs Division, Library of Congress, Washington, DC.

the leadership of women like Elnora Babcock and Eliza Gifford, county-level club membership grew to 1800 members.[98] Membership in other clubs around the state also burgeoned. For example, when the Millers established the Geneva Political Equality Club with the help of the New York State Association organizer Harriet May Mills, they counted 400 members, and it grew to be the largest club in the state by 1907.[99] In 1905, the New York State Woman Suffrage Association counted ninety-seven suffrage societies in the state, representing thirty-one counties and 3,403 members. By 1910, there were 155 suffrage clubs affiliated with the New York State Woman Suffrage Association, representing thirty-six counties and 55,000 members.[100]

As upstate leaders nurtured local and county suffrage clubs, nominal efforts were underway to centralize state activity. In February 1901, the founding meeting of the New York Political Equality League was held at the New York City home of Dr. Mary Putnam Jacobi. At the meeting, members drafted a constitution and "great interest was shown among some of the most influential suffragists of the city."[101] Within a few weeks, the home of Harriet May Mills, on West Genesee St. in centrally located Syracuse, became the state headquarters for the New York league. Across the state, suffrage workers traveled through often inclement weather to recruit new members and initiate new clubs.[102] League members did whatever they could to contribute to the cause of suffrage. The Redford League, in a hamlet south of Plattsburgh, held rummage sales to raise money for the state and national associations and to defray publishing costs for the monthly newsletter. In Geneva, club leaders decided to hold their meetings in the members' parlors to circumvent the expense of building rental.[103] Lack of finances plagued leaders and suffrage organizations across the state. Many relied on the personal contributions of members to sustain their organizations. Cayuga member Emily Howland not only contributed to the Sherwood Equal Rights Association but also became one of Susan B. Anthony's top two financial backers, second only to Eliza Wright Osborne, a daughter of Martha Coffin Wright, of Auburn. The Monroe County Woman Suffrage Party depended on the $450 annual contribution from the Mary S. Anthony Trust Fund.[104]

Some lobbying activities by suffragists, such as those aimed at securing the right to vote for school board representative or county school commissioner, proved more successful than others.[105] But suffragists had to fight continually to keep whatever rights they won. New York State Woman Suffrage Association executive board members feared that women would lose the right to vote in school elections if they did not regularly exercise their rights. Five years after winning school suffrage, they sent speakers to every county to encourage women to vote in school elections and prevent the "annul[ment of] such power and protection as we now have" in the state legislature.[106] A few years after that, they followed the directive of the New York State Woman Suffrage Association vice president, Harriet May Mills, to "write, write, write like those in Jamestown, Ithaca, Newburgh, Oswego, Little Falls, Norwich, and Union Springs already have." In addition, some of those writers attended Senate hearings at the state capitol to seek passage of the Woman Taxpayers' Bill.[107] Triumph for the suffragists came in April 1901 with the passage of the bill. Senator Otto Kelsey of Livingston County had "been at it" for five years when he "finally succeeded in getting through the Legislature an act giving women limited suffrage." New York Governor Benjamin B. O'Dell, Jr., signed the bill authorizing women taxpayers in towns and villages to vote on local tax questions. Suffrage leaders, including Carrie Chapman Catt and Anna Howard Shaw, had also been instrumental in getting the legislation passed.[108] Women in the larger "first-class" cities like New York and Buffalo and medium-sized "second-class" cities including Rochester, Syracuse, Albany, and Troy had tax matters decided for them by a Board of Estimate. Only a few of the smaller "third-class" cities with a population of under 50,000 gave women the right to vote on local tax questions.[109]

The Evolution of Ithaca's Clubwomen

Tracing the roots of Ithaca's Political Study Club provides an example of the evolution of a small town club. By the turn of the century, as far as politics and cultural mores were concerned, Ithaca, surrounded by the vastness of rural Tompkins County, remained a somewhat isolated and conservative town of about 11,000 residents. When Susan B. Anthony spoke in Ithaca in 1869 at the invitation of Ezra Cornell, few attended her speech, and the cause of woman suffrage proved unpopular. The New York State Woman Suffrage Association chair for Tompkins County, Carrie E. Bouton, who hailed from Ithaca, observed at the close of the 1894 state constitutional convention petition drive that the "women of the country are better informed and more intelligent upon this subject [of suffrage] than women of our city." Bouton also pointed out that the rural reaches of the county had elected a female school commissioner and that two of the county's newspaper editors supported woman suffrage.[110]

Whenever women in Ithaca gathered informally, discussions concerning temperance, literature, and education proved acceptable; talk about women's rights did not. Louisa Riley and her husband, William, a cousin of Lucretia Mott, moved to Ithaca in the summer of 1894 from New Jersey to be near their son Howard, a student at Cornell University. Both Louisa and her husband had been avid suffrage supporters while living in Orange, New Jersey, where Louisa had started a suffrage club. Although disappointed to find that Ithaca lacked a similar club, Riley remained passionate about women's rights.

However, the opportunity for political engagement presented itself within months of Riley's relocation. The executive board of the New York State Woman Suffrage Association decided to hold its annual convention at a university center—Ithaca—despite, or probably because of, the lack of a local organization there. At the November 1894 convention, state association leaders decided to go beyond submitting petitions to the general legislature in Albany and to adopt more proactive tactics such as the personal petitioning of legislators on an individual basis, a suggestion from the dynamic Lillie Devereux Blake.[111] Over the course of the convention, Louisa Riley assisted national leaders, including Susan B. Anthony and Anna Howard Shaw, as they attempted to organize an Ithaca chapter of the state suffrage association. But, to their dismay, "not enough women could be found who were sufficiently interested in suffrage."[112]

Refusing to be deterred, in the months following the convention, fifty-eight-year-old Louisa Riley worked relentlessly to establish a club for Ithaca women. The innocuously-named Women's Club of Ithaca first convened in January 1895, seeking "to awaken in its members an interest in topics of general and social importance by means of essays and discussions." Members of the club adopted the motto, "All are needed by each one." When Riley became the club's first president, her husband recorded the organization's by-laws and constitution. Though, at first appearance, the club may seem like a compromise in Louisa's suffrage principles, it was not. Every fourth week, the Equal Suffrage Section of the Women's Club presented talks devoted to the topic of woman's attainment of equal suffrage to its members.[113]

Members of the Equal Suffrage Section, already considered "a club within a club," decided to form a separate Political Study Club to explore and debate the cause of women's rights in 1899. Thirteen women, about half of whom identified as widows or teachers, attended the first meeting on March 27 at the home of Carrie Buckliss. They accepted an account of work from the State Charities Board and discussed school suffrage matters, including the dearth of women school board members in Ithaca.[114] A month later, twenty-three women, including the savvy Louisa Riley, signed the roster. Ithaca women received tremendous support from state and national leaders, including a congratulatory letter from the New York State Woman Suffrage Association president Mariana Wright Chapman, as well as visits from Susan B. Anthony and Syracuse activist and Cornell graduate Harriet May Mills. In addition to maintaining close ties to the Ithaca Women's Club, the Political Study Club established working relationships with the Woman's Christian Temperance Union, the Daughters of the American Revolution, the Child Study Club, the Campus Club, and the Political Equity League of Sage College.

Activist women in Ithaca also ignited suffrage forces in surrounding Tompkins County. In October 1899, Lucy Calkins proposed the formation of a Tompkins County Woman Suffrage Association. The towns of Groton, Newfield, and Ithaca sent representatives to the first meeting, where members elected Calkins as the president of the new organization.[115] When the organization changed its name, in 1914, to the Tompkins County Woman Suffrage Party, under the tenure of Juanita Breckenridge Bates, the organization listed 124 members, including bookkeepers, milliners, telephone operators, housecleaners, teachers, and the daughter of the president of Cornell, representing an intriguing cross-section of the local population.[116]

By the time the New York State Woman Suffrage Association held its 43rd Annual Convention in 1911 in Ithaca, the political landscape had changed dramatically. In December 1914, the Ithaca Political Study Club announced that the Tompkins County Pomona Grange had adopted a resolution endorsing woman suffrage.[117] Like countless others around the state, the club served as a base for local suffrage activities and education and undoubtedly convinced many to join the cause. John Grace, the owner of the *Weekly Ithacan*, did his part by publishing articles supportive of the club and advocating universal suffrage and temperance.[118]

More Auxiliaries for the State Association

Leaders reported the intensification of suffrage activities at each annual state convention, highlighting the influence of the New York State Woman Suffrage Association around the state and beyond. For example, at the 32nd annual convention in October 1900, in Glens Falls, the state organizer Harriet May Mills reported on her activities: editing the monthly *Newsletter*, a short-lived publication for political equality clubs; visiting fifteen counties in New York State; and doing fieldwork in Michigan and Ohio.[119] Mills bolstered newly-formed clubs with her compelling speeches, one of which a farmer pronounced the best address "by man or woman" ever heard.[120] Mills continued to work with state and national leaders in her capacity as association vice president. That fall, Mills publicized woman suffrage in the main building at the New York State Fair in Syracuse, where she and the other workers distributed souvenirs and literature. In addition to addressing large audiences at public venues, like fairs and churches, organizers spoke in private homes. Some may have preferred this more intimate environment where they did not have to shout through megaphones.[121] At a typical parlor meeting in Groton, Tompkins County, attended by seventy-five young people, "Miss Mills' pleasing manner of arguments" won many adherents.[122] In 1903, Mills reported that she had spoken at a legislative hearing in Albany, at the annual meeting of the Grange, and in the State Fair auditorium on Suffrage Day.[123]

By 1908, Mills and other suffragists hoped to solicit more rural women by participating in the Women's Institutes sponsored by the State Agricultural Department, held in twenty counties over the course of two months. Mills spoke at all but one. She reported to the New York State Woman Suffrage Association's annual convention: "In this way we were able to come into touch with thousands of men and women whom we could not reach in our suffrage gatherings." Separate meetings held in Institute towns benefitted existing suffrage organizations or helped to create them in unorganized towns, such as when Mills organized a suffrage club in Seneca Falls in 1905. Increased organizational activities, as well as extended favorable newspaper coverage, helped the New York organization become the largest suffrage association in the nation by the time state and national headquarters relocated to New York City in 1909.[124]

In September 1910, six women in the picturesque village of Clinton, in Oneida County, organized a political equality club at the home of its first president, Delia Avery Williams. The club grew to fifty-six members, including nine men, by the following year. For a fee of thirty-five cents, the club welcomed those willing to sign the constitution and those "not yet ready to sign the constitution but who desire[d] to join the club for educational purposes."[125] The Clinton club attracted primarily community leaders and those from well-established families, some with a history of reform activism. Reform organizations such as the Woman's Christian Temperance Union and the Grange maintained an active presence in Clinton, also home to a number of private educational institutions. Men who belonged to the Clinton Political Equality Club tended to be business owners, professors connected to Hamilton College, or ordained ministers affiliated with the Presbyterian Church. Many of the women members participated in the Women's Missionary Society and the Monday Club, a literary group.[126] As in Ithaca, the home of Cornell University and Ithaca College, the presence of Hamilton College seemed to encourage an intellectual climate that fostered liberal-minded reform.

The Clinton Political Equality Club's first year proved to be one of its most active. The club used the *Clinton Courier* as a propaganda tool to recruit new members. Its editor and publisher, Henry B. Sykes, belonged to the club and rarely gave press to the village's anti-suffragists, many inspired by Clinton native Elihu Root. Instead, the paper emphasized the club's success with headlines like "A Flourishing Organization," praising the club's members for the "orderly and intelligent manner" of its meetings, and lauding the men who had exercised "the courage of their convictions" when they became members.[127] In August 1911, the club sponsored a highly successful and entertaining staging of *How the Vote was Won,* a satirical play set in London, and a "convincing address" by Harriet May Mills, the president of the New York State Woman Suffrage Association. Club members also helped elect two women to the Clinton school board, sponsored suffrage movies, and erected two popular traveling exhibits in Hart's Store. Club women began a discussion about organizing a county political equality club since Oneida County remained the only county in the state without a county organization. The Political Equality Club ended a successful year by sending representatives to the first Oneida County Suffrage Convention in September and to the State Convention in October 1911.[128]

While not many farmers or their family members joined the Clinton Political Equality Club, the Delhi Equal Suffrage Club, organized the same year, appealed more broadly to rural families in small towns and villages across Delaware County. Summer suffrage work remained crucial in rural areas, where farm families had time to spare once they planted their crops. Taking care not to intimidate or insult potential supporters, suffragists approached rural residents with caution. The Delhi club president, Jennie Curtis Cannon, suggested that "only the best speakers and organizers should be sent to rural districts; the intelligence of the farmer, his wife, and his daughter requires this."[129] Cannon's records include reports to headquarters detailing the multifaceted efforts to establish suffrage operations in Delaware County. With organizing efforts in their infancy, in 1912, the Delhi club held a number of evening meetings with speakers that included Anna Howard Shaw and Max Eastman. Cannon also invited the professional organizer May Bell Morgan to come to Delaware County "to do organization and propaganda work" in the summer. Morgan spoke at two fairs, at parlor meetings, and at numerous outdoor meetings. She also spoke in Delhi at the annual convention of the Woman's Christian Temperance Union and at a "Moving Picture performance" at the Delhi Opera House. Especially proud of the special entertainment provided by "New York professionals" sponsored by the Delhi Equal Suffrage Club during Old Home Week, Cannon enthused that "every seat was taken and people were turned away."[130]

Jennie Curtis Cannon (the woman seated beside the driver) held the presidency of the Delhi Equal Suffrage Club and served as the New York State Woman Suffrage Association's Delaware County Chair. Used with permission from the Delaware County Historical Association, Delhi, NY.

Energetic efforts paid off. While Cannon's penchant for organizing was tied to her sensibilities regarding farm families, Harriet May Mills approached the task more systematically. Mills designed a program specifically to attract men to suffrage meetings—invite men and their wives for the forenoon and give them a good dinner followed by a "rousing suffrage meeting, which the men in common courtesy must attend." Mills also insisted on a training school for speakers and organizers, a clerk for the headquarters, and printed educational pamphlets for every aspect of study to be provided to new clubs. Although Mills often expressed her appreciation for in-kind donations of carriages, automobiles, or telephones, she could not help but point out that, "We could use more money." Suffrage workers' lack of funds troubled Mills, as it did other organizers.[131]

From trudging through blizzards to obligating farmers to attend suffrage talks, women who lived and organized in rural areas faced more obstacles than urban dwellers. Nevertheless, they erected an unsurpassed foundation for suffrage advocacy. With the failure of the 1894 Constitutional Convention to sway legislators to present a suffrage referendum to voters, rural women realized that they had to expand their power base. At the suggestion of the more assertive leaders, suffragists moved from mass petition drives to lobbying male politicians and voters individually. Utilizing tactics honed in their respective organizations, individual women made tremendous advances in their quest for suffrage. Some, like Stanton and Blake, found their voices on the lecture circuit. Frances Willard also led her women-centered organization in a new direction—away from evangelicalism. After her death in 1898, the Woman's Christian Temperance Union shifted its tactics to exert political pressure on both candidates and legislators. The reform-minded Eliza Gifford pushed past the constraints of her organization at the state level, and then at the national level, to guarantee that the resolution supporting woman suffrage would be endorsed by male grangers. Location mattered. Living in one of the most progressive counties in the state helped Gifford move up through her organization and provided an opportunity to be a part of the early political equality club movement. In college and university towns like Ithaca and Clinton, reform sentiment found a more welcome reception. People in rural communities became a critical part of the complicated and disparate New York State coalition working to enfranchise women.

 Chapter 3

The Quest for Industrial Citizenship

Woman Suffrage and Immigrant
Garment Workers

Just as icy spring rains began to melt the record-breaking snow of 1893, an unnamed eighteen-year-old homeless woman, weak with hunger, collapsed on a downtown Rochester street. Not knowing what else to do, patrolmen carried the unconscious woman to their station to revive her. Although similar events generally escaped public notice, this one did draw attention. When the city's most distinguished woman citizen, Susan B. Anthony, heard that the woman awoke in a jail cell, Anthony resented the implication that the poor woman's destitution linked her to wrongdoing. She resolved to safeguard the welfare of the city's poor and working women, many of whom were immigrants. Rochester had experienced tremendous growth in the previous decade, with 39,000 residents (of a total population of 133,000) having been born overseas. By 1900, immigrants comprised forty percent of the city's population.[1] Despite Rochester's long-standing tradition of political activism and benevolent sentiments, this 1893 incident exposed a raw reality: neither the municipal, state, or federal government cared to solve the problems of women, some of the city's neediest people.[2] It also marks the point when activist women's attitudes began to shift from a need to dispense charity to a recognition of the importance of directly empowering women. Disturbing incidents—such as women collapsing of hunger in the streets—supported suffragists' contention that only when women had the right to vote would they have the power to alleviate the injustices associated with urban poverty.

Suffrage reformers reasoned, and the majority of women workers came to agree, that once women won political rights, their economic rights—including fair wages, shorter hours, and safer conditions—would follow. From the onset of the fight to recognize women's rights in the 1840s, several upstate woman suffrage leaders took an interest in the issues confronting women workers. Early suffragists believed in the ballot as the answer to empowering and improving the lives of working women. On April 14, 1852, Anthony served as secretary for a committee of seamstresses advocating the need to reform wages and working conditions.[3] The appointment of Anthony and Elizabeth Cady Stanton as delegates to the 1868 National Labor Union convention demonstrates the early connection forged between the political and industrial aspects of the suffrage movement.[4] Anthony asserted that women should earn the same pay as men for the same work and often told her audiences that the ballot held the solution to their problems.[5] Rochester reformer Helen Barrett Montgomery echoed Anthony's sentiments: "The political condition largely determines the industrial condition."[6] State and local middle-class suffrage activists fought on behalf of working women, agitating for protective labor legislation and the right to join labor unions. However, until the 1890s, they made only sporadic attempts to enlist working women into the ranks of the suffrage campaign.

The suffrage movement, as represented by the New York State Woman Suffrage Association, progressed irregularly, apparent in its unbalanced connection to working women and labor unionism. Dominated by an elite leadership primarily located in New York City, suffragists did not systematically court working-class women. Eventually, New York City leaders sent organizers out from the state association headquarters (after 1909) into upstate garment-producing cities such as Utica, Troy, Gloversville, and Rochester. While suffragists continued to struggle throughout the movement to gain the support of the native-born population, their influence with working-class immigrant newcomers required different strategies. For example, the leadership deliberately recruited ethnic organizers to appeal to specific immigrant groups. Events in rapidly industrializing Rochester illuminate the relationship between suffragists and working women.

At the 1894 twenty-sixth annual New York State Woman Suffrage Association Convention in Ithaca, Sarah Fleming Bradstreet, president of the Monroe County Woman Suffrage Association, pronounced her hometown, Rochester, "the hotbed of woman's suffrage."[7] Over the course of the suffrage movement the city served as home to three generations of women's rights and suffrage activists, including Amy Post, Frederick Douglass, Susan B. Anthony, Mary Anthony, Jean Brooks Greenleaf, Emma Goldman, Hester Jeffrey, Mary Thorn Lewis Gannett, Helen Barrett Montgomery, Lillian Wald, Alice C. Clement, and Florence Cross Kitchelt. Rochester women's activism resulted in the establishment of the Women's Educational and Industrial Union (1893), the election of the city's first woman school commissioner (1898), the entry of white women into the University of Rochester (1900), and the use of public schools for social centers (1907). Over the course of the movement, these advances, along with the founding of several settlement houses and the advocacy for protective labor legislation, helped to improve the lives of working women. Although far more is known about these efforts in and around New York City, the record of upstate industrial cities such as Buffalo, Syracuse, Utica, and Rochester parallels that of the much larger metropolis.

By the late 1880s, Rochester suffragists joined Susan B. Anthony in the Woman's Political Club (renamed the Political Equality Club in 1891). The club focused on political education, gathering signatures on petitions, enlisting the aid of men in the cause, and hosting prominent suffrage speakers.[8] They persisted in their activities, under the leadership of the first generation of women's rights and suffrage activists, into the new century. After Anthony's death, in 1906, suffragists temporarily retreated, but they reasserted themselves within a decade. State and national leaders, headquartered after 1909 in New York City, prescribed more proactive tactics that they hoped would culminate in a suffrage victory.[9] By including immigrant working women in the organizations and institutions they built, Rochester women held fast to the promise of progressivism in an otherwise politically conservative city. The next generation of activist women in Rochester, including Helen Barrett Montgomery, Mary Thorn Lewis Gannett, Florence Cross (Kitchelt), and Alice C. Clement, recognized the necessity of broad support for suffrage.[10] Consequently, working-class immigrant women became a dynamic aspect of the suffrage coalition.

Rochester Women and the Tradition of Reform

In order to broaden their appeal and ultimately their effectiveness, suffrage leaders realized that they had to make a more conscious effort to incorporate immigrant women workers across the state into the suffrage movement. By the early twentieth century they had been fighting for working women for decades. Participants at the 1848 Woman's Rights Convention in Rochester resolved to investigate and report on women's wages in the community and formed the Woman's Protection Union.[11] A Mrs. Roberts, the union's first president, vowed to campaign for the voluntary increase of working girls and women's wages. In 1853, Susan B. Anthony organized a small group of seamstresses and, at a state teachers' convention later that year, called for women to be admitted to the profession and for better pay for women, who made less than one-half of what men teachers earned.[12] After the Civil War ended, she advised a group of working women in New York City to seek higher wages by "get[ting] the ballot" first so that when they did strike, trade union men would sustain them with money and assistance.[13] She continued advising working women and soon formed the Workingwomen's Central Association; its members elected her president.

Working women did not immediately flock to middle-class allies when summoned. Women who worked often found pursuing activism difficult because they spent the majority of their waking hours at their jobs. If women had husbands or children they also faced a second round of work, cooking, cleaning, and mending once they returned home. Pieceworkers who sewed by hand prepared for the next day by threading hundreds of needles to use in the workplace. An article that appeared in the *New York Tribune* lent insight into this dilemma in the headline: "What with Washing, Cooking and Sewing at Home after Factory Hours, Working Women Have No Time to Think of Suffrage, their Labor Leaders Explain."[14] Some women labor leaders thought that working women would accomplish more of their goals by joining a labor union rather than a suffrage organization.

To that end, reformers in Rochester founded the Women's Educational and Industrial Union both to help working women and promote their political activism. After the incident involving the collapse of the young homeless woman, Anthony met privately with Harriet Townsend, the president of the Buffalo Women's Educational and Industrial Union. She invited Townsend to speak at a mass meeting in Rochester on April 10, 1893. Townsend so impressed the audience with her description of her city's organization that Rochester women decided to form their own branch of the union with the explicit purpose of "increasing fellowship in order to promote the best practical methods for securing their educational, industrial, and social advancement."[15] Anthony viewed the union as a suffrage recruiting ground for working-class women otherwise at the mercy of male-dominated workplace politics.[16] Honoring Anthony's commitment to working women, middle-class Rochester reformers sought to protect and offer services and activities to the city's working women, especially, as Mary Gannett pointed out, in cases where "no existing organization" was available to help.[17] The organization served as a social service agency as it connected working women to suffrage and women's rights activists.

Union members, including Gannett and Montgomery, had worked for women's rights for decades. Both Gannett and Anthony supported Montgomery in her successful bid to become Rochester's first female school commissioner in 1898.[18] Also holding membership in the New York State Woman Suffrage Association and the Rochester Political Equality Club, the three women formed an impressive nucleus of activists who guided the women's movement in Rochester. Montgomery's biographer asserts that, although the trio cooperated for the same causes, the strategies they used and the rhetoric they employed reflected their different generations and priorities. With Montgomery's departure from the union's presidency, in 1911, to become more active in mission work, Mary Gannett, the head of the union's legal protection committee, assumed the presidency and became increasingly involved in suffrage activities from her executive post.[19]

The Women's Educational and Industrial Union's work exemplifies the link between Rochester's progressive social reform movement and its women's movement.[20] Women leaders in the organization held classes, established an employment bureau, ran a legal aid department with free advice to working women, and created lecture and recreation programs. The union raised funds to build playgrounds in poor areas, held mothers' meetings (a forerunner of the Parent Teacher Association), and opened a shop where women could sell their homemade goods.[21] It also hosted conventions for local political equality clubs.[22] Union members placed works of art and water fountains in public schools and supported school nurses and penny lunch programs. Eventually the Rochester organization helped to establish a branch of the National Consumers' League and operated a "Noon Rest" lounge and lunchroom for working women on Clinton Street. With its model of cross-class cooperation, the Women's Educational and Industrial Union became the city's most influential progressive-era civic reform organization, earning the respect of city officials.[23]

Moving Toward Modernity

Rochester suffragists watched as the city grew from a hinterland canal town to a modern urban industrial center. In the process of transitioning to a manufacturing economy, Rochester's workforce underwent a marked transformation. Where once flour mills powered by the rushing waterfalls of the Genesee River provided the majority of employment opportunities in the nineteenth century, by 1910 one-quarter of Rochester's approximately 200,000 residents worked in factories. Recently arrived immigrants from Italy, Poland, Russia, and Lithuania made up an ever-increasing proportion of the city's working population.[24] Immigrant laborers lived in poor enclaves, segregated by ethnicity, while the native-born moved from out-lying farms and villages into the better neighborhoods. George Eastman's Kodak Company, conceived during late night experiments in Eastman's mother's kitchen, became both a world leader in the production of photo-graphic equipment and the city's largest employer. Eastman preferred white native-born workers; the Eastman Kodak Company's employment policies reflected its owner's xenophobia. The paternalistic Eastman reasoned that a homegrown workforce would be less likely to succumb to the threat of unionism or, worse yet, the socialism that certain ethnic groups had a reputa-tion for supporting. A staunch Republican, the Kodak patriarch and his cro-nies wielded a formidable influence on the city's politics and work force for over three decades of the twentieth century.[25] To encourage worker loyalty and discourage unions, Eastman joined the ranks of welfare capitalists who offered benefits to workers that included paid vacations, company housing, and health services.[26]

Not all Rochester workers benefitted from these munificent practices, known as "the social spirit."[27] With Kodak's doors closed to them, newly-arrived immigrants, along with their children, turned to the shops in the men's gar-ment industry for work. The city's second largest industry—the production of men's suits and overcoats—had begun in earnest in 1883 when the three Adler brothers—Levi, Simon, and Abram—opened their factory on cloth-ier's row on St. Paul Street. Stein Bloch, Michaels-Stern, and Hickey Free-man followed the Adler model.[28] Early industrialists included a number of German-Jewish tailors and button makers, often better versed in socialist doc-trine than in matters of local politics. Their companies quickly grew to domi-nate the almost two hundred garment firms located in Rochester. As leaders in the business world they joined the native-born capitalists in allying with the Republican Party and in conducting open-shop anti-union campaigns under the auspices of the Clothiers' Exchange.[29] They welcomed immigrant new-comers as a source of cheap labor.

The city, which had hosted three women's rights conventions in the pre-vious century, came to serve as a bastion for conservative politicians and elite entrepreneurs who exhibited little empathy for the less fortunate. The nascent efforts of nineteenth-century women activists to attain rights for themselves and for immigrant and working-class women left little impact outside the suffrage circle, and virtually none on wealthy business owners. By 1912, Eastman and the Republican politicians he commanded had deliber-ately (albeit discreetly) suppressed the efforts of women's rights and suffrage activists in the city. Suffragists fought back, to the point that debates over the right of women to vote grew more intense with every passing year.[30]

Suffrage and the Immigrant Question

Rochester suffragists watched as the suffrage contest unfolded at the legislative level in Albany, drawing attention to immigrant women and their place in participatory democracy. Senator Henry W. Hill of Buffalo and member of the assembly Frederick Toombs of New York introduced a concurrent resolution that would strike the word "male" from the state constitution. On February 23, 1909, pro-suffrage and anti-suffrage women testified before members of the Judiciary Committees of the Senate and Assembly. Anti-suffragist Mary Dean Adams, an investigator for the New York State Commission of Immigration, described the immigrant woman as "a fickle, impulsive creature, irresponsible, . . . as capable of understanding as much about political matters as a man deaf and blind would [be] of the opera," and who "would sell her vote for a pound of macaroni." An irritated Anna Howard Shaw, the president of the National American Woman Suffrage Association, expressed her dissatisfaction with Adams's speech in "audible comments."[31] Regardless of any individual's suffrage sentiments, the subject of immigrant citizenship rights continued to be contentious at all levels.

Although prejudice ruled the lives of immigrants, garment factory owners preferred a primarily immigrant work force that they could pay less and work longer than they could native-born employees. The primarily Italian and Eastern European Jewish immigrants who had arrived in Rochester most recently (referred to as "greenhorns," like all new immigrants) proved especially vulnerable to exploitation by employers. Without union support and lacking any legal recourse, immigrants could be forced by their employers to work long days in vile conditions for a pittance. Women endured an additional form of abuse: sexual harassment on the job from male shop owners and foremen. In part to avoid the pitfalls of the shops, some women took hand finishing home and worked alongside their children far into the night.[32] Both women and men suffered the disadvantage of not being able to negotiate their positions in the workplace due to their limited English language skills. Shop owners preyed upon workers with large families to support. With the possible exception of the Adler brothers, garment manufacturers seemed to be more concerned with making profits than with the welfare of their workers, turning a blind eye to cruel practices or denying knowledge of dangerous workplace conditions.[33]

In the first decade of the twentieth century, 4,500 women totaled more than sixty-one percent of the Rochester garment manufacturers' entire workforce. Immigrants or, even more commonly, daughters of immigrants, made up over half of the female workforce.[34] Approximately one-third of female garment workers operated sewing machines, while the majority performed hand-finishing tasks, like sewing buttonholes or felling (finishing seams), that high-end men's clothing required. Regardless of age, ethnicity, race, marital status, or any other variable, most women worked out of economic necessity rather than for "pin money" to purchase life's luxuries.[35] After ten- to twelve-hour workdays, women returned to dilapidated and overcrowded homes that offered little respite from factory pressures.

Jewish and Italian workers had optimistically immigrated to what they believed would be a new industrial order in the United States. Instead, they were met with disheartening living and working conditions. Some immigrant women had developed strong political views prior to emigrating. The doctrines of Karl Marx and the Bund, a revolutionary Jewish workers' group, particularly influenced Eastern European Jewish women. Counter to the perception that Italian workers were especially difficult to organize, some Italian women became politically radicalized as they sought to escape the destitute poverty of peasant life in rural Italy.[36] Unwilling to settle for less than what they had anticipated, these women applied their political sensibilities to formulate a new vision of citizenship that could be easily adapted to their new circumstances. Women like the New York City capmaker-turned-suffragist Rose Schneiderman, who "laid the groundwork for working-class women's activism" for the first half of the twentieth century, considered democracy to be a two-fold process. According to Schneiderman, attaining "industrial citizenship"—safe conditions, decent hours, and fair wages—would be only the first step for women on the way to their "right to citizenship."[37]

The fullest form of citizenship encompassed a definition of democracy that extended beyond the workplace. Citizenship, in the words of Schneiderman, entitled one to "the right to be born well, the right to a happy and carefree childhood, the right to education, [and] the right to mental, physical and spiritual growth and development."[38] Immigrant women in Rochester and across the state hoped to attain "happiness" for themselves and "all the money that [they] wanted," reshaping their vision of democracy and aspiring to "a higher idea of happiness . . . the happiness of others."[39] Immigrant women's increasing political consciousness allowed them to look beyond workplace justice and formulate an enlightened version of citizenship where votes for women related directly to "regular hours, better conditions, and the enforcement of the laws."[40] Contending with employer exploitation and frustrated by being excluded from the democratic process in the workplace and in the wider polity, immigrant women decided to act.[41] When invited, they joined middle-class women in suffrage advocacy, because the reality of their experiences as workers in a country that had promised equality to all fell short of the ideal.

Settlement Houses as Centers of Activism
for Working Women

For many working-class immigrant women, settlement houses offered a convenient place of refuge, providing them with meeting spaces and a place to socialize. The Women's Educational and Industrial Union helped to finance the establishment and maintenance of Rochester's two largest settlement houses.[42] A group of German Jewish women philanthropists from B'rith Kodesh Temple, who possessed a sense of social responsibility and desired to teach immigrant women the "basic tasks and responsibilities of life in the United States," established the Baden Street Settlement in 1901. Led by Therese R. Katz, a volunteer teacher, and Fannie Adler Garson, the daughter of one of the city's largest clothing manufacturers and wife of another, the settlement coordinated activities like evening classes and dancing twice a week for the Eastern European immigrants who populated the city's Jewish Eighth Ward. As the settlement expanded, so did its programming. In addition to social and athletic activities for children, it hosted an informal kindergarten, public bathing facilities, a day care center, and the operation of a "milk station" to distribute safe milk to neighborhood children.[43] Publicly-spirited, Rochester settlement women championed social and political reform. Their concerns included the abolition of child labor, obtaining desirable legislation as tied to women's workplace conditions and political rights, and "awakening the membership to its responsibilities as intelligent voters."[44] While New York City settlement leaders, especially in the Jewish neighborhoods, tended to affiliate with suffragists, Rochester Jewish settlement leaders did so on a more limited basis.[45]

Suffragists fared better in the Italian neighborhoods. In 1907, the suffragist Florence Ledyard Cross, born into a prominent Rochester Unitarian family, founded the Practical Housekeeping Center (later the Lewis Street Center), in Rochester's Sixteenth Ward, to promote "better race relations" with recent Italian immigrants.[46] The sympathetic young Cross defended Italians against racist newspaper attacks and went to great lengths to understand the best way to educate and uplift her Italian neighbors.[47] Early in her career, Cross recognized that rather than emphasizing charity or Americanization programs, empowering immigrants would be the most effective approach to aiding them.[48] Cross offered adult English classes and dedicated much of her work with women and men to helping them become citizens.[49] Like the majority of women on the settlement's board, Cross belonged to both the Rochester Political Equality Club and the Women's Educational and Industrial Union. She considered suffrage a responsibility of citizenship. The cooperative efforts Cross made in the Italian community and the respect she earned for her work encouraged community members to follow her lead.

The Florence Ledyard Cross Kitchelt and Richard Kitchelt "suffragist wedding" highlights the connection between suffrage, socialism, and settlement houses in Rochester, New York. Richard's support of Florence's suffrage work reflects men's advocacy for woman suffrage. Image courtesy of the Arthur and Elizabeth Schlesinger Library on the History of Women in America, Radcliffe Institute, Harvard University, Cambridge, MA.

In June 1911, with a dozen young settlement women serving as brides-maids, Cross married the socialist Richard Kitchelt in what one local paper described as "a suffragist wedding." The couple composed their own vows, omitting the word "obey," and pledged to work together as "comrades." The participation of Catherine Rumball, the wife of the Unitarian minister Edwin Rumball, as an officiant in the ceremony symbolized "the equality of man and woman."[50] Florence Cross Kitchelt went to work shortly thereafter for the Bureau of Information and Protection of Foreigners and the North American Civic League, where she continued to serve the ward's Italian pop-ulation by providing advice to "foreigners who are in any kind of trouble," promoting education in the factories, and advocating support for workers in labor disputes. In 1914, Florence Kitchelt ran an unsuccessful campaign for the office of Secretary of State in New York.[51] She kept her membership in the Rochester Political Equality Club, writing suffrage stories for local newspapers. Kitchelt also served in a paid capacity as canvasser and organizer for the Monroe County Woman Suffrage Party and as an Industrial Section Leader and delegate to the National American Woman Suffrage Association convention in 1916.[52]

Workers' Need for Suffrage

Events in other upstate cities and in New York City influenced Rochester working women and suffragists. Convinced of the value of political equality in the fight for industrial equality, Harriot Stanton Blatch, the founder of the Equality League of Self-Supporting Women and daughter of Elizabeth Cady Stanton, saw the vote as aiding in trade union work "as nothing else could."[53] For suffragists and trade union women, it became a question of allegiance. Some, like Rose Schneiderman, who identified as a trade unionist and social-ist, readily supported suffrage. Schneiderman overcame the anti-immigrant sentiment held by some of the reformers in New York City to become a valu-able suffrage ally. Between suffrage demonstrations and working women's "self-assertions," women extended the boundaries and raised the stakes for the women's movement.[54] The allure of the vote as the solution to their problems drew working-class women into the suffrage movement in the first decade of the new century.

By 1906, suffrage leaders realized that the movement had to confront the changing nature of the nation's urban industrial centers. They began to use innovative techniques that helped to raise the visibility of suffrage to a level that more readily attracted the working-class constituency. Maud Nathan, president of the New York City Consumers' League, traveled to

Rochester to address its political equality club on "Working Women and the Ballot."[55] Harriet May Mills, the dynamic vice-president of the New York State Woman Suffrage Association, traversed the state promoting votes for women. Mills began by speaking to working women in and around New York City. In 1910, the Syracuse Political Equality Club invited Mills to be the principal speaker at a meeting of the women's branch of the Garment Cutter's Union and the Political Equality Club. The local paper hailed the joint meeting as the first of its kind in the city. At the same time, activists published their appeals for suffrage in twenty-six languages. Through these combined efforts, "thousands of working women united in the movement to secure franchisement for women."[56] These overtures to working women would continue until the eve of the 1915 vote on the referendum, when places like the industrial towns of Gloversville and Johnstown hosted leaders such as Lucy Carlisle Watson, the president of the Utica Political Equality Club, at their "splendid meetings."[57]

Rochester suffrage leaders did not fully commit to pledging working women until Alice C. Clement replaced Mena C. Brown as the Rochester Political Equality Club president in 1912.[58] The National American Woman Suffrage Association president Anna Howard Shaw and state suffrage leaders headquartered in New York City, including Harriot Stanton Blatch, Alva Belmont, Harriet Burton Laidlaw, and Mary Garrett Hay, had long realized that the success of their movement depended on working women's signatures on petitions and their husbands' votes on Election Day.[59] Garment workers also felt strongly enough to form their own suffrage organization run by and for factory workers. On March 22, 1911, a group of New York socialist suffrage leaders created the Wage Earners' League for Woman Suffrage. Leonora O'Reilly became president; fellow waistmakers Clara Lemlich and Mollie Schepps and laundry worker Margaret "Maggie" Hinchey acted as cofounders.[60]

Three days later, on March 25, the Triangle Shirtwaist Factory fire in Manhattan exposed shocking garment factory conditions to the entire nation. One hundred and forty-six young, mostly Jewish and Italian women died in the tragedy. Trapped on the upper floors of the Asch Building when the fire broke out, many jumped to their deaths. In the wake of the Triangle fire, upstate factory conditions fell under closer scrutiny. State legislators established a Factory Investigating Commission to research and conduct hearings on working conditions throughout the state. Advised by suffrage reformers such as the shirtwaist union leader Clara Lemlich and the Consumers' League executive secretary Frances Perkins, the commission's work resulted in more than thirty New York State factory fire and safety laws.[61]

The Triangle fire mobilized the Rochester Political Equality Club to hold its first ever series of open-air meetings outside a number of large factories during the summer of 1911. Suffrage speakers, including Harriet May Mills, Anna Cadogan Etz of Hornell, and Portia Willis of New York City, helped to distribute literature and spoke three times daily to curious groups of workers who wanted to know what "votes for women" meant.[62]

The suffragists and socialists Catherine and Edwin Rumball closely monitored the conditions of working women in Rochester. They used their monthly publication, the *Common Good*, to expose troubling industrial conditions. According to the Rumballs, in 1912 the New York State Legislature passed a fifty-four hour law pertaining to women workers, meaning that women could not start work before 6 a.m. or end after 9 p.m. and were to have sixty minutes for meals. But most employers failed to mention the law, and their workers continued to "work overtime as if there were no new law."[63] One report on women workers in the men's clothing trade found excessive "nervous strain" because of the "extreme monotony" of the processes and "the speed with which they are carried on." Rochester operatives worked on sewing machines that sewed between 1,500 and 2,000 stitches per minute. In the knitting mills of Utica, the machines moved almost twice as fast, advancing 3,500 stitches per minute.[64] As Schneiderman reported in the *Woman Voter*, unorganized women are "at the mercy of the employer."[65] The Rumballs devoted the February 1913 issue to studying "The Working Girls and Women of Rochester." After elaborating on the degrading conditions, including speeding, fatigue, and low wages, inherent in "the cruel system of piece-work" found in hundreds of Rochester factories, the Rumballs concluded that working women had to fight to live because they "have not the suffrage."[66]

Rochester Garment Workers Rise

Revolutionary workplace politics assumed a new exigency after the Triangle Shirtwaist Factory fire. In the wake of the disaster, activism on the part of both middle-class suffrage workers and working women intensified. Middle-class women sought to bridge the class divide, and working-class women more readily accepted their help. When Women's Trade Union League organizers like Leonora O'Reilly and Maggie Hinchey traveled upstate, they found that Rochester had a radical tradition of activism that extended beyond the workplace to suffrage.[67] The anarchist Emma Goldman lived in Rochester with her older sister's family for several years. Like countless other Rochester immigrants, Goldman found work at a local garment shop with other

Russian-Jewish immigrants before she relocated to New York City to carry on in the anarchist movement.[68] The reformer Lillian Wald grew up in Rochester before moving to the Lower East Side of Manhattan, where she founded the Henry Street Settlement in 1893. For Wald, and for increasing numbers of activists, immigrant rights and suffrage rights became synonymous.[69]

There had been prior attempts by men's clothing workers to enact improvements in hours, workplace conditions, and wages that led to strikes in Rochester from 1903 to 1904 and again in 1905, but due to the lack of union strength and the open shops of the city, the strikers in both instances failed.[70] Although, in the aftermath of the Triangle fire, the United Garment Workers enjoyed an active organizing stint in the industry, they did not directly recruit women into their ranks. Rochester women garment workers earned approximately 60 percent of what male workers earned. As large garment manufacturers in the city drove out their smaller competitors, including subcontracting shops and manufacturers who employed homeworkers, they hired more workers and purchased the latest mechanical equipment that could more quickly produce quality garments. In this competitive industrial environment, as employees became acutely aware of their exploitation, male labor leaders began to realize that as factories employed larger numbers of women, unions could no longer neglect them.[71]

In late 1912, a group of militant New York City tailors—dubbed "foreign agitators" by the *Democrat and Chronicle*—traveled to Rochester seeking solidarity with workers filling orders for New York City firms with striking employees.[72] By appealing to garment workers in English, Italian, Polish, and Yiddish, the organizers reached unprecedented numbers of workers who, at a mass meeting in Convention Hall on January 22, 1913, voted overwhelmingly to strike.[73] During the eight-week "great struggle of the Garment Workers of Rochester," thousands of female factory workers demanded relief from their oppressive working conditions.[74] The women strikers who filled the streets possessed attributes similar to those of the Triangle Shirtwaist Factory fire victims; they were young, single, mostly Jewish and Italian immigrants or daughters of immigrants whose families relied on their earnings for survival.

After walking off their jobs in mid-January, strike leaders publicized their grievances in the local media. Edwin Rumball printed a list of the workers' demands, including a forty-eight hour workweek, wage increases, union recognition, and the right to arbitrate disagreements. One garment worker described the clothing workers' plight as "ten times worse than the White Slave trade."[75] Striking women voiced additional complaints about the sexual harassment they experienced at the hands of abusive bosses and foremen.

Women marchers demanded justice in the workplace and political rights during the 1913 Rochester Garment Workers' Strike. Image courtesy of the Albert Stone Negatives Collection, Rochester Museum and Science Center, Rochester, NY.

Although strike leaders did not include women's specific grievances in the list of formal demands, airing them helped to expose complaints unique to women.[76] One contingent of men carried American flags and signs that read: "We want better homes for our wives and our babies." They demanded a family wage.[77] Pushed to their limit, male and female clothing workers insisted on "bread and roses"—fair wages, full citizenship, including voting rights, and dignity.[78] Women workers recognized the reciprocity of the relationship between economic and political rights in the "assertion of their entitlements as women," connecting workplace demands to enfranchisement.[79]

After the shooting death of Ida Braiman, an eighteen-year-old striker, by a shop owner in late January 1913, women reformers opened a commissary in conjunction with the Rochester Central Trades and Labor Council to feed and lend support to striking workers. As in the Little Falls strike the previous year, the Socialist Party and the Industrial Workers of the World sent speakers and otherwise came to the strikers' aid.[80] Marching together, the sympathetic women in the Women's Educational and Industrial Union, the Rochester Political Equality Club, and the city's settlements displayed a sense of camaraderie with the strikers. The Lewis Street Center held extra meetings and classes "owing to the strike." Florence and Richard Kitchelt both addressed crowds of strikers.[81] Anna Cadogan Etz, the founder of the

Hornell Wage-Earning Women's Club for Equal Suffrage, and the Women's Trade Union League leader Leonora O'Reilly, an organizer for the New York State Woman Suffrage Association, spoke to the strikers.[82] After police brutality escalated, concerned middle-class women intervened by stepping in as observers to discourage rough treatment. For example, Mary Gannett, Florence Kitchelt, Catherine Rumball, and Alice Clement joined the approximately fifty women who attended a meeting in early March. Gannett and Rumball spoke to women strikers, invited them to address meetings of middle-class women, and walked the picket line.[83] Although less visible than in the New York City strikes, other middle-class Rochester women, virtually all suffragists, also offered their support to the women strikers.

The strike ended in March, eight weeks after it began, when the Clothiers' Exchange finally agreed to honor the majority of the strikers' demands: the abolition of subcontracting, a fifty-two hour workweek with time-and-a-half for overtime, five annual legal holidays, and an agreement that workers would not be discriminated against for joining a union. They did not get the right to arbitrate disagreements with their employers. Collective bargaining would have to wait another six years, until the more militant Amalgamated Clothing Workers of America replaced the United Garment Workers in Rochester's garment factories.[84] Members of the Rochester Political Equality Club, the Socialist Party, and the settlements, all of whom supported women workers during the strike in 1913, intensified their suffrage activism among workers. The New York City laundry worker and co-founder of the Wage Earners' League for Woman Suffrage, Maggie Hinchey, addressed women in Rochester, making a direct link between women's poor working conditions and their lack of suffrage.[85] Judging by the crowds that turned out to hear Hinchey and other socialist suffrage speakers, growing numbers of clothing workers supported woman suffrage.

Rochester Suffrage Revived

In 1912, the Rochester Political Equality Club continued to mobilize as it had after the Triangle Shirtwaist fire, electing the vivacious Alice Clement to succeed the tactically conservative president Mena Brown.[86] Clement had supervised the music education program in the Rochester City Schools prior to her election to the club. A relative newcomer to suffrage work, Clement attempted to resurrect the vitality of the Rochester suffrage movement, seeking to restore it to the level it had reached under the direction of Susan B. Anthony and her sister Mary.[87] Clement earned praise for her efforts to increase the visibility of the cause when she set up an office to distribute literature and sponsor public activities. She did her best to modernize suffrage publicity tactics by selling buttons, hosting mass meetings, and encouraging "house-to-house" and "shop-to-shop" canvassing work.[88]

Clement borrowed New York City strategies to lead Rochester suffragists, who attracted the attention of working-class people through meetings, pageants, and parades. The Rochester Political Equality Club made a special effort to invite speakers who would appeal to working-class women. In March 1913, the club invited the suffragist and lawyer Inez Milholland to speak. She addressed an overflowing assembly hall at East High School, making a plea for "the entrance of the humane into politics." According to the "capable, charming, and earnest" Milholland, seven million women in the United States needed to work or they would starve to death. She argued that the working woman should be afforded the same protections as the working man who "with the ballot [is] sovereign; without [it] he is a slave."[89] Others on the platform included younger members of the Rochester Political Equality Club attired in white frocks trimmed with yellow sashes lettered with "Votes for Women."[90] In July, the women's float made its way past a crowd of approximately 50,000 in an evening pageant on the banks of the Genesee River. The float, "entered in the interest of woman suffrage," depicted a mother perched on a wicker throne holding a clinging baby, and appeared among the boat and canoe club entries. The suffrage float evoked "generous applause from the onlookers."[91]

In 1914, local suffrage women took to the streets to target primarily male factory workers at lunch time and again at quitting time. After securing the permission of authorities, suffragists dressed in purple, white, and green and spoke to "giggling girls and jeering men." Gradually they won over the growing crowd, especially when "the prettiest girls announce[d] that they [were] going to speak to no man who is not wearing a suffrage button."[92] That summer, a procession of sixty suffragists, clad in white-hooded robes or "dominos" and carrying placards, paraded through downtown streets, offering a rather eerie spectacle. The women, hiding "their charming faces under masks so that the public's gaze may not rove from the placards," advertised the upcoming visit of Dr. Anna Howard Shaw. Led by six mounted policemen, the suffragists, in rows of three abreast, carried the names of the states where suffrage had already been won. Women bearing signs with information about Shaw's appearance the following week wore blue robes trimmed in gold. To attract even more attention, two buglers followed the procession. The day before Shaw's arrival, suffragists held a second parade led by the Ontario Beach Park Band.[93] The innovative tactics stopped bystanders in their tracks.

Suffragists from all over the state organized "motor caravans" to travel to Rochester for the forty-sixth New York State Woman Suffrage Association annual convention in October 1914.[94] The "automobile pilgrims" held meetings and rallies along the way to Rochester, taking advantage of every opportunity to promote suffrage to working-class and rural voters.[95] The *Sun* reported on all the "casualties," especially among the drivers, of the caravan led by the New York State Woman Suffrage Association president Gertrude Foster Brown. One woman dropped out for medical reasons, while Maud Nathan stopped in Utica to remind Theodore Roosevelt of "what women expected" of him, and Cora L. [Mrs. Arthur] Dunlavey, whose husband acted as her chauffeur, stopped at farms and in outlying villages to give speeches. When Brown's car would not start again, she and her companions had to take a train into Syracuse. She claimed that she'd had such a "splendid time that nothing could worry her now." The socialite Rosalie Jones, the "general" who had led hikers to Albany just the year before, kept her automobile, named "Victory," in top running order. The New Yorker Jane Olcott unexpectedly but willingly transported fire fighters to a burning house in Cortland. She then took advantage of her honorary status as a member of the fire department to hold a suffrage meeting.[96] At their brief layover in Syracuse, the women held a banquet and a series of street meetings.[97]

Once they arrived in Rochester, suffragists traveled in "gaily decorated cars" to Exposition Park. At the opening session in Convention Hall, Mayor Hiram Edgerton cordially welcomed the women to his city. While he initially claimed that he did not support woman suffrage, by the time he left the platform and the five hundred enthusiastic delegates to the convention, he had changed his mind.[98] Much of the convention focused on hearing reports from various groups, ranging from the congressional committee of the national association to smaller gatherings "of workers for each Campaign District with their Chairmen."[99] The National American Woman Suffrage Association president, Carrie Chapman Catt, reported that 141 of the state's 150 assembly districts had been organized. The New York Women's Trade Union League president, Melinda Scott, also addressed the convention, highlighting the cross-class connections between suffragists and working women.[100] Rochester's residents could not help but be impressed by the suffrage energy that spilled from open-air meetings to parades, churches, automobile clubs, moving picture performances, and suffrage booths at local fairs. One anti-suffrage newspaper conceded, "A cause presented in so fair and reasonable manner must receive the respect due and the earnest consideration it deserves."[101]

In the months leading to the referendum, suffragists employed even more "dramatic appeal[s]" to publicize their claims. In March 1915, Florence

Kitchelt led an army of black-robed college graduate suffragists wearing "Votes for Women" sashes down the aisle of the Naturalization Court in Rochester. Kitchelt and the other women intended the demonstration not to be "a slur upon the men being naturalized" but to be "a silent protest against a system of government which had given the ballot to men who scarcely understand our language and denied it to women."[102] Taking her cue from labor organizers, Catt appealed to religious groups. She encouraged campaign workers to make preliminary visits to each and every church in their communities. She informed them that "on the last Sunday before the election an appeal will be sent out from clergymen high in the councils of every church—Protestant, Catholic and Jewish—to their brother clergymen," asking them to make a strong plea for the suffrage bill.[103] At least some religious officials answered her plea. In October 1915, the *Catholic Journal* featured a statement by the Reverend John H. O'Rourke, claiming that "women shop workers receive less pay than men for the same work, labor longer hours, and have less protection from fire and for health." He announced himself in favor of "giving women a chance to influence legislation by the vote."[104]

Anti-suffrage forces upstate responded to increased suffrage support by hiring "scores of paid Italian and Polish agents to do missionary work and to give voting instructions to voters of respective nationalities."[105] The Rochester *Democrat and Chronicle* carried large advertisements, sponsored by the anti-suffragists, urging voters not to support woman suffrage in the months prior to the election. One advertisement claimed that New York already had better protective legislation for women and children in the workplace than any of the suffrage states and that eighty percent of the state's women did not want the right to vote.[106] With only two pro-suffrage advertisements during the same period, anti-suffrage sentiment appeared stronger in the city.[107] Anti-suffrage attitudes extended to the press, where four of the five daily papers opposed woman suffrage in their editorials and in the lack of attention they afforded suffrage events. On the eve of the referendum, with leading politicians and their male supporters remaining staunch in their anti-suffragism, suffrage support in Rochester remained uncertain.

Suffrage Setbacks in Rochester

By the turn of the century, Rochester's industrial growth outpaced most other upstate cities. Immigrant women in the city's garment factories proved especially vulnerable to workplace issues including low wages, long hours, sexual harassment, and unsafe conditions. For immigrant women workers in particular, attaining full industrial citizenship replete with the ballot promised a better life for them and for their children. Like immigrants in other

upstate cities like Buffalo and Utica, Rochester's immigrants patronized settlement houses and the other local organizations that sponsored activities
for them. In 1907, Rochester reformers set the precedent for using schools to
spread the word of democracy in what became known as social centers. The
social centers' community forums could become training grounds for participatory democracy and, by extension, for suffrage. Rochester's Republican
political machine fought against the increasing involvement of the immigrant population in politics and brought the centers to rather abrupt ends.
The objections began in 1910, when a Jewish girls' club held a masquerade
dance on a Sunday afternoon, offending some within the Christian community. A few months later, the suffrage supporter and University of Rochester professor Kendrick Shedd further offended the conservative community
when he held a discussion on socialism. Financial backers pulled their funding from social centers across the city, forcing many to close. In the process,
Shedd lost his faculty position.[108]

Progressive reformers worked hard to address the city's problems, but
the Republican Party's conservative grip on business and politics presented
a more formidable obstacle than in other upstate cities. Though he initially
made some concessions to suffragists, such as endorsing Helen Montgomery's school board candidacy, the Republican leader George W. Aldridge later
took advantage of the suffrage movement's lull in the first decade of the
twentieth century to turn hostile toward the reformers. He arranged to have
Montgomery removed from the school board in 1910, just as the director
of the social centers, Edward Ward, left to organize a social center program
for the University of Wisconsin; Montgomery's removal spelled the end of
social centers in the city.[109] Between 1911 and 1915, George Eastman, George
Aldridge, and their counterparts stifled reform activities just as suffragists
tried to build a solid base for woman suffrage. Suffragists defiantly held their
first ever series of open air meetings outside factory gates. They orchestrated
noontime meetings close to Kodak Park, Eastman's main manufacturing
complex, and near the entrance of Bausch and Lomb Optical Works, so that
women workers could attend.[110] Despite these efforts, suffragists found it
difficult to overcome opposition from male industrial and political leaders.

The influence of the indomitable Women's Educational and Industrial
Union waned as well when a number of the organization's key personalities
left to pursue reform goals elsewhere. President Helen Barrett Montgomery
departed to lead the ecumenical woman's missionary movement under the
auspices of the National Federation of Church Women. With her departure,
"feminist activist" Mary Gannett assumed the presidency. A more assertive
suffragist than Montgomery, Gannett found success by appointing suffragists

to the union's board more so than by recruiting new members—working-class or otherwise—to become part of the organization.[111] In the wake of the Triangle Shirtwaist fire, when factories across the state came under scrutiny, the union, together with the Women's Relief Corps and the Rochester Political Equality Club, commissioned the Crane Sanitary Survey.[112] Caroline Bartlett Crane, a social reformer known as "America's Housekeeper" for her efforts to improve urban sanitation, conducted an extensive investigation and compiled a detailed description of health and living conditions in Rochester.[113] Crane's findings highlighted several slum areas and exposed dangerous unsanitary practices, including water contamination and unsafe milk distribution. This negative publicity outraged many of the city's leading citizens, who withdrew financial support from the union.[114] This might help to explain the weakening power of Rochester's women's activist groups and the subsequent rise of the organized anti-suffrage movement.

Since Rochester lacked a strong mainstream reform movement, working-class activists could not rely on support from any but the most radical labor and suffrage advocates, like the Kitchelts. Richard Kitchelt and several of Rochester's liberal ministers and socialist sympathizers, including William Gannett and Edwin Rumball, supported suffrage. The demise of the *Common Good* began in 1913 when the Rumballs published a special issue on "Working Girls," causing offended financial backers to withdraw their support. Before it folded in 1914, the *Common Good* suggested a number of remedies to Rochester's social problems, including the organization of workers into labor unions, protective legislation, and, of course, woman suffrage.

Hard hit by the death of the Anthony sisters almost a decade earlier, the city's suffrage forces entered a period of transition. They occasionally retreated to the parlor politics of the past rather than fully embracing the tactics of the new urban repertoire. Under Mena Brown's tenure, the Rochester Political Equality Club did little to advertise its cause or to support Rochester workers until 1911. The next president, Alice Clement, energized the political equality club by working at the state and local levels, and in her capacity as chair of the Seventh Assembly District, to help to increase suffrage activity, until 1915.[115] She invited the nationally and internationally renowned suffragists Maud Younger, Sylvia Pankhurst, and Charlotte Perkins Gilman to speak to members of the club and to workers at the Labor Lyceum. In addition to spectacular stumping efforts such as the open-air meetings, club members intervened in strikes and began to court the workers' votes at the Lyceum.[116] These attempts to entice the labor vote, however, proved sporadic rather than systematic and failed to win the support of disheartened local labor leaders who believed that "any electoral challenge to business was futile."[117] Although the efforts of Rochester suffragists, including those in the Women's Educational and Industrial Union and the political equality club, resulted in some success, they failed to win the support of significant numbers of male voters.

By 1914, the anti-suffragists presented a well-organized force with access to the upper echelons of Rochester's political and economic power. The antis had strong ties both to Republican leaders and to business, including the Eastman Kodak Company, prominent nurserymen in the "Flower City," the Bausch and Lomb optics families, and the major department store owners. Rochester businessmen, with the exception of those in the garment industry, successfully kept unions out of their factories. Employers perceived the strong link between unions and suffrage activity as a threat to worker loyalty. Upper-class professional women and men, including the president of the University of Rochester and some faculty wives, stood in opposition to votes for women, because to hold otherwise risked people's professional positions—as happened in the case of Professor Shedd.[118]

In the 1915 referendum, the Italian Sixteenth Ward stands out as the only immigrant ward to pass the referendum in an anti-suffrage city, in an anti-suffrage county—a testament to Florence Kitchelt's suffrage work.[119] While the activism of suffragists alone could not effectively challenge oppositional forces, activists learned that they had to form alliances on all levels to grasp full industrial citizenship. The most militant had to reach out to women of diverse backgrounds to help them in their fight. They moved past traditional trade union circles to realize their rights in the workplace and beyond. A few middle-class allies, some influenced by socialist doctrines, introduced recruits to a world of power and influence that, through suffrage and lobbying, insured that the state would protect their welfare. Above all, suffrage activists learned that they had to build cross-class coalitions with union men, progressive middle-class and upper-class women, and the working women they sought to organize.[120]

CHAPTER 4

A Fundamental Component

Suffrage for African American Women

Sarah J.S. Garnet, representing the Colored Women's Equal Suffrage League of Brooklyn, and Irene L. Moorman, the president of the Negro Women's Business League, met with the wealthy and fervent white suffragist Alva Vanderbilt Belmont in January 1910 at the office of Belmont's Political Equality Association. They arranged a February 6 meeting to be held at Mount Olivet Baptist Church on West Fifty-Third Street. Belmont, like Ella Hawley Crossett and the civil rights activist Fanny Garrison Villard, wanted to expand the base of support for woman suffrage and sought ways to include black women in a "colored" branch of her association.[1] At the invitation of Garnet and Moorman, two hundred women and men gathered to hear Belmont "endorse the idea of racial equality and the expansion of suffrage to all American citizens."[2] She promised to fund a meeting place for the black women's branch of her Political Equality Association when it enrolled one hundred members.

Black women had already established a strong coalition of suffrage activism; they did not need white women to organize them. As a consequence, they responded only halfheartedly to Belmont's call.[3] According to the report of the meeting in the influential black newspaper the *New York Age*, the pro-suffrage speeches by the white women "did not evoke much applause," and some of the women who joined the African American branch of the Political Equality Association planned to support the branch financially but not to participate regularly in its activities.[4] Crossett, then in her final year as the president of the New York State Woman Suffrage Association, invited African American suffragists to send a delegation to Albany on March 9, 1910, to appear before a state legislative committee at the hearing on the woman suffrage bill.[5] She also invited them to affiliate with the state suffrage organization, which some individual women did.[6]

True to their commitment to "uplift" the race, black women wove agitation for the vote into their activism for civil rights, moral reform, and community improvement. Because black women typically had more power within their own communities than did white women in theirs, black women saw the need for suffrage differently than white women did. Issues that occupied the energies of white women, such as the need for "equality within their families, political rights, and access to paid work," did not mean as much to black women.[7] Some black women did not feel the necessity to press for the vote as much as they felt the need to agitate to "emancipate their race from the oppressive conditions under which they lived."[8] However, core groups of black women certainly agitated for the vote throughout the movement, with or without a connection to white women's suffrage organizations. They saw the vote as a way to solve the problems the black race—and especially women—faced, including segregation, lynching, and other forms of systematic racism.[9]

Generally more financially stable and educated than blacks who migrated from the south after the turn of century, many activist women came from families long established in the north. Most of these middle- and upper-class women and men supported woman suffrage.[10] The network of elite African Americans in the major cities of the coastal northeastern states included

This group portrait of young black women originally graced the first page of an article in support of woman suffrage that appeared in the NAACP's *Crisis: A Record of the Darker Races*, August 1915. Image courtesy of the Herman B. Wells Library, Indiana University, Bloomington, IN.

dynamic women reformers. Mary Burnett Talbert of Buffalo and Hester Jeffrey of Rochester focused their efforts in upstate New York. Sarah Garnet, the first African American female school principal in New York City; her sister, Susan McKinney Steward, the first African American woman to practice medicine in New York State; Victoria Earle Matthews, founder in 1897 of the White Rose Mission; Maritcha Lyons, the first black school principal to supervise both black and white teachers; Verina Morton-Jones, another doctor and a founder of the Lincoln Settlement House in 1908; and businesswoman Irene Moorman all worked in the New York metropolitan area.

These and many other black women actively sought the right to vote at the same time that white women agitated for voting rights. Black women had organized for woman suffrage decades before, although most often within organizations devoted to broader social activist agendas. Belmont tried to take advantage of both the strong suffrage sentiment black women already harbored and their firmly-established networks to enfold them into the New York State suffrage coalition. Though the history of black women's suffrage has been rendered nearly invisible by the paucity of archival materials, it is still possible to reconstruct a compelling portrait of the commitment and sacrifice of these dedicated reformers.[11] They did not rely on white women to tell them they needed the right to vote; they began organizing for the franchise in New York State as early as the 1880s and, in spite of the racism they faced, they would actively seek their enfranchisement throughout the entire struggle.

African American women rarely separated the quest for the vote from the other activism in which they engaged. Many black women came to fear that white women would "devise something akin to an exclusionary 'grandmother's clause'" to keep black women from voting once they won the vote.[12] Some scholars argue that, in fact, "racist attitudes provided additional impetus" for black women's struggle.[13] Much of their activism and work for woman suffrage and women's rights occurred as a fundamental component of their activities in clubs such as the Negro Women's Business League or in the National Association of Colored Women's Clubs or its affiliates, such as Phyllis Wheatley Clubs, the Empire State Federation of Women's Clubs, or the Northeastern Federation of Colored Women's Clubs.[14] Most women who supported enfranchisement did so as part of their goal to improve the status of black women in addition to that of black men and children.

The early twentieth century was "characterized by racial segregation, defamation of the character of Black women, and lynching of black Americans, both men and women," making it a dangerous period to have been a person of color in the United States.[15] The very years when "racial prejudice became acceptable, even fashionable, in America" marked greater respectability and broad acceptance of the woman suffrage movement.[16] Not radical in their thinking, these women reformers believed that the vote would give them the power to change what was wrong with the social and political systems in the United States.[17] Their first task was to obtain racial equality; obtaining women's rights would come next.[18] Black women also formed a fundamental component of the woman suffrage movement, adding their voices to the coalition working for women's right to vote.

Activist Limits and Support

Black women had a deep-rooted reform tradition and had long supported woman suffrage in spite of numerous challenges.[19] Fannie Barrier Williams blamed slavery for the problems faced by black women of the time, arguing that "slavery left her in social darkness, and freedom has been slow in leading her into the daylight of the virtues, the refinements and the blessed influences that center in and radiate from the life of American free women."[20] During the debates following the Civil War, all too many of the reformers "fell into the trap of assuming black to be male and women to be white." Black women struggled to keep their enfranchisement goals in the minds of other reformers.[21] However, as Jane Dabel points out regarding the nineteenth century, the activism of black women "was not explicitly feminist." They focused on the needs of their communities rather than on women's needs exclusively.[22]

Enfranchisement simply made perfect sense to black women. Louisa Jacobs, the daughter of Harriet Jacobs, who escaped slavery in the 1850s, served as a speaker for the American Equal Rights Association in the next decade. She helped to spread a message of universal suffrage and equal rights for women and men, black and white. Later she attended meetings of the New York-based National Woman Suffrage Association.[23] A few other black activists supported the national association and attended white women's suffrage meetings.[24] Before and after the Civil War, Sojourner Truth, also a member of the American Equal Rights Association between 1866 and 1869, passionately called for the right of black women to vote, along with equality and justice.[25] In what became her last appearance at a women's rights meeting, Truth attended the 1878 National Woman Suffrage Association convention in Rochester.[26] Attendees commemorated the thirty years since the first Woman's Rights Convention held at Seneca Falls, but by that point many members felt discouraged because women still did not have the right to vote.

Few black women attended, but Truth, who did attend, entreated her audience to "take their rights" rather than beg for them.[27]

Truth's long-time friend, the venerable activist Harriet Tubman, had supported votes for women since at least the Civil War, "faithfully" attending suffrage meetings in upstate New York.[28] According to one of her biographers, Catherine Clinton, whenever Tubman heard about a woman suffrage meeting, she would "grab her shawl and hat and head for the Auburn train station" and board the next train going in the direction she wanted to go.[29] At the twenty-eighth annual New York State Woman Suffrage Association convention, held in Rochester in 1905, Susan B. Anthony, holding Tubman's hand, introduced her to the delegates as a "living legend."[30] A year later, Tubman rode the train with the white suffragist and philanthropist Emily Howland to attend another suffrage meeting in Rochester. Tubman sat up all that night in the train station, knowing that no hotel in the city would give her a room. The next day, when a "horrified" Howland found out what Tubman had endured, she insisted that conference organizers provide lodgings for women of color who attended suffrage meetings.[31] Other white suffragists also made connections with Tubman. For example, Elizabeth Smith Miller sponsored her as a life member of the Geneva suffrage club.[32]

Another early black suffrage supporter, Charlotte E. Ray, also attended National Woman Suffrage Association meetings, as did her sister, the poet H. Cordelia Ray. The daughter of a pastor well known for his work on the Underground Railroad and his editorship of the New York newspaper, the *Colored American*, Charlotte was the first woman to graduate from Howard Law School in 1872.[33] She engaged in the discussions about resolutions at the 1876 ninth annual convention of the association held at the Masonic Hall in New York City.[34] When the National and American Woman Suffrage Associations merged in 1890, many black women supported the National American Woman Suffrage Association, although the alliance remained fraught with racial tension.[35] While there are instances of black and white suffragists working together in the wake of the Civil War, for the most part they and their organizations remained segregated. For black women, racism and classism discouraged their involvement in white women's suffrage organizations. The *New York Times* reported in 1911 that when Harriet Alice Dewey, wife of the Columbia University professor John Dewey, tried to host an interracial suffrage meeting in her uptown apartment, the landlord insisted that she cancel it. He emphasized that the attendance of black women was the reason.[36] Most women preferred to work through separate organizations even into the twentieth century.

Any study of women of color confounds our understanding of class. The suffrage activist Addie Jackson, for example, took in washing and ironing, "day's work," or housecleaning, in the Brooklyn area during the 1880s.[37] Her class status improved significantly over the decades, as illustrated by her mobility and volunteerism. As soon as her life stabilized, Jackson found more time to devote to activist causes. By the 1910s she lived in Tarrytown, and the New York Age noted her as a participant in a number of activities related to suffrage and other activism. She also attended the fifth annual meeting of the Empire State Federation of Women's Clubs in Buffalo for a two-day session in July 1913. Members of the club made sure that the New York Age announced its support for woman suffrage.[38] Alice Wiley Seay founded the federation in 1908 to coordinate the influence of the black women's clubs in the state and to help support Harriet Tubman and her home for the aged in Auburn.[39] Jackson served as its financial secretary, an office she held for several years.[40]

While many New York activist women joined clubs between the 1860s and the 1910s, not all African American women agreed on how to improve their status or bolster their "collective prospects," of course.[41] However, most black women believed that they made more progress through their own organizations because white women's clubs not only barred them from participation, they sometimes interfered with their efforts.[42] Although some black women's clubs and organizations that concentrated solely on woman suffrage existed, out of necessity most clubs focused on far more than just getting the right to vote for black women. Virtually all of the women who agitated for woman suffrage deeply committed themselves to a range of progressive causes such as establishing homes for orphans and the elderly, trying to guarantee the protection of Fourteenth Amendment rights, racial uplift, education, settlement house work, and public health. Ending the lynching of black women and men, anti-miscegenation, and Jim Crow legislation also expended the energies of these civil rights activists.[43] The multitude of problems and challenges that black women and the black community faced was such that to concentrate exclusively on woman suffrage was a luxury few could afford.

Church membership also proved integral to black women's organizing and activism during this period.[44] As the historian Evelyn Higginbotham points out, "clubwomen themselves readily admitted to the precedent of church work in fostering both a 'woman's consciousness' and a racial understanding of the 'common good.'"[45] Most women learned leadership and organizational skills in the churches, which gave them "the collective strength and determination to continue their struggle for the rights of blacks and the rights of women."[46] The churches, especially the Baptist and African Methodist Episcopal denominations, proved particularly welcoming to the speeches and debates of women advocating for enfranchisement. Women turned to church membership in order to carry on their work for woman suffrage. For example, when Mabel E. Brown began canvassing for support for woman suffrage in Rochester in early 1917, she asked W. E. B. Du Bois to write letters of introduction to ministers.[47] Church newspapers and publications also offered black women opportunities to articulate and promote their views regarding women's rights.

Some black men, like some white men, opposed woman suffrage. A prevailing attitude dictated that black men take on the responsibility of financially supporting their women, implying that black women ought not need to work—contrary to the reality for many black households.[48] Countering these attitudes, Nannie Burroughs, the principal of the National Trade and Professional School for Women and Girls in Washington, DC, argued along with others that black women needed the vote because black men did not understand its value.[49] Many black men also tried to block female membership in their organizations, especially in the most intellectual of them. Only after Anna Julia Cooper, the educator and author, protested women's exclusion from the American Negro Academy in Washington, DC, the society for intellectual and educational achievement founded in 1897, did the Reverend Alexander Crummell, a prominent minister and scholar, invite the New York educator Maritcha Lyons to speak at the academy.[50] A resolution passed at the 1910 National Association of Colored Women convention called men to account, stating, "we urge our men to show greater respect to the women of our race."[51]

Still, many black men joined the women who met in the churches, clubs, and other places to debate the topic of woman suffrage. W. E. B. Du Bois, taking "Frederick Douglass's place as the leading male feminist of his time," observed that "votes for women means votes for black women."[52] He, like most activists, realized that women's enfranchisement benefited everyone. Black women believed in the power of the vote to "acquire advantages and protection of their rights," particularly their rights to be free from sexual exploitation, to increase their access to education, and to protect their labor.[53] The ballot had come to signify "private self-respect and public dignity for women," a dramatic change in attitude since the latter half of the nineteenth century.[54] The meaning of citizenship had, by the 1910s, expanded to include aspects of social justice.

New York Women in the Broad Networks of Female Activism

Black women began collaborating in local self-help groups to achieve common goals after the end of the Civil War.[55] Just prior to the 1876 national centennial celebration in Philadelphia, the American-Canadian activist and journalist Mary Ann Shadd Cary, writing on behalf of ninety-four black women in the District of Columbia, appealed to the leaders of the New York-based National Woman Suffrage Association. They wanted their names added to the list of signers of the Declaration of Rights of the Woman, to be presented by Matilda Joslyn Gage and Susan B. Anthony at the celebration.[56] Cary applied the "universal-rights arguments developed by white suffragists to address the specific needs of black women," with the result that many more black women began to support woman suffrage.[57] Just four years later, Cary founded the first organization of black women with a broader reach, the Colored Women's Progressive Franchise Association, which had as one of its goals the promotion of equal rights and woman suffrage. Cary argued that the vote would "empower" women to make needed reforms in education, professionalize them in a wider array of occupations, and enable more independent thought.[58]

The need to vote pervaded virtually all of black women's club work. In 1892, Ida B. Wells, the guest of honor at a rally in New York to raise funds for her work in anti-lynching, brought together the suffrage advocates Victoria Earle Matthews, Maritcha Lyons, Sarah Smith Garnet, and Susan Smith McKinney of Brooklyn, among others.[59] They organized the Women's Loyal Union of New York and Brooklyn with Matthews as president. Drawing at least 150 members by 1894, the union sought to educate African Americans about their ability to support issues important to all black people, to encourage the "intelligent assertion of their rights," and to use every means possible to "retain the unmolested exercise" of those rights.[60] Those rights included a right to the ballot.

By the 1890s, New York women also served on the executive boards and committees of newly founded national-level associations for black women. At one meeting, Victoria Earle Matthews presented "The Value of Race Literature," contending that black women could dispel negative stereotypes through their own writing.[61] Sarah Garnet and others representing the Woman's Loyal Union also attended national meetings.[62] In Buffalo, Mary Burnett Talbert, Susan Evans, Mrs. Charles Davis, and several other women established the Phyllis Wheatley Club, as an affiliate of the National Association of Colored Women, to develop strategies and programs to uplift black communities and encourage suffrage support.[63] But negative images of black women as "promiscuous" or "immoral" hampered their work.[64] To counter this attitude, the national association celebrated the contributions of African American women and supported women's rights activism.[65] Members considered political activism and securing voting rights for women important focus issues.

In July 1904, at the fourth convention of the National Association of Colored Women, held in St. Louis, Missouri, Sarah Garnet gave "an excellent talk" on the suffrage question. At that same meeting a Mrs. Thurman made a motion that a suffrage department be organized under the supervision of the association for the "purpose of teaching our women the principles of civil government, political economy, etc., that they may thus be prepared to become intelligent voters and responsible citizens of this republic."[66] The motion, seconded by Rochester resident Hester Jeffrey, carried. Eventually, Sarah Garnet served as the superintendent of the suffrage department of the National Association of Colored Women, which had merged with the National Council of Women by 1905.[67] The umbrella organization "provided the infrastructure for local clubs to organize for the social, economic, and political improvement of black communities." The national association helped to nurture networks of women who, in turn, influenced the membership of their local organizations.

In May 1908, to celebrate the sixtieth anniversary of the first Woman's Rights convention in Seneca Falls, organizers invited Mary Church Terrell, the president of the National Association of Colored Women, to commemorate Frederick Douglass's work on behalf of the women's rights movement. Harriot Stanton Blatch represented her mother, Elizabeth Cady Stanton; Eliza Wright Osborne represented her mother, Martha Coffin Wright; and Fanny Garrison Villard represented Lucretia Mott. Antoinette Brown Blackwell, Lillie Devereux Blake, Annis Ford Eastman, Maud Nathan, and Anna Garlin Spencer also attended the ceremony. The women installed a large bronze tablet dedicated to the first convention. Suffragists began the summer campaign with a trolley trip through the Mohawk Valley, traveled by automobile to the Republican National Convention in Chicago, held open-air meetings for working class women across New York State, and ended with an Erie Canal boat trip from Albany to Buffalo before returning to New York City. Having found the U.S. women's movement "boring" and "repelling," Blatch had arranged the ceremony as part of this summer-long effort to infuse energy into the movement.[68]

Energy at the State Level

Sarah Garnet founded the Equal Suffrage League of Brooklyn in the late 1880s, and she eventually affiliated her organization with the National Association

The educator Sarah Jane Smith Thompson Garnet founded the Equal Suffrage League of Brooklyn in the late 1880s, continuing her work for woman suffrage until her death in 1911. The organization continued after her death. Image courtesy of the Schomburg Center for Research in Black Culture, New York Public Library, New York, NY.

of Colored Women's Clubs.[69] In the early years of the league members met in the back of her seamstress shop. Garnet argued that women had the "same human intellectual and spiritual capabilities as men," and that it opposed the tenets of democracy to deny women the right to vote.[70]

Initially many black women had reservations about supporting woman suffrage, fearing that "involvement in public, political activities would compromise their femininity."[71] But over time, women became convinced that the vote would protect them as workers, allow them to improve education for their children and themselves, and challenge black men's disenfranchisement. Increasing numbers of women found suffrage arguments convincing.[72] Eventually, the growing membership required that meetings be held in a larger space at the Young Men's Christian Association on Carlton Avenue.[73] Usually attendees enjoyed a musical performance, a report recounting the group's accomplishments since the previous meeting, and suffrage speeches by members or special guests.

Because the Equal Suffrage League remained active for at least thirty years, it drew a number of eminent activists into its fold. Sarah Garnet's social justice work ranged from her efforts to abolish race-based discrimination against black teachers to a commitment to equal rights for African American women relative to pay and suffrage.[74] Her younger sister, Dr. Susan Maria Smith McKinney Steward, helped to found the Equal Suffrage League and remained active in the suffrage and temperance movements.[75] In 1870, she had graduated as valedictorian from the New York Medical College for Women, founded by the staunch suffragist Dr. Clemence S. Lozier, a woman Steward considered a friend.[76] Addie Waites Hunton, better known for her anti-lynching work and her support of the Young Men's Christian Association, the Young Women's Christian Association, the National Association for the Advancement of Colored People (NAACP), the National Association of Colored Women, and the Empire Federation of Women's Clubs, regularly participated in league activities.[77] Alice Wiley Seay, the president of the Northeastern Federation of Women's Clubs, also maintained her membership in the league.

Another prominent member of the Equal Suffrage League, Verina Harris Morton-Jones, practiced as a physician in addition to her suffrage activism and volunteer social work.[78] A member of the board of the NAACP, Morton-Jones also helped to found organizations such as the National Urban League, the Association for the Protection of Colored Women, and the Cosmopolitan Society of America, which sought to end discrimination in New York City public facilities.[79] In 1908, Morton-Jones founded the Lincoln Settlement House in Brooklyn, providing both social services and moral uplift.[80] Like Garnet, Morton-Jones joined the National Association of Colored Women, eventually serving as the director of its Mothers' Club in Brooklyn. She also held membership in the Empire State Federation and the Northeastern Federation of Women's Clubs.[81]

Under Morton-Jones, who assumed the presidency of the Equal Suffrage League by 1906, the organization continued its suffrage activism.

Morton-Jones presided over the meeting when the league honored Susan B. Anthony following her death that year.[82] She invited Congressman William H. Calder, a native of Brooklyn, to speak at a meeting of the Equal Suffrage League at the Carlton Avenue Branch of the Young Men's Christian Association on March 28, 1908. As Morton-Jones presided, Garnet, then serving as suffrage superintendent of the National Association of Colored Women, presented an Equal Suffrage League petition "asking for the enactment of such legislation by Congress as will enforce the Fourteenth Amendment to the Federal Constitution" to Calder, who "assured the assemblage" that he would do "all he could for justice to all citizens."[83] In the fall of 1908, Morton-Jones took up residency at Clark University in Atlanta.[84] She remained president of the Equal Suffrage League nevertheless and returned to Brooklyn for a reception given in her honor in June 1909. Sarah Garnet, who remained active in the league after her tenure ended, took over the league in the absence of its president.[85]

Equal Suffrage League members continued to expand their activities to educate and recruit members. By February 1910, the league vice-president, Mary E. Eato, a teaching colleague of Sarah Garnet, presided over most of the Equal Suffrage League meetings and events.[86] The club hosted a celebration in honor of Abraham Lincoln and Frederick Douglass on February 16. According to the *Brooklyn Daily Eagle*, Attorney D. Macon Webster gave an "excellent" speech on suffrage for women before he gave his speech on Douglass, a man he had known personally. Some members read papers or poems. Alice Davis accompanied attendees singing woman suffrage songs. They also voted to accept the invitation of the Interurban Association, a New York City umbrella organization coordinating the efforts of twenty-three local clubs, to cooperate in its suffrage work. The league then elected Lydia C. Smith and Maria C. Lawton as delegates to attend state legislative proceedings in Albany on March 9.[87] During the March meeting, members sang suffrage songs before they heard an address given by Ida Craft, the president of the Kings County Organization of the New York State Woman Suffrage Association.[88] The league also celebrated the ninety-ninth anniversary of the birth of Harriet Beecher Stowe, the author of *Uncle Tom's Cabin*, at a public meeting in June 1910.[89] W. E. B. Du Bois spoke on the advancement of the race at another meeting of the Equal Suffrage League in April 1911.[90] These examples of suffrage activities highlight black women's commitment to woman suffrage.

Other prominent league members included Maritcha Rémond Lyons and Victoria Earle Matthews. Lyons, who grew up in a home that served as a station on the Underground Railroad, supported organizations such as the New York African Society for Mutual Relief and held membership in St. Philip's

Protestant Episcopal Church.[91] Deeply involved in social reform, Lyons supported the Howard Colored Orphanage Asylum in Brooklyn as well as woman suffrage.[92] Matthews, in spite of marriage and motherhood, found time to be active as a journalist and as a clubwoman.[93] Her writing, often in dialect in her early body of work, prompted the predominately white Women's National Press Association to invite her to join its ranks.[94] In addition to her leadership in the Woman's Loyal Union of New York and Brooklyn, Matthews cofounded the National Federation of Afro-American Women, serving as its first chairperson, and the National Association of Colored Women, where she acted as chair of the Executive Board and a national organizer.

Because of her activism at the national level, Matthews rose to become one of the most prominent and well-regarded black activists in the country.[95] When her sixteen-year-old son died, the tragedy impelled her to become more deeply involved in helping less fortunate people in New York City.[96] She founded the White Rose Mission to counter the dominance of the so-called employment agencies that forced naive young women into debt and "depravity."[97] Although many women, including Maritcha Lyons, supported Matthews's White Rose Mission, the activist and educator Frances Reynolds Keyser served the mission as Matthews's foremost assistant. Keyser's devotion to the mission freed Matthews to travel and speak extensively. As a result, Matthews played an important role in the "national African American women's club movement and interracial social reform efforts."[98] The networks of reform that she and other women built strengthened black women's suffrage activism and attracted new members.

Having worked with Sarah Garnet and Verina Morton-Jones, Irene L. Moorman, a businesswoman, eventually took over as a prominent leader for suffrage. Moorman represented the Metropolitan Business Women's Club in the Northeastern Federation of Colored Women's Clubs.[99] At about the same time, she became more deeply involved in activism and reform, joining the Equal Suffrage League of Brooklyn in December 1907, when she spoke at a meeting held in tribute to the radical abolitionist John Brown.[100] Notable activist women such as Margaret Murray Washington, Fannie Barrier Williams, and Mary Church Terrell visited Moorman in her Brooklyn office, signifying her increasingly respected role as a social activist.[101] By 1908, members of the Empire State Federation of Women's Clubs had elected her as treasurer. She rubbed elbows with Lyons as well as Keyser and spoke at fundraisers for Verina Morton-Jones's Lincoln Settlement House.[102] In October 1910, she represented the Negro Men's and Women's Branch of the Political Equality Association at the forty-second annual New York State Woman Suffrage Association convention in Niagara Falls. There, Moorman and representatives of the Harlem Club and the Wage Earners' League spoke about the ways that settlement house workers promoted suffrage and political equality in the city.[103]

Other clubs supporting woman suffrage existed in the Greater New York area. For example, Maria C. Lawton, one of the presidents of the Empire State Federation of Women's Clubs, also served as president of the Harriet Beecher Stowe Equality League of Kings County, founded in July 1910. In addition to the goal of securing the ballot, members expected to promote the advancement of the race and to give women a voice in government decision making. To help meet their objectives, members intended to reach out to young laborers in department stores to enlist their aid in the campaign.[104] New Rochelle hosted a Colored Women Suffrage League by 1915, offering events such as musicals to the public.[105] These organizational and membership efforts helped to increase the visibility of black women's suffrage involvement.

African American women and men often debated woman suffrage in their churches, lyceums, and elsewhere. Typically, a prominent leader like Frances Reynolds Keyser would read a paper about her views on woman suffrage, followed by presentations by other suffrage proponents.[106] The Brooklyn Literary Union, an "anchor for intellectual discussion and social reform," hosted lectures on a variety of topics, including woman suffrage.[107] Maritcha Lyons had once served the organization as vice-president, and the membership included several women who worked for woman suffrage.[108] Occasionally women and men would give their views on the opposing side of the issue, as happened in Brooklyn in April 1909. Anti-suffragists Sarah Brown, Miss A. A. Sampson, John D. Jones, and Mrs. Stuart articulated their views in opposition to women's enfranchisement at a meeting of the Equal Suffrage League at St. Mark's Lyceum.[109] The league sponsored mock conventions at the lyceum on two consecutive Thursdays that same month. Those who took part in the general discussion included Keyser, Lyons, Moorman, Wiley, Garnet, and Ida B. Wells-Barnett.[110] Several weeks later, people again discussed woman suffrage at the lyceum of the Metropolitan United African Methodist Episcopal Church.[111] The topic of suffrage drew large audiences of African American women and men in the city, as it did across the state.

Suffrage Clubs in Upstate New York

Victoria Earle Matthews served as a link between New York City and Rochester activists. She participated in the birthday celebration of Frederick Douglass, held on February 15, 1897 at Plymouth Church in Rochester, three years after the death of the beloved statesman. Those paying tribute also discussed the erection of a monument to commemorate his work as an abolitionist who championed civil rights, including suffrage for women. Because of his skills as a mediator, women of both races could come together to celebrate his life. In a letter composed for the occasion, Elizabeth Cady Stanton wrote, "He was the only man I ever knew who understood the degradation of the disfranchisement of women."[112] Those on the platform at the birthday celebration included Hester Jeffrey, the president of the local Colored Woman's Club; Susan B. Anthony, who read the letter from Stanton; and the Reverend Anna Howard Shaw of the National American Woman Suffrage Association. Jean Brooks Greenleaf, the retired president of the New York State Woman Suffrage Association, and Matthews, representing the National Association of Colored Women and recently returned from a national tour "in the interests of women of her race," joined them at the dais.[113]

Introduced as the "speaker of the evening" by Anthony, Matthews immediately took umbrage with Stanton's suggestion that a fitting tribute to Douglass would be to build a schoolhouse or a tenement for the poor and with Stanton's criticism of the proposed monument as "so many useless shafts of marble and granite." Acknowledging that many African American children "are naked and ignorant and in need of schools," Matthews argued that it was important for the black community have a person to whom "they can point as an example, an incentive, to their children . . . [to] stimulate a higher type of the youth of our race."[114] Her friend and colleague Frances Reynolds Keyser described Matthews as "enthusiastic, forceful . . . [with an] eager, restless spirit" that often caused her to seem intimidating or to be misunderstood.[115] Characteristically, Matthews dared to contradict a revered white women's rights activist publicly.

Matthews's companion on the platform, Hester C. Jeffrey, also devoted her life to civil rights activism and the uplift of her race. Jeffrey was born in Norfolk, Virginia, in 1842, to Robert and Martha Whitehurst Smith, both free people. At her childhood home, a station on the Underground Railroad, she met William Lloyd Garrison, Charles Sumner, and John Brown.[116] She married Jerome Jeffrey, a political activist who stored Frederick Douglass's *North Star* printing press in the basement of the Favor Street African Methodist Episcopal Church in Rochester.[117] Religiously devout, she attended services at the First Unitarian Church, ministered by the Reverend William Channing Gannett, after she and her husband moved to Rochester. Her church attendance stimulated a friendship with the minister's wife, Mary Thorn Lewis Gannett, who, like her husband, actively supported suffrage. Jeffrey also worshiped at the Memorial African Methodist Episcopal Zion Church.[118]

Hester Jeffrey founded the Susan B. Anthony Club in Rochester. Activism for woman suffrage com-
plemented her dedication and efforts for racial uplift. Image is from *An Authentic History of the
Douglass Monument* by J. W. Thompson (1903).

Jeffrey's leadership in a number of organizations and her commitment to social and political activism kept her at the forefront of black women's club work in Rochester from the 1890s into the 1910s. Alongside colleagues such as Victoria Earle Matthews, she functioned as an integral member of a broader, statewide community of black activist women.[119] Jeffrey founded organizations such as the Climbers to encourage "both improvement and protest, combined in the concept of 'uplift.'"[120] As the most highly educated black woman in Rochester and a role model, she funded a scholarship for young women to attend the Mechanics Institute in Rochester (now the Rochester Institute of Technology) through the Hester C. Jeffrey Club of the African Methodist Episcopal Zion Church.[121] In 1901, she helped establish a nine-member branch of the Woman's Christian Temperance Union; the president, Mrs. A. K. Mason, and most members hailed from the Zion Church.[122] In addition to her church work, Jeffrey held a position as an organizer for the National Association of Colored Women; she once presented an address on the "Pioneers in Woman's Suffrage" to its membership.[123] She also served as organizer for and president of the Empire State Federation of Women's Clubs.

Hester Jeffrey supported woman suffrage even before she met a colleague of Susan B. Anthony sometime in the 1890s, and through her met Anthony. Although Anthony is often criticized for her "willingness to accept racist allies and racist arguments in the name of political expediency," locally she supported the political and social aims of the Rochester-area African American community, clearly recognizing their right to a political voice.[124] Jeffrey was not the only black woman to work closely with Anthony. Ida B. Wells-Barnett stayed in the Anthony home during a visit to Rochester. When Anthony's secretary refused to do some clerical work for Wells-Barnett, Anthony fired her.[125] Jeffrey had a place on the platform during a mass meeting to protest Negro disenfranchisement held at the Central Presbyterian Church in Rochester on April 28, 1903, when Anthony spoke about the similarities between the situations of white women and African Americans.[126] Jeffrey accepted Anthony's invitation to join the Rochester Political Equality Club; she steadfastly sought to bridge the divide between black and white suffrage activists.

In 1902, the tireless Jeffrey organized Rochester's Susan B. Anthony Club for Colored Women, serving as its first president. The club met to discuss the importance of obtaining woman suffrage but also sought to get young black women admitted to the University of Rochester.[127] At the 1903 celebration of Susan B. Anthony's birthday, club members joined other "special guests" in presenting Anthony with an enamel green and white pin in the shape of a four-leaf clover bearing the initials of their club.[128] The club drew many members from the Zion Church, including Lucy J. Sprague, a colleague of Jeffrey in her church work as well as her suffrage and civil rights activism.[129]

Jeffrey also attended the New York State Woman Suffrage Association annual convention in Rochester in 1905, representing the Empire State Federation of Women's Clubs and her suffrage club. Jeffrey's report at the convention focused on the club movement among black women, including "mothers' clubs, domestic science clubs, and literary clubs," and black women's work in "hospitals, homes, and social settlements."[130] In discussing the work of the Susan B. Anthony Club, Jeffrey shared examples of activism, including visiting the financially needy, beyond just suffrage-related work.[131] That same year, Jeffrey invited Anthony to speak at the African Methodist Episcopal Zion Church in Rochester to celebrate the centennial of William Lloyd Garrison's birth. There, the eighty-five-year-old Anthony presented her last public speech.[132]

The only black woman to eulogize Anthony at the funeral following her death on March 13, 1906, Jeffrey expressed her profound grief to the other mourners. Speaking for members of her race, she pledged "to devote our time and energies to the work thou hast left us to do."[133] Two years later, Jeffrey and other members of the Susan B. Anthony Club oversaw the installation of a stained glass window commemorating Anthony's work for woman suffrage at the African Methodist Episcopal Zion Church, the first of several memorials to commemorate the esteemed suffrage leader.[134] Anthony's is one among eight memorial windows installed in the church; others commemorate Frederick Douglass, Harriet Tubman, and Lucy Sprague. Jean Brooks Greenleaf also attended the dedication, presenting a speech entitled "Susan B. Anthony as a Window."[135]

The National American Woman Suffrage Association also commemorated Susan B. Anthony on February 15, 1907, at its annual convention. Fannie Barrier Williams, the first black graduate of Brockport Normal School (now the College of Brockport, State University of New York), spoke in tribute to Anthony. She pointed out that Anthony "never wavered, never doubted, never compromised" in her "unremitting struggle for liberty, more liberty, and complete liberty for negro men and women in chains and for white women in their helpless subjugation to man's laws."[136] Williams frequently spoke and wrote on behalf of black women's intellectual and cultural advancement. Many of the suffrage and rights activists of both races possessed extraordinary reform energy.

A "whirlwind in her work for justice," Mary Barnett Talbert of Buffalo involved herself in an array of activist organizations including the Empire State Federation of Women's Clubs, the National Association of Colored

Women, the Niagara Movement, the NAACP, and the Anti-Lynching Crusaders. She and other members of the Phyllis Wheatley Club, founded in Buffalo in 1899, helped to support Harriet Tubman and her charity projects in Auburn, and they facilitated the development of a branch of the NAACP in Buffalo in 1915.[137] During World War I, Talbert would work for peace at the international level.[138] Reports of the activities of the Buffalo Phyllis Wheatley Club appeared regularly in "Buffalo Briefs," a column in the *New York Age*, highlighting the connections among black women throughout New York.[139]

New York black women continued to champion woman suffrage to their audiences, further developing their political activism and sometimes having a lot of fun in the process. For example, in Buffalo, in 1910, Annie Thomas of the Anihita Club and William Powell of Alpha Beta Sigma debated the "Enfranchisement of Women," eliciting enough interest from the audience that they later presented a playlet, "Why We Never Married," under the supervision of Mrs. H. H. Lewis, director of the choir at the First Methodist Church.[140] The performance suggested that the popular suffrage debate had devolved into a battle of the sexes rather than a discussion of the merits of women entering politics. Contingents of black women spoke about, wrote about, and debated political rights, as part of a viable and vibrant movement encompassing an extensive network in support of woman suffrage across the state.

Woman Suffrage in Jeopardy

Irene Moorman administered the Afro-American branch of the Political Equality Association, with its headquarters at 83 West One Hundred and Thirty-Fourth Street, New York, from its founding. Following the meeting called by Alva Belmont in February 1910, Moorman had presided and introduced all of the speakers. The "comfortably furnished" rooms of the suffrage branch, "well supplied with suffrage literature," remained open in the evenings of the fall and winter. There, women and men met for "various lecture courses and study classes in the season." If the group expanded, Belmont promised to move it to a "regular suffrage settlement house."[141] Moorman took an increasingly visible and more dynamic part in activities related to woman suffrage from this point on. On December 8, 1910, for example, as the organizer of the Political Equality Association, she presided over a Literary League meeting focused on woman suffrage. Moorman herself "waxed eloquent" on the subject as she introduced speakers Nettie A. Odell, Mrs. O. P. Morgan, and Harriet May Mills, the president of the New York State Woman Suffrage Association. Following the women speakers, Hubert Henry Harrison, the president of the Liberty League, and D. E. Tobias, a

British pan-Africanist who wrote about the status of blacks in the United States, spoke in favor of woman suffrage. Apparently the speechmaking continued well into the night, and the "evening was declared a grand success for the 'cause.'"[142]

New York suffragists also took advantage of travel opportunities to speak and learn about suffrage. In July 1911, Sarah Garnet traveled to London to attend the first Universal Races Congress, where her sister, Susan McKinney Steward, presented a paper entitled "The Afro-American Woman," highlighting the condition of black women in the United States. The league held a reception for Garnet in her home on September 7, 1911, with music and poetry. Garnet distributed suffrage literature she had gathered at the congress to members of the league. In addition to Steward's rereading of the paper she had presented at the congress, both W. E. B. Du Bois, who had also attended the congress, and Addie Hunton spoke on related topics. Many prominent people attended, including college president and professor John Hope and his wife, Lugenia Burns, from Atlanta; Verina Morton-Jones; Maritcha Lyons; and other members of the Equal Suffrage League.[143] Garnet died within twenty-four hours of that reception, and Brooklyn lost one of its foremost activists.

Black women's suffrage groups in New York encountered other difficulties as they sought to strengthen their connections to the broader woman suffrage movement. By October 1911, Alva Belmont had apparently lost interest in the branch headed by Irene Moorman. Moorman remarked on the club's "loneliness" and members' desire to "ally themselves with a good live suffrage organization."[144] Sarah Mulrooney Ruhlin, the president of the Women's Progressive Political League, took over the Negro branch of the Political Equality Club that month.[145] Then, in a March 1913 column for the *New York Age*, the journalist May Martel demanded that more black women participate in the suffrage struggle and criticized those who led the clubs but had been chosen more for a "glib tongue and suave manner" than for a commitment to the suffrage movement. She claimed that the organization under Mrs. O. H. P. Belmont had "gone to pieces." A thinly-veiled criticism of Moorman, the column seemed to presage a dearth of suffrage club reporting in the black newspapers.[146]

In spite of less publicity concerning their activities, quite a few black women retained their commitment to woman suffrage. Annie K. Lewis and the "stepladder speaker" and socialist Helen Holman led suffragists in Harlem, a place where the New York State Woman Suffrage Party estimated at least 15,000 African American women would be eligible to vote once enfranchised.[147] Holman contended that "woman's work has moved from the home to the factories, to the trusts. We must therefore enter politics to rear our race with health. If women don't know any more about politics than the average man, I'll guarantee we will get along."[148] The Empire State

Federation of Women's Clubs continued to hold meetings throughout the suffrage campaign. Maria Lawton hosted Mary Talbert, Mrs. Charlotte Dett of Niagara Falls, and Mrs. M. A. Lee of Rochester during a July 1914 federation meeting.[149] Lyda Newman worked through the Negro Suffrage Headquarters in Manhattan, while Annie K. Lewis and the Colored Women's Suffrage Club of New York City led the "final push in Harlem."[150] The club had been meeting right along, hosting suffrage speakers—often white women, such as when Mrs. H. Edward Dreier and Mrs. D. W. Barker addressed club members at Carlton Hall in 1914.[151]

Black women's suffrage activism began in the years after the Civil War and continued unabated throughout the battle for women's voting rights. Black women leaders, often forerunners in their professions, dominated efforts for suffrage in New York. Seldom free to concentrate on just one aspect of racial uplift, they sought political rights and racial equality. The historian Rosalyn Terborg-Penn contends that black women "could not afford to dismiss class or race in favor of sex as the major cause of oppression among Black women."[152] Far too many issues required their attention, and they could not promote racial uplift nor ignore racism and economic woes in the sole interest of enfranchisement. Their club work helped them to "challenge institutions in society that restricted black rights."[153] Beyond their activism as members of the Equal Suffrage League, the Susan B. Anthony Club, or other suffrage organizations, black women incorporated suffrage goals into virtually all aspects of their activism.

Although some black and white women tried to integrate the movement, which would have added greater strength to the woman suffrage coalition in New York State, the groups for the most part remained separate from each other.[154] Despite their frustration with racist aspects of white women's organizations, black women usually cooperated when white women made overtures, while remaining loyal to the goal of racial uplift. Black women forged inroads, connecting to white women's suffrage activism, by establishing relationships with white suffrage activists, affiliating their organizations wherever possible, attending white women's conventions, and involving themselves in state-level legislative efforts. However, black women refused to accept marginalization. Fannie Barrier Williams counseled women against discouragement by writing that black women "are furnishing material for the first chapter and shall some day recite the discouragements endured, the oppositions conquered, and the triumph of their faith in themselves."[155] In the meantime, black women's suffrage contributions were critical to the ultimate victory of women's enfranchisement.

 CHAPTER 5

Persuading the "Male Preserve"

Men and the Woman Suffrage Movement

On May 6, 1912, half a million New Yorkers watched in awe as one row of suffragists after another paraded along Fifth Avenue. The women, representing "every grade of society and every walk of life," impressed onlookers with their dignified solidarity.[1] Toward the end of the parade, a "solid cluster of men," led by the prominent banker James Lees Laidlaw and the writer and political activist Max Eastman, appeared following the ranks of women. An observer described the men as "grinning and a little sheepish," carrying banners, one reading: "Welcome Girls! Glad to Have You with Us." The catcalls and hisses explicitly reserved for the men faded as the last of more than 600 male suffragists passed by. A *New York Times* reporter speculated on the "inducement[s]" that would "make men march in a woman's parade." Perhaps a few, like the waistmakers and dentists, "may be looking for customers. . . . But the majority must firmly believe in the righteousness of the cause."[2] Men first marched in New York women's suffrage parades in 1911, and their presence became increasingly commonplace as the movement accelerated.

When it came to men's public support for woman suffrage, men usually deferred to the women who led the way. James Mott, the husband of Lucretia Mott, and Frederick Douglass had both shown their encouragement as early as the first Women's Rights Convention in Seneca Falls, in 1848. In addition to attending other women's rights meetings, Samuel J. May attended the founding convention of the New York State Woman Suffrage Association, in 1869, in Saratoga. The most fortunate suffragists, according to the *New York Tribune*, welcomed the support of their "husbands, brothers, and sweethearts."[3] Many a man aided and sustained suffragist women with money and personal sacrifice, making a significant difference to the woman suffrage movement. Male suffrage support, which had been sporadic and uneven in the nineteenth century, grew as the century waned.

The Unitarian minister William Channing Gannett of Rochester vigorously encouraged his wife's suffrage activism. In 1894, Mary Thorn Lewis Gannett attended the New York State Woman Suffrage Association Convention in Ithaca. Jean Brooks Greenleaf, the president of the state association, introduced Mary Gannett, by now an enthusiastic suffragist who had "left her two babies at the request of her husband to come and tell you why she wants the ballot." Gannett made a compelling speech to the convention, imploring women to "share the duties and responsibilities of the larger home—the City, the State, the Nation" with male citizens. Although William Gannett provides us with one example of a male suffrage advocate, men, either of their own volition or with their wives' encouragement, clearly became an integral part of the suffrage coalition.[4] By the dawn of the twentieth century, however, no organization of men dedicated to working toward woman suffrage yet existed in New York.[5]

Individual middle- and upper-class men of course supported their suffragist wives, sisters, mothers, and daughters, but most men generally avoided public displays of encouragement.[6] Men who visibly championed woman suffrage, such as those who marched in the May 1912 parade, surprised onlookers, and many men obviously felt uncomfortable openly admitting their sentiments. Over time, however, the sight of men working in tandem with women suffragists became more acceptable, thereby encouraging reluctant men to express their support.[7] While women had already made significant inroads in persuading the electorate, as men rallied to the women's cause, more (male) voters could now imagine an electorate that included women. Just a few short years before, seeing women in parades had shocked spectators; now seeing men willingly trailing behind contingents of marching women added a unique dimension to the strengthening suffrage coalition.

The Origins of the Men's League for Woman Suffrage

Women often faced a hostile environment when it came to promoting their right to the elective franchise. When suffragists adopted more daring tactics after 1908, male supporters stepped forward to defend women's entry into

the public arena while, simultaneously, male detractors of the suffrage movement continued to voice their opposition. In addition to trying to win over
men on the street, certain suffrage leaders realized the crucial need to win
state legislators to the side of suffrage. Elizabeth Cady Stanton's daughter
and the founder of the Women's Political Union, Harriot Stanton Blatch,
launched an aggressive campaign that began to focus more on cultivating
political support to encourage the legislature to respond favorably to a
woman suffrage referendum.[8] Once they had the support of the legislators
responsible for putting a referendum on the November 1915 ballot, the wom-
en's job would be to convince the majority of male voters to vote "yes" on
the referendum. Women found men useful as part of their suffrage coalition.

Suffragists rolled out a dynamic repertoire replete with speaking tours,
mass rallies, soapbox stumping, and parades, but even these tactics could
not guarantee success quickly enough to satisfy them. "Women," as Max
Eastman observed, "need all the help they can get."[9] Suffrage leaders like
the National American Woman Suffrage Association president Anna Howard Shaw (who tended to be more moderate than Harriot Stanton Blatch)
realized the necessity of expanding the association's influence along with
its tactics. At the same time suffragists campaigned in urban areas, they also
traveled outside the state's major population centers to tap into bases of
support found in the granges and other rural organizations.[10] Male suffrage
supporters, like their female counterparts, had to be willing to commit their
resources to broadly appeal to the New York legislature as well as to male
voters both upstate and downstate. As the suffrage struggle entered its sixth
decade, the establishment of a separate men's league seemed logical.[11]

A series of letters between Shaw and the *New York Evening Post* editor
Oswald Garrison Villard helps to unravel the origins of the Men's League
for Woman Suffrage.[12] On December 30, 1907, Shaw, advancing her efforts
toward cultivating new networks of allies, including women and men, wrote
to Villard. Acting on the suggestion of Villard's suffragist mother, Fanny Garrison Villard, Shaw invited him to speak at the National American Woman
Suffrage Association's annual convention in Buffalo.[13] Avoiding a commitment to a future speaking engagement, the over-taxed Villard asked Shaw
why a men's equal suffrage club could not be started. Villard did not volunteer to initiate such an organization, asserting instead, "if the right person
could be found . . . a men's club favoring suffrage could be formed in this city
which would have excellent names on it, and would be a useful organization
with which to impress the public and legislatures." Villard asked Shaw what
she thought of his suggestion.[14]

In Villard, Shaw found a well-connected man amenable to helping her
meet one of her suffrage goals. She responded that she had "thought much"

about forming a men's league that would ultimately become national.[15] Apparently she had been considering the idea for years but had concluded that "the men, whose influence and interest would enable them to draw [prominent names]... are too much occupied with other things to give their time and thought to Woman Suffrage." Shaw contended that "many men don't consider [woman suffrage] at the present time a vital issue." In addition, Shaw and other women feared that men would "encroach" upon and patronize their movement. With Villard willing to help initiate recruiting, however, Shaw happily offered a list of possible male supporters and let him know at the onset that she planned to relinquish any control of the potential organization.[16]

When it came to woman suffrage, Oswald Garrison Villard and Anna Howard Shaw seemed to be of a similar mindset. While Shaw had no intention of allowing the men any authority over the women's campaign, men's public support of woman suffrage was long overdue. The active enlistment of men into the movement and men's active participation in movement events would go a long way to lend credibility to woman suffrage among male voters. Anticipating the formal creation of a New York men's league, Villard added the names of several potential members to Shaw's list and proposed the organization "should be worked for all it is worth" by the local press. Furthermore, members should be ready to speak at hearings or participate in other events organized by woman suffragists. Villard reiterated the need for an organizing secretary to build the men's organization and encouraged National American Woman Suffrage Association affiliation. He asked Shaw if she knew anyone who would be willing to act as secretary.[17]

In the meantime, Villard conferred with his good friend Rabbi Stephen Wise about starting a league, well aware of the sarcastic remarks and the humiliation that members might face. Villard and Wise had been working together to promote the nomination of the New York governor Charles Evans Hughes for Supreme Court Justice and readily "agreed to share the ignominy, provided someone turned up to do the work" of organizing. Elated by the promise of a men's league, Wise could not contain his excitement and prematurely announced the plans for a men's league at the Fortieth Convention of the National American Woman Suffrage Association in Buffalo in October 1908.[18] New York suffragists at the convention, including Fanny Garrison Villard, Carrie Chapman Catt, Eliza Wright Osborne of Auburn, the socialist Jessie Ashley of New York City, Harriet May Mills, Lucy Calkins of Ithaca, and others assuredly greeted the plan with enthusiasm.[19]

Early the next year, a leader for a men's league presented himself in the person of Max Eastman. By the time the charismatic twenty-seven-year-old "turned up" in Rabbi Wise's office after a spring suffrage rally, Eastman had

MAX EASTMAN

The principal organizer for the Men's League for Woman Suffrage and a frequent speaker at colleges, Max Eastman left a wave of college suffrage clubs in his wake. He continued speaking on behalf of woman suffrage after he became the editor of the *Masses* in 1913. Image courtesy of the Prints and Photographs Division, Library of Congress, Washington, DC.

already begun to "attract notice as a suffragist."[20] A *New York Herald* reporter covering the event published Eastman's remark that he planned to start a men's league. Compelled to "make good" on the statement, Eastman approached Wise as a well-known suffrage supporter. Wise's enthusiastic response disarmed the young man. Eastman later remembered, "I could see at a glance that I couldn't keep up with his pace as a reformer."[21] Eastman visited Oswald Garrison Villard next. In Villard's spacious and "bookish" *New York Evening Post* office, Eastman learned that Villard had already corresponded with Anna Howard Shaw about a men's league. Villard, who "dwelt more upon the ease than the glory of the task," gave Eastman the confidence necessary to begin the formidable task of organizing the Men's League for Woman Suffrage.[22]

Max Eastman Helps Launch the League

Max Eastman's predilection for feminism may be traced to his upstate New York childhood in a matriarchal household. By the time of his birth, Eastman's mother, Annis Ford Eastman, maintained an interest in a number of reform causes, including the fight for suffrage. One of the first women ever to become an ordained Congregationalist minister, Annis counted Oswald Garrison Villard among her many influential acquaintances. Max's older sister Crystal, a lawyer with a "zeal for feminism[,] . . . pulled [Max] toward the social problem."[23] After completing an undergraduate degree in classics at Williams College, in 1907, Max confronted his fear of urban life by moving into Crystal's Greenwich Village apartment. With no clear plan for his future, he wanted to explore possibilities that only a post-graduate interlude in New York could offer.

Annis Eastman had long nudged her son toward reform work. Eastman remembers in his autobiography how Annis wrote to him that she wished he "had a life of doing things" and "had some *real* work like speaking."[24] Eastman earned his mother's approval, along with some money, when Paul Kellogg, the editor of *Charities and the Commons*, appointed Max "tuberculosis impresario" for the Charity Organization Society. Coordinating and staging lectures on the prevention of tuberculosis in East Side union halls and churches satisfied Max Eastman's "thirst for activity and experience." However, traipsing from place to place in an unfamiliar city carrying heavy stereopticon equipment proved too much for Eastman. He rated his performance a "complete flop."[25]

A rare opportunity presented itself when Crystal's friend Vladimir Simkhovitch, a bibliographer at Columbia University, told Eastman about a job opening, saving the young man "from the disgrace" of losing his lecturing gig. Despite a complete lack of preparation, Eastman found himself "lifted" out of his bedroom, "landing" in an office in the Department of Philosophy and Psychology as an instructor in the Principles of Science. The brilliant colleagues that surrounded Eastman included John Dewey, then at the beginning of what would become an acclaimed academic career.[26] Max Eastman began work toward a doctorate under Dewey, an "instinctive democrat and ardent feminist" with a sincere concern for social problems. Under Dewey's influence, the floundering young man realized that it would not be necessary to choose between making a living and pursuing a fulfilling life.[27]

Never content with a singular focus, by 1909, Eastman added his work as a paid organizer for the Men's League for Woman Suffrage to his list of "too-many activities."[28] He remembered his pivotal work organizing a Men's League for Woman Suffrage as part of "the big fight for freedom in my time." On a practical level, it offered a welcome distraction from his intense graduate studies as well as a much-needed source of income. Villard supplied Eastman with cards of introduction to a dozen leading New Yorkers and, even more importantly for Eastman's commitment to the nascent organization, two dollars toward league dues. After he "corralled" ten of the twelve men on Villard's list, Eastman appealed to prospective members with a letter elevating league status by advertising the names of those who had already joined. Acknowledging men's fear of standing alone, the letter guaranteed that no public announcement would be made until the list of members reached at least one hundred. At first, according to Eastman, "the essential activity of the league would be to exist."[29]

Over the next months, Eastman and his mother coordinated a mailing campaign that reached several thousand men. His efforts "capture[d] a hundred members" across New York State, including the banker and philanthropist George Foster Peabody, whose "generosity made the rest possible."[30] Dewey, whose wife Harriet Alice Chipman Dewey passionately supported suffrage, also signed an early league membership card.[31] Years later, Eastman explained the rationale behind his clandestine efforts. While he engaged in the process of recruiting the first one hundred men, the "plan was to keep [the] first activities private," so that the league could make its public debut "with a large and powerful explosion."[32] In May, however, a *New York Times* reporter spoiled Eastman's plan when he published the news of the league's formation and leaked the names of its earliest members.[33]

League Activities

The Men's League for Woman Suffrage of the State of New York held its first official meeting at the City Club late in the afternoon of November 29,

1909.[34] More than fifty elite men attended the event. They believed that women's access to the vote would prove to be in the "best interests of all men and women."[35] Across the city, newspapers sensationalized members' photographs and published statements of the men's serious intentions, noting the thousands of dollars they committed to the movement.[36] Although the league's constitution allowed any voter in the state of New York to become a member, the majority claimed religious, political, business, or academic affiliations, often holding membership in multiple reform causes.[37] Peabody consented to serve as the first president. In Eastman's mind, "the League owed its pecuniary life" to Peabody.[38] Within a week after announcing the league, the men lived up to their promise of "making a showing in Albany."[39]

Cognizant of the men's activities, Anna Howard Shaw complimented the boom in suffrage activity and Carrie Chapman Catt remembered 1909 as the year New York State became the "storm center of the movement."[40] Members of the men's league worked in conjunction with the New York State Woman Suffrage Association's state legislative committee to "assist with mass meetings" in the twenty-six districts represented by members of the state legislature's Joint Judiciary Committee.[41] In December, Peabody, representing 200 men's league members with hundreds more in the professional and business world "who would find it a satisfaction to show this tardy justice," met with Governor Hughes alongside the New York State Woman Suffrage Association president Ella Crossett and state grange and Woman's Christian Temperance Union leaders. Villard asked Hughes to take action on the woman suffrage referendum by "recommending that the question be submitted to the people." He asserted that other civilized nations were moving in the direction of granting suffrage to women and that the president of the United States ostensibly supported it but would not yet declare his public support "until all women want it."[42] Men's league members vowed to encourage women and men to *want* women to vote.

Under Peabody's guidance, the league continued to gain momentum. He took seriously the constitutional directive to help women attain full suffrage "by public appearances on behalf of the cause, by the circulation of literature, [and by] the holding of meetings."[43] An elegant public dinner at the Aldine Club on Fifth Avenue in December 1910 attracted over 600 guests who paid two dollars each to honor the British suffragist Ethel [Mrs. Phillip] Snowden and to hear other suffrage speakers elaborate on the importance of the cause. The following year, the men's league cosponsored a Cooper Union meeting and drew an overwhelmingly male crowd to hear the Idaho governor James Henry Brady's inspiring speech on winning state suffrage. The men cheered late into the night.[44] Events like these attracted additional male support.

Men's league members collaborated with the New York State Woman Suffrage Association and other women's organizations to publicize the cause of woman suffrage. Together they planned rallies, dinners, dances, theatrical performances, and pageants to raise money and popular support for suffrage. More entertaining than rallies or parades, pageants, especially, provided "a relatively safe but glamourous new venue for entering the public sphere."[45] Pageants helped to close the divide between "positive associations of public men and negative associations of public women."[46] In addition to displays of talent, pageant planners capitalized on big name speakers like Theodore Roosevelt, who spoke at a Men's Suffrage Pageant in New York City.

To democratize the reach of the woman suffrage message, league members explored the new medium of moving pictures. Film had the potential to reach rural and working-class audiences unable to attend the events staged for more privileged participants. Along with nationally known suffrage leaders like Anna Howard Shaw, Max Eastman and his wife, Ida Rauh, acted in the 1911 production *Votes for Women*, one of many films made to appeal to general audiences.[47] Using the latest technology, "banner-waving suffragists" hoped to showcase their speaking skills while promoting their cause. In addition, they intended to make a historic film, one that audiences one hundred years in the future could appreciate. However, the finished project actually highlighted the actors' discomfort with the medium and fell short of the producer's expectations. Disappointment temporarily dampened the suffragists' enthusiasm for the new medium.[48]

Men's league members also directly supported women suffragists in the public arena. They appeared with them on film and on theater stages, accompanied them to hearings, helped them lead rallies and protests, marched with them in parades, and peopled pageants, dinners, and other events. When men harangued women as they spoke from atop soapboxes in Hell's Kitchen, women complained to the police commissioner. The commissioner ignored the women, but after James Lees Laidlaw, a prominent banker and a respected "man of affairs," voiced his dismay, the police provided protection at the next rally and it proceeded without incident.[49] Repelling disparaging remarks became second nature as both men and women became more experienced publicly sharing their pro-suffrage perspectives.

League founders could not have anticipated the excitement generated by the events they sponsored. After the establishment of the men's league, a few magazines and newspapers, most notably the *New York Tribune* and the *Sun*, began to devote increasing space to suffrage and material contributed by league members. However, popular press coverage of league events did little to accurately reflect the surge of interest in "the glories of the Men's Movement," as Eastman put it.[50] Men lent their support to women's activities while at the same time they expanded their reach to sponsor their own innovative endeavors. One men's league in Kings County went as far as building a new two-story headquarters with a garage to hold at least five automobiles and serve a "flying squadron of speakers" on the ground floor, with sleeping quarters on the top floor for the orators. Teams of two speakers would travel together to establish new political equality clubs or to reinvigorate failing clubs.[51]

While the majority of league activities remained centered in or immediately around New York City, some rural areas upstate began to form their own men's leagues. In the North Country, Marion Sanger Frank, the daughter of a New York City alderman and Board of Education president, persuaded her husband, Julius, the mayor, to start the Ogdensburg Men's League for Woman Suffrage. At the same time, Marion served as head of the Ogdensburg Political Equality Club.[52] The Franks worked in tandem to fulfill their political aspirations. He supported his wife's suffrage activities, which included fund raising and letter writing campaigns, and she helped him win his reelection to a second term as mayor.[53] In towns and cities without separate men's leagues, suffragists worked closely with sympathetic men to form local equality leagues or men's committees on a county-wide basis. In some sparsely-populated areas, like Delaware County, women and men joined mixed equal suffrage clubs.[54]

Elizabeth Smith Miller and her daughter Anne Fitzhugh Miller founded the Geneva Political Equality Club in 1897 and included male members from the onset. The daughter of the abolitionist Gerrit Smith, Elizabeth had a close relationship with her cousin Elizabeth Cady Stanton. In October 1907, the Millers hosted an evening reception at their home for "delegates, officers, speakers and visitors" attending the New York Woman Suffrage Association annual convention in Geneva. Welcoming their guests to Lochland, a palatial estate overlooking Seneca Lake, Anne remarked, "Of all factors in the success that Geneva has achieved, I count . . . the fact that the men of this place are with us."[55] Since the Millers founded the Geneva club, it had grown to 362 members. The Millers counted the Geneva mayor, Arthur Rose; the president of Hobart College, Langdon C. Stewardson; and a number of local newspaper editors as club members.[56] The mother and daughter team had spent many hours working with the male leaders of the Geneva Federation of Labor to secure an endorsement for woman suffrage. With the Millers' help, the club sent a delegation to the 1910 Union Square suffrage rally to represent their city. Anne appointed her friend, the prominent banker William G. Ver Planck, to lead the delegation, which protested the failure of legislators to live up to their promise to "obliterate the word male from the Constitution."[57]

Anne Fitzhugh Miller and her mother, Elizabeth Smith Miller, stand beneath the wisteria on the veranda at Lochland, their estate overlooking Seneca Lake. They frequently hosted suffrage events and offered a quiet retreat during the summer lull in suffrage activities. Image courtesy of the Prints and Photographs Division, Library of Congress, Washington, DC.

Throughout their lives, the Millers hosted social activities at their lakeside home and nearby camp. Anne built a summer camp along the shore that she called Fossenvue. Guests included civic leaders and suffrage supporters such as college professors Felix Adler, Francis Nash, and Joseph McDaniels. Max Eastman, who first visited the Millers as a child with his family, continued to make summer visits and to bring his close friend, the Cornell professor Nathaniel Schmidt, to Lochland well into adulthood.[58] Affluent and well-connected, the Millers coordinated a successful campaign to incorporate males into the suffrage movement in a way that few other leaders replicated.

Several men gained fame for their suffrage work. Max Eastman, who traveled across the northeast and became one of the league's most popular speakers, is a prime example of a man who bolstered his professional reputation with suffrage-related work. Engaging in an "accidental career" as a male suffragist—in an increasingly fashionable movement—enabled him to command as much as fifty dollars for each appearance.[59] When asked how he became a committed suffragist, Eastman expressed his penchant for "women with brains, character and independence." Suffrage conventions and speeches by women like the British suffrage maven Emmeline Pankhurst, whom Eastman described to his mother as "a complete and triumphant soul," deepened his commitment to the cause of woman suffrage. Eastman's debonair good looks, along with his simple message, drew enormous crowds. Referring to his ability to dazzle his audience, in his autobiography Eastman described one of his first lovers, the suffragist Inez Milholland, and himself as "twin rising stars on the feminist horizon . . . her female beauty and my masculine oratory providing just the combination that the movement wanted."[60] Few men who joined the league rivaled Eastman's energy or visibility. Suffrage never represented a primary focus of their lives as it did for many of their female counterparts.[61]

As Max Eastman's status on the suffrage circuit soared, his speeches, reprinted in pamphlet form, rose to the top of the National American Woman Suffrage Association's list of "what to read on woman's suffrage."[62] His unadorned message concentrated on the democratic necessity of extending the protection of citizenship to women. In his speeches and literature, Eastman countered the classic anti-suffrage claim that "woman's sphere is the home" made by "domestic idealists," informing women and men in his audiences that women worked not by choice but most often because of their social or financial situation.[63] Eastman explained that "many of them are working under conditions that corrupt health and motherhood." He concluded by suggesting that the conditions of industry should be "compatible with the physical and moral health of women." For Eastman and his audiences, the situation of working women in the United States posed "a vital problem for the future of our race."[64] He argued that once women could vote they would have the power to alleviate the strain of working conditions that compromised the health of childbearing women.

Max Eastman also attracted large audiences on college campuses, including Cornell, Vassar, Wellesley, and Bryn Mawr.[65] Certainly in part drawn to his magnetic good looks, college students flocked to hear Eastman's suffrage message. He varied his speeches to appeal to individual audiences, but several consistent themes ran through his discourse. From Eastman's perspective, women in a democracy deserved full citizenship and the right to the vote, and women needed the ballot so they could achieve their highest potential as reformers. Eastman's oratory often relied on the expediency argument: by granting women the right to vote, the state would benefit from women's unique moral perspective, thereby elevating the broader society.[66] According to Eastman, the nature of the political act would alter "the character and status of women in society to the benefit of themselves, their husbands, their children and their homes."[67]

Male Activism in the Legislative Halls

In 1910, in an aggressive move that temporarily put her at odds with the more moderate mainstream leaders, Harriot Stanton Blatch announced that she planned to go on the offensive to "change the state legislature from an indifferent body to one responsive to our ideas." More determined than ever, Blatch questioned legislators regarding their stand on the suffrage issue during the nominating conventions instead of during the opening day of the legislature. She threatened "to work against the man who is against woman suffrage."[68] When she hired a female lobbyist to conduct a systematic investigation concerning the legislators' sentiments, Blatch learned that many districts did not have even one legislator who supported a woman's right to vote.[69] Furthermore, many of the men lacked sound rationale to articulate their opposition effectively. Blatch realized the possibility of changing their minds.

Blatch undertook an extensive mission to educate herself about how to force a reluctant committee to act. She enlisted an unlikely ally, the "master of the legislative process," Republican Assembly Speaker James W. Wadsworth, Jr. Wadsworth, one of the state's staunchest anti-suffragists, fretted about the "calamity" of the votes of "hordes of women of the lowest class, who have no ideas or convictions as to political economy or National policies."[70] Ever the consummate politician, however, Wadsworth agreed to share the intricacies of the legislative process with Blatch. A quick learner, Blatch penetrated the "male preserve" of politics.[71] Newly empowered thanks to the patronage of Wadsworth, Blatch deliberately placed herself and her colleagues in a position to infiltrate the legislative nucleus. In the meantime, members of the men's league, accompanied by the leaders of the New York State Woman Suffrage Association, descended on suffrage hearings in Albany.

Women had been petitioning the state legislature and turning out *en masse* for decades when the Men's League for Woman Suffrage joined them in their "annual pilgrimage of the fighters for the franchise" in 1910.[72] The New York Woman Suffrage Party chair, Mary Garrett Hay, led the charge, accompanied by George Foster Peabody. He addressed the State Assembly in an effort to bring the Toombs Bill—which would delete the word "male" from the constitution—out of the Assembly Judiciary Committee to the floor for a vote. Men's league member, the attorney Samuel Untermyer, also addressed the Assembly, noting that "women are eligible with men for the electric chair, the prison and the tax roll. It seems intolerable that they should be ineligible for the ballot, the jury box, and to have their part in framing the law under which they are required to live."[73] Max Eastman and Professor Nathaniel Schmidt, who distributed cards that read: "Men who love Freedom which Your Fathers won for You; Pay Your Debt by Winning Freedom for Your Daughters," rounded out the men's contingent.[74]

In response to the Assembly's negative vote, suffragists representing sixty-three New York districts led a protest in automobiles, ending in a massive rally in Union Square, well-attended despite a downpour. Women suffrage leaders called on men for their support. Assemblyman Frederick R. Toombs and Judge William Wood joined Anna Howard Shaw and Harriet Burton Laidlaw, the wife of James Lees Laidlaw, then chair of the Executive Committee of the men's league, on the platform.[75] Robert Elder, the assistant district attorney of Kings County, whose wife also supported suffrage, devised an effective argument for woman suffrage: "if a woman is not fit to vote than she is not fit to be the wife of a voter."[76] While the men spoke, women distributed literature and Votes-for-Women buttons to the crowd.

In late February 1911, Max Eastman returned to Albany to address an over-capacity crowd at a hearing of the Joint Judiciary Committee on "Woman's Suffrage and Sentiment."[77] This time Eastman attacked employers who preferred that women remain unprotected without the ballot. Denied their political rights, workers had no choice but to continue to endure long hours, low pay, and poor conditions. Eastman repeatedly cited census data to support his claim that one-fifth of the women in the United States worked to earn a living, with the number steadily increasing.[78] League members tried to "do whatever they could" to influence legislation and bring the issue of woman suffrage "before federal and state legislatures."[79] The presence of Eastman and his league colleagues at legislative hearings and their efforts to strengthen political connections reinforced women's suffrage activism.

Men on the March

On May 6, 1911, the New York State Woman Suffrage Association leaders organized the first annual parade that included a delegation of men among the multitude of women marchers.[80] The eighty-nine courageous men's league members, including John Dewey, Oswald Garrison Villard, and their supporters, marched up Fifth Avenue to the jeers of the crowd. The investor Frederick Nathan, the playwright George Middleton, and Max Eastman led the way while James Laidlaw and professors Vladimir Simkhovitch and John Dewey bore the standard.[81] Laidlaw remarked on "the derision of the men in his own clubs, as they sat in their windows and watched" the procession.[82] An anonymous "husband of a suffragette" described the experience as being part of a "forlorn little corporal's guard marching at the tail end." He felt every "hostile taunt and mirth of a mob," which accused the men of "tagging along after the girls."[83] In spite of "the populace dissolv[ing] into a mush of laughter along the curbs," the journalist Will Irwin, son of a suffragist, forever regretted his decision to remain on the sidelines, because his sentiments truly lay with the marchers.[84]

Others already dedicated to the suffrage cause found the men's participation stimulating. Frances Perkins, the future New York State Commissioner of Labor, later credited Laidlaw with inspiring courage in many "young and doubtful" participants. She recalled his encouragement as she waited to " 'fall in' with the great suffrage parade."[85] By the time marchers reached Union Square, the end of the two-mile hike, curbside insults gave way to feminine appreciation. A New York newspaper reported, "the enthusiasm was at its height when, with a blare of 'La Marsellaise,' the crowning feature of the parade came into view." The crowd hailed the members of the Men's League for Woman Suffrage with a "cheer that defied the lungs behind the brasses."[86]

In 1912, James Lees Laidlaw, the chair of the Executive Committee of the men's league, assumed the presidency. League membership grew to include the New York mayor, John Purroy Mitchel; George Harvey, the editor of the *North American Review*; Dr. Simon Flexner, the director of the Rockefeller Institute; the novelist William Dean Howells; the attorney Samuel Untermyer; Cornell president Jacob Gould Schurman; Vassar president Henry Noble McCracken; and other influential progressive figures. Even William Sulzer, the New York gubernatorial candidate, joined the league. Sulzer, who had worked closely with Susan B. Anthony in the years before her death, devoted the openings of his campaign addresses to woman suffrage.[87] While motivation for supporting suffrage varied from personal interest to potential political or professional gains, these men all had the power to vote for woman suffrage.

Much to the joy of Harriet Burton Laidlaw, who had converted her husband to woman suffrage, James Lees Laidlaw, the new president, promised to do his part to win the suffrage contest in the state.[88] Laidlaw proved to be an invaluable ally. Once he assumed the helm, the men's league evolved from an organization that some assessed as taking "no active part in the fray" to one of noteworthy activism.[89] James Laidlaw's "ardent spirit" and dedication to woman suffrage also helped the organization coalesce around common strategies. Between 1910 and 1912, the league sent representatives to over forty meetings, including some in the upstate cities of Buffalo, Rochester,

James Lees Laidlaw assumed the presidency of the Men's League for Woman Suffrage in 1912 and, with his wife, Harriet Burton Laidlaw, continued his activism until the passage of the Nineteenth Amendment in 1920. He is the only man listed on the Suffrage Memorial Plaque installed by the New York League of Women Voters in the New York State Capitol in Albany in 1931. Image courtesy of the Arthur and Elizabeth Schlesinger Library on the History of Women in America, Radcliffe Institute, Harvard University, Cambridge, MA.

and Syracuse. League representatives also traveled to New York Woman Suffrage Association state conventions as speakers. Initially, some men's league members disagreed over the degree of support that the league should lend to women. One newspaper reported that "some members think men ought to sit back and let women do the work of getting themselves the vote." Others believed that men "ought to lift the burden entirely from their shoulders." A third group agreed that "both sexes should work together" since "women can do [some things] better than men and vice versa."[90] Ultimately the men presented a united front in support of women's enfranchisement to an increasingly interested public.

Men in states across the country established men's leagues, modeled after the New York league. By 1912, men's league members had assisted with the establishment of eighteen other leagues.[91] In addition to cooperating with women's associations, Laidlaw embarked with Harriet, an officer in both the New York City Woman Suffrage Party and the National American Woman Suffrage Association, on two speaking tours. They traveled across the country to facilitate league activities in Georgia, Montana, California, Nevada, Colorado, and a number of other western states.[92] Encouraging other men to become national organizers, James Laidlaw had founded the National Men's League for Woman Suffrage in 1910. Several individuals expressed surprise that a man of his standing headed the national men's organization. Significantly, Laidlaw's distinguished presence and high visibility helped to normalize woman suffrage and attract more elite and middle-class supporters.

In preparation for the 1912 suffrage parade, the New York league secretary, Robert Cameron Beadle, sent out over one thousand letters asking men to march in the men's contingent. Hundreds of men marched four abreast through New York City in what was quickly becoming a highly publicized annual suffrage event. At the front of the men's contingent, Laidlaw and other supporters carried a large purple banner trimmed in gold that read: "Men's League for Woman Suffrage." The banner's purple color and white lettering lent homage to Harriot Blatch's Women's Political Union, while the gold trim gave a salute to the Woman Suffrage Party.[93] This time the journalist Irwin positioned himself in the front lines of the men's division and "felt like an early Christian in the arena." He recalled that "the masculine adherents of the woman suffragists" deflected taunts like "Sissy" and ignored questions like "Does your mother know you're out?" and "Did your wife make you?" Oswald Garrison Villard kept order at the rear, ignoring the hecklers.[94]

The novelist Fannie Hurst described watching the marching men interspersed with squads of women and interludes of brass bands in the parade from the curb. According to Hurst, the next thing she knew she was in the formation marching up Fifth Avenue, clutching one end of a banner that read, "Move Over Gentlemen. We Have Come to Stay." At the other end of the banner was "a brilliant dark-haired mite" who introduced herself as Marie Jenny Howe. Her husband, Frederic C. Howe, who would soon become the commissioner of immigration at Ellis Island, marched with the men's group.[95] Beadle estimated that labor union men made up fifty percent of the group, which also included hundreds of men from Harvard, Princeton, and Yale. About two hundred Columbia men rounded out the contingent that represented "every trade and profession."[96] Later, when asked by a reporter about his motivation for joining in the parade, Laidlaw responded,

"We are marching to give political support to the women and moral support to the men."[97]

The Men's League Expands its Influence

Although a few league members initially seemed reluctant to take an "active part in the fray," they soon followed Laidlaw's lead as he pushed the organization forward. Between January and May 1912, in an appeal for funds, league members "distributed upwards of 40,000 booklets and letters, held one large dinner attended by 300 people[,] and [had] been represented at almost all of the meetings held in the city by various organizations." League members who owned businesses displayed "Member of Men's League for Woman Suffrage" placards in their establishments.[98] They also did whatever they could to bring woman suffrage before legislators and influence legislation.[99] As women had done all along, men began to take advantage of every opportunity to discuss women's enfranchisement at the local, state, and national levels.

New York league members announced plans to go to Washington to try to affect legislation there as well.[100] At the annual National American Woman Suffrage Association convention in the fall of 1912, women delegates held a men's night to recognize the support of the National Men's League for Woman Suffrage, also led by Laidaw. It served as an umbrella organization for state-level organizations.[101] In addition to men's league officers assisting with campaigns in other states, male members spoke at congressional committee hearings and sent delegates to the National American Woman Suffrage Association. In 1913, the same year that James Laidlaw reported to the House of Representatives that his organization had branches throughout the country with over 5,000 members in New York alone, the New York Men's League for Woman Suffrage sent representatives, including Oswald Villard, to march down Pennsylvania Avenue in the Washington, DC, suffrage parade.[102]

Meanwhile, as New York suffragists gained ground, anti-suffragists reacted with more vehemence. The New York City lawyer Everett P. Wheeler, passionately opposed to woman suffrage, formed the Man-Suffrage Association Opposed to Woman Suffrage in 1913. Wheeler claimed to have almost 600 members at the inception of the organization. The affluent and powerful men who joined the Man-Suffrage Association argued that decisions regarding suffrage should remain in the states and eventually commandeered the fight from anti-suffrage women.[103] Wheeler's organization also entered into a number of debates with suffragists. In 1914, suffrage and anti-suffrage men debated the topic of "What Men Think about Suffrage." Wheeler, speaking for the anti-suffrage side, argued that women's wages would not be improved by the ballot, and that women did not need the vote to be protected.[104] In a climate of growing suffrage support, Wheeler, whose wife also worked for anti-suffrage, and his followers continued to represent a significant portion of the electorate.

Despite challenges from the anti-suffragists, the year 1913 marked a watershed in New York State suffrage history. Growing numbers of men followed the lead of Theodore Roosevelt and openly converted to the cause. Roosevelt is a prime example of a reluctant suffrage supporter who converted for political purposes. He had remained ambivalent on women's voting rights until forced to take a stand supporting woman suffrage in 1912.[105] When he ran for the presidency on the Progressive ticket that year, since the party supported suffrage, the once cautious Roosevelt came out in favor of female participation in politics. Other prestigious politicians, including William Jennings Bryan, followed Roosevelt's lead.[106]

At the opening session of the New York State Legislature in 1913, the newly-elected democratic governor and longtime suffrage advocate William Sulzer thrilled the suffragists when he honored his election pledge to support woman suffrage in any way possible. He recommended "that the Legislature declare in favor of submitting to the voters of the State, as soon as possible, the Woman Suffrage Constitutional Amendment."[107] On January 27, 1913, both houses signed legislation proposing an amendment to the state constitution striking out the word "male" and "enfranchising every citizen over the age of twenty-one years . . . providing that a citizen by marriage shall have been an inhabitant of the United States for five years."[108] The platform of every party in the state stood for submission of woman suffrage to the voters in 1915. A referendum to decide woman suffrage finally appeared to be on the horizon in New York State.

Beginning in early 1914, suffragists exerted intense pressure on legislators to pass the woman suffrage bill a second time, as required by the state constitution.[109] That summer, suffragists turned out in force at the three largest state party conventions and talked all three parties—Democrat, Republican, and Progressive—into adopting planks that promised to approve the woman suffrage bill a second time. Only then could the woman suffrage referendum go before the voters.[110] Suffrage proponents had made tremendous advances in the course of just three years. When Harriot Stanton Blatch approached the convention chair, Senator Elihu Root, at the Republican convention in Saratoga, in 1912, party members had backed his adamant anti-suffrage stance—that suffrage "would be a loss to women . . . because it would be an injury to the State and to every man and woman in the State."[111] By 1914, a significant number of Root's party disagreed with him.

The Republican governor Charles Whitman not only joined the Men's League for Woman Suffrage but also openly declared his support for women's enfranchisement.[112] Whitman had sympathized with the suffrage movement for years. In early December 1914, he welcomed suffragists who visited him seeking support for the suffrage bill. "I am very glad to see you and I am interested and impressed by what you say," he told them. Suffragists saw their goal on the horizon when Whitman promised to address a mass meeting early the next year.[113] Following the lead of others in their parties, legislators began to lean toward enfranchising women as the referendum drew nearer.

Men in New York State acted first as individuals and then as members of the Men's League for Woman Suffrage to assist women as they struggled to attain their suffrage goals. Laidlaw led the organization from one dominated by men with "quiescent attitudes" to a vital and active group whose increasingly assertive members readily participated in public activities and whose generosity enabled the organization "to reach large numbers of voters throughout the state."[114] The league gradually progressed from nominally supporting the cause to sponsoring and organizing a number of highly visible public events in the name of woman suffrage. In April 1914, the men's league hosted a pageant to promote women's right to the elective franchise. They orchestrated a production that included a 500-member cast to represent six periods of American life, with "Indians, Pilgrims, Colonists, slaves, soldiers, housewives, milkmaids, woodsmen, nurses, blacksmiths and many other elaborately costumed figures." Society women, college students, authors, artists, wage earners, businessmen, and suffragists of "every class and creed" made up the cast. The *New York Evening World* reporter Marguerite Mooers Marshall suggested that this time "the most significant thing about the glorification of the women's cause is that men are responsible for it."[115] In addition to extravagant demonstrations of support, men continued to organize and strategize at their regular weekly meetings, speaking at women's meetings, and organizing male support for events like Suffrage Days.[116]

Although it is impossible to quantify the impact that the Men's League for Woman Suffrage had on the New York movement as a whole, it undoubtedly went a long way toward recognizing women's right to vote. Members of the men's league readily cooperated with women and their autonomous organizations. When conducting independent activities, men's league members proved especially effective "in reaching the denizens of community chambers of commerce and fraternal organizations," though perhaps less so among the working-class or immigrant men.[117] Not surprisingly, men did not devote as much time to suffrage work as women did. Most league

The Men's League for Woman Suffrage contingent marched in a 1915 New York City parade. Men marching for the cause attracted attention from onlookers as well as the media. Image from the Carrie Chapman Catt Papers, courtesy of Bryn Mawr College Special Collections, Bryn Mawr, PA.

members had professions, leaving them little extra time for the day-to-day commitments that so deeply engaged women suffragists. Men were late-comers to the formal suffrage battle, but their participation and the outward signs of their dedication to the right of women to the ballot spoke volumes to observers. As they marched bravely through city streets, their demonstration of support for the women assuredly won many other men to their side. Just back from a weeklong organizing stint in Rochester, for example, James Laidlaw confidently expected 10,000 men to march in the men's contingent of an October 1914 parade.[118]

Throughout 1914 and 1915, men's league leaders like Rabbi Wise and Frederic Howe grew even more vocal in their support of woman suffrage.[119] The January 1915 issue of the *Woman Voter* carried suffrage arguments from more than thirty state and local officials, continuing a practice that began in November 1914. These men unanimously agreed with Judge William H. Wadhams, who declared, "As a matter of common justice those who are subject to the obligations are entitled to enjoy the privileges of citizen-ship."[120] Hope ran high on the eve of the suffrage vote in 1915. Many league members certainly worked behind the scenes to inspire others to act. These men and the men who openly spoke, marched, and participated in pageants and other league-sponsored events helped forge a movement that eventually appealed to working men as well as to middle-class and professional men.

Despite the failure of male voters to pass the 1915 referendum that would have extended suffrage to New York women, increasing numbers of men came to support women's right to vote. Some male suffrage leaders like Oswald Garrison Villard and Max Eastman had grown up in households rich with reform sentiments, including woman suffrage, from an early age. Others, like Theodore Roosevelt and Charles Whitman, had only recently converted to the cause upon the realization that woman suffrage "is humanly right and socially just" (and politically expedient).[121] Frederic Howe represented those who foresaw the future implications of women's political rights. He and others, such as the Rochester reformer Edward Ward, asserted that in addition to the influence of women's "public housecleaning" on the governmental and social service sectors, "the changes in industry and society demand the participation of woman in politics."[122] Irrespective of the reasons why men sympathized with the cause of suffrage, the members of the New York State Men's League for Woman Suffrage, and others outside the organization who actively took a "stand for the enfranchisement of women, contributed sub-stantially to the success of the movement."[123] Their efforts increased the vis-ibility and, ultimately, the power of the woman suffrage coalition.

CHAPTER 6

Radicalism and Spectacle

New Women Modernize the Suffrage Movement

By 1907, the editor of the *New York Times* described the changing persona of the suffrage activist: "the old days when a gaunt, masculine, and forbidding appearance seemed to fit the woman with thoughts have long since passed; the old-time 'war horse' of woman suffrage has passed."[1] The impetus for this change came from the suffragists themselves, especially from the most radical and irreverent among them. Suffragists became acutely sensitive to the presentation of their appearance and arguments. Well aware that support directly related to appealing to a fickle public, they deliberately adapted the way they displayed their suffrage and women's rights ideology. Intensely conscious of how powerful beauty, pageantry, and imagery could be in directing public opinion, suffragists creatively engaged in a brilliant, complex, and exciting marketing campaign. Expanding beyond conventional strategies of petitioning and canvassing to reach individual legislators and voters, "new woman" suffragists used unconventional and often innovative tactics to attract mass attention and win votes.

Of course, not all suffragists agreed on how to orchestrate this modernized movement, just as from the beginning women had disagreed on how best to achieve the vote. New York State had long harbored many suffrage organizations, some adhering to the idea that coordination, gentle persuasion, and patience would win enfranchisement. By the second decade of the twentieth century, more activists contended that only "headlines, emotion, and activism" would draw the attention of legislators and (male) voters.[2] While this conflict over strategy often resulted in personal disagreements, it also encouraged suffragists' efforts to appeal to a broader and more diverse audience. Facing the persistent arguments of anti-suffragists likewise helped suffragists develop strategies to outwit their opponents. Perhaps most important, activists "idealized" their "public identity" to reach voters.[3] The techniques suffragists developed, modified, and appropriated to positively affect public opinion about suffrage included marketing suffrage events, publishing cartoons and advertisements, and commissioning novelty items, always drawing on the newest and most creative technologies. Suffragists even influenced fashion, pageantry, and film. By thus expanding their repertoire, they made themselves and their aim impossible to ignore. As the mainstream movement activities intensified, other members of the loose coalition of suffrage activists—rural, urban immigrant, black, and elite women, as well as men—attracted new supporters.

Cooperating to a greater or lesser extent through the New York State Woman Suffrage Association, the Woman Suffrage Party of New York City, Alva Belmont's Political Equality Association, Harriot Stanton Blatch's Equality League of Self-Supporting Women (founded in 1911 to break the state legislative deadlock), the Women's Political Union, and Katherine Mackay's Equal Franchise Society, as well as hundreds of political equality clubs, Woman's Christian Temperance Union chapters, and granges throughout the state, suffragists concentrated on enhancing, and ultimately transforming, the suffrage image. Suffrage organizations drew incredibly diverse groups of people, not always working in tandem. In fact, many of the women who identified as suffragists agreed on virtually nothing but the right to vote. According to Laura Ellsworth Cook, an organizer and speaker for the Women's Political Union, "All faiths and all types of women work[ed] for suffrage," representing a "complete cross-section" of people. Despite conflict, controversy, or strained relationships, Cook continued, all suffrage supporters worked for the political enfranchisement of women, feeling "cooperation and admiration," and "great unanimity on the whole."[4]

By 1909, suffrage, as Gertrude Foster Brown exalted, had become "fashionable!"[5] Everywhere one turned, signs of suffrage and anti-suffrage sentiments barraged the New Yorker. In the process, suffrage became more commonplace. The National American Woman Suffrage Association moved its headquarters from Warren, Ohio, to New York City. Alva Belmont paid most of the moving costs in addition to paying a year's rent for the office in a skyscraper. When the landlord refused to allow her to erect an electric "National American Woman Suffrage Association" sign on the top of the building, she purchased a nearby building for the sign.[6] Suffragists played on the idea of women's proper sphere of activity with bake sales, wash days, and canning demonstrations to raise money and promote their need for the vote. Many suffragists deliberately highlighted their domesticity in an effort to show how easily voting could be incorporated into women's domestic duties. Most suffrage cartoonists and artists, too, realized the importance of using non-threatening domestic images in their artwork, which appeared virtually everywhere.[7] Yet, this was also the epoch of the "new woman," and radical suffragists who merited this moniker sought exciting, creative, and thoroughly modern ways to express themselves. Changes in the appearance of the fashionable woman of the day, regardless of her social class, readily enhanced the spectacle of suffrage.

The New Woman

Over the long course of the suffrage movement, ideals of beauty and fashion changed, and the movement welcomed the so-called "new woman" into its ranks. Sarah Grand, an English author who toured the United States after the publication of her book *The Heavenly Twins*, first used the phrase "new woman" in 1894. In a provocative article for the *North American Review*, she described the new woman as needing to "set the human household in order, to see to it that all is clean and sweet and comfortable for the men who are fit to help us make a home in it."[8] The new woman, at first symbolized most recognizably by the Gibson Girl, from the pen of artist Charles Dana Gibson, frequented educational institutions, the work place, and public suffrage events.[9] In many ways a transitional ideal with "tightly corseted waist and lavish bust and impressive hips," the hourglass figure of the Gibson Girl would soon be replaced by a "slim, youthful figure with a natural waistline . . . more fitting to th[e] new woman."[10] The principles of the new woman defied the conventions of the times. As described by the historian Margaret Finnegan, the new woman "combined the age-old virgin and whore archetypes into a model of fun-loving, modern, youthful, yet morally pure femininity."[11] Although marriage remained her ultimate goal, the new woman experimented with sexual freedom, athleticism, and physical image. The reaction of the new woman to the prevailing political and social conservatism still prevalent in the early decades of the new century drew increasing attention from the public.[12]

In the 1910s, working-class women also adopted fashionable habits such as dancing, treating (accepting gifts or money in exchange for their company), petting (amorous kissing and caressing), smoking, drinking, and other behaviors once linked only to prostitutes.[13] The more "decorous" of these

Mrs. John Blair, Vira Boarman Whitehouse, and Harriet Burton Laidlaw, all prominent leaders in the New York State movement, epitomize the "new woman" suffragist. Image courtesy of the Prints and Photographs Division, Library of Congress, Washington, DC.

behaviors eventually transferred across class lines to middle-class women and ultimately reached upper-class women.[14] The new woman label is easily applied to striking professional women prominent in the suffrage movement, including Inez Milholland, Portia Willis, Mary Elizabeth Pidgeon, Vira Boarman Whitehouse, Katherine Duer Mackay, Harriet Burton Laidlaw, Edna Buckman Kearns, and many others admired by their contemporaries. These women spoke publicly and advocated for the right to vote as they used their money and their influence to bolster the campaign.[15]

Women cast aside their corsets, bobbed their hair, revealed their necks and exposed their wrists, raised their hemlines, and painted their faces. The change in fashion from the tightly corseted figure to a slimmer, less restricted shape allowed more uninhibited movement on the part of women.[16] Although these changes in deportment and dress were striking, the focus on self-development and the emphasis on independence made the new woman truly new. The consummate new woman resisted male control, taking charge of her own social, economic, and political life.[17] Even women less interested in fashion and appearance recognized the value of using dress and adornment in reaching audiences. Gertrude Foster Brown, for example, applied make up, piled her hair up under a stylish hat, and donned an evening gown to appear on the vaudeville stage when she gave one of her suffrage speeches.[18]

Many of the new women can also be linked with feminism. Carrie Chapman Catt considered feminism a "world-wide revolt against all artificial barriers which laws and customs interposed between women and human freedom."[19] But, as the journalist Rheta Childe Dorr articulated, "feminism was something with dynamite in it . . . like trial marriage or free love."[20] Edna Kenton considered feminism "a great personal, joyous adventure with one's untried self."[21] A term relatively unknown to earlier suffrage activists, feminism, as the historian Nancy Cott points out, exemplified the ideas surrounding the new woman and her potential political rights.[22] Furthermore, "women who lifted the banner of Feminism had . . . already welcomed the idea of radical and irreverent behavior in the labor movement, art, or politics."[23] The radical and innovative tenets of feminism certainly influenced the women of the suffrage movement.

Dress Reform and Fashionable Behavior

In the early twentieth century, trends in women's fashion reflected social and cultural changes in the broader society. Highly sensitive to the power of appearance, suffragists carefully crafted a modern, vibrant, and competent image of themselves for the public. Carrie Chapman Catt paid close attention to how the press portrayed suffrage and suffragists and once remarked that cartoonists had depicted Susan B. Anthony as unkempt, "with a dress hanging in uneven scallops," as she wielded her umbrella to drive home her points. After 1893, the clothing of suffrage became increasingly fashionable, as suffragists themselves actually influenced clothing styles.[24] At the same time, suffragists' public demeanor became softer and more feminine, thereby drawing more popular attention. For example, Gabrielle Stewart Mulliner, a financially successful New York lawyer and women's rights advocate, described suffragists sent to Washington in 1910 as "frumps." Inez Milholland responded by saying that it "might be good politics for those in the suffrage ranks to put their most attractive members forward" when seeking to influence legislators.[25] As Margaret Finnegan posits, "suffragists used physical appearance, dress, and personality" to convince men that "potential women voters . . . were attractive, stylish, charming, dignified, and virtuous."[26]

Suffragists had been linked with dress reform since the days of the bloomer costume. The less restrictive clothing, introduced by Elizabeth Smith Miller, featured full trousers gathered at the ankles and worn under a knee-length dress. Suffragists argued that the cumbersome garments women typically wore endangered their health, because of the heavy weight of the clothing and the long skirts dragging in the mud and muck of the streets. In addition, corsets cinched women's waists, not only compressing organs but also making it difficult to bend or move. Many suffragists adopted the bloomer style, but boys chased and taunted women wearing bloomers on the streets. After discovering how distracting the costume was, most suffragists abandoned wearing the garments in public. Their next target was the corset. Over the decades of the nineteenth century, women's styles and silhouettes changed, but the corset remained a staple of most women's wardrobes. The new woman wanted to be comfortable in her clothing, thereby making it easier to function athletically and in public settings. By 1905, Anthony mused that "people should dress to accommodate whatever business or pastime they pursue . . . if women ride the bicycle or climb mts [sic], they should don a costume that permits use of the legs."[27]

Many suffragists belonged to a social and economic class that could afford the most comfortable and fashionable clothing. But by 1910, virtually all items of women's clothing could be mass-produced and ready-made and were widely available in department stores or mail order catalogues at a reasonable cost to the consumer. Finally freed from the time-consuming fittings previously required of all well-to-do women needing clothing, suffragists could pursue other activities. However, fashion affected all classes of women, and all benefited from the ready availability of attractive, less expensive clothing. Because clothing manufacturers wanted to keep their sales high, fashions changed rapidly.[28] One of the most dramatic changes in women's fashion came from the creative imagination of Paul Poiret, a French fashion designer who "liberat[ed]" women "from the corset." His models displayed natural waists, comfortable fabrics, and less formal clothing, and the silhouette became narrow and youthful. While Poiret is responsible for "hobble skirts," which forced women to take tiny, mincing steps when they walked, his ideas also "revolutionized" women's clothing and the clothing industry.[29] The pages of the *Woman Voter* are filled with pictures of dresses and other articles of clothing available to suffragists. A suffragist even invented the one-piece dress. Agnes Morgenthau designed a "ready-to-wear-to-anything-and-not-at-all-expensive" suffrage blouse, demonstrating both creativity and practicality on the part of suffragists.[30] In New York City, suffragists unabashedly promoted Macy's department store as a source for purchasing suffrage supplies and regalia. They used their clothing as a kind of uniform, suggesting suffragists wear particular garments or colors to parades, pageants, and other public events.[31]

College Women and Suffrage

Dr. S. Josephine Baker once quipped that when asked to join a college equal suffrage club, "the average college woman acted as if you had suggested she play Lady Godiva at a stag-picnic."[32] Although college women certainly supported the right of women to education and economic independence, they often found the idea of votes for women too extreme.[33] For example, one of the students in the newly coeducational University of Rochester, Julia Crowe Maxfield, did not want the vote. She met Susan B. Anthony when Anthony visited the university in 1903. Anthony warmly embraced her and called her "one of my girls." Maxfield long felt guilty that she did not support suffrage and that Anthony had "pressed a viper to her bosom."[34] However, because the numbers of U.S. women who attended college increased from 11,000 to 85,000 between the years 1870 and 1900, many women learned about the goals of the suffrage movement and came to support it during their college years.[35]

With another surge in women's college enrollment between 1900 and 1912, suffragists intentionally and assertively focused their efforts on college women, marking another interesting shift in attitudes toward suffrage.[36] Once Max Eastman joined the suffrage movement through his membership in the Men's League for Woman Suffrage in 1909, he played a major role in attracting college women; many college organizations were founded after his visits to campuses. Anti-suffragists also recognized the appeal of the new suffrage movement to young college women and so developed their own branches on campuses in an effort to counter the exciting influence of the suffrage movement.[37] By 1915, state suffrage organizations supported college women's branches, with the goal of drawing support and active workers from a dynamic group of educated, enthusiastic young women. At the same time, support for suffrage in colleges among faculty and administrators proved uneven at best, with some administrators refusing to allow any campus meetings on the topic.

The world outside the college campus often intruded nonetheless. Under the auspices of the Equality League of Self-Supporting Women in May 1908, Harriot Blatch and Maud Malone organized a "trolley car campaign" from the sixtieth anniversary celebration in Seneca Falls to Syracuse, Albany, and Troy, holding open air meetings along the way. The trolley campaign ended in June just before Vassar's commencement in Poughkeepsie.[38] The Vassar president, James Monroe Taylor, had forbidden suffrage meetings on campus, so Inez Milholland, then in her junior year, led a group of two dozen students to a nearby cemetery and introduced four notable suffragists: Blatch, an 1878 Vassar alum; the author and economist Charlotte Perkins Gilman; the young lawyer Helen Hoy; and the trade unionist Rose Schneiderman, all of whom made quite an impression on the young women gathered to hear the speeches.[39] Milholland not only delighted in defying male authority, she deeply admired the women who spoke on behalf of women's rights.[40] This cemetery meeting became famous in the annals of suffrage literature, but it represents only one of a multitude of such entertaining and provocative marketing ploys on the part of suffragists.

Soon, colleges other than Vassar began to support suffrage clubs and issue invitations to suffrage speakers.[41] Student interest in the topic increased as the interest of the broader society grew. After a talk and reception hosted by members of the Syracuse Political Equality Club, students at Syracuse University formed a branch of the College Equal Suffrage League.[42] College women often connected to the movement through the friends they met, who, in turn, had family or other connections to the suffrage movement. For example, Laura Ellsworth Cook met Nora Stanton Blatch, the daughter of Harriot Stanton Blatch, through her elder sister Elizabeth Ellsworth Cook when they both attended Cornell University. Nora Blatch often visited the Ellsworth home in Ithaca, where the topic of woman suffrage frequently arose. After Elizabeth and Nora graduated in 1908, Elizabeth moved to New York City to work with Harriot Blatch, eventually becoming vice president of the Women's Political Union.[43]

Laura, seven years younger, and not yet as enthusiastic as her sister about the topic, participated in a suffrage debate in high school, then also entered

Cornell University. Although Max Eastman lectured on woman suffrage at the college in 1911, it took until the following year, when Laura's fiancé "smugly" commented that Laura did not believe in the "nonsense" of votes for women, for her to become politically involved. She founded a suffrage club at the college, claiming to have drawn about seventy-five members from the approximately three hundred women students.[44] It seems that membership in college suffrage clubs fluctuated as students entered college and graduated, for Helen Brewster Owens, a math professor, also founded a suffrage club at Cornell in 1911.[45] At her sister's request, Laura marched in the 1912 New York parade, led by Inez Milholland, and found herself quite impressed by the hundred or so men who also marched.[46] Back at college, the Cornell suffrage club met mostly to discuss suffrage, but members did agree to hold a suffrage debate in conjunction with the visit of a male student's prominent anti-suffragist mother, in spite of how intimidating it must have been.[47]

Suffragists attempted to organize college women in a more stable, statewide association. In 1904, Caroline Lexow helped found and served as the president of the College Equal Suffrage League of New York State. Women who joined included Carrie Chapman Catt, Crystal Eastman, Harriet Burton Laidlaw, Alice Duer Miller, Inez Milholland and her sister, Vida Milholland, Josephine Baker, and dozens of others. Lexow traveled across the state to recruit other college graduates, women and men, until M. Carey Thomas, the president of Bryn Mawr and of the National College Equal Suffrage League (affiliated with the National American Woman Suffrage Association), asked her to serve as the executive secretary of the national organization. Lexow traveled across the country, recruiting college graduates to support suffrage and the league.[48]

Thereafter, Katrina Brandes Ely [Mrs. Charles] Tiffany served as the president of the New York branch of the College Equal Suffrage League. An 1897 graduate of Bryn Mawr, she married into the prominent jewelry family in 1901. Donating time and money to the suffrage movement, she also joined the New York City Woman Suffrage Party and served as chair of its Manhattan borough branch.[49] She traveled all over the state speaking and recruiting new adherents to the cause. Following Tiffany's tenure, Jessie Ashley, a lawyer and member of the Socialist Party, headed the college league for another two years.[50] Rather than playing a political role, the league considered itself an educational organization, with the goal of drawing the attention of undergraduate and graduate students to seriously consider and support suffrage.

The national association often sent speakers, supplied suffrage literature, and enrolled new members in the state-level college league. Members gave talks on topics such as "What Women Can Do Before They Vote."[51] League members made quite an impression on one occasion when thirty women college graduates, wearing their regalia, attended a naturalization ceremony for seventy-five immigrant men who acquired the right to vote with their citizenship papers.[52] The incident typified the increasingly radical activities of suffragists in this period. But not all college-age suffragists openly affiliated with the league. For example, Vassar students met secretly for years after the "graveyard incident," until 1915, when the Vassar president James Taylor allowed the suffrage club to affiliate with the College Equal Suffrage League.[53] With support and encouragement from the state-level organization, college league members went on to influence others in their communities.

Collegiate suffragists enriched the movement's ranks in other ways as well. Alice Duer Miller, the finance chair for the Woman Suffrage Party, recruited Mary Elizabeth Pidgeon as an attractive, college-educated, career-oriented young activist, gifted at reaching rural and working-class women and men.[54] At once a Quaker and a new woman, Pidgeon chose not to marry. Working her way through the ranks, she began as a field secretary in Buffalo, earned a promotion as an organizer and speaker for the Eighth District, and then served Cayuga County as Assembly District Leader. "Self-sufficient, intelligent, capable, and active," she became skilled at averting class, generational, and perhaps even racial conflicts.[55] Pidgeon tempered her love for modern dress with her concern for respectability. She knew instinctively when to change out of her suffrage blouse and single strand of pearls into her blue silk and serge suit "trimmed with nickel buttons."[56] Downstate, other, more radical, college-educated suffragists found their way to the Heterodoxy network.

Downtown Radicals

Greenwich Village harbored a community of middle-class, college-educated women, many of whom, rather than returning home after college, made unconventional choices. They often remained single, took apartments in the Village, and lived "according to [their] own lights."[57] They supported themselves most commonly with social work, freelance writing, or jobs in male-dominated fields such as law or medicine.[58] Embracing the personas of new women, virtually all of these women—often termed "downtown radicals"—considered suffrage "a tenet of democratic politics."[59] Furthermore, these feminists rejected the separate spheres ideology, thriving instead on "female bonding" and a worldview that encompassed combinations of career, marriage, and motherhood, sometimes involving lifestyle experimentation.[60]

Marie Jenney Howe founded the Heterodoxy Club in Greenwich Village in December 1912. Howe, a Unitarian minister and the author of "The Anti-Suffrage Monologue," a parody written to entertain the New York State Woman Suffrage Party and other suffrage organizations, also chaired the "Fighting" Twenty-Fifth District for the National American Woman Suffrage Association.[61] Capped at forty members, the club required only that a woman "not be orthodox in her opinions." Members attended weekly lunch meetings to discuss self-fulfillment, self-development, politics, and a myriad of popular topics of the day.[62] Heterodites identified with liberal politics and all sexual orientations and found themselves radically committed to "militant" activism.[63] The most radical of all affiliated with the Socialist Party.[64]

United by ideals of feminism and woman suffrage, these unconventional women epitomized the new woman and her openness to new ideas. Prominent members included Alice Duer Miller, an author of satirical suffrage poetry; Ida Sedgwick Proper, the art editor of the *Woman Voter*; the anthropologist Elsie Clews Parsons, wife of Herbert Parsons, known for his unfailing suffrage support in the state legislature; the radical lawyers Crystal Eastman and Inez Milholland; the novelist Fannie Hurst; Vira Boarman Whitehouse, a member of the Women's Political Union and an officer in the Empire State Campaign and the New York State Woman Suffrage Party; Elizabeth Ellsworth Cook, the vice president of the Women's Political Union; and Grace Nail Johnson, the black civil rights activist and wife of the writer and activist James Weldon Johnson.[65]

Thoroughly optimistic, Heterodites expected enfranchisement to help women eliminate political corruption, influence social justice legislation, and prevent wars.[66] At meetings, held two Saturdays a month, members ate lunch and then spent about two hours hearing a talk or presentation, sometimes from an invited guest, or discussing whatever topics interested them, such as politics, current books, music, theater, art, or social problems.[67] Rheta Childe Dorr reflected that whatever the topic, they discussed themselves: "not ourselves personally, but the feminine half of creation, subjectively and objectively."[68] On occasion, Heterodites organized public meetings, such as the "feminist mass meetings," with both male and female speakers, held at Cooper Union in 1914.[69] Heterodites, with their radical, unique perspective, made up an important, though controversial and exclusive, component of the suffrage coalition.

Raising Funds and Attracting Affluence

The suffrage campaign had long relied heavily on donations from supporters. Emily Howland regularly donated significant sums to the suffrage movement, beginning with her $1,200 donation prior to the 1894 New York State Constitutional Convention.[70] Anthony consistently contributed liberal amounts of money to the campaign. Over her lifetime, Eliza Wright Osborne, the daughter of Martha Coffin Wright, also donated large sums of money to the cause.[71] Newspapers alerted the public to the biggest donations, such as the time when an anonymous woman gave $35,000, of a total of $45,056, collected during a campaign fund drive in October 1914. Suffragists put the money to good use, purchasing a suffrage van to "patrol" lower Manhattan and distribute suffrage literature and opening a "suffrage shop" at 663 Fifth Avenue.[72]

Suffragists did not hide the fact that suffrage activism and promotion required a lot of money. At every opportunity, suffrage workers sought donations, knowing that every dollar helped. When the Women's Political Union sent out speakers to stand on soapboxes on street corners, their companions passed hats to collect donations. Other times, workers gave away or sold buttons, fans, tea sets, dolls, postcards, and many other items endorsing both woman suffrage and domesticity.[73] Several women opened suffrage shops in busy shopping areas. Suffrage souvenirs appealed to those who collected political memorabilia or to those who simply enjoyed the ephemera.[74] Carefully selecting items that defended "their right to the public [sphere] while promising they would not abandon the private [sphere]," suffragists appropriated consumer culture for political and monetary gain.[75] In addition, suffragists frequently held benefits to raise money, as for instance when the Nineteenth Assembly District of the Woman's Suffrage Party presented a "recital of folk lore and folk music" at the McDowell Club in April 1912.[76]

Harriot Stanton Blatch actively recruited women she considered capable of charming donors as well as supporters. She had lived in England from the time of her marriage in 1882 until 1902, when she returned to New York to be with her dying mother. In addition to her admiration for "militant British suffragette theatrics," she had become particularly sensitive to the need for wealthy and eye-catching women to represent the woman suffrage movement.[77] She recruited Caroline Lexow, first as executive secretary, then as field secretary for her Women's Political Union, positions Lexow held simultaneously with her duties for the college suffrage leagues.[78] Traveling for the union from Albany to Buffalo to establish branches, Lexow concentrated on communities where the competing New York State Woman Suffrage Association had less coverage. She often attended legislative sessions so activists constantly knew that body's decisions relative to suffrage. In later years, she recalled that women positioned themselves right on the floors of the Assembly and Senate, not yet being confined to the galleries. Suffragists also stood as sentinels at the doors of key committees in the hopes of keeping woman suffrage from being "buried" in the halls of the legislature, as so often happened. The women "became accustomed to evasion, to slights, to derision, to open hostility," targets of the resentment men demonstrated toward them in the legislature.[79]

Blatch also recruited the "strikingly beautiful" Katherine Duer Mackay, married to the founder of the International Telephone and Telegraph Company, to the woman suffrage movement.[80] Already involved in activism in her local community, Mackay joined the woman suffrage campaign in 1908. Desirous of adding a more "genteel" element to the movement, Mackay sought to influence wealthy and politically well-placed women and men in drawing rooms and other refined venues.[81] That December, she founded the Equal Franchise Society, also recruiting Caroline Lexow as executive secretary.[82] Mackay drew other elite women to the movement, including Alva Vanderbilt Belmont. Belmont had a reputation for being difficult to work with.[83] The conservative Mackay and the more radical Belmont became adversaries, often entertaining suffragists and other observers with their arguments. Mackay also disagreed with Blatch about marketing tactics. According to Blatch, Mackay "beat the table with her hands" when her board of directors disagreed with her refusal to have her society march with the parade Blatch organized in May 1910.[84] In spite of disagreements between suffrage leaders, they sought common ground. In this case, Mackay eventually calmed down and entered into discussion relating to the logistics of the parade. The competitiveness between suffragists and rival suffrage organizations is inherent to all dynamic movements.

Yet, Blatch expected the support of the Equal Franchise Society, which, including its state branches, had reportedly grown from 16 to 625 members by March 1910. Mackay set up "lavish" headquarters in the Metropolitan Building at Madison Square, procuring enough money to support three secretaries to publicize the activities of the society.[85] Mackay had presented her first speech on January 15, 1909, when she spoke before the Interurban Woman Suffrage Council, a city-wide coordinating organization founded, in 1903, to systematically unite all suffragists and affiliated suffrage societies. Modeled after the dominant political parties, it divided the city into sixty-three assembly districts with captains for its over two thousand election districts. It sought to influence legislators by forming public opinion through canvassing voters directly.[86] Mackay spoke on woman suffrage whenever possible.

For the next few years, Mackay's suffrage activism preoccupied reporters and audiences throughout the state and beyond. In February 1911, Mackay's society hosted a reception at the Hotel Ten Eyck in Albany, with Fola La Follette reading the one act comedy *How the Vote was Won*.[87] La Follette had begun giving performances of this enormously popular suffrage entertainment just the year before. The daughter of the "maverick" governor of Wisconsin, she had had little success with an acting career in New York until she offered private readings of the British play, written by Cecily Hamilton and Christopher St. John in 1910.[88] La Follette presented the play around the country, and, like Mackay, La Follette challenged the criticism of suffragists as frumpy and unattractive. Mackay, however, dropped out of suffrage activism two months later, when she left her husband and children for a love affair.[89] The Equal Franchise Society dissolved soon after, and some of its members joined other suffrage groups.[90]

Blatch prided herself on bringing the affluent Vira Boarman Whitehouse into the suffrage fold. Born to a wealthy New Orleans family, Vira Boarman married the New York stockbroker James Norman de Rapelye Whitehouse in 1898.[91] In the early years of her marriage, Whitehouse prioritized her active social life. Then she met Nora Blatch, who introduced her to her mother, Harriot Blatch.[92] The elder Blatch, in her autobiography, quotes Whitehouse as saying, "I can't remember when I didn't believe in suffrage . . . but I didn't know how to do anything except dance and go to dinner parties, and then last spring I found there was something I could do. I could march in a parade and carry a banner. And here I am making a speech. . . . I am so glad I have come to myself before the cause was quite won."[93] The young socialite wooed reporters with her "beguiling southern accent" and turned her work for the New York suffrage movement into a career.

Whitehouse marched in the 1913 New York suffrage parade and six months later gave her first outdoor suffrage speech—an experience she called "the proudest moment in her life." She immediately demonstrated an extraordinary gift for fundraising in the leadership positions she assumed.[94] Whitehouse had the talent, the time, and the passion for suffrage advocacy. By 1913, she served as chair of publicity for one suffrage organization and found time to tend the Women's Political Union suffrage shop.[95] "Young, beautiful, and brimful of energy," Whitehouse embodied the new woman in the woman suffrage movement during these years when she fully committed herself and her resources to the campaign.[96]

Another woman who personified the new woman, the Long Islander Edna Buckman Kearns, also had a gift for attracting suffrage publicity. Often the creative endeavors of the New York suffragists caught the attention of newspaper editors elsewhere in the country. No longer forced to choose between activism and homemaking, the new woman could do both. One example of this is the day that Kearns put up seventeen cans of peas and six jars of raspberries before she made a "good speech" at a suffrage meeting.[97] Women

Edna Buckman Kearns and her daughter Serena rode in the suffrage wagon on Long Beach to advertise votes for women. Image courtesy of Marguerite Buckman Kearns, granddaughter of Edna Buckman Kearns, and used with the permission of Rose Gschwendtner.

in the audience asked her how she had managed the peas, and several subsequent articles in various newspapers around the state reported that Kearns clearly made the point that she could give suffrage speeches and fulfill her responsibilities as a homemaker.[98] Yet, she had a more independent streak as well. Usually accompanied by her young daughter, Serena, she often traveled to meetings or participated in parades riding in an old wagon, using the wagon as another way to draw attention to the movement.

Adventures in Technology and Transportation

It makes sense for innovative women to be drawn to the most advanced and dramatic technology of the day. New and updated forms of transportation—trains, automobiles, and airplanes—inspired creative publicity stunts on the part of women suffragists as they sought to reach the "man on the street."[99] The development of automobiles coincided with activists' increasing sensitivity to the advantages of schemes and gimmicks to market woman suffrage. Although suffragists could not claim to be the only women's political group to use consumer culture, over time they became masters of its power. To a significant extent, suffrage may be seen as another product in the consumer marketplace, "one more commodity to be fashioned or refashioned for public consumption."[100] And suffragists everywhere enjoyed the attention they drew to their crusade.

Suffragists employed political motifs, symbolism, memorabilia, and color to construct their public identity.[101] The manufacture and distribution of useful and novelty items highlighted visible support for the cause as purchasers carried decorative fans, used automotive accessories such as fleur-de-lis-shaped radiator caps painted with suffrage colors or "Votes for Women," or wore buttons with suffrage slogans.[102] They set their sights on ever more dramatic merchandise. Suffragists appropriated motorcars, useful as a symbol of independence as well as a practical way to disperse the ideas of suffrage to outlying areas, for use in political campaigns. Initially too expensive for ordinary Americans and more common in cities, automobiles came to be associated with elites. In fact, Alva Belmont, an early motorcar enthusiast and perhaps the first person in the United States to import an automobile from France, had been motoring to suffrage functions at least since 1911.[103]

While it remained challenging for women to invade the supposed male sphere of automobiles, suffragists used them for auto tours, parades, and "open-air revivals" across the state, drawing new supporters in increasingly inventive ways. Women drivers still drew a great deal of attention to themselves, especially in outlying and rural areas of the state. Driving also "embodied a new female sense of self, more mobile, more active, more public," ideal for the new woman, who rejoiced in "pursuing thrills" and excitement as she sought political rights for herself.[104] Suffragists also found the open automobiles convenient as portable speaker platforms. Some rural people certainly attended the open-air meetings simply for the novelty of seeing an automobile. Even though they had felt dirty and exhausted, suffragists would remember these as some of the best times of their lives.

Suffragists found automobiles appropriate for both fundraising and making a living. The motorist Olive Schultz, for example, operated a taxi service for suffragists and other women in New York City, beginning in 1913, splitting her profits with Harriot Stanton Blatch's Women's Political Union. Willing to drive even at night, she had a reputation for being a mechanical genius, able to "do more to improve a peevish carburetor with a hairpin than most mechanics can with a hydraulic drill and an assortment of monkey wrenches."[105] Her business represented the growing goals of suffragists—that political enfranchisement would expand "social and economic options" for women.[106] Realizing the advantages of the automobile for women's independence, Crystal Eastman, Inez Milholland, Mary Beard, and Mary Garrett

Hay collaborated with the Maxwell Motor Company to hire women on an equal basis with men for motorcar sales positions.[107] Ever the opportunists, suffragists devised practical as well as spectacular uses for the automobile.

New York suffragists also found ways to integrate aviation into their publicity stunts, as in September 1913, when "General" Rosalie Jones, a socialite and the daughter of an anti-suffragist, organized an "aviation meet" on Hempstead Plains.[108] Portia Willis, the daughter of a Civil War infantry captain, loved the pageantry and excitement of the suffrage movement. Willis attended the meet and auctioned off a cake, challenging one of the pilots to join the Men's League for Woman Suffrage. Marion Simms led a "procession of flying machines" into the air, dropping "yellow suffrage roses and literature" from the cockpits.[109] Enthusiasm for airplanes infected anti-suffragists, too, who used them when they could. In 1915, for example, antis hired "Flying Johnson" to drop pink anti-suffrage flyers on the Olean fairgrounds from his plane.[110] In these early years of aviation, flying had no gender association and many women enjoyed the freedom of the skies over New York.

Getting the Word Out

Suffragists learned to respond spontaneously and in increasingly innovative ways to get the word out to those they wanted to reach. So, for example, when the Colorado judge Ben V. Lindsay, long recognized as a strong advocate for woman suffrage, cabled the Women's Political Union to say that he would be available for whatever they needed while he visited Albany, suffragists chalked the announcement on the sidewalks and distributed flyers to let people know they would hold a special suffrage meeting in the Assembly chamber. Interested and curious people attended in large numbers.[111] In expanding on the directives of nineteenth-century suffragists to "employ agents, circulate tracts, petition the state and national legislatures, and endeavor to enlist the pulpit and press," the activists of the new century discovered that being conspicuous garnered them "free advertising" and additional supporters.[112]

The most extroverted women made the best speakers for suffrage and drew the largest crowds. Well-educated, intelligent, and worldly, Inez Milholland had trained as a lawyer and committed herself to activism for world peace as well as woman suffrage. Her dynamic personality made her especially effective as a spokesperson for the suffrage movement. Born into a well-connected family in 1886, Milholland possessed a myriad of benefits right from the beginning of her life. Her father made a fortune in developing a pneumatic system for transporting mail between major cities.[113] He committed himself to social justice and fighting racism; both parents instilled in their children a strong sense of obligation to serve others.[114] Well aware of her good looks, Milholland "reveled" in her effect on observers and allowed suffrage leaders such as Blatch and Alice Paul to exploit her beauty in the promotion of woman suffrage. In essence, she helped to create her dazzling image.[115] Milholland embodied the movement's "idealism and influenced its most spectacular campaigns."[116]

Suffragists recruited other speakers right out of college. Laura Ellsworth Cook worked for a short time as the paid head of the Women's Political Union's Speakers' Bureau, training and assigning orators, as well as speaking herself. The union expected women to donate their time, although a few salaried women received a nominal sum to cover expenses.[117] After obtaining permits from the police department, "every night of the week," ten or twelve women carried soapboxes to stand on. The women worked in pairs; one would speak while the other distributed suffrage literature or novelties. Their work could be risky. Sometimes people would throw stones or other projectiles at the women or the gathered audiences.[118] Perhaps suffragists, too, believed, like Rheta Childe Dorr, that it was "better to be stoned than to be ignored."[119]

Members of the Women's Political Union continually sought publicity through stunts and by inviting and cultivating reporters. At one point, women made speeches from horseback at City Hall Park. They attached boards announcing a meeting to the sides of the horses, annoying the animals. While Nora Blatch aptly presented her speech from horseback, a "horrible little office boy jabbed a pin" into Laura Cook's horse, which reared and took time to calm. Cook did not give her speech that day.[120] On another occasion, the two young women hired a motorboat for a stunt, running the boat parallel to the shoreline yelling "Suffrage votes for women" at any men they saw. Fishermen thought it would be funny to circle the women's boat, creating waves that threatened to sink them; none too pleased, the two male anti-suffrage reporters with them had to bail out the boat with their hats. Despite Nora Blatch's admonition to give the suffragists good publicity, the stunt garnered just one brief paragraph in the newspaper. One of the reporters promised Cook they would get front-page coverage if they drowned the next time.[121]

Suffragists found all kinds of ways to promote suffrage to the broader public. The "voiceless speech," first used by the Women's Political Union, offered a simple but innovative publicity stunt. Anna Constable first used the technique when she held up large placards printed with simple suffrage statements in the window of a rented shop on Fifth Avenue. Standing silently, she displayed the cards one by one to gathering crowds. Eventually

Voiceless speeches offered women a non-threatening and unique way to communicate their message to the public. Women often stood in shop windows, slowly turning pages as spectators crowded around. Image from the Carrie Chapman Catt Papers, courtesy of Bryn Mawr College Special Collections, Bryn Mawr, PA.

the police arrested her for "causing a crowd to collect and block the sidewalk" but released her with a warning. Suffragists continued using silent speeches in rural areas as well, especially in public venues such as fairs and Old Home Days, finding that women less extroverted than Inez Milholland could still broadcast the suffrage message.[122] This individualized approach surely reached a limited number of people, but suffragists continually sought opportunities and techniques to reach any potential voters.

Pageants, Parades, and Hikes

For a brief period during the suffrage movement, pageants of as many as five hundred costumed suffragists, standing motionless and silent as they depicted "historical and allegorical scenes," held the rapt attention of audiences. Certainly, having to remain silent and still would not have appealed for long to the women working to counter the image of the mute and obedient woman. Yet, suffrage pageants, with women dressed in rich colors and standing so that they created specific patterns, or dressed all in white wearing flowers or crowns, held a certain appeal. The sentimentality evoked by such displays could leave as lasting an impression on viewers as suffrage speeches could.[123] Suffragists and onlookers also flocked to "Yellow Rallies." Held at night and lit by lanterns carried by marchers wearing yellow capes over white dresses, these rallies or torchlight parades drew a lot of attention.[124]

For the boldest suffragists, parades held great appeal. Warnings published in newspapers prior to the date of the first parade coordinated by the New York State Woman Suffrage Association on May 7, 1911, made it quite clear that some people worried that too much physical activity could be harmful for women. As Rheta Childe Dorr dryly remarked, walking "might be all right for women in perfect health, but for women *in any way incapacitated*, the results might be very serious." Her point is punctuated by the marchers' "mirth" as they observed a dozen ambulances standing by in the side streets, waiting for delicate women to collapse from the excitement. Delayed at the start by a group of "marathoners" trying to sidetrack the parade, the marchers let out a "big equal rights cry" for the right of way.[125]

Inez Milholland joined the three thousand women marchers for the parade along Fifth Avenue, witnessed by 150,000 spectators. She and two other women carried a banner lettered with the words of an English hymn: "Forward, out of error, Leave behind the night/Forward through the darkness, Forward into light." These words would become closely associated with Milholland. Behind her, Fola La Follette led the division of actors, and many other prominent suffragists marched with contingents of farmers, dressmakers, athletes, women workers, society women, and representatives of the various woman suffrage organizations. Floats, one decorated with an old-fashioned hearth and women spinning and weaving and another with Quakers and a liberty bell made of flowers, rode between the contingents of marchers.[126]

Parades in New York drew thousands of participants and curious watchers, eliciting more publicity and enthusiasm for the suffrage movement than any other single suffrage activity. The newspapers loved the marching women, who publicly unified their movement by wearing the same colors, or types of clothing, and carrying similar accessories at the request of parade organizers.[127] Mounted on a spirited horse, Milholland, a perennial favorite, rode at the head of 8,000 marchers, including 619 men, in a 1912 Fifth Avenue parade.[128] In 1913, she led a torchlight parade along Fifth Avenue in a golden chariot representing the first suffrage state, Wyoming, celebrating women gaining the right to vote in Arizona, Kansas, and Oregon.[129] However, marchers were vulnerable to violent responses from unsupportive onlookers, who threw garbage or wet sponges at them.[130] After violence erupted during the

Participants lined up in preparation for a suffrage parade in Albany in 1914. Image from the Miss Bessie Little Collection, courtesy of Kevin Franklin and the Weare C. Little Memorial Park Association, Colonie, NY.

March 3, 1913, suffrage parade in Washington, DC, even the often "acidulous" and conservative (especially in regards to woman suffrage) *New York Times* admitted that women should be able to march and "were entitled to protection," regardless of their reasons for marching.[131] Nevertheless, as the scholar Linda Lumsden posits, women risked physical safety as they sought political power in public spaces.[132] These spectacles attracted both favorable and unfavorable attention yet earned steadily increasing support from those who stood along the parade and transportation routes.

Hikes, especially those led by Rosalie Jones, the president of the Nassau County suffrage organization, presented yet another example of the pageantry of the suffrage movement. Jones basked in the publicity related to her thirteen-day hike from Long Island to Albany in December 1912. The twenty-six hikers arrived at the capital in time to meet the newly-elected governor, William Sulzer, presenting him with their "sacred parchment" and its "secret" message for woman suffrage.[133] Jones's exploits garnered broad newspaper coverage beyond the state of New York. From February to March 1913, she led a pilgrimage from New York to Washington, DC. As they traveled the two hundred grueling miles, the women gave speeches and distributed suffrage literature. More important, they received press coverage every day. Once they reached Washington, they joined more than 5,000 National American Woman Suffrage Association members in a parade, deliberately held at the time of Woodrow Wilson's inauguration. People paid virtually no attention as Wilson disembarked from the train bringing him to the city; most of them found the suffrage parade far more intriguing.[134]

Suffrage in Print and Advertising

The deliberate and concerted efforts on the part of suffragists to influence public opinion through print media in New York State can be traced to 1868 with the publication of the radical periodical, the *Revolution*. Founded by Elizabeth Cady Stanton and Susan B. Anthony, the periodical readily endorsed a range of commercial products, tying their use to suffrage. For example, as the editors of the *Revolution* pointed out, "Blanchir" soap worked so well that women voters "shall always have the washing done early on election day." The office in the Women's Bureau actually offered the product for sale.[135] Taking advantage of the newspaper's position at the juncture of the suffrage cause and the consumer marketplace, the editors willingly adapted the content as necessary to gain the financial support of advertisers.[136] Regardless of how the philosophy of woman suffrage changed over the decades of the campaign, activists found that packaging their arguments in consumer-friendly messages helped to brand woman suffrage. As suffragists gained expertise over the decades, they advertised clothing, cleaning solutions, and an array of other products in the *Woman Voter* as well as in other suffrage publications.

New York women had editorship of many publications over the years, including Amelia Bloomer's *Lily* (1849–1856), Victoria Woodhull and Tennessee Clafin's *Weekly* (1870–1876), Matilda Joslyn Gage's *National Citizen and Ballot Box* (1878–1881), the *New York Suffrage Newsletter* that Harriet May Mills edited for the New York State Woman Suffrage Association (1899–1913), the *Woman Voter* (1910–1917), and Harriot Stanton Blatch's *Women's Political World* (1913–1916).[137] These periodicals published articles to keep women informed about meetings, conventions, activities, and pertinent news related to woman suffrage. They made available for purchase books and pamphlets on topics related to woman's rights, as well as novelty items to appeal to new women consumers. As the referenda neared, they increasingly focused on legislative developments related to their enfranchisement. Part of their support came from advertisements placed by women-owned businesses. In addition, suffragists sought to influence public opinion through the mainstream press.

Throughout the suffrage campaign years, conventional newspapers and magazines also helped to shape popular opinion and to spread news about the suffrage movement more broadly throughout the state. Daily papers upstate found an ever-increasing readership. Although they covered suffrage events, with few exceptions—such as the *New York Evening Post*, edited by Oswald Garrison Villard—newspapers and their respective editors did not openly support suffrage. Acknowledging this point as late as 1915, Carrie Chapman Catt lamented, "Newspapers are not ready to fight for us."[138] Although general interest magazines, such as the popular *Saturday Evening Post*, attracted women readers, most women subscribed to women-centered periodicals. In 1907, Arthur T. Vance, the former editor of the *Women's Home Companion*, transformed the *Pictorial Review* from a small, unassuming monthly to a reform-minded magazine that appealed to middle-class women. Committed to social change, Vance published Charlotte Perkins Gilman's article on divorce and the muckraker Rheta Childe Dorr's explanation of why women wanted to be self-sufficient.[139] By June 1915, the *Pictorial Review*, with a readership of 1.2 million women, ranked second behind the *Saturday Evening Post*, and Vance became one of the few editors to declare unequivocally his support for equal suffrage.[140] His backing was unusual in the male-dominated world of publishing, which largely ignored or even opposed women's voting rights.

Suffrage in Theater and Film

Whereas the relatively staid publishing world opposed votes for women, the theater and film industries welcomed the theatrical potential of the lively suffrage appeal. The spectacle of the theater contrasted superficially with the more conservative arguments some suffragists promoted: that the state needed women's moral attributes and domestic expertise. However, the simultaneous growth of the entertainment medium and the suffrage movement actually enhanced both. Radical and savvy new woman suffragists advocated their goals in ways that satisfied audiences craving the "drama, excitement, [and] 'color and dash'" of performance.[141] In addition, new movie houses demanded reels of film to show to eager moviegoers, just as suffragists sought new methods of conveying their cause to voters. This confluence enriched both entities.

Suffragists loved great theater and had a long tradition of performing plays. When the Broadway actor Edson R. Miles and a cast of amateurs performed in the comedy *How the Vote Was Won* in Clinton, New York, in 1911, the audience thoroughly enjoyed itself.[142] Beatrice Forbes-Robertson organized a "suffrage matinee" at the Maxine Elliot Theater on Broadway, built in 1909 by the popular and controversial actress, who donated her venue for the event. Harriot Stanton Blatch spoke and Charlotte Perkins Gilman recited a suffrage poem during an intermission. Cast members of the three plays *Before the Dawn*, *A Woman's Influence*, and the audience favorite, *How the Vote Was Won*, included prominent actresses and suffrage workers. All proceeds benefited Blatch's Equality League of Self-Supporting Women.[143]

Suffragists hosted other plays as fundraisers, too—for instance, when they held a performance of Bernard Shaw's *Press Cuttings* at the Broadway Theatre in April 1912. Relying on volunteer actors and the addition of two one-act plays, suffragists showed their expertise in raising money.[144] Letting no opportunity pass them by, some suffragists even sold cigarettes labeled "Votes for Women" at the Victoria Theatre just five months later. Despite local ordinances banning women from smoking in public, some new women adopted the habit. However, when word got out about suffragists selling cigarettes, Harriet Laidlaw expressed her disapproval of them doing so, because to her "Votes for Women" meant "purity of life, manners, and morals." She regretted the alignment of suffrage with a habit often associated with vice. Other suffragists wore yellow armbands with black edging to acknowledge the mistake. Mainstream suffrage groups blamed members of the Women's Political Union, and the controversy earned coverage in the local papers.[145]

By the 1910s, suffragists could take advantage of film to reach diverse groups, knowing full well that the demand for movies guaranteed suffragists audiences for their productions.[146] Plays and silent suffrage films produced by the National American Woman Suffrage Association and the Women's Political Union eventually came to rural areas just starting to build theaters to accommodate such productions.[147] Virtually all nationally known suffragists starred in films. For example, in 1912, Anna Howard Shaw, Jane Addams, Max Eastman, James Lees Laidlaw, Harriet Burton Laidlaw, Inez Milholland, and numerous others appeared in a dramatic silent film, *Votes for Women*, featuring lengthy footage of one of the suffrage parades. The following year, Harriot Stanton Blatch starred alongside Emmeline Pankhurst, the head of the radical English movement, in *What Eighty Million Women Want*. It challenged these suffragists to get their points across to audiences who could not hear them.[148] In spite of the silence, viewers eagerly thronged movie houses, sometimes unintentionally absorbing the suffrage message.

Suffrage and Art

The Buffalo artist and suffragist Evelyn Rumsey Cary designed a dramatic art nouveau–style gold-bordered suffrage poster with a far more deliberate message in 1905. Widely disseminated in magazines and suffrage propaganda, the poster depicts a woman with arms outstretched. The message on the poster below the figure of the woman reads, "Give her of the fruit of her hands and let her own works praise her in the gates," drawn from Proverbs 31:31. The ethereal quality of the poster represents one powerful image of the woman suffrage campaign, whereas the work of a number of other artists expressed diverse and nuanced ideas about women's voting privileges. Suffrage artists also helped to publicize and raise money for the benefit of the movement. The artwork produced took myriad forms, from cartoons published in local papers to nationally recognized paintings and sculpture.

An increasing number of people could see what a suffragist looked like, since advertising found the new woman so appealing to draw and to photograph. Young, fashionable, and feminine (hence, nonthreatening), her attributes included intelligence, sophistication, and competence. Many professional women artists, also identified with the new woman, supported women's right to vote and functioned as feminist activists. As the historian Laura Prieto articulates, "women artists' contribution to the suffrage movement serves as a powerful example of women's using their cultural influence to change social and political status."[149] Simultaneously, the suffrage movement eliminated some of the barriers for professional women artists.[150] While suffragists sought to remove gender barriers from electoral politics, women artists sought to "overturn gender-based exclusions."[151] The heady combination promised professional success, creativity, and excitement for many women artists.

Cartoonists and illustrators knew full well the power of humor to ease people's discomfort with new ideas and the ability of images to evoke sympathy for those who suffer oppression or abuse.[152] Cartoonists had long delighted in portraying suffragists as unattractive and masculine, the antithesis of the pious, feminine, domestic womanly ideal of the nineteenth century. Learning more every year about the value of appearance, presentation, and drawing attention, women illustrators and artists drew images of the "new women" as suffragists while actively serving the suffrage movement. May Wilson, for example, studied at the Art Students' League and at the New York School of Art, where she met Edith Dimock. Wilson married James Moore Preston and Dimock married William Glackens, thereby associating themselves informally with the Ashcan School, an art movement that portrayed the daily life of poor New Yorkers. May Preston became a popular illustrator of magazines and books, including *How It Feels to be the Husband of a Suffragette*, probably written by Arthur Brown, the husband of Gertrude Foster Brown.[153] Women artists, many of whom associated "in one way or another" with the Ashcan School, marched along Fifth Avenue in the 1913 suffrage parade. The ranks of artists included Abastenia St. Leger

Eberle, best known for her controversial sculpture, "The White Slave," which appeared on the May 3, 1913, cover of the *Survey*, and Edith Dimock Glackens, while Glackens's husband marched with the men toward the back of the parade.[154] The Heterodite artists Lou (Annie) Rogers and Ida Sedgwick Proper, the art editor for the *Woman Voter*, maintained active roles in the suffrage movement.

Suffragists with creative talents in the varied artistic styles of the period directed their energies toward raising money for the cause with an exhibition held at the Macbeth Galleries from September 27 to October 16, 1915. New York professional artists, such as the lead organizer, Ida Sedgwick Proper; Anne Goldthwaite, a "New Yorker by adoption" who painted in the style of French post-impressionists; and the sculptor and recording secretary of the New York State Woman Suffrage Party, Alice Morgan Wright, made clear their attitude toward equal suffrage. These artists drew nearly one hundred contributors from Boston, Santa Monica, England, and elsewhere to the gallery, which expressed "a certain freshness and energy," representing the mood of the season as well as the mood of suffrage. Several hundred people attended the opening day, and attendance "remained strong" during the exhibit.[155]

One critic described "political conviction," not "artistic affinity," as the organizing factor of the exhibit, but only two artists actually created artwork directly related to the woman suffrage theme.[156] Helena Dayton contributed several rather "cartoonlike" sculptures, including "Suffrage Girls" and "The Two Antis." The painter Theresa Bernstein, whose career remarkably spanned the entire twentieth century, entered a piece called "The Suffrage Meeting." Suffrage artists joined in the ongoing efforts to modify the public perception of suffragists. For example, photographs of Dayton, Proper, and Wright appeared in the *Illustrated Milliner* "looking very glamorous in stylish hats."[157] Highbrow or lowbrow, virtually anyone could find something interesting in the appeal for woman suffrage. At the end of the show, the exhibitors donated half of their proceeds to the Empire State Campaign of the New York State woman suffrage movement.[158]

The Empire State Campaign Committee

In spite of strenuous efforts, the years of the suffrage marketing campaign to change public perception and affect legislation continually met with frustration. The disheartening refusal of legislators to seriously consider woman suffrage in 1912 forced suffragists to admit that an even more systematic campaign would be necessary to achieve women's enfranchisement in New

York. The New York State Woman Suffrage Association had approximately 450 branches across the state and claimed an estimated enrollment of 350,000 members.[159] While women's membership numbers continued to grow, leaders concentrated on building a tighter organization, headquartered in New York City, that would bring supportive male voters into the fold. The tactics

Suffragists often traveled outside of New York to assist with suffrage campaigns in other states. The New Yorker Portia Willis stands with elephants Jennie and Lena carrying the "suffrage plank" prior to the national suffrage parade held in Chicago during the Republican National Convention in 1916. Image courtesy of the Women's History Archives, Sophia Smith Collection, Smith College, Northampton, MA.

of the state association differed from those of the New York City Woman Suffrage Party. The merger of the *Woman Voter* and the New York State Woman Suffrage Association *Newsletter* in January 1913 prefaced the power shift. Rural adherents to the Woman Suffrage Association who prioritized school, tax, and township suffrage over state suffrage reluctantly witnessed the leadership forces regroup in New York City.[160] Suffragists needed a more dynamic approach to win voter support.

In the fall of 1913, while serving as the president of the International Woman Suffrage Alliance, Carrie Chapman Catt launched the Empire State Campaign Committee. Temporarily relieved of her national level suffrage responsibilities, Catt had served as the chair of a coalition comprised of the New York State Woman Suffrage Association, the Woman Suffrage Party of New York City, the College Equal Suffrage League, the Equal Suffrage Society, and the Men's League for Woman Suffrage.[161] Catt made what her supporters considered an ingenious move in modeling the Empire State Campaign Committee's hierarchal machinery after the Democratic forces of Tammany Hall. Determined to reach each and every potential voter in the state, Catt divided the state into twelve districts, each with its own chairperson who supervised the assembly district leaders, who, in turn, controlled the election district captains. To employ a more methodical approach to changing legislation, Catt attempted to gain some control over upstate suffrage work.[162] However, Blatch disagreed with Catt over the tactics the suffragists should use and felt that Catt focused on the achievements of the New York City headquarters while too often neglecting the needs of upstate suffragists.[163] Refusing to join what she viewed as an all-too-conservative coterie, Blatch dissolved her Women's Political Union and, with Alva Belmont, shifted her energies to the federal amendment.[164]

New York suffragists pushed past conventional boundaries to revitalize a movement that, after six decades, still had not achieved its goal. Radicalism, or the willingness to be more boldly public, on the part of many of the new women and feminist suffragists accentuated the goal of the movement. By playing on consumer consciousness and appropriating new technologies in travel and media, all while engaging in exciting pageantry and parades, suffragists drew funding and support from increasing numbers of voters. The suffrage influence in theater and film helped to spread the growing enthusiasm to people far from the centers of suffrage activism. At the same time, suffrage artwork drew appreciative audiences and helped to raise funds to support the cause. In fact, most of the marketing efforts of suffragists proved financially successful. Making suffrage fun, and, at the same time, commonplace, went a long way toward changing public opinion, a factor essential to changing legislation and winning suffrage.

CHAPTER 7

The Great Interruption

World War I and Woman Suffrage

Abandoning woman suffrage for war work remained one of the journalist Rheta Childe Dorr's lifelong regrets.[1] At first, in a "stirring" editorial for the *Suffragist*, she erroneously predicted that "war could have no effect on the struggle of American women for the ballot."[2] Wrestling with the notion that no cause demanded more attention than the war, however, she soon gave up virtually every connection she had with the suffrage movement, including editing the *Suffragist*, the journal of the National Woman's Party, and membership in the Greenwich Village radical group, Heterodoxy. As she recalled, the "world-shaking event affected [her] so deeply that it changed [her] whole viewpoint if not [her] whole life."[3] Dorr eventually found her way to Europe as a war correspondent. Many women—patriotic, pacifist, or merely compliant with governmental policies—faced similar choices; upheaval and contradictions marred the final years of the suffrage campaign in New York.

Although the United States delayed entry into World War I—or the Great War, as it was called at the time—until April 1917, most New York suffragists early on turned some of their attention from suffragism to war relief, war preparedness (opponents would call it militarism), pacifism, or patriotism, between 1914 and 1917.[4] Never members of a monolithic movement, pro-suffrage women and men hailed from such diverse groups that no one philosophy regarding war dominated their decisions or behavior.[5] Conversely, virtually every anti-suffragist actively turned her attention from the suffrage contest to war preparedness, eliminating some of the resistance to the suffrage campaign. Some suffragists, such as Carrie Chapman Catt, Crystal Eastman, Mary Heaton Vorse, Inez Milholland, and Madeleine Doty, fervently opposed war and clearly proclaimed their support for peace, a radical and controversial stance at the time. Others sold war bonds, knit socks, rolled bandages, raised money for war relief or the purchase of war materiel, and fully backed the government's evolving stance on war. Still others essentially ignored the war to concentrate on suffrage.

Many suffragists argued that because war affected women just as it did men, they should not be denied a voice in the war councils.[6] Support for or opposition to the war became a point of contention between mainstream suffragists and more radical suffragists. Mainstream suffragists preferred to distance themselves from those who expressed any opposition to the war.[7] The conundrum for New York State voters, as Gertrude Foster Brown, the president of the New York State Woman Suffrage Party, asserted, was that the state "could not afford to refuse democracy to its own women" as long as the United States "engaged in a war for democracy."[8]

The unevenness of the suffrage reaction challenges the impression given by accounts of the movement that claim either that suffragists ignored the war to push forward with their goal for enfranchisement or that voters rewarded women for their war work.[9] Not only do these perspectives disregard the decades during which thousands of women devoted their energies to the suffrage movement, they also overlook the widening support suffragists had gained over the years. According to the historian Sara Hunter Graham, when "weighing only women's patriotic service," legislators could have decided to reward anti-suffrage dedication to the war effort, rather than the work of suffragists.[10] Suffragists joined peace societies; anti-suffragists did not. Otherwise, suffragists, both black and white, and anti-suffragists alike sold Liberty Bonds, raised money for the war effort, and even joined some of the same organizations, such as the Red Cross, related to war relief. Suffragists, more talented than anti-suffragists at raising funds, could donate money for war-related causes and still have some to spare for the suffrage cause. Desperate for full citizenship after almost seven decades of agitation, few suffragists could remain completely neutral during the war years.

Suffrage and Isolationism

The years prior to the Great War seemed filled with the promise of progressive reform and social and economic equality.[11] While the majority of citizens opposed U.S. involvement in European wars, they generally supported the intervention of the United States in conflagrations in the western hemisphere. For example, the Mexican Revolution, fought between 1910 and 1920, caused some people in the Woodrow Wilson administration to pressure the president to use military force to protect "American interests."[12] While border patrols had been "on the alert" since 1910, by late 1913, Wilson threatened to depose the dictator Victoriano Huerta. This threat angered Mexicans, not so much because they supported Huerta, but because the United States was interfering with events in Mexico. Francisco ("Pancho") Villa, a general under Huerta's opponent, Venustiano Carranza, and a man who appealed to the imagination of Americans, welcomed U.S. intervention in April 1914.[13] The United States occupied Veracruz for only seven months, accomplishing little but cleaning up the city.[14]

During the months leading to the U.S. occupation of Mexico, many suffragists voiced their strong objections to military action. Fanny Garrison Villard, the suffragist, civil rights activist, and pacifist, chaired a meeting at Cooper Union on April 23, 1914, protesting the invasion of Mexico. Harriot Stanton Blatch observed that working people "do the killing, they do the dying, and they do the paying for it," while those in power who send them to war remain safe behind the lines.[15] To highlight their refusal to support war, a few of the most radical suffragists connected with the Women's Political Union took the "will and won't pledge," vowing they would not support philanthropic causes until they secured the right to vote. Carrie Chapman Catt denied the existence of such a pledge, inspiring a few editorial rejoinders.[16] Anti-suffragists, in contrast, declared that the "decision of the policy of peace or war" should be left "to the men of the nation" and sent telegrams to Woodrow Wilson and Red Cross secretary Mabel Boardman pledging the support of their organization to the war effort.[17]

When people in the United States first heard the news of the June 28, 1914, assassination of Austrian archduke Franz Ferdinand and his wife Sophie, most did not pay much attention. As Dorr put it, the "Hapsburgs were always being assassinated."[18] But, as Americans in Europe could attest, Europeans seemed to be itching for a fight, and the assassination triggered events that led to the German invasion of Belgium on August 4, and, subsequently, to the Great War. Many suffragists naturally found it difficult to focus solely on their enfranchisement. War news increasingly preempted suffrage news.[19] As a result, Vira Boarman Whitehouse, the chair of the New York State Woman Suffrage Party, and Helen Rogers [Mrs. Ogden Mills] Reid, the treasurer, raised additional money for vigorous advertising campaigns to keep as much attention as possible focused on suffrage.[20] Suffrage speeches

and articles, while still addressing woman suffrage, now also included refer-
ences to the war. Many suffrage events resulted in the donation of at least
some of the money they raised for war relief and, especially after the United
States entered the war, for war matériel.

Many people in Wilson's administration and throughout the country
resisted any U.S. involvement in the European war, regardless of the provo-
cation. On May 7, 1915, a German submarine sank the *Lusitania* off the coast
of Ireland, killing 1,200 passengers, including 124 Americans. In addition to
its passengers, the luxury liner had carried food and a significant amount of
ammunition, violating rules of neutrality during times of war. Three days
after the attack, Wilson appeared cowardly to many who heard him say in a
speech in Philadelphia that "there is such a thing as a man being too proud
to fight. There is such a thing as a nation being so right that it does not need
to convince others by force that it is right."[21] Clearly, the leader of the United
States wanted to avoid engagement in a major war. As the war in Europe
intensified, public opinion shifted gradually in the direction of military commitment to the war, forcing New York suffragists to take an official stance
on the conflict.

Meanwhile, in September 1914, the *Woman Voter*, the official organ of
the Woman Suffrage Party of New York City, began running a "Women and
War" column and publishing articles making reference to the war. These
articles linked enfranchisement with protecting home and country "from
the horrors of war."[22] Artists contributed images that evoked the suffering
of especially the women and children victimized by military conflict. Other
images highlighted the responsibilities of women to heal and comfort the
suffering. The language of war entered the language of suffrage writing and
rhetoric. Collectively, the poetry, cartoons, and excerpts reprinted from other
publications strongly suggest a pacifist, or sometimes antagonistic, attitude
on the part of the editors. The Woman Suffrage Party president, Gertrude
Foster Brown, pronounced that "wherever democracy is strongest the war
spirit is the weakest." She had no qualms about arguing that war is incompatible with full democracy.

In the earliest months of the war, suffragists ignored it except when
reminded by a strong advocate for peace. In preparation for the woman suffrage convention in Rochester in October 1914, Brown called on suffragists
to conduct open air meetings in every district in the state as part of a "whirlwind campaign" to keep the goals of suffrage before the voters, whatever
their position on war.[23] During the convention, the Hungarian suffragist and
pacifist, Rosika Schwimmer, in her talk on women and war, encouraged her
listeners to "make a new patriotism which says not that you must die for

your country, but that you must live and work for it."[24] As long as the vote remained a priority and the war played out in European trenches without American soldiers, most suffragists paid little attention to foreign affairs.

Suffrage, War Relief, and War Preparedness

Reports of the "wanton slaughter" of innocent civilians from the first days of the August 1914 German invasion of Belgium formed the "basis of the Belgium atrocity stories," compelling even the German commander to describe it as "brutal."[25] So many women's organizations offered relief that fall that "their activities were marked by duplication and confusion."[26] Able to draw on significant resources and already established networks, suffragists raised relief funds in conjunction with their suffrage activities. By November, the Brooklyn Woman Suffrage Party chair, Ethel Dreier, proud of the money suffragists raised for relief efforts, remarked that "no more fundamental work for peace can be done than to work for enfranchisement for the women of New York State, for to win New York will be the next step toward the civilized world."[27] Knowledge of the horrors Belgians faced, coupled with activity in war relief, persuaded some women to embrace the war preparedness cause.

Anti-suffragists, arguing that suffragists "put a price on their war service activities," renewed their pledge of support and resources to the president of the United States and the Red Cross in late 1914.[28] Josephine Jewell Dodge, the president of the National Association Opposed to Woman Suffrage, used New York newspapers to encourage women of "all shades of political faith" to support the work of the Red Cross.[29] New York antis encouraged the relief organization to use their headquarters one day a week, rolling bandages and replacing typing with sewing. They consistently raised money for the Red Cross and war relief throughout the period of the suffrage campaign.[30] Antis argued that doubling the electorate by granting women the right to vote would increase the cost of democracy by requiring more voting booths, more election inspectors, and the need to count more votes. Antis thereby took credit for helping to save the government "an amount sufficient to buy five hundred million rounds of ammunition a year" by preventing women from voting.[31] Likewise, the anti-suffrage publication the *Woman's Protest* ran Red Cross and war relief news rather than news about their work to prevent enfranchisement.[32] Anti-suffragists even advocated for a "truce" with suffragists until the war ended, promising to donate all funds raised to the Red Cross if suffragists agreed to the truce.[33]

In spite of the war and an awareness of its attendant atrocities, suffragists continued to make connections with the need for women's voting rights. So, for example, when the British nurse Edith Louisa Cavell was executed for helping Allied soldiers escape occupied Belgium, Gertrude Foster Brown asserted that since women suffer the same as men, they require the same protections granted them.[34] Because women bore sons who fought in wars, their position outside of the political decision-making process especially galled suffragists.[35] They increasingly called for women's voice in government.[36] By the summer of 1916, most cities held preparedness and patriotic rallies, such as the one in Buffalo in June. The fifty thousand marchers who participated in the parade included suffragists; suffragists participated in similar events in Albany, Rochester, New York, and elsewhere.[37] Other suffragists argued that "the military state" is one in "which woman has no place."[38] Anti-suffragists accepted the conventional gender role division relative to war: men conducted the business of war and women performed the duties of relief.[39] Others could not see the dichotomy so clearly defined, and governments at both state and national levels had no idea what to do with the overwhelming offers women made on behalf of war preparedness or relief. It took nearly two years for the government to acknowledge and accept the help of women and their efficient organizations in any work related to war.[40]

Those involved in war relief efforts argued that food conservation constituted the "first line of defense" during times of war. A group of home economists had founded the American Home Economics Association in Saratoga Springs, in 1885. By the summer of 1916, they established an Emergency Committee to address the needs they saw arising in conjunction with the war in Europe. That fall, women such as the anti-suffragist Annie Nathan Meyer taught camp cooking and street cooking in case of an invasion, part of a new feminine campaign for preparedness.[41] Meyer chaired the Home Economics Committee during a New York City conference called to address the issues of feeding families during wartime. They looked for innovative ways to convey their ideas, recruiting students from Columbia Teachers' College to go into the field and people's homes.[42]

After the United States entered the war on April 6, 1917, the committee enhanced its emergency relief efforts to extend its reach into rural areas. The work of the committee included opening a library, creating educational films, publishing instructional information regarding cooperative buying and food conservation, demonstrating food preparation, and demonstrating how to cook under adverse conditions. It also offered programs to accommodate the needs of educational institutions, as well as those of diverse ethnic and

The United States government encouraged women's involvement in certain feminine arenas during World War I, as can be seen in this "Feminine Patriotism" poster. Image courtesy of the National Archives and Records Administration, Washington, DC.

religious groups. It addressed the problems related to the food riots on the east and west sides of New York City, resulting in "greater pressure on nurseries and settlements."[43] With the U.S. declaration of war, the Emergency Committee of the Home Economics Association acted in a national advisory capacity, overseeing local committees in cooperation with the National League of Women's Services.[44] For their part, suffragists cooperated with the Red Cross and other relief groups, inviting "contingents of Red Cross women, office workers, and 'farmerettes'" to participate in their suffrage parades.

Alva Belmont appropriated a journalist's term, "farmerette," originally intended to be a "sassy, diminutive" combination of the words "farmer" and "suffragette," when she referred to the workers in a pilot agricultural program on one of her estates in 1911.[45] What began in March 1917 as an experiment to address potential farm labor shortages under the auspices of the New York City mayor John Purroy Mitchel's Committee of Women on National Defense grew with positive publicity.[46] Virginia Gildersleeve, the dynamic dean of Barnard College, chaired the Standing Committee on Agriculture and supervised the farmerettes.[47] The farmerettes, a group composed of teachers, college students, and unemployed trade union women, worked during summers as part of a unit plan to increase agricultural production. The surplus crops could go to Europe for war relief. The women earned a wage based on a piece rate and lived in camp-like quarters. For working women in New York City, the prospect of patriotic work in the fresh air had a great appeal.

Suffrage and Pacifism

Suffragists who eschewed war work engaged in writing and activism related to the peace movement and anti-war protests prior to and after direct U.S. involvement. During the period from 1914 to 1917, anti-suffragists advertised the untrustworthiness of the suffragists and the lack of patriotism on their part. The more public the suffragists' peace activism, and the more well-known the pacifist-suffragist, the more time and money they spent refuting anti-suffrage accusations of disloyalty.[48] An unsigned article in the *Nyack Journal*, for example, attacked Harriet Laidlaw for her criticism of a government that would continue to deny the vote to women deeply engaged in war work. The article also condemned suffragists for "putting a price on patriotism." Suffragists who opposed the war also faced accusations of socialism.[49] Furthermore, many people, including anti-suffragists, found pacifism and patriotism incompatible.[50] Contradictions arose for women who wanted full citizenship and its attendant rights, but who could not support the many people in New York calling for war preparedness or more formal U.S. involvement in the war in Europe.

On August 29, 1914, an estimated fifteen hundred women, wearing mourning garb and marching to the somber beat of muffled drums, paraded along Fifth Avenue to protest the carnage in Europe.[51] While ostensibly not a suffrage parade, many women carried yellow flowers to represent the suffrage movement, and organizers contended that they could not have staged the protest without the help and experience of suffragists.[52] Drawing many more participants than anticipated by Fanny Garrison Villard, the chair of the planning committee, the parade included Portia Willis as grand marshal, Alice Carpenter carrying a peace flag, Harriot Stanton Blatch, Eleanor Garrison, Lillian Wald, Harriet Burton Laidlaw, Charlotte Perkins Gilman, Mary

Ware Dennett, and the prominent peace activists and suffragists Fanny May Witherspoon and Tracy Mygatt.[53] Small children rode with their mothers in automobiles, and at least twenty women of color marched in the ranks. Marchers adhered to the admonishment that they refrain from laughing, smiling, or bowing during the procession. A regiment of mounted police led the parade past a crowd of thousands along the route.[54] After being reviewed by Villard, the women dispersed, moving into different venues of reaction to the war.[55]

The peace movement changed with the Great War. Previously, men had dominated the peace movement and focused on "legalistic devices" such as "international arbitration and the world court" to end war. The peace movements of the World War I era, now dominated by women, sought to end war with "economic and political democratization."[56] Suffragists and members of other women's organizations founded the Woman's Peace Party in Washington, DC, in January 1915. Crystal Eastman, Mary Heaton Vorse, Madeleine Doty, and others established a much more radical branch of the Peace Party in New York around the same time. Inez Milholland, Ida Rauh, and many other "new women" joined the Woman's Peace Party, believing that war represented "another argument why women clearly needed the vote."[57] The party included suffrage on its plank, so anti-suffragists accused suffragists of being "lukewarm" patriots.[58] Anti-suffragists such as Annie Nathan Meyer refused to join the Woman's Peace Party, claiming that men should dominate peace societies, for without male "guidance and political experience," women alone could not make sense of the "right ideas of nations."[59]

According to the Heterodite S. Josephine Baker, radical groups such as her own found it necessary to meet in a different place every week to keep from being watched by the Bureau of Investigation, forerunner of the Federal Bureau of Investigation.[60] Some members of Heterodoxy suspected that a patriotic club member alerted the authorities about their meeting places and activities.[61] Charlotte Perkins Gilman, like Rheta Childe Dorr, resigned her membership in Heterodoxy in protest of the club members' anti-war sentiments.[62] To Dorr, her colleagues in the club represented the conflicting attitudes of the intellectual elites of the time. The group included several German sympathizers, two of whom Dorr identified as "disloyal Americans," but the majority of the Heterodites viewed war, in the words of the British pacifist, journalist, and author of The Great Illusion, Norman Angell, as "irrational and uncivilized."[63] Dorr frankly assessed most members as too self-absorbed to care much about the outside world, war or no war.[64]

Dorr could not have been referring to Madeleine Doty, Mary Heaton Vorse, Alice Carpenter, or Leonora O'Reilly, all of whom simply could not ignore the war. They joined about twelve other delegates from New York State who boarded the *Noordam* on April 13, 1915, to attend the International Congress of Women at The Hague in an effort to stop the war. Sent off by a raucous, jeering crowd of critics, who, much like Theodore Roosevelt, considered the women's cause ridiculous and futile, the ship, sporting a homemade blue and white peace banner, sailed through treacherous waters.[65] The approximately fifteen hundred women who participated in the Amsterdam gathering prioritized their protest "against the madness and the horror of war."[66] Many women knew each other through their membership in the international suffrage movement, but this marked the first time such a large and diverse group—the women hailed from a dozen belligerent and neutral countries—met to protest war. An observer commented that "contained grief" dominated the mood of the assembly.[67] The most notable achievement of the congress came when delegates selected a group of envoys to meet with the leaders of both warring and neutral nations to exert moral pressure, mediate the war, and enact a message of everlasting peace.[68]

Unwilling to concede defeat on peace mediation, the peace activists Rebecca Shelley and Rosika Schwimmer convinced Henry Ford, the automobile tycoon, financially to back another mission to implement the plan of the International Congress of Women.[69] An interested Ford met with Jane Addams, representatives from the Woman's Peace Party, and the Henry Street Settlement House. Less than a week later, Ford and the journalist Louis Lochner, acting as Ford's secretary, met with President Wilson to request an official appointment of a neutral commission to seek an end to the hostilities. Although Ford offered full financial support, Wilson remained uncommitted. Nevertheless, Ford pressed forward and chartered a ship, the *Oscar II*, thereafter known as the Ford Peace Ship, to transport American delegates to Europe, promising to "have the boys out of the trenches by Christmas." His boast subjected the entire peace movement and its adherents to derision.[70]

The teacher and ardent suffragist Katherine Devereux Blake, daughter of Lillie Devereux Blake, joined the Ford Peace mission. Arguing that "man's ability to bear arms has no relation to his right to vote," she contended that women, too, bore the burden of war. Other New York suffragists who joined the mission included the cartoonist Lou Rogers, Inez Milholland, the journalists Mary Alden Hopkins and Alice Lawton, Gertrude Steinman Oliphant, and the social investigator and settlement worker Elizabeth C. Watson.[71] In spite of the prominent and talented participants, from the beginning the mission seemed doomed. Peace activists did not get along with each other. A number of them, in particular Ford, found Schwimmer, a woman described by her detractors as "autocratic," abrasive and annoying.[72] To make matters worse, an influenza epidemic broke out on board ship, resulting in the death of one of the delegates. Henry Ford, apparently feeling ill himself, abandoned the mission, leaving the "pilgrims" in disarray. Some members met with European leaders in an attempt to carry out the goals of the mission, with virtually no success.[73] They returned to the States, disheartened and embarrassed.

It is possible that Milholland resigned from the Woman's Peace Party because she found the mission so disastrous. Instead, she joined Lillian Wald's American Union Against Militarism.[74] Members of the union contested conscription and military preparedness, seeking peaceful resolutions to international disputes. They also offered legal and other advice to conscientious objectors.[75] Again, suffragists were conspicuous on the membership rosters. Those who resigned from peace activism to devote themselves to Red Cross or other home front causes also disrupted the work of suffrage and peace organizations. Observers could see the escalating fear and uncertainty building in the United States. Attitudes of Americans toward the war in Europe began to change, and more people questioned their country's neutrality.

Suffrage and Patriotism

The New York State Woman Suffrage Party was the suffrage organization most supportive of U.S. involvement in the Great War. It established a Patriotic Committee that oversaw the staffing of Red Cross workers in stores, collected money for the United War Work drive, sold $35,000 worth of War Saving Stamps, and donated hundreds of knitted garments to the relief organization. The committee used preexisting district resources to assist with conducting the official state census, actually a county-based military census to determine the number of young men eligible for the draft. Narcissa Cox [Mrs. Frank A.] Vanderlip took charge in Westchester County, where her suffrage followers gathered information from virtually every house.[76] Counties all over the state followed suit. Vira Boarman Whitehouse called the statewide effort the "most effective suffrage propaganda possible," since suffragists could take advantage of canvassing opportunities to promote their cause.[77] They used their patriotic endeavors to keep their enfranchisement goals alive during a time of intense distraction. Mainstream suffragists sought to convince voters that they deserved enfranchisement by connecting woman suffrage to patriotism.[78]

Suffragists often evoked military and patriotic themes in the years before and during U.S. involvement in the Great War. New woman Katerina Ely Tiffany, the president of the New York branch of the College Equal Suffrage League, carries a flag in a patriotic suffrage parade held on October 27, 1917. Image courtesy of the Prints and Photographs Division, Library of Congress, Washington, DC.

Suffragists, by this point, had the serious attention of some men in power, at both the state and national levels. Even before the official entry of the United States into the war, several U.S. senators, both Democrats and Republicans, signed a statement recognizing women's cooperation in the defense and other industries, their willingness to abide by the laws, nurse the wounded, bury the dead, and make myriad sacrifices in "the great conflict now raging over three continents." Under the circumstances, it had become more difficult for legislators to accept that federal or state constitutions could continue to deny women the same rights to the franchise as men had. The statement recommended abolishing restrictions on voting rights based on sex.[79] Women's patriotic work, which suffragists by now knew exactly how to publicize, made a bold declaration, impossible for legislators to ignore.

The suffrage campaign in New York took on a growing urgency; suffragists had less than a year to persuade male voters to pass the referendum. At the Forty-Eighth New York State Woman Suffrage Convention, held in Albany in November 1916, suffragists evaluated the previous referendum campaign. Berating themselves for campaigning in a less than professional manner, they regretted not adhering more closely to their motto of "Suffrage First." Suffragists deeply lamented the distraction of the war.[80] In contrast, anti-suffragists had long agreed to support the government's position on the war, and since 1914 their motto had been "America First" and anti-suffrage second.[81] Anti-suffragists contended that *all* political activity should be set aside until the war ended and normal life could resume. Alice Hill Chittenden, the president of the New York State Association Opposed to Woman Suffrage, and other antis often reiterated their commitment to national preparedness and universal military service, as well as the willingness of all anti-suffragists to render services to the nation with no expectation of any reward.[82] Suffragists accused antis of being "war mongers" and intensified their campaigns for woman suffrage.[83]

On February 8, 1917, Vira Boarman Whitehouse, the chair of the New York State Woman Suffrage Party, announced the decision of the executive board to commit the loyalty and services of the state organization to Governor Charles S. Whitman.[84] She contended that the decision did not represent a "stand on the question of war or peace" but a commitment on the part of suffragists to act as partners with the government. She urged members to wear their suffrage buttons prominently as they engaged in any war-related work, reminding her workers that "war or preparation for war . . . is an additional reason for the immediate granting of woman suffrage."[85] The New York State Woman Suffrage Party commanded a large contingent of women experienced in speaking before the public, a highly efficient publicity service, a talented and resourceful membership, and a well-organized recordkeeping system. Nevertheless, many suffragists resented the idea that the resources of a suffrage organization, one established for the purpose of gaining women the right to vote, would be used to support a war they opposed. Those who disapproved of the decision elicited anger and dissention within and outside of the organization.

Crystal Eastman resigned her membership in the suffrage association, noting her aggravation that the state suffrage leaders would so lightly pledge the organization "to a government which has denied to them . . . a fundamental democratic right."[86] The Suffrage Party also officially met hostile opposition to the decision to support the war from the Woman's Peace Party of New York, which passed a resolution on March 13, 1917, expressing its displeasure. Contending that the Woman Suffrage Party "as an organization, could be of no service to the Government in times of war" and had "no power over the members of the organization as individuals," the Woman's Peace Party "protest[ed] against the highhanded and undemocratic action of the Executive Committee."[87] This discord highlights the complicated relationships and diverse personalities converging around woman suffrage activism.

Carrie Chapman Catt, well-known for her international peace activism, postponed the commitment of the National American Woman Suffrage Association, representing about two million members, to Wilson until February 23, 1917, long after the antis had dedicated their organization and resources. Even then, executive board members of the suffrage organization found compromise difficult, since so many members had publicly criticized war.[88] The politically astute Catt "instructed her people to work for both the war effort and suffrage."[89] The association, working at multiple levels, mobilized a range of resources and effective organizations at every level in nearly every state. Most importantly, with years of experience, suffragists knew exactly how to raise vast sums of money quickly.[90] It is unfortunate that government leaders at the state and national levels did not better appreciate or know how to utilize the extraordinary talents and resources the organized suffragists placed at their disposal in 1917.

The United States Declares War

Although Wilson won reelection on the campaign slogan "He kept us out of war," it became impossible for the United States to remain neutral.[91] In January 1917, British intelligence intercepted an encoded German telegram from Arthur Zimmermann, the German Foreign Secretary, to the German ambassador in Mexico. The telegram suggested that Mexico's dictator, Carranza, could regain the territories of New Mexico, Arizona, and Texas if the United States declared war on Germany. Several weeks later, German submarines sank three more American ships. The inherent threat of the telegram, coupled with the devastating loss of American life and property on the high seas in the years since the sinking of the *Lusitania*, finally compelled Wilson to ask Congress to approve a declaration of war.[92] On April 6, 1917, the United States officially entered the war against Germany.

From January to September, newspapers reported far fewer events related to suffrage campaigning in New York and sharply increased their coverage of war-related activities. The National League of Women's Services, founded on January 26, 1917, in anticipation of direct U.S. involvement in the war, existed to coordinate the war work of women and their organizations.[93] Suffragists and anti-suffragists eagerly joined the league, established in thirty-five states by the time the United States entered the war. They structured the league along lines of "Constructive Patriotism." Rather than simply waving a flag, patriotic women sought practical methods of contributing labor and resources to the war effort. They devised programs of voluntary rationing, such as abiding by suggestions for "meatless Mondays" and "wheatless Tuesdays" to reserve these foods for the troops. They strove to eliminate kitchen waste and to grow and preserve their own fruits and vegetables.[94]

League members also collected the names of women experts in agricultural, industrial, commercial, and professional fields, all ready to offer their services to replace men potentially called to serve in the military.[95] Despite the existence of the league, in April the government appointed Anna Howard Shaw to oversee the newly established Woman's Committee of the Council for National Defense. Members agreed to focus on "Americanization" and patriotism through an educational "propaganda department," in addition to food conservation efforts.[96] The committee, with active suffragists occupying two-thirds of the positions, duplicated much of the work the league had already done, competing bitterly with it.[97] Shaw "groaned" that poor funding, red tape, and having virtually no authority hindered her efforts, and she prayed to be delivered from the "pettiness of public officials."[98]

Suffragists assumed new responsibilities, relative to the federal and state governments, based on experiences with war preparedness and relief organizations. As Gertrude Foster Brown related, New York suffragists "almost forgot their own campaign as they plunged into war work."[99] They fought to protect women's workplace rights when the government attempted to strike down laws that prohibited women from working more than twelve-hour days in war-related industries.[100] In May 1917, suffragists worked with the New York City Committee on National Defense to visit public places such as retail establishments, hotels, and telegraph offices to collect signatures pledging loyalty to the government. They also established new War Service and Emergency Committees within their organizations.[101]

The War Service Committee of the New York State Woman Suffrage Party raised and donated money to units of troops being trained in the YMCA. Over a twenty-four hour period, suffragists raised $12,000 to "supply, equip, and maintain" a unit of New York City-based troops organized by the Young Men's Christian Association and pledged to help with other units.[102] Committee members donated $10,000 to a unit at the Plattsburgh YMCA camp. In October 1917, they donated another $10,000 to the "colored troops" of the YMCA Unit at Camp Upton, Yaphank, Long Island. The chair of the committee, Mrs. Caroline M. [F. Louis] Slade, announced that they "would enjoy making life pleasant for colored soldiers." Black women, represented by Annie K. Lewis, were surprised but happy about the donation. The War Service Committee had no members of color, although a few black women suffragists did affiliate with the party. Lewis announced that her colleagues were "gratified to find that the Woman Suffrage Party lives up to its verbal declarations of democracy."[103]

Suffragists also proposed farmerettes as a solution to the farm-labor problem facing the nation, as men, including farmers, enlisted or accepted the wartime draft. Women belonging to organizations such as the Women's National Farm and Garden Association, the Young Women's Christian Association, the Woman Suffrage Party, and the Committee of the Women's Agricultural Camp met with representatives of the grange, Cornell Agricultural College, and the Farmingdale State School of Agriculture to form an advisory council to "stimulate the formation of a Land Army of Women."[104] Elsewhere, Hester Jeffrey, like many other women, contributed her war work efforts stateside. Mary Burnett Talbert "emphasized the patriotism of black women" and expressed their willingness to aid the government in any way possible when she spoke before the Council of National Defense in 1918.[105] Suffrage workers dominated the mobilization of New York women during the Great War.

Suffragists Report on the War

Additionally, suffragists, empowered by their experiences in the movement, sought to understand or explain the war. Mary Heaton Vorse, Madeleine Doty, Rheta Child Dorr, and Inez Milholland stood out among the journalists who risked traveling to Europe to report on the war for U.S. publications. Anticipating adventure, women found that the reality of prejudice against women in combat zones hampered their ability to report accurately on war events. Authorities forced them to the periphery of the action. They sought alternative angles from which to assess and evaluate the effects of the war on those living in the belligerent countries. Some expressed unexpected enthusiasm for the experience. Doty, for example, traveled to Europe to survey the conditions of women under wartime pressures, the reporting of which she found thrilling.[106]

Inez Milholland had traveled to Italy as a war correspondent in 1915, just two weeks after the sinking of the *Lusitania*. Although many of her reports remained unpublished due to her lack of training in the "craft of gathering and synthesizing facts," she often wrote more about her anger at the conditions she observed than she did about the actualities related to the war.[107] A series of her pacifist articles offended the Italian government, which then asked her to leave the country.[108] Upon her return to the United States, in October 1916, she traveled to the West as the "special flying envoy" for Alice Paul's Congressional Union, which intended to punish the party that withheld the vote from women. As Milholland's biographer, Linda Lumsden, points out, the demand was "revolutionary" because it asked women voters to "align themselves politically with their sex instead of the male political parties."[109] Exhausted, her pallor become more noticeable as the trip progressed. Nevertheless, the media attention and the applause of the audiences energized her.[110] Milholland collapsed in Los Angeles on the evening of October 23, succumbing at the age of thirty to aplastic, or pernicious, anemia a month later. She immediately became a martyr for the cause of woman suffrage, "usher[ing] in the final, most militant phase of the suffrage movement."[111]

A colleague of Milholland, Madeleine Zabriskie Doty, also a feminist, suffragist, peace activist, and lawyer, worked as a social reformer and journalist. She reported on the International Congress for Women at The Hague for the *New York Evening Post* in 1915 and continued her involvement with the Woman's Peace Party throughout the war.[112] She published a book, *Short Rations: An American Woman in Germany* in 1917, based on her two wartime trips across Europe. She later covered the Russian Revolution on an assignment for *Good Housekeeping*, contending that "Russia had swung clean out of the Twentieth Century," in response to the overwhelming changes taking place under Bolshevik rule. Her book, *Behind the Battle Line, Around the World in 1918*, appeared that same year. She also wrote about woman suffrage in Europe during the war.[113] Mary Heaton Vorse, who had likewise traveled to The Hague, represented the New York State Woman Suffrage Association there. While attending the conference, she reported on the war for *Good Housekeeping*, *Century*, and *McClure's* magazines.[114]

In contrast to these three suffragists and peace activists, Rheta Childe Dorr, personally supportive of the United States entering the war, determined to return to Europe to see the war for herself. However, it took her until the spring of 1917 to secure a newspaper assignment reporting on the Russian Revolution for the *New York Evening Mail*.[115] In September she returned to the United States, but soon after she went back to Europe in search of her son, a soldier, and to report on the war in France, although she knew editors hesitated to trust a woman's reporting on the aftermath of war.[116] Soon after, Dorr suffered a tragic motorcycle accident that caused brain and leg injuries, effectively ending the trajectory of her journalistic career.[117] These path-breaking journalists provided a female perspective on the war and gained respect for their reportage and ability to handle themselves in the war arena.

Home Front Efforts

On the home front, Alice Hill Chittenden had worked with both anti-suffragists and suffragists to raise $46,000 for Red Cross efforts.[118] In addition to selling Liberty Bonds, both suffragists and antis enrolled in the Hoover food campaigns and worked in factories, taking the place of men stationed overseas.[119] Organized anti-suffrage women, already fewer in number, could not effectively campaign against suffrage and do war work at the same time; they had to make a choice to do one or the other. In contrast, suffragists had the political wherewithal to work for various goals simultaneously and enrolled many more members in their suffrage organizations in the last months of the campaign. Their professionalism and their unwavering commitment to war and suffrage work won many men over to the side of suffrage.

By September 1917, alarmed at the proximity of the referendum on woman suffrage, New York suffrage leaders "made strenuous efforts to rally their scattered forces" to bring their attention back to their primary goal.[120] Reinvigorating their campaign, suffragists canvassed women, spoke in every possible venue, including training camps for soldiers, printed and distributed leaflets, posters, and newspaper articles asserting that more than a million New York women demanded that voters pass the suffrage referendum on November 6. Suffragists acquired lists of the men serving overseas from the secretary of state and sent them literature to influence their absentee ballots.[121] Suffrage supporters in the upper echelons of the federal government conceived of the idea to reconsider woman suffrage as a "war measure," an idea the president supported as "wise." The idea of enfranchising women as a war measure had been bandied about for some months, apparently originating with Harriot Stanton Blatch. Chittenden and others had commented that rewarding women with suffrage for their war work amounted to "penalizing" anti-suffragists for their war efforts. But Wilson probably welcomed the opportunity to yield to suffrage pressure, for he had long been reluctant to publicly support women's enfranchisement.[122] The idea of woman suffrage as a war measure also allowed Congress, which had vowed not to consider any issue unrelated to the war, to discuss woman suffrage in committee.[123] Furthermore, it had the effect of influencing voters in New York State.

Regardless of the raging "war to end all wars," suffragists intended to finally win the vote in New York State.[124] As Election Day approached, with the woman suffrage referendum on the ballot, suffragists intensified their efforts. By this point they had collected over a million signatures from women who wanted the right to vote. Criticizing a planned suffrage parade, Chittenden warned women "not to be misled" by its displays of patriotism. Vira Whitehouse countered that the parade should express patriotism, and she really did not expect any anti-suffragists to march unless they agreed to convert to woman suffrage.[125] The competition for men's votes escalated as the day of reckoning drew near. On October 25, 1917, with only twelve days remaining, one hundred women from the New York State Woman Suffrage Party kept a coveted appointment with President Wilson to ask him to voice his support for the impending state suffrage referendum. Spokesperson Whitehouse reiterated the activities that suffragists had performed in active support of the war. She asked the president to "send to the voters a message so urgent and so clear that they, on Election Day, cannot fail as patriotic men to place the women of their State on an equal footing with the women of the allied countries." Wilson responded evasively that "it is time for the people of the states of this country to show the world in what practical sense they have learned the lessons of democracy," and gave the women permission to convey his message to the voters of New York.[126]

As these events took place, the most radical suffragists exercised their democratic rights. National Woman's Party picketers had long been applying pressure on the president. Suffragists, known as "silent sentinels," picketed the White House every day except Sundays beginning January 10, 1917, and continuing until June 1918, holding aloft banners decorated with quotes from the president himself. Hundreds of party members from all over the United States supported the picketers, or joined in the protests in front of the White House; more than sixty hailed from the state of New York.[127] The women's civil disobedience resulted in jail terms for some of the picketers, drawing some public sympathy. However, in a nation experiencing heightened patriotism, the demonstrations initiated "a storm of protest and hostility."[128]

Anti-suffragists accused all suffragists of betraying the democratic ideals of the United States, but anti-suffrage arguments no longer had the power they once commanded.[129]

The war in Europe profoundly influenced the suffrage movement in New York State. In spite of the disruptions of the Great War, the New York campaign for women's enfranchisement encompassed an extensive effort on the part of suffragists to canvass women and men, circulate special literature, target soldiers in training camps and overseas, and advertise their cause everywhere in the state to reach male voters.[130] Whether or not they experienced criticism for their lack of patriotism, suffragists worked relentlessly for their enfranchisement.[131] In general, suffragists entered the war effort and Liberty Bond drives more reluctantly than anti-suffragists, especially in the earliest years. Once suffragists committed their resources to the aid of the government, in whatever capacity, they made tremendous advances for women's rights.[132] The entry of the United States into the Great War shifted the perception of voters relative to woman suffrage, complicating reactions of men for or against women's voting. Many men saw women as partners in the war effort, whereas others found suffragists too closely linked to the peace movement or too radical to consider them patriotic. Women and men on both sides of the issue learned a great deal about politics and government during the war.

CHAPTER 8

Rising from the Ashes of Defeat

The Woman Suffrage Victory in New York State

In early August 1917, from her suffrage post in Auburn, New York, Mary Elizabeth Pidgeon wrote home to her "folks" apologizing for her lapse in correspondence. Pidgeon admitted to her exhaustion after being on "the hard rush all day," trying to involve women and men in the woman suffrage movement. Before the day ended, Pidgeon had successfully "hunted a member of the men's committee" so that he could "present a suffrage resolution to the Letter Carriers Union." She had also recruited "the husband of the proposed [Auburn] city chairman" to speak at the Cayuga County Fair in Moravia on behalf of suffrage.[1] On the verge of exasperation, Pidgeon recounted more of her activities that day. "I have also been soliciting cakes to take to the soldiers on Friday. Have women promised up to get 30. Also searched speakers for the fair. Also got two news stories in each of the two newspapers—great feat that."[2] As for her remaining task, she elaborated, "I have been . . . trying to get a city chairman. The most hopefully inclined was doing her washing when I called, has poor help, a houseful of company, and a delicate baby. But she will consider it seriously. The wealthiest lady I went to was taking a nap and wasn't interested in suffrage. Another would have been [willing] but she had just accepted presidency of the Parent-Teachers [Association]."[3] Clearly, the day-to-day work of suffrage organizing required relentless energy.

Mary Elizabeth Pidgeon, Auburn, N.Y.

Mary Elizabeth Pidgeon, sent by the National American Woman Suffrage Association to organize suffrage clubs and elicit broad support in upstate New York, rose quickly through the ranks to become assembly district leader in the Fifth Campaign District. Image courtesy of Bryn Mawr College Special Collections, Bryn Mawr, PA.

Shortly after graduating from Swarthmore, Mary Elizabeth Pidgeon had left a teaching job to organize for the National American Woman Suffrage Association in the battleground state of New York. The sheer intensity of Pidgeon's work as Cayuga County assembly district leader meant that no two days ever seemed to be the same. Her responsibilities kept her so busy that she neglected writing the letters home her parents longed for, instead adopting a "diary plan" to keep track of her activities. Pidgeon's letters offer invaluable insight into the world of suffrage workers between 1915 and 1917 in New York.

In these years, New York State activists campaigned for two separate referenda on woman suffrage, one in 1915 and one in 1917. Over the course of both campaigns, war news captured the headlines, usually relegating suffrage and anti-suffrage news to the back pages of newspapers, yet suffragists expended extra effort to keep their movement in the forefront of people's minds and as topics of their conversations. Greater numbers of supporters joined the cause as suffrage activities escalated across the state. Women and men on both sides of the suffrage issue agitated for or against the right to vote in the countryside, on the streets of cities, and in the state legislature. A new generation of college-educated women, like Mary Elizabeth Pidgeon, played an instrumental part as organizers during the final stages of each campaign. Increasingly, suffragists recognized the need to confront individual lawmakers directly as critical to the overall success of the campaign.[4] With diverse suffrage groups applying pressure on reluctant legislators, suffragists stood an excellent chance of winning the state.

The 1915 Campaign

Virtually all of the state suffrage societies pledged support to Carrie Chapman Catt's "Victory in 1915" Empire State Campaign.[5] As a reflection of the more politically-charged stance the suffragists assumed, a number of political equality clubs changed their names to include the word "party" rather than "club."[6] Although the New York State Woman Suffrage Association claimed the rural organizations, Catt's nascent Empire State Campaign Committee marked a more concerted effort to bring them under New York City control. Women worked tirelessly to recruit men into their ranks. Members of the New York City branch of the Woman Suffrage Party became ever more innovative and confident. They went so far as to staff a booth at the prestigious Westminster Dog Show. The organizer Maggie Hinchey and others suggested recruiting the widest range of working men, which required reaching them in their places of employment, where women rarely ventured. Women approached letter carriers, conductors, motormen, subway workers, elevated guards, street sweepers, ticket sellers, firemen, and police. Mary Garrett Hay, for example, worked through Police Commissioner Arthur Hall Woods to "make friends with the police" so that "in the event of trouble" they would protect campaigning suffragists.[7] As the 1915 election drew near, suffragists also worked hard in New York's upstate cities, towns, villages, and hamlets.

Both Catt and Anna Howard Shaw readily understood the need for greater organization in rural areas and both lectured in virtually every county in the state.[8] To reach new audiences, suffrage speakers traveled long distances over

unpaved roads, enduring poor accommodations, isolated by infrequent telegraph or telephone access, to the farthest reaches of the state. Catt spoke at
the Universalist Church in Canton, in May 1914, where her family had distant
roots. On her speaking tour, Shaw gave a memorable speech in June 1915
on "The Fundamental Principle of a Republic" at the Ogdensburg Opera
House.[9] Trained suffrage organizers often encountered apathetic crowds
during their systematic canvassing and appeals for support. Nancy Schoonmaker, an Ulster County Fair suffrage speaker, approached every potential
voter at the fair from "dog trainers to snake charmers" but found that many
"men showed no real opposition or real interest."[10] Despite the gargantuan
efforts of the Empire State Campaign Committee, certain areas of the state
proved less receptive to the idea of women's enfranchisement than others.
Despite the resistance, the remarkable dedication of suffrage workers would
ultimately result in their success.

Carrie Catt wrote to the district chairs in the Empire State Campaign
concerning summer meetings in various towns across upstate. She urged a
contingent of 130 New York City teachers under the leadership of Katherine
Devereux Blake to sacrifice their summer vacations so that they could "get
down into the trenches." Catt reasoned, "If you can win the local politicians
you will get the men in their districts, and if you can get the county politicians there is less likelihood of the bigger politicians giving orders for votes
against suffrage."[11] Rural organizers hoped to establish "a man's league or
committee" in each of their respective counties with the assistance of the
New York Men's League. Leaders encouraged men, especially working-class
and farmers, to appear at public suffrage meetings whenever possible.

Suffrage organizers echoed Catt's concern that the "suffrage movement
is pretty weak in a large number of these towns," since many rural dwellers
had yet to hear of woman suffrage. The district chairs encouraged speakers
(often male) on the Redpath Chautauqua lecture circuit, already participating
in their annual summer speaking tours, to include suffrage with their usual
topics.[12] Catt also personally corresponded with district leaders when their
spirits lagged, such as happened to sixth assembly district chair Helen Brewster Owens and several of her organizers, who expressed discouragement
over their failure to make significant progress in rural Tioga and Chenango
counties. Catt goaded Owens, insisting that she "go out in the field" and
spend "a very great deal of time there." Family responsibilities, health issues,
and the lack of funds allocated by headquarters for travel and canvassing voters presented continual problems for organizers.[13]

In addition to using all resources possible, including established suffrage
networks, Catt paid attention to details that could potentially result in gains

for the Empire State Campaign. Because of the campaign's long-term connection to the Woman's Christian Temperance Union, many Americans associated suffragists and their work with Protestantism. Catt realized the value of appealing to Catholics, Protestants, and Jews, and encouraged campaign workers to do preliminary work by visiting each and every house of worship in their communities. She instructed suffrage workers to contact the leaders of these religious institutions so that on the weekend before the election they could make a strong plea for the passage of the suffrage referendum.[14] In addition to paying close attention to where organizing took place, Catt monitored the suffrage workforce. To Helen Owens, for example, she expressed her pleasure about the appearance of a "good-looking" professional organizer she planned to send in from Ohio. The Empire State chair believed "that some of these middle-aged women are good assets" because "it does not do to give the impression that we have only young girls working."[15] No detail seemed to escape Catt's attention.

With the suffragists pressing forward, James Laidlaw lent his considerable men's league membership to Catt, including vast ranks of marchers for an October suffrage parade.[16] In what they anticipated would be a final surge on election eve, members of the league worked late into the night. Election Day

Suffragists wanted to be sure that women knew how to participate in the electorate. In 1915, Gertrude Foster Brown trained women as poll watchers to ensure that poll activities followed proper procedure. Image courtesy of the Prints and Photographs Division, Library of Congress, Washington, DC.

began with 200 cars carrying speakers, banners, and literature to a meeting at the Battery. After the men dispersed to hundreds of separate rallies across Manhattan and the Bronx, they reassembled to hear more speeches and discuss poll watching stints. Rabbi Stephen S. Wise, addressing a crowd of 2,500 people, suggested that women should refuse to bear children until they had the right to vote.[17] The outpouring of support seemed to predict success.

For all their hard work, suffragists lost the 1915 referendum by almost two hundred thousand of the over 1.2 million votes cast.[18] Both John Purroy Mitchel, the mayor of New York City, and Charles Seymour Whitman, the governor of New York State, had announced earlier in the year that they would vote for woman suffrage, but almost fifty-eight percent of the men who cast ballots in the referendum voted against it. Only six counties, mainly rural in nature, approved woman suffrage: Broome, Chemung, Chautauqua, Cortland, Schenectady, and Tompkins.[19] The rest of the counties opposed it by a range of fifty-two to seventy-three percent, with one third of all counties coming out against suffrage at sixty percent or more of the vote.[20] Generally, suffragists won where their level of organization appeared the strongest; antis won in places with weak suffrage organization.[21] Suffragists had made progress, but they still had a long way to go.

Changing the New York State Constitution

At midnight, after seeing an overwhelming number of adverse election returns pour into headquarters, activists realized to their dismay that voters had defeated the woman suffrage referendum on November 2, 1915. Undaunted, Harriet Burton Laidlaw, the chair of the Manhattan Borough, "sprang up, her head held high, her lovely color heightened," and shouted to the tired, drawn faces of the suffragists in the room with her, "Who'll go with me now and start a new campaign with a street meeting?"[22] Inspired to action, the women trooped out into the still-crowded streets and renewed their campaign for woman suffrage. Refusing to stay downhearted for long, Laidlaw epitomized the persistence and resilience of suffragists over the ebb and flow of the New York State suffrage movement. Mary Garrett Hay considered it "a great day in New York State." In her eyes, "half a million men saw their duty, and they did it. Defeated? No. Only postponed."[23] Despite a general preoccupation with the war in Europe on the part of the public, the Empire State Campaign Committee had managed to wage a dramatic and energetic drive for woman suffrage.

After scrutinizing the results, Carrie Chapman Catt realized that New York voters had finally taken woman suffrage seriously. Forty-two percent of voters favored suffrage, as she told her audience at a Cooper Union meeting two days after the loss. The New York State Woman Suffrage Association president, Gertrude Foster Brown, expressed the surprise echoed by many of her colleagues that such a high percentage of ballots remained blank on the suffrage question, however. Renewing their optimism, suffragists could now see potential converts to the suffrage cause in the half a million men who had not voted either for against woman suffrage.[24] All they needed to do would be to convince those men of women's right to the vote. Catt praised the women suffrage workers who "had done it alone, without endorsement from a single political party."[25] She then presented her revised strategy to her supporters, which included an evaluation of the work that had been done across the state for suffrage.[26] To reaffirm their commitment, suffragists raised almost $100,000 to invigorate the new campaign. Then, at the New York State Woman Suffrage Association Forty-Seventh Annual Convention, held from November 30 to December 2 at the Hotel Astor in New York City, suffragists systematically analyzed the success and failure of their varied activities district by district, demonstrating their attention to detail.[27]

Virtually all campaign leaders believed in the value of publicity but felt that suffrage workers' efforts fell short when it came to following up education with both personal canvassing and encouraging political leaders to support the amendment. Although radical and moderate suffragists often disagreed on the best strategies to reach voters, they knew audiences appreciated their attention-drawing public events. The diversity of the male electorate, coming from every class, ethnicity, and locale, demanded ever-increasing creativity, energy, and political savvy on the part of suffrage workers to advance the campaign. As the movement matured, suffragists adapted their strategies as they deepened their understanding of the fundamental right of women to full citizenship. Most knew that they would not stop with state-level enfranchisement but would work to obtain national enfranchisement. In linking state campaigns to the federal effort, Carrie Chapman Catt designed what would soon become known as her "Winning Plan," structured around the goal of contacting each and every potential voter from the largest cities to the smallest hamlets. State leaders made plans to formally reorganize the New York movement, launching their campaign for "Victory in 1917."

They immediately concentrated their efforts on securing a second state referendum.[28] Suffrage leaders consulted with Judge William H. Wadhams and other men who informed them that it would be "entirely possible" to schedule another referendum in 1917.[29] On the evening of January 4, 1916, suffragists arrived in full force in Albany. The state amendment recognizing women's right to vote had to be resubmitted to the legislature. Before legislators drafted the new amendment, suffragists discreetly but intensely pressed legislators on the assembly and senate committees to pass the new bill.[30] The New York State Woman Suffrage Party representatives Harriet Burton Laidlaw and Helen Rogers Reid called on Senator George Whitney of Saratoga County and Assemblyman Henry Brereton of Warren County to move the suffrage bill from its place before the Judiciary Committee onto the floors of their respective houses.[31]

The suffrage bill sponsors introduced the bill a second time, as required by the state constitution. On February 22, 1916, Vira Boarman Whitehouse, Harriot Stanton Blatch, and other suffragists appeared before the New York State Assembly Judiciary Committee during the debates over the Whitney-Brereton suffrage bill and the feasibility of a referendum in the general election of November 1917. The anti-suffragists Alice Hill Chittenden and Everett P. Wheeler argued that it was too soon to consider another referendum on the question because the "state had spoken emphatically against woman suffrage" at the fall 1915 referendum. The chair of the committee asked Whitehouse and Blatch if women would be satisfied with a bill allowing women to vote only for presidential electors. Whitehouse replied to the question, "Most emphatically no." Soon after, the Assembly committee reported favorably on the bill, but the Senate committee deferred action on the companion measure for two weeks.[32]

On March 14, by a vote of 109 to 30, the state assembly of New York passed the Whitney-Brereton Bill, providing for a woman suffrage referendum in 1917. However, due to political maneuvering on the part of the bitter anti-suffragist Senator Elon R. Brown, the senate delayed the bill's passage for almost a month.[33] In the meantime, male suffragists telephoned their senators urging them to stand firm in their support for woman suffrage.[34] Legislators, many of them relatively new to the cause, began to encourage their colleagues to join them in supporting women's voting rights. The *New York Times* reported that "when the referendum finally reached the upper house it had a large majority, due to the efforts of the women advocates of the measure."[35] After passing both houses, the secretary of state slated the woman suffrage referendum for the November 1917 ballot.[36]

Invigorating the Suffrage Movement

Hoping to guarantee women's enfranchisement via the 1917 referendum, Carrie Chapman Catt reorganized the New York State Woman Suffrage Association into the New York State Woman Suffrage Party, and its members unanimously elected her to serve as chair.[37] The name change reflected a more intensely politicized methodology and involved creating a single organization committed to a single platform—winning votes for women— by uniting virtually all state suffrage groups in a coalition.[38] Members of the New York State Woman Suffrage Party focused a great deal of attention on upstate urban areas, with their immigrant and working class voters, but they "gave top priority" to New York City because it contained almost half of those eligible to vote in the state.[39] The suffrage party promised stronger unity and increased commitment to the suffrage cause.[40]

But New York suffragists would be operating without Catt's undivided attention. By early 1916, Carrie Chapman Catt reluctantly gave into the demand of a "committee of one hundred women" and accepted the presidency of the National American Woman Suffrage Association when Anna Howard Shaw resigned the position.[41] Vira Boarman Whitehouse, serving as first vice-chair of the New York City Woman Suffrage Party, became the chair of the New York State Woman Suffrage Party. With the able assistance of Treasurer Helen Rogers Reid, Whitehouse took over the New York State campaign, renting an empty Fifth Avenue shop for suffrage meetings, and prepared to win the next referendum.[42] From 1916 to 1917, Whitehouse headed the state suffrage party, building it "on the twin pillars of money and steady organizational work."[43] Whitehouse and Reid surrounded themselves with a highly experienced cadre of women suffrage workers.[44]

Catt had long realized that the key to success lay in building an effective statewide organization, cultivating strong leadership with an emphasis on training workers and personal canvassing, and employing both long-range and short-term planning strategies. Catt's resignation letter to the state suffrage party outlined a three-tiered strategy for winning the state: push a referendum through the 1916 legislature, enroll a million women for suffrage, and campaign for more women converts and workers to persuade male voters.[45] In the interest of reaching those voters, Catt had advocated education and organization to replace the focus on public activities, and Whitehouse followed suit. According to the new chair of the state suffrage party, "the first task of the great new campaign is to increase our organization among women themselves, until behind every door of every house . . . there is a suffragist."[46] Well-advertised parades, pageants, and speakers continued as an integral part of the movement, yet door-to-door canvassing took priority.

The campaign struggled with delays and interruptions, however. War work, for some women, frequently took precedence over suffrage labors. Canvassing efforts came to a standstill during the summer of 1916 when an epidemic of infantile paralysis rendered it "not possible to canvass house to house for enrollments." Suffragists suspended all public activities including street meetings, and many women devoted time to "working with the health authorities to check the spread of the disease." After an emergency convention, suffragists finally returned to work to "take up the campaign with renewed vigor." Charged with a multitude of activities, including fund-raising and enrolling supporters, suffragists seemed to be on track again by mid-September.[47] The organization, in all its complexity, had deliberately built its strength to enable it to withstand virtually any challenge and winning seemed within reach. On November 7, 1916, Jennette Howell Deal Prior, the wife of Lewis Prior, a Yates County farmer, made a telling entry in her diary: "This has been a beautiful day. Lewis sowed some patches of rye this forenoon. This afternoon he went down to vote." She and other New York women determined that this election marked the very last time they would have to watch forlornly as their menfolk left them behind and went off to vote.[48]

Campaigning for the 1917 Referendum

Whitehouse and other New York State leaders pledged their full commitment to winning the vote in 1917, knowing its importance for the ultimate goal of a federal amendment. By this point, the movement had attracted over a million dues-paying women to the New York State Woman Suffrage Party.[49] Victory in New York, the most densely populated state in the nation, with its forty-five Congressional delegates (forty-three seats in the House of Representatives and two in the Senate) and forty-five electoral votes, would force national party leaders to support suffrage.[50] "No longer a loose association of upstate coteries but a modern campaign organization whose diverse activities were increasingly coordinated by New York City headquarters," the membership drew from its experience in the first referendum campaign.[51] Whitehouse sent downstate emissaries, including field secretaries, into the nine upstate districts. Depending on its size, each county had at least one leader, and each city within the county had at least one chairperson. Regrouping after the 1915 defeat meant that field secretaries acted as "executives" in the larger campaign districts and oversaw paid professional organizers to penetrate every level of society from the large state election districts down to the smallest village.[52] They had less than a year to win over enough women and men to pass the suffrage referendum.

Both by example and persistence, suffrage efforts persuaded many. In November 1916, the *Woman Voter* carried a story entitled "How I Became Converted to Woman Suffrage," by Lawrence Abbott, the president of the company that published the progressive *Outlook* magazine. Abbott considered the suffrage movement "that has swept over the civilized world . . . so rapidly and so extensively" as one "that no thinking man would regard with indifference." Abbott admitted that other countries that had granted the right to vote to their women citizens had done the right thing.[53] Although raised by the prominent anti-suffragists Abby Hamlin and Lyman Abbott, Lawrence Abbott came to understand that women had the right to elect officials who enacted the laws that affected their daily lives.[54]

Abbott cited the stellar examples of the Hull House founder, Jane Addams, and Josephine Goldmark, the author of *Fatigue and Efficiency*, a study of women in industry, in an effort to highlight women's accomplishments. He disputed the common criticism that granting women suffrage would result in undesirable women voting. He agreed that "heartless and corrupt" women may in fact cast their ballots, but they would be "enormously outnumbered" by "thoughtful, intelligent, righteous and patriotic women."[55] Abbott's rationale seemed to represent a shift in many men's suffrage sentiments. By 1916, all three major parties included planks favoring woman suffrage as part of their platforms and, although few dared to say it aloud, suffrage in the Empire State seemed inevitable.

Promoting education, a critical aspect of expanding an organized movement, became an easier task when women requested suffrage information. Mail order suffrage correspondence schools presented an innovative solution for upstate women who consistently sought information on how to become suffrage activists.[56] Under the direction of Gertrude Foster Brown, the vice-chair of the New York State Woman Suffrage Party, and Mrs. Howard Mansfield, the chair of the educational section, workers in the Suffrage Training School in New York City designed a program to reach rural women who lived "seven miles from the nearest post office, ten miles from a railroad, tied down by a multiplicity of housekeeping duties, and . . . hampered by the difficulties of transportation."[57] Suffrage students paid a twenty-five cent fee to cover the cost of tuition. The course consisted of a series of twelve lessons mailed on a weekly basis with a test mailed monthly. The approximately fifty lectures contained in the course covered suffrage history and organization, civic responsibility, public speaking, parliamentary law, and civil government.

Suffrage schools so impressed campaign leaders in other states that they requested materials from New York so that they could start their own educational programs.[58] The National American Woman Suffrage Association headquarters *Newsletter* ran an article in its May 1916 issue entitled "How to Organize a Rural County," based on New York's example. Workers built on a predetermined organizational structure with the smallest unit of precinct leaders (or captains) at the base, overseen by town committees, then legislative or district committees, and finally by the county committee. Standing committees recommended for each unit included propaganda, press and publicity, literature, finance, organization, and enrollment. The plan outlined the specific tasks of each of these committees.[59]

Personal canvassing of both women and men played a vital part in the new state campaign strategy. Suffrage leaders scrutinized the 1915 campaign district returns and contribution records, many of which, according to a party worker, Dorothy Hubert, spoke for "the need of work here!"[60] The election district captains contacted political leaders as well as individual voters in an effort to persuade them to support woman suffrage. Women continued to lobby legislators throughout 1917, their efforts made more effective by their highly systematic approach and more frequent confrontation. Alliances that could be forged with local party leaders would play an important part in achieving a victory at the polls. A mere guarantee that politicians would not work against the woman suffrage amendment could be enough to shift district sentiment.[61]

All this work took money, and the entire movement relied on the contributions of devotees. Every suffragist, whether comfortable about it or not, learned to ask for donations during every public event. Sometimes the movement received anonymous donations, such as when an unnamed woman donated $35,000 to the New York campaign.[62] Wealthy upstate women such as Emily Howland and Martha Coffin Wright's daughter Eliza Wright Osborne were notable as the biggest and most consistent financial benefactors of suffrage in New York State.[63] Carrie Chapman Catt had inherited a fortune from Mrs. Frank Leslie, publisher of *Frank Leslie's Illustrated Newspaper*, who trusted Catt to use the money for the suffrage campaign. After more than two years of court and legal haggling, and with most of the money being siphoned off by lawyers, in February 1917 Catt finally received a portion of what rightfully belonged to her. She immediately turned $10,000 over to Whitehouse for the New York State campaign and gave Mary Garrett Hay $15,000 for the New York City campaign. Ultimately, Leslie's bequest amounted to just under $1,000,000 in cash and jewels.[64] Regardless of the amount of monetary gifts, every suffrage worker faced long hours of hard work "begging of money, meeting problems of personality, [and] paying her own expenses."[65]

Workers experienced a higher level of success when two volunteers visited each rural household armed with suffrage literature.[66] In their homes and at public events, district residents received pamphlets with titles such as "Great Men who Favor Suffrage" and "To the Farmers of New York." Copies of the inspirational 1867 speeches by George William Curtis and John

Stuart Mill also proved popular.[67] Disseminating the arguments and theories of woman suffrage more broadly informed rural voters of the logic of the campaign and alleviated some of the entrenched fears of a conservative electorate. Suffrage campaigners simultaneously approached urban voters. For example, in the fall of 1917, the New York State Woman Suffrage Party arranged a Men's Experience Meeting in Carnegie Hall so that twelve prominent men, ranging from labor leaders to the governor of Rhode Island, could give five-minute speeches describing why they supported suffrage.[68] While public events attracted large crowds, suffragists concentrated heavily on personal interactions with prospective male supporters.

Aside from suffrage leaders, very few workers left detailed records of their activities behind. Mary Elizabeth Pidgeon, recruited into the movement during the "Victory in 1917" campaign, is an exception. Her papers are rife with examples through which we might understand the level of commitment of thousands of suffrage workers who labored diligently with little public acknowledgment. The National American Woman Suffrage Association leaders recognized Pidgeon's promise early in her suffrage career and acted quickly to move her into their ranks as a paid organizer.[69] Catt insisted leaders choose speakers with the utmost care so that the suffrage message would appeal to the broadest possible audiences. Pidgeon made a flawless transition from her teaching job into Catt's "great army in perfect discipline," just as it moved "forward toward its goal."[70] In addition to being well educated and an articulate speaker, Pidgeon possessed an awareness of rural conditions and class divides that enabled her to interact with and influence a variety of New Yorkers. She criticized some of the other young workers who, because they had graduated from elite women's colleges, often appeared to hold a "highbrow attitude," or to be "stuck-up."[71] At twenty-six, her youthful good looks, combined with her sense of style and propriety, enhanced Pidgeon's charisma as a speaker.

Mary Elizabeth Pidgeon's letters reveal rich details about her daily life as a suffrage worker. Raised in rural Virginia and educated in Quaker boarding schools, Pidgeon initially became involved in the suffrage movement while an undergraduate in English at Swarthmore College. Active in Swarthmore's branch of the College Equal Suffrage League, she was elected president in her junior year. In 1913, with her degree in hand, she secured a teaching job at Friends' School in Media, Pennsylvania, where she enjoyed the company of her students and coworkers but found the work tedious and the pay "poor." Seeking to circumvent what she anticipated could become a rather mundane existence, Pidgeon soon volunteered her services to the National American Woman Suffrage Association.[72] Shortly thereafter, a suffrage organizer invited her to speak at a meeting near Media, and Pidgeon began her life as a suffrage activist.

Pidgeon's only formal education as an organizer consisted of a two-day training session at the National American Woman Suffrage Association's Fifth Avenue offices. Pidgeon believed that she and the other field secretaries required only minimal training, especially in the area of public speaking, since most already had experience as lecturers.[73] The training session leaders concentrated on the history and policies of the state and national associations and devoted only one hour to the subject of organization. As evidenced by her handwritten notes on the training session program, as well as her notes on the 1915 Annual Report of the New York State Woman Suffrage Association, Mary Elizabeth Pidgeon paid close attention to this information.[74] She seemed to find the interactions with the many leaders from other states as valuable and enlightening as the more formal classroom sessions.[75]

The constant travel Pidgeon's work required is striking. By her own admission "footloose" and free to traverse the country, Mary Elizabeth Pidgeon represented many young women new to the movement.[76] Single women made ideal professional organizers partly because they could endure sometimes "miserable" conditions on the road. Yet Pidgeon loved the trips. While in Washington awaiting her first assignment, she lamented, "I surely do wish I were to stay here awhile—just as you get interested and learn about one place, you get sent to another."[77] During her stay in Washington, Pidgeon assisted with a conference, attended by Secretary of War Newton D. Baker, announcing the commitment of the two million members of the suffrage association to war preparedness and the United States government. In mid-February 1917, Pidgeon learned she would be sent from Washington to the New York headquarters for a brief training period and to await a more specific assignment as a field secretary.[78] She wrote to her parents that the first vice-president of the National American Woman Suffrage Association, Mrs. Walter McNab Miller, mentioned that once the New York campaign ended, the national office in New York would be reorganized and Pidgeon might be able to have an executive position with the national because they considered her "abilities in that line [would] be most valuable."[79] Pidgeon had enjoyed "the great privilege of sitting at a table twice with Mrs. Catt, Miss Alice Stone Blackwell and others" by the time she arrived at the New York headquarters for training.[80]

Direction for the organizers' work came in the form of weekly letters from the New York association's Executive Board members. The organization chair, Gertrude Foster Brown, sent Pidgeon one of her first pieces of official correspondence. In a letter dated February 23, 1917, Brown warned the organizers not to be dissuaded by women who "shirk suffrage work because they have very little time for it." She relayed Catt's suggestion that each organizer recruit other women to serve as volunteers so that they could help "parcel out names of 35 men who are registered voters to convert to suffrage and to see that they vote for suffrage, or as many of them as she can persuade to do so."[81] Catt's vision for the victory centered on paid organizers coordinating the necessary arrangements for contacting all voters prior to the November 1917 vote.

Mary Elizabeth Pidgeon's first official assignment as a field secretary placed her in Buffalo, where she "did campaign work from February to July 1917" and received $75.00 a month.[82] New York leaders perceived Buffalo as the most pro-suffrage upstate city and as less dependent than other districts on organizational help from suffragists. Buffalo headquarters sponsored its own schools for young suffrage workers. Pidgeon's time in Buffalo afforded her the opportunity to see how innovative "new women" applied Catt's revamped organizing repertoire both inside and outside the city. Nettie Rogers Shuler, the chair of the Eighth District to which Buffalo and its surrounds belonged, conveyed the need to employ "different methods to reach the wide-varying people of New York State."[83]

Buffalo suffrage workers used energetic tactics to reach diverse populations ranging from working-class immigrants in densely populated neighborhoods to remote hinterland farmers. Buffalo leaders like the attorney Helen Zaidee Rodgers, a charter member of the Buffalo Political Equality Club and the vice chair of the Erie County Woman Suffrage Party, took part in suffrage parades and traveled to Albany to plead the suffrage cause. Along the way from Buffalo to Albany, organizers forged strong ties with the many community organizations that already existed in Buffalo. Suffrage speakers like Maggie Hinchey of New York City attended ward and labor meetings in Polish and Italian neighborhoods and observed as the Buffalo branch of the State Federation of Labor endorsed woman suffrage.[84] They also spoke at Parent Teacher Association meetings, union meetings, and grange functions. Some activists, like Mary Talbert, the president of the National Association of Colored Women, assisted in forming new organizations supportive of suffrage.[85] Shortly after the United States entered the war, suffragists began to participate in meetings of war-related organizations. For instance, Pidgeon attended the first meeting of the Home Gardening League, along with housewives and boy scouts, to promote gardening as a means for civilians to increase the food supply.[86] Apparently Pidgeon followed Catt's lead in temporarily suspending her pacifist principles in the interest of furthering the suffrage cause.

Throughout their sojourns in upstate towns, field workers anticipated weekly written instructions from the New York leaders. In May 1917, Mary Elizabeth Pidgeon received a letter from the New York State Woman Suffrage Party sales manager offering a variety of suffrage pamphlets and merchandise ranging from calendars to automobile radiator caps for purchase. Headquarters expected suffrage workers to buy these items with their wages so that they could distribute them within their districts.[87] The organizers incurred travel expenses along with the cost of suffrage novelties. They planned and paid for their own accommodations when they traveled. If they invited speakers into their districts, they paid for their accommodations as well.[88] The organizers found it necessary to cut costs whenever possible, sometimes at the risk of their own comfort.

In late July, after Mary Elizabeth Pidgeon had proven her worth as an organizer and speaker for the Eighth District, the leaders transferred her to Auburn and promoted her to a position in charge of Cayuga County. Technically speaking, Pidgeon became one of two assembly district leaders in the Fifth Campaign District, with Syracuse serving as headquarters. She moved into the Auburn YWCA, where she began to plan the entire district campaign. Describing her elderly partner as "not too mobile," Pidgeon assumed all of the responsibilities for speaking, including hosting prominent speakers and generating publicity for suffrage events.[89] Soon after relocating to Auburn, Pidgeon received a letter from Violet Morawetz, the chair of the speakers' bureau for the New York State Woman Suffrage Party. In her letter, Morawetz reemphasized the need for "leaders" to "gain an entrée into every possible club or association." She insisted that "arrangements should be made for a meeting solely devoted to Woman Suffrage." She recommended sending speakers to "political clubs, chambers of commerce, labor unions, trade associations, professional associations, civic clubs, patriotic clubs, university clubs, benevolent associations, religious organizations, YMCAs," and a number of other organizations.[90]

After coordinating and participating in a three-day series of suffrage events at the county fair in Moravia, Pidgeon confessed to her parents that at the end of the day she felt "tired to death" and literally "fell into bed."[91] Pidgeon's correspondence waned in October 1917, the last month of the campaign. Intensely occupied with a last-ditch effort to garner more suffrage support, she could not find time to jot down even the briefest entries in her diary. Pidgeon and other organizers had more than exhaustion to contend with. While Pidgeon acknowledged that she found upstate audiences generally receptive to speakers, women suffrage workers often had to confront male hecklers who shouted that the suffragists should be home minding their children. Like all suffrage activists, Pidgeon quickly learned how to deflect sarcastic taunts with humor.[92]

Victory in the Air

At the end of August 1917, Pidgeon went to Syracuse so that she could ride with Gertrude [Mrs. Frank J.] Tone, then the Eighth Campaign District leader, to the final state convention in Saratoga before the November vote. According to the New York Tribune "to suffragists' eyes all roads lead to Saratoga."[93] Participating in the 300-mile long caravan to the convention, carloads of women stopped in Little Falls and other towns to hold street meetings, both on their way and on their return. At the convention, held from August 29 to August 30, Pidgeon watched intently as Catt gave her speech to "Madam Chairman and Comrades."[94] A number of notable men, including the New York City mayor, John Mitchel, and the New York governor, Charles Whitman, attended the convention where leaders announced that over 900,000 women believed in their right to the ballot.[95]

Members of the Colored Women's Suffrage Club of New York City, including Annie K. Lewis, Mary M. Sharperson Young, Helen Christian, LeRue Sand, Ella Cunningham, and Lizzie B. Sims, attended the convention in Saratoga as affiliates of the New York City Woman Suffrage Party. Lewis found the notable speeches reflecting the importance of the suffrage movement in the state impressive.[96] However, soon after the women returned from the meeting, discussion arose about the treatment of the delegation and their position relative to that of white women. Deeply angered, Mary Young complained of discriminatory treatment at the meeting. Lewis and Mrs. John Humphrey Watkins both argued that the black members should have the same status as the white members and that any woman paying her dues and abiding by the rules of the suffrage club should be entitled to full membership.[97] Members of the club also traveled to Syracuse and spoke there about the Saratoga convention.[98] As imperfect as the suffrage movement, dominated by white middle-class and elite women, appeared to them, black women remained staunch supporters of the need for all women to continue agitating for their right to the elective franchise.

The suffragists who had attended the Saratoga convention implemented their plans for the remaining nine weeks of the campaign. As the last phase of their systematic efforts, the state headquarters issued a "Plan to be Submitted to State Committees," bearing the notation "This plan to be kept secret" until those last weeks. Most of the leaders' directives concentrated on "circularization" and inundating individual voters with pro-suffrage postcards. The Executive Committee of the party instructed workers to send a postcard to every enrolled member "urging her to turn in at least one favorable vote for suffrage."[99] The plan also provided directions for Election Day work, including instructions for poll watchers, and enlisted men with autos to transport voters to the polls. It required election district captains to be present at polling places to be sure that each male suffrage supporter voted. If they discovered any man shirking his duty, "he should be sent for."[100]

Pidgeon and the other organizers received notice of the upcoming October suffrage parade scheduled to begin at Washington Square Park. The parade coordinators capitalized on the suffragists' patriotic efforts. For example, they billed one parade division as "Mothers, Wives, and Sisters of Soldiers and Sailors," and another as "Women Who Have Rendered Patriotic Service." Suffrage leaders went to great lengths to standardize the appearance of parade participants. Ever concerned with respectability, but more so in a time of war, Catt issued parade announcements that instructed suffragists participating in the parade to wear "a costume of dark suit [with a] small dark hat."[101] Constantly aware of the need to draw support for the suffrage cause, the women still knew they had to adjust their appearance and message to reach an audience deeply troubled by war.

An unexpected source of support came when the Tammany Hall and Democratic Party boss Charlie Murphy withdrew his opposition to suffrage. Newspapers announced in early fall that thirty-four women had been appointed as members of Tammany Hall. Finally realizing that women voters might be of some use to him, Murphy promised Carrie Chapman Catt that his organization would not act to prevent the passage of the state suffrage amendment. Murphy was not the first, nor would he be the last, politician to act on his own political convictions concerning woman suffrage.[102] In 1917, rather than opposing the suffrage campaign, Tammany Hall maintained a neutral stance allowing voters to "express their own convictions at the polls."[103] The withdrawal of his opposition effectively translated to Tammany support for women's right to vote.

Although the historian Paula Baker maintains that voters in rural regions, often informed by churches and newspapers, tended to be politically conservative, there is evidence that men in rural areas supported suffrage more extensively than initially believed.[104] After the women of Roxbury, at the eastern end of Delaware County, formed the Equal Suffrage League in 1916, the league's president, Anna Palen, surmised that it was mostly women joining the anti-suffragists. According to Palen, "the men of the town seemed tolerant or neutral at worst—and most of them voted for suffrage."[105] Organizers made efforts to appeal to suffragists, anti-suffragists, and "indifferents" at various fairs and gatherings.[106] A transition on the part of some rural residents can be detected in newspapers, many of which came to favor suffrage by 1917. For example, in the town of Delhi, newspapers "advocating the Cause and refuting certain anti-suffrage arguments" prevailed.[107]

In the final months of the campaign, suffragists advertised everywhere. They advertised in theater programs, in subways, on elevated cars, and on trolleys. Announcements of parades appeared in newspaper headlines, and advertisements ran instructing voters to vote "yes" on Election Day. Suffragists inundated potential voters with literature, distributing it at every meeting, picnic, country store, and post office. They held mass meetings and political rallies with speakers provided by the New York State Woman Suffrage Party speakers' bureau. Workers contacted political leaders and sought endorsements from the county committee chairs of the major parties. During the final year of the campaign, the state suffrage party printed over eighteen million pieces of literature aimed at distinct groups including Catholics, labor unions, farmers, and military personnel.[108]

Suffragists continued to raise money and meet for speechmaking and other purposes in the last few weeks of the campaign. Observing "sacrifice week," they held card parties, teas, rummage sales, parcel post parties, dances, and a children's dance in their efforts to fund their activism. Because much of their money had gone for "patriotic work for the government," suffrage clubs grappled with a perpetual lack of funds.[109] To keep the war news from obscuring the suffrage campaign, women raised an additional $200,000. Of the over $500,000 total contributed to the final campaign, only a small amount went toward paying organizers or office help. Treasurer Helen Rogers Reid revealed that the financial statement of the New York State Woman Suffrage Party for the 1917 campaign reflected a deficit at its close.[110]

Suffrage Victory in the Empire State

High level government officials had hailed suffrage as a war measure in September, acknowledging women's patriotic commitment.[111] Suffrage leaders continued to promote the screening in local movie houses of the comprehensive one-reel film, "Women's Work in War Time," which debuted at the Saratoga convention.[112] Special speakers went into state military encampments to spread the suffrage message to the 150,000 soldiers in training. Placards distributed to those in military service read: "Stand by the women of your country; they have stood by you."[113] Workers saw to it that appeals went to every man serving in the military, using lists provided by the secretary of state. Suffragists even sent absentee ballots to soldiers stationed in Europe. The special attention devoted to soldiers and sailors both at home and abroad cast the 1917 referendum campaign as uniquely different from the previous campaign.

All of the suffragists' hard work came to fruition on November 6, 1917, when New York State granted women full suffrage.[114] Although suffrage headquarters were just as crowded as they had been in 1915, the atmosphere this year turned "electric with hope and anticipation" as returns began to roll in with suffrage victories in every borough of New York City. The wires began to vibrate with news of upstate triumphs. Then, according to Gertrude Foster Brown, one of the suffragists dashed in, shouting "the *Times* has just flashed a white light showing suffrage has carried the state!"[115] Harriet Burton Laidlaw and her husband, James Lees Laidlaw, celebrated along with their jubilant compatriots. As the *Woman Voter* had predicted, "in 'the bright lexicon' of suffrage there is no such word as fail."[116] Carrie Chapman Catt offered the keynote of the evening: "The victory is not New York's alone. It's the nation's. The 66th Congress is sure to pass our federal amendment."[117]

The Cayuga County Political Equality Club celebrated the suffrage victory in November 1917. Seated at the desk to the left is Mary Elizabeth Pidgeon, the assembly district leader, while to the right is Sara Wadsworth of Auburn, who long served as the Cayuga County chair. Emily Howland, the president of the Cayuga Political Equality Club, is seated second from the left. Image courtesy of the Friends Historical Library of Swarthmore College, Swarthmore, PA.

In spite of relatively low voter turnout due to its being a midterm election, the house-to-house canvassing on the part of hundreds of suffrage activists, along with the Leslie money and the support of soldiers and sailors, won the day. Mary Garrett Hay of the New York City Woman Suffrage Party had relentlessly and successfully fought resistance from Tammany Hall. New York City and its surrounding area, with a strong immigrant vote, carried the referendum for women by more than fifty-three percent. A few cities in upstate New York, including Rochester, Utica, and Albany, did not pass the measure, although the counties around those cities came out in favor of the referendum. The Southern Tier generally supported suffrage, as it had in 1915.[118] Despite pockets of resistance, women in New York had finally won, in Catt's words, "the very greatest victory."

When suffrage won in New York State, Anna Howard Shaw "ceremoniously pinned on the brooch given to Susan B. Anthony by the women of Wyoming, the pioneer suffrage state." As each state had enfranchised women, they had added a diamond to the brooch. Since 1869, thirteen states had enfranchised women, and now New York became the fourteenth state to recognize women's right to vote. Remembering Anthony's 1906 prophecy that "federal suffrage would come in 1920," Shaw remarked that the year would mark the centennial of Miss Anthony's birth.[119] Many New York women took their experience, their success, and their zeal and directed their attention toward the passage of a federal amendment. Thousands of fascinating and dynamic women in the Empire State served the New York State Woman Suffrage Association and other organizations in myriad ways during the campaign. The importance of the campaign lay in the achievement of critical victories for the larger cause of women's rights, leading to the acceptance of their right to vote nationwide, and ultimately to broader political and social rights for women.

Conclusion
Winning the Nation

In 1917, after sixty-nine years of suffrage activity, New York women won full suffrage. To commemorate the victory, suffragists held a woman citizens' dinner at the Hotel Biltmore, where Vira Boarman Whitehouse, the guest of honor, accepted a wax replica of a wreath she would receive later. Members of the New York State Woman Suffrage Party then traveled to the National American Woman Suffrage Association headquarters in Washington, DC—where it had relocated from New York in December 1916.[1] They presented Whitehouse with the 18-carat gold laurel wreath, said to have cost $1,000. The inscription read, "To Vira Boarman Whitehouse from the women of New York State whom she led to victory November 8, 1917."[2] Regarding the conferring of the wreath—some called it a crown—the *New York Times* published a letter from Whitehouse to the head of the gift committee. Whitehouse contended that if she had known what the members of the committee had planned, she would have stopped them. But since the wreath had already been created, she had decided to accept it with the "greatest gratitude." Critics who felt the money should have been better spent, including Mary Garrett Hay, the head of the New York City Woman Suffrage Party, argued that a crown represented a most undemocratic gift.[3]

The controversy surrounding the wreath illustrates some of the complications inherent to the winning of woman suffrage in New York State. Mary

Garrett Hay's criticism reveals both the underlying class tensions and conflicting interpretations of democracy. Although the cost of the wreath may have seemed extravagant to some, it symbolizes the vast sums of money suffragists could raise during their campaign. It also emphasizes their generosity and heartfelt devotion to the cause and its leadership. Without a mastery of civics combined with theatrical skill, attaining the goal of suffrage may have been delayed even further. Suffragists across the country lauded the Empire State victory as a crowning achievement. Carrie Chapman Catt called the New York win the "Gettysburg of the woman suffrage movement," while Massachusetts suffragist Maud Wood Park referred to it as the "handwriting on the wall."[4] With these affirmations of their winning strategies, New York suffragists anticipated the work that remained on the road ahead to the federal amendment enfranchising all women in the United States.

New York Women Picket the White House

Losing patience with the increasing gap between what they saw as the rights and responsibilities of American women and the "promise of liberty empty," suffragists from all over the country traveled to Washington, DC to take the fight for a federal suffrage amendment to the next level.[5] Although Catt and her by now conventional National American Woman Suffrage Association denounced radical demonstrations, more than sixty New York women, including Edna Buckman Kearns and her twelve-year-old daughter, Serena, joined Alice Paul and the National Woman's Party to picket the White House between January 1917 and the spring of 1919.[6] Inspired by their British counterparts to hold the ruling party responsible for their disenfranchisement, suffragists determined "to organize women to act aggressively on their demands—to *take* their rights."[7] As a result some of the most militant activists, including the New Yorkers Lucy Burns, Dorothy Day, Kathryn Lincoln, Louise Bryant, Amy Juengling, and Maud Malone, earned the moniker "Iron-Jawed Angels" after their arrests and subsequent hunger strikes in the Occoquan Workhouse. Of the approximately five hundred women arrested, one hundred and sixty-eight of them spent time in jail.[8]

Police arrested Vida Milholland, sister of Inez Milholland, on July 4, 1917, and she spent three days in jail.[9] She responded to the harsh treatment women received at the hands of male authorities by singing ballads, love songs, and "The Woman's Marseillaise" to relieve the monotony and lift the spirits of the other prisoners. Ada Davenport Kendall, a Buffalo woman, suffered solitary confinement and a bread-and-water diet and was forced to wear the same clothing for eleven days after protesting the demand that she scrub the floors on her hands and knees. Only when her friends created a ruckus did prison authorities give her clean clothes and release her from confinement.[10] Alice Paul and the New Yorker Rose Winslow, a Polish immigrant, initiated hunger strikes and, like many other women, suffered forced feedings to prevent their becoming martyrs for the cause.[11] The New Yorker M. M. Young, a black woman, offered to help with the picketing, although it is not clear that she actually picketed.[12]

Despite national headlines exposing the cruel and inhumane treatment of women simply demanding the recognition of their rights of citizenship, women across the country, young and old, flocked to participate in the picketing demonstrations, taking up the banners as women dropped out, were arrested, or went to jail. As activists faced condemnation for picketing a wartime president, the fact that the United States engaged in a war to "make the world safe for democracy" struck suffragists and increasing numbers of observers as ironic.[13] The more moderate suffragists in the National American Woman Suffrage Association criticized the picketers for causing a rift in the movement. In reality, although the "silent sentinels" and their picketing caused tremendous controversy, they assuredly pushed the woman suffrage campaign forward.

Finishing with the Business of the War

However radical or moderate in nature, suffrage involvement provided an exceptional training ground for women as they ventured into new realms of activity. For many suffragists, taking part in the movement represented a political coming of age moment in the story of their lives. Regardless of their age, they had acquired speaking, organizing, and fund-raising skills, self-confidence, knowledge about how to overcome adversity, and, most important, the opportunity to learn the meaning of full citizenship in the United States. Involved in an undeniably multifaceted venture, women took what they needed from their education and experience in the movement, and headed off into a wide variety of endeavors. The vote had been a rallying battle cry. Some participants could rest on their laurels and faded from the public eye altogether; others felt compelled to take on new challenges.

New York women who had spent years on one side or the other of the suffrage movement finally enjoyed the freedom to turn their attention to other arenas. Utilizing speaking, organizing, marketing, and fund-raising skills from their suffrage days, they worked at the local, state, national, and even international levels in careers ranging from government service to endorsing beauty products. While women like Alva Belmont sold Pond's Cold Cream, others used their suffrage skills to bolster their personal and professional autonomy.[14] Skills honed in the New York movement easily transferred to other kinds of occupations. For example, when Vira Whitehouse went to Washington to attend the National American Woman Suffrage Association convention, she expressed her desire for war work to her friend George Creel, a journalist and the chair of the Committee on Public Information.[15] Woodrow Wilson had appointed Creel to supervise the systematic distribution of "America's message" around the world.[16] Whitehouse accepted Creel's invitation to serve the committee in Switzerland, thereby becoming one of the first female diplomats for the United States.[17]

The war presented the most immediate concern for many New York suffragists. Some, like the Buffalo attorney Helen Zaidee Marie Rodgers, volunteered their time in the name of patriotism. Rodgers spoke for the Red Cross, the War Stamp drive, and Liberty Bond drives, sometimes alongside the New York governor, Charles Whitman. While retaining her post in the New York State Woman Suffrage Party, Harriet Burton Laidlaw continued her public service career, serving in 1918 as the chair of a division of the United States Food Administration. Ella Crossett, who spent her life working for suffrage, founded a local chapter of the Red Cross in Warsaw, New York.[18] Another former president of the New York association, Gertrude Foster Brown, spent 1918 in France working as a liaison for the Women's Overseas Hospitals, while Addie Waite Hunton served with the Colored Troops of the American Expeditionary Forces. Mary Talbert served as a nurse for the Red Cross in Romagne, France.[19] After the war, Madeline Doty married her longtime friend Roger Baldwin, founder of the American Civil Liberties Union, and continued her commitment to peace activism.[20] With the end of the Great War, activists could again turn their attention to politics.

Creating the League of Women Voters

Harriet May Mills was one of the many suffragists who continued to work with the New York State Woman Suffrage Party during the years it took to transition to the League of Women Voters. At a convention a few weeks after the win, the party voted to remain dedicated to woman suffrage at the federal level while pursuing a distinct agenda emphasizing civic education. At first, the suffragists maintained their organizational structure while they concentrated on turning suffrage activists into informed voters. Mills suggested that the organization change its name to the League of Women Citizens to reflect the new emphasis on education and research activities related to making use of the vote as a tool of citizenship.[21] With their attention never wavering from the federal amendment, the New York suffrage leaders began to reorganize the party to match existing legislative districts and pledged themselves to nonpartisanship until the federal amendment proved successful.

Aligning with a broad spectrum of progressive reform causes, the Woman Suffrage Party of New York City, in 1918, transitioned to the Woman Voters' Council to monitor New York governmental activities and to investigate health, working, and other conditions related to women and children.[22] Optimistically, Gertrude Brown coordinated informal talks at woman suffrage party headquarters on "What Every Voter Should Know" even before New York recognized women's right to vote. Within two months of the passage of the state suffrage referendum, the Woman Voters' Council hosted a citizenship drive and announced a six-lesson lecture course, "The Business of Citizenship," to inform new voters about their rights and responsibilities at various levels of government. Brown and Violet Morawetz, the acting chair of the educational section, underwrote the expansion of the citizenship education offerings taught by faculty at Barnard and Hunter Colleges.[23] The council also responded to women's demands for information and conducted a general registration campaign, using telephones and personal canvassing to distribute and explain voter registration forms and candidates for upcoming elections.

Education became the new activism. Helen Zaidee Rodgers organized the first course of political study for the new League of Women Voters branch in Buffalo. The curricula and courses duplicated many of the suffrage school lessons in the effort to educate voters. At a New York City Board of Directors meeting on May 29, 1918, Mary Garrett Hay and the chair of the industrial section of the New York State Woman Suffrage Association, Mary Dreier, decided to concentrate only on educating foreign-born women eligible to vote. Citizenship and worker education courses took place in Russian, Italian, and Yiddish at local centers where league members believed that the information would be "a tremendous help to men as well as women."[24]

In the wake of the New York victory, black women's activism paralleled that of white women in many ways. Black women formed clubs to educate themselves about their political responsibilities and encourage black women to register and to vote. Early in 1918, Harlem women formed the Women's Non-Partisan Political League to "make the women voters of Harlem a factor in politics and to actively further the interests of the race." League members learned how to complete a ballot, observed debates between representatives of the various parties, and listened to speakers on political topics.[25] Dr. Gertrude Curtis McPherson, the first black woman to earn a license to practice dentistry in New York State, cofounded the league. In addition to having a dental practice, Curtis McPherson belonged to the Loyal League of Brooklyn, supported the building of a hospital in Harlem, and served on the staff of the Colored Orphan Asylum at Riverdale-on-the-Hudson.[26] The newly-founded Negro Women Voters, situated in Queens County, established branches in Jamaica, Coram, Flushing, and Richmond Hill. Curtis McPherson and another black woman, Mrs. Laura E. Fisher, both living in New York City, served as delegates to the New York State Republican Convention in 1918. Bessye B. Bearden, a member of the New York Urban League, founded the Colored Women's Democratic League in 1922 and served as its first president.[27] At the same time, racism and the tendency of white women to exclude black women from their activist organizations continued to complicate the relationship between black and white suffragists.

According to the report from New York in the *1919 Handbook of the National American Woman Suffrage Association*, the New York State Woman Suffrage Party "had just passed through the most unique year" in the history of any suffrage organization. With war as a backdrop, suffragists had dramatically rebounded from their painful loss in 1915 to achieve a resounding win in 1917. Relying on its solid foundation and its ability to adapt to the needs of the newest portion of the electorate, the party remained intact. After years of intense campaigning, the focus of the organization had "sober[ed]" into a "constructive, educational" agenda to inform women about voter registration, candidate qualifications, governmental structure, and the "responsibilities that came with suffrage."[28] In addition to teaching citizenship courses at educational institutions, the activists did "intensive work among new women voters," holding lectures in stores, factories, churches, movie houses, and halls, reaching 500,000 New Yorkers and registering over 414,000 women. Outreach into rural counties to distribute literature and register both women and men voters took place concurrently.[29] Like-minded and optimistic women across the country could see the need for preparing similar programs.

Carrie Chapman Catt initiated plans for a new organization to emerge from the National American Woman Suffrage Association at the Jubilee convention held in St. Louis in late March 1919.[30] Thinking ahead, Catt and other leaders sought to use the power of women's coordinated efforts to enact change, and they looked forward to setting new agendas with the force of approximately two million enfranchised women behind them.[31] The next month, New York became the first state to affiliate with the nascent National League of Women Voters.[32] The headquarters of the New York State Woman

Suffrage Party became the headquarters of the New York League of Women Voters. Some important leaders, including Harriet Burton Laidlaw, Narcissa Cox Vanderlip, and Mary Garrett Hay, assumed posts in the new league. The new League of Women Voters branch in Westchester County opened its membership to men because, as the Westchester County league president said, "We decided discrimination is not the proper attitude."[33]

Running for Office and Affecting Legislation

One of the reasons it took so long for women to get the right to vote is that men feared the "entry of women into the ranks of voters, party activists, candidates, and office holders." Furthermore, voting rights radically shook the "relationship between gender and citizenship."[34] Men had no idea what kind of political power women could wield and consequently perceived women as a threat. Yet, in following the old adage that one should keep one's friends close but one's enemies closer, the major party members competed with each other to convince as many new voters as possible to register with their respective parties. Both the Democratic and Republican parties in New York State appointed women to nearly every district to work toward registering women. The efforts of suffragists and party workers paid off. 679,618 women in New York State were registered to vote by May 1918. Sixty percent registered as Republicans, in gratitude for woman suffrage having had a place on the party platform since 1916.[35] By that fall, 1.2 million total voters, most of them women, had registered.[36]

Male politicos feared that newly registered women would vote as a bloc and shape politics in ways that challenged male authority.[37] Voting had been quintessentially male for centuries, and, as the New York State woman suffrage campaign attests, it can take decades to change deeply engrained attitudes and behaviors for both women and men. The vote had long expressed "masculine power" in the "male sphere of public life," and many men resented the entry of women into those realms.[38] In spite of women's registering with political parties, it quickly became evident that women would not be as loyal to their party as men tended to be. Women did not behave like typical male voters. New York women had long distrusted party politics. Many preferred not to support a party candidate, voting instead for candidates based on their position on issues important to women as voters. In the post-suffrage years, women continued their tradition of non-partisanship and volunteer activism.[39] The long-awaited recognition of women's right to vote had happened to come at a time when fewer voters actually believed in the power of the vote.[40] The party leaders quickly realized that they could not predict how individual women would vote, and the fears of a women's bloc dissolved within a few years of women's enfranchisement.

In keeping with his promise to stay with the cause until women won suffrage, James Laidlaw aided in expanding the fight for other issues meaningful to women. In January 1919, Laidlaw led a delegation of women to Albany in an effort to persuade the legislature to ratify the "federal dry amendment."[41] Activism related to the prohibition of alcohol had long drawn women's attention, and many wanted to use their votes to influence policy and to elect candidates sympathetic to their desire to control or ban the manufacture, sale, and distribution of alcohol. Some women, such as the Woman's Christian Temperance Union leader, Ella Boole, took advantage of the suffrage victory to run for U.S. Senator on the Prohibition Party ticket in 1920.[42]

Most women who sought elective office at the time descended from the ranks of suffrage activism, and some experienced more success than Boole.[43] Mary Lilly and Ida Sammis both won election to the 142nd session of the New York State legislature, although each served only one term. Suffolk County voters elected Sammis, a Republican, to the Assembly. Legend has it that her first act involved polishing her brass spittoon, filling it with flowers, and setting it prominently on her desk. In 1919, she introduced a bill to protect women who worked as elevator conductors, requiring them to be over the age of twenty-one, limiting their hours to between 7:00 a.m. and 10:00 p.m. during a maximum fifty-four hour week, and providing seats for them to rest. Governor Alfred Smith signed the new bill into law. In fact, ten of the fifteen bills Sammis introduced passed into law.[44]

Already involved in social and political reform with a particular interest in prison reform, Mary Lilly, a Democrat and lawyer from New York County, won her campaign for the New York Assembly in November 1918. She immediately advocated for the passage of the federal suffrage amendment. As a member of the Assembly, she wrote bills to protect the rights of children, including one to establish the right of children born out of wedlock to share in their fathers' estates, one to raise the age of delinquency to eighteen, and another to abolish the death penalty for minors. For a time she served as the director of female prisoners at Blackwell Island, drawing criticism for accepting a city salary at the same time she drew a state salary.[45] As did Sammis, Lilly set important precedents for what women at the state level could do politically.

Some notable former suffrage leaders sought to integrate themselves into the formal political process, with varying degrees of success. In July 1920, members of the Democratic Party nominated Syracuse native Harriet May

Mills to run for Secretary of State. Encouraged by her male colleagues in the party, Mills believed she had a duty to run for office to help pave the way for other women's candidacies. Although Mills, the first woman nominated for a statewide office by a major political party, lost her election bid, she continued to speak out against "discrimination on the grounds of sex." Through her political activism Mills became friendly with Eleanor and Franklin Roosevelt and, by the early 1920s, served as the first female State Hospital Commissioner.[46] At the same time, the trade unionist Rose Schneiderman ran for U.S. Senator on the Farmer-Labor ticket, in spite of her having been labeled unpatriotic in 1918. She lost the election.[47] A past as a suffragist could hinder women in their post-suffrage political careers. Conversely, it could launch a career, as it did for Mary Elizabeth Pidgeon, who became a director of citizenship education at the University of Virginia.[48]

In spite of women's struggle to enter politics and the fact that they came to politics to stay, the "levers of power did not change hands."[49] Women in both major parties found themselves relegated to segregated spaces within those parties.[50] Although women made a few remarkable gains, party politics, including voting patterns and partisan alignments, did not change much regardless of the essential doubling of the electorate.[51] Nevertheless, a subtle, long-range transition occurred as women's particular issues permeated state and national politics increasingly over time. Aspects of women's reform agendas, especially in the areas of protective legislation for women and children, women's rights, consumer protection, industrial health and safety regulations, and social welfare programs, more often appeared in the halls of state and federal legislatures and more likely became laws.[52] "Women's collective presence made a difference in politics," and consequently elected officials gradually took the responsibility for the well-being of their female constituency more seriously.[53]

Victory for the Nation's Women

Carrie Chapman Catt, the president of the National American Woman Suffrage Association, had tested her "Winning Plan," a two-pronged approach designed to campaign simultaneously for state and federal suffrage, in New York State. Her consummate organizational skills proved to be a determining factor in the New York victory. Catt's plan for gaining women's enfranchisement in every state of the union openly deviated from the approach employed by Alice Paul. The National Woman's Party pushed for visibility and media exposure and held the party in power (the Democratic Party) responsible for the government's failure to recognize women's right to the vote. Catt, in contrast, believed that Congress would not move on suffrage until enough women, in their respective states, could vote for suffrage supporters in national elections to make ratification a reality.[54] Once Catt could celebrate the New York suffrage referendum as "a great step toward national victory," she turned virtually all of her attention to the federal campaign in Washington, DC.[55] At the same time, the triumphant New York suffragists turned the "full force of [their] organization to bear on the passage of the Federal Woman Suffrage Amendment."[56]

Before New York women won enfranchisement, there had been virtually no hope of a federal amendment. After the New York win, Catt grew increasingly optimistic about securing the federal amendment to enfranchise all female citizens in the United States. Fifty-two years had passed since Congress ratified the Fourteenth Amendment, adding the word "male" to the United States Constitution. Since that time, three generations of suffragists had waged a total of 909 campaigns at state and federal levels—including at state constitutional conventions and presidential party conventions—and nineteen successive campaigns with nineteen successive Congresses to remove the offending word.[57] Conflict regarding support of the Great War and controversy over picketing the White House had complicated the transition to agitation for a federal amendment.

Determined to move ahead in spite of her disapproval of the picketers, Catt used her own systematic and purposeful tactics to reach President Wilson and members of Congress. National American Woman Suffrage Association members flocked to the Capitol to confront and discuss woman suffrage with legislators, a tactic that reporters dubbed the "front door lobby." The strategy helped the association win additional backing in the House and Senate.[58] Although Wilson instructed members of Congress to support women's enfranchisement, it still took several separate Congressional votes to pass the measure. The fact that the number of presidential electors hailing from equal suffrage states had risen from 91 to 339—including the 47 from New York—obviously had an impact.[59] By June 1919, when the amendment had finally passed both houses of Congress and had gone to the states for ratification, Catt expressed a feeling common among many suffrage workers that "the final victory lay not at hand, but somewhere in the future."[60] In other words, plenty of work for women's equality remained to be done. New York ratified the amendment in a special session, becoming the sixth state to do so. The ratification by a total of thirty-six states complete, the Nineteenth Amendment officially became part of the United States Constitution, by the certification of Secretary of State Bainbridge Colby, on August 26, 1919.[61] Not a single suffragist observed Colby as he signed the amendment, and many women had to wait to vote until the amendment went into effect in 1920.

Despite all the excitement around the years of campaigning for women's right to vote, and despite a tendency for women's rights activists to pursue woman suffrage single-mindedly, suffrage leaders realized that work on behalf of women still needed doing. Although many of the rights that women had demanded in 1848 with the Declaration of Sentiments had been won, women still did not have all of the rights freely accorded to white men.

Emily Howland's activist career would span over seven decades at the national, state, and local levels. She is remembered for being one of the most generous financial contributors to the movement. Here she is, at the age of ninety, in 1918, on her way to cast her vote. Used with permission of the Friends Historical Library of Swarthmore College, Swarthmore, PA.

Native American women (and men, for that matter) would not win United States citizenship rights until 1924. However, because voting rights are determined by individual states, some states prohibited Native Americans from voting until the 1960s.[62] Legislation continues to ensure the rights of native people in the face of challenges to those rights.[63] Women could not serve on juries in many states. In New York State, for example, it took until 1937 for a state law to grant permission to courts to include women on juries.[64] Black women (and men) continued to struggle for their rights long after the passage of the Nineteenth Amendment. The civil rights movement in the 1960s won for minorities and white women more rights equal to those of white men, but none of those rights came easily or is, even now, completely secure.

If we allow that the suffrage movement was born with the Women's Rights Convention in Seneca Falls in 1848, it took sixty-nine years in New York State, and more than seventy-two years in the nation, to win for women the right to vote. The incredible dedication and perseverance of suffrage women and men, who devoted such energy to a movement where so many separate factions worked together in a loose coalition, made the win possible. Thousands of women demanded, argued, and fought to have members of the state and federal governments finally recognize their right to vote. What members of these disparate groups did was nothing short of remarkable—it was amazing, unprecedented, and unique. Yet in spite of how hard these women worked throughout the suffrage movement, some had the time of their lives. Many made like-minded and lifelong friends of the other women they had met during one or another of the suffrage campaigns. For others, movement activities determined their career trajectories. Never again have New York women organized as they did to win the vote. With an irrepressible drive, motivated by a moral vision, suffrage workers altered the nature and actions of the masculine state and polity.[65] Their example continues to inspire.

New York State Suffrage Conventions, 1869–1917, Map and List

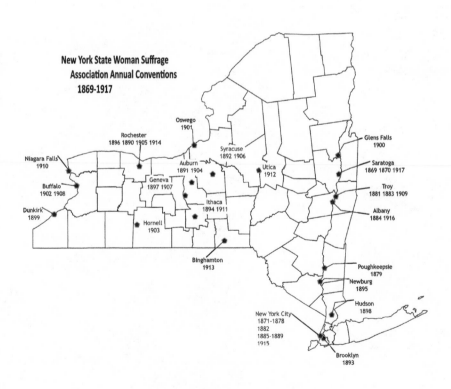

New York State Woman Suffrage
Association Annual Conventions
1869-1917

Oswego
1901

Rochester
1896 1890 1905 1914

Syracuse
1892 1906

Glens Falls
1900

Niagara Falls
1910

Auburn
1891 1904

Utica
1912

Saratoga
1869 1870 1917

Buffalo
1902 1908

Geneva
1897 1907

Troy
1881 1883 1909

Dunkirk
1899

Ithaca
1894 1911

Albany
1884 1916

Hornell
1903

Binghamton
1913

Poughkeepsie
1879

Newburg
1895

Hudson
1898

New York City
1871-1878
1882
1885-1889
1915

Brooklyn
1893

Table 1

YEAR	PLACE HELD	YEAR	PLACE HELD	YEAR	PLACE HELD
1869	Saratoga	1886	New York City	1902	Buffalo
1870	Saratoga	1887	New York City	1903	Hornell
1871	New York City	1888	New York City	1904	Auburn
1872	New York City	1889	New York City	1905	Rochester
1873	New York City	1890	Rochester	1906	Syracuse
1874	New York City	1891	Auburn	1907	Geneva
1875	New York City	1892	Syracuse	1908	Buffalo
1876	New York City	1893	Brooklyn	1909	Troy
1877	New York City	1894	Ithaca	1910	Niagara Falls
1878	New York City	1895	Newburgh	1911	Ithaca
1879	Poughkeepsie	1896	Rochester	1912	Utica
1880	No convention	1897	Geneva	1913	Binghamton
1881	Troy	1898	Hudson	1914	Rochester
1882	New York City	1899	Dunkirk	1915	New York
1883	Troy	1900	Glens Falls	1916	Albany
1884	Albany	1901	Oswego	1917	Saratoga
1885	New York City				

APPENDIX 2

New York State Suffrage Organizations and Political Equality Clubs Map and List

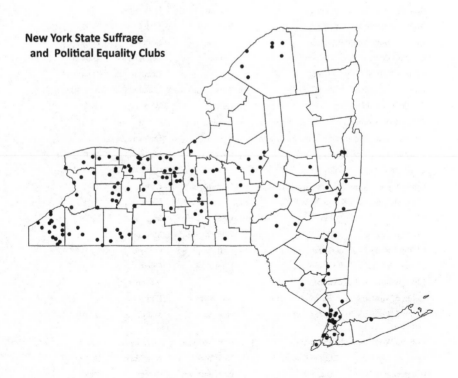

New York State Suffrage and Political Equality Clubs

Table 2

NAME	PLACE	COUNTY	DATE FOUNDED
Akron [Political Equality Club]	Akron	Erie	1906
Albany Political Equality League/Club	Albany	Albany	1902
Albany Woman Suffrage Society	Albany	Albany	1880
Allegany County Woman Suffrage Association	Belmont	Allegany	by 1912
Allens Hill Suffrage Society	Allens Hill	Ontario	1906
Alton [Political Equality Club]	Alton	Wayne	1907
Andover Equal Suffrage Club	Andover	Allegany	—
Arcade [Political Equality Club]	Arcade	Wyoming	1905
Batavia Political Equality Club	Batavia	Genesee	1895
Bath Political Equality Club	Bath	Steuben	by 1900
Bedford Political Equality League	Bedford	Westchester	1894
Belmont Political Equality Club	Belmont	Allegany	by 1907
Binghamton [Political Equality Club]	Binghamton	Broome	1912
Bolivar Political Equality Club	Bolivar	Allegany	1912
Bradford Political Equality Club	Bradford	Steuben	1892
Brasher Falls [Political Equality Club]	Brasher Falls	St. Lawrence	1914
Brooklyn Progressive Suffrage Association	Brooklyn	Kings	—
Bronxville Civic Club	Bronxville	Westchester	1914
Buffalo Political Equality League	Buffalo	Erie	1912
Bushwick Political Equality Club	Brooklyn	Kings	1900
Byron Women's Suffrage Club	Byron	Genesee	before 1893
Camillus Political Equality Club	Camillus	Onondaga	1904
Carroll Political Equality Club	Carroll	Chautauqua	1888
Cassadaga Political Equality Club	Cassadaga	Chautauqua	by 1893
Castile Political Equality Club	Castile	Wyoming	by 1896
Cattaraugus County Political Equality Club	Randolph	Cattaraugus	1890
Cayuga County Woman Suffrage Association	Auburn	Cayuga	1891
Cazenovia [Political Equality Club]	Cazenovia	Madison	1902
Charlotte Political Equality Club	Charlotte	Chautauqua	1888
Chautauqua County Political Equality Club	Jamestown	Chautauqua	1888
Cherry Creek Political Equality Club	Cherry Creek	Chautauqua	1888
Chili Political Equality Club	Chili	Monroe	by 1900
Churchville Club	Churchville	Monroe	by 1902
Clifton Springs Political Equality Club	Clifton Springs	Ontario	by 1905
Clinton Political Equality Club	Clinton	Oneida	1912
Clyde Woman Suffrage Club	Clyde	Wayne	—
Colored Women's Equal Suffrage League	Brooklyn	Kings	late 1880s
Colored Women's Suffrage Club of New York City	New York City	Manhattan	by 1917
Colored Women's Suffrage League	New Rochelle	Westchester	1912
Co-operative Woman Suffrage League	New York City	New York	by 1909
Cooperstown Political Equality Club	Cooperstown	Otsego	1896
Cortland Political Equality Club	Cortland	Cortland	1898

NAME	PLACE	COUNTY	DATE FOUNDED
Dansville Political Equality Club	Dansville	Livingston	1904
Delaware County Political Equality Club	Delhi	Delaware	by 1916
Delhi Equal Suffrage Club	Delhi	Delaware	1912
Dundee Political Equality Club	Dundee	Yates	1907
Dunkirk Political Equality Club	Dunkirk	Chautauqua	by 1890
East Groton Political Equality Club	East Groton	Tompkins	1907
East Syracuse [Political Equality Club]	East Syracuse	Onondaga	1904
East-Side Political Equality Club	Buffalo	Erie	by 1892
East Side Equal Rights League	New York	Manhattan	1908
Easton Political Equality Club	Easton	Washington	1891
Eaton Political Equality Club	Eaton	Madison	—
Elizabeth Smith Miller Club	Geneva	Ontario	by 1907
Ellery Political Equality Club	Ellery	Chautauqua	1890
Ellington Political Equality Club	Ellington	Chautauqua	1888
Elmira Club	Elmira	Chemung	1896
Equal Franchise Association	Tarrytown	Westchester	by 1913
Equal Franchise League	Buffalo	Erie	by 1914
Equal Franchise League	Rye	Westchester	1913
Equal Franchise League of New Rochelle	New Rochelle	Westchester	1912
Equal Suffrage League of Wappinger Falls	Wappinger Falls	Dutchess	1877
Equal Suffrage League of Self-Supporting Women	New York City	New York	1907
Equal Suffrage League of the City of New York	New York City	New York	by 1910
Erie County Political Equality Club	Buffalo	Erie	by 1910
Etna Political Equality Club	Etna	Tompkins	1898
Political Equality Club	Buffalo	Erie	by 1893
Flatbush Political Equality Club	Brooklyn	Kings	1902
Fluvanna Club	Fluvanna	Chautauqua	1891
Friendship Political Equality Club	Friendship	Allegany	—
Fredonia	Fredonia	Chautauqua	by 1889
Frewsburg [Political Equality Club]	Frewsburg	Chautauqua	1888
Gainsville Political Equality Club	Gainsville	Wyoming	1898
Genesee County Woman's Suffrage Association	South Byron	Genesee	by 1902
Geneseo Political Equality Club	Geneseo	Livingston	1910
Geneva Political Equality Club	Geneva	Ontario	1897
Glens Falls Political Equality Club	Glens Falls	Warren	by 1900
Gouverneur [Political Equality] Club	Gouverneur	St. Lawrence	—
Green Point [Political Equality Club]	Brooklyn	Kings	1905
Greenleaf Political Equality Club	Cuba	Allegany	by 1899
Greenwood Club	Brooklyn	Kings	1905

(Continued)

Table 2 (Continued)

NAME	PLACE	COUNTY	DATE FOUNDED
Groton Political Equality Club	Groton	Tompkins	1898
Hamburg Political Equality Club	Hamburg	Erie	1902
Hamilton County Political Equality Club	Kingston	Hamilton	by 1916
Hannibal Suffrage Club	Hannibal	Oswego	1913
Harlem Club of the Political Equality Association	New York City	New York	1910
Harlem Rights Equality League	New York City	New York	1905
Harriet Beecher Stowe Equality League of Kings County	Brooklyn	Kings	1910
Hastings-on-Hudson Political Equality Club	Hastings-on-Hudson	Westchester	—
Holley Political Equality Club	Holley	Orleans	1902
Honeoye Political Equality Club	Honeoye	Ontario	1906
Hornellsville Club	Hornellsville	Steuben	1896
Hudson Falls Political Equality Club	Hudson Falls	Washington	by 1915
Hudson River Equal Franchise League	Dobbs Ferry	Westchester	by 1910
Irondequoit Political Equality Club	Irondequoit	Monroe	1891
Italian Woman Suffrage Association	Rome	Oneida	by 1911
Ithaca Political Study Club	Ithaca	Tompkins	1899
Jamaica Political Equality Club	Queens	Queens	1904
Jamestown Political Equality Club	Jamestown	Chautauqua	1887
Jasper Political Equality Club	Jasper	Steuben	1906
Johnson Creek Political Equality Club	Hartland	Niagara	1894
Junius Civic Club	Junius	Wayne	1907
Kennedy Political Equality Club	Kennedy	Chautauqua	by 1889
Kiantone Political Equality Club	Kiantone	Chautauqua	by 1889
Kings County Political Equality League	Brooklyn	Kings	by 1894
Kingston Political Equality Club	Kingston	Ulster	by 1912
Lawton Station Political Equality Club	Lawton	Erie	—
Lily Dale Political Equality Club	Lily Dale	Chautauqua	1891
Livingston Political Equality Club	Livingston	Columbia	1886
Locke Political Equality Club	Locke	Cayuga	1906
Lockport Political Equality Club	Lockport	Niagara	1894
Lyons Political Equality Club	Lyons	Wayne	1902
Marengo Political Equality Club	Marengo	Wayne	1906
Mayville Political Equality Club	Mayville	Chautauqua	by 1889
Medina Political Equality Club	Medina	Orleans	1896
Middletown Political Equality Club	Middletown	Orange	1895
Monroe County Political Equality Club	Rochester	Monroe	1890
Mount Vernon Political Equality Club	Mount Vernon	Westchester	by 1897
Moravia Political Equality Club	Moravia	Cayuga	1906
Niagara Falls Political Equality Club	Niagara Falls	Niagara	1894
Nassau Political Equality Club	Nassau	Rensselaer	1898
Negro Men's and Women's Branch	New York City	New York	1910
Negro Suffrage Club	New York City	New York	1910

NAME	PLACE	COUNTY	DATE FOUNDED
Newark Political Equality Club	Newark	Wayne	1902
New York City Woman Suffrage Party	New York City	New York	1909
New York County Political Equality Club	New York City	New York	—
Norfolk Campaign Club	Norfolk	St. Lawrence	1914
North Chili Political Equality Club	North Chili	Monroe	by 1914
North Eaton Political Equality Club	Eaton	Madison	1902
Norwood Political Equality Club	Norwood	St. Lawrence	1914
Ogdensburg Political Equality Club	Ogdensburg	St. Lawrence	1912
Olean Woman Suffrage League	Olean	Cattaraugus	1887
Oneida Political Equality Club	Oneida	Madison	1898
Onondaga County Political Equality Club	Syracuse	Onondaga	by 1901
Orleans County Political Equality Club	Albion	Orleans	—
Oswego County Political Equality Club	Oswego	Oswego	1896
Ontario County Political Equality Club	Canandaigua	Ontario	1904
Parishville Political Equality Club	Parishville	St. Lawrence	1914
Pavilion Political Equality Club	Pavilion	Genesee	by 1904
Pelham Manor Political Equality Club	Pelham Manor	Westchester	—
Penn Yan Political Equality Club	Penn Yan	Yates	1913
People's Political Equality League of Brooklyn	Brooklyn	Kings	1908
Perry Political Equality Club	Perry	Wyoming	by 1893
Phelps Political Equality Club	Phelps	Ontario	1898
Phoebe Benton Club	Ithaca	Tompkins	1906
Pittsford Political Equality Club	Pittsford	Monroe	1902
Political Equality Club of Auburn	Auburn	Cayuga	by 1891
Political Equality Club of Cattaraugus County	Little Valley	Cattaraugus	1892
Political Equality Club of Richmond County	Staten Island	Richmond	by 1905
Political Equality Club of Sage College	Ithaca	Tompkins	by 1909
Political Study Club	Garden City	Nassau	by 1916
Political Study Club	Newburgh	Orange	by 1915
Pope Mills Political Equality Club	Pope Mills	St. Lawrence	1915
Port Jefferson Political Equality Club	Port Jefferson	Suffolk	1896
Prospect Political Equality Club	Prospect	Oneida	1904
Prospect Heights Political Equality League	Brooklyn	Kings	by 1894
Queens County Political Equality Club	Queens	Nassau	by 1897
Randolph Political Equality Club	Randolph	Chautauqua	1888
Rensselaer County Woman Suffrage Association	Troy	Rensselaer	1905
Rochester Political Equality Club	Rochester	Monroe	by 1891
Rockland Assembly District League	New City	Rockland	by 1916
Roxbury Equal Suffrage League	Roxbury	Delaware	1916
Salamanca Political Equality Club	Salamanca	Cattaraugus	by 1909
Scarsdale Equal Suffrage Club	Scarsdale	Westchester	1914
Scio Political Equality Club	Scio	Allegany	1905
Schenectady Political Equality Club	Schenectady	Schenectady	—
Seneca County Political Equality Club	Seneca Falls	Seneca	by 1917

(Continued)

Table 2 (Continued)

NAME	PLACE	COUNTY	DATE FOUNDED
Sherwood Equal Rights Association	Sherwood	Cayuga	1891
Sinclairville Political Equality Club	Sinclairville	Chautauqua	1888
Sodus Political Equality Club	Sodus	Wayne	1902
South Chili Political Equality Club	South Chili	Monroe	—
South Stockton Political Equality Club	South Stockton	Chautauqua	1888
Stockton Political Equality Club	Stockton	Chautauqua	1888
Susan B. Anthony Club	Rochester	Monroe	by 1898
Susan Look Avery Club	Wyoming	Wyoming	by 1901
Syracuse Political Equality Club	Syracuse	Onondaga	1892
Tappan Political Equality League	Tappan	Rockland County	—
Tenth Ward Equal Suffrage Club	Yonkers	Westchester	by 1916
Tompkins County Woman Suffrage Association	Ithaca	Tompkins	1899
Trenton Political Equality Club	Trenton	Oneida	—
Troy Political Equality Club	Troy	Rensselaer	1905
Ulster Political Equality Club	Saugerties	Ulster	—
University Political Equality Club of Syracuse	Syracuse	Onondaga	by 1907
Utica Political Equality Club	Utica	Oneida	1900
Valley Falls Political Equality Club	Valley Falls	Rensselaer	1903
Warren County Political Equality Club	Glens Falls	Warren	—
Warsaw Political Equality Club	Warsaw	Wyoming	by 1891
Washington County Woman Suffrage Association	Hudson Falls	Washington	—
Waterloo Political Equality Club	Waterloo	Seneca	1907
Wayne County Political Equality Club	Lyons	Wayne	1902
Webster Political Equality Club	Webster	Monroe	—
Weedsport Political Equality Club	Weedsport	Cayuga	1904
Wellsville Political Equality Club	Wellsville	Allegany	1898
Westchester County Woman Suffrage Association	Yonkers	Westchester	1910
Westfield Political Equality Club	Westfield	Chautauqua	1888
White Plains Equal Franchise Club	White Plains	Westchester	by 1916
William Lloyd Garrison League	New York City	New York	by 1909
Williamson Political Equality Club	Williamson	Wayne	1902
Williamsville Political Equality Club	Williamsville	Erie	1904
Woman Suffrage Study Club	New York City	New York	1909
Woman Wage Earners' League	New York City	New York	1911
Woman Workers Suffrage League	Buffalo	Erie	1908
Woman's League for Civic Education	Poughkeepsie	Dutchess	1913
Wyoming County Political Equality Club	Wyoming	Wyoming	1890
Yonkers Woman Suffrage Club	Yonkers	Westchester	1909
Young Men's Woman Suffrage League	New York City	New York	1874
Young People's Suffrage League	Brooklyn	Kings	1904
Young People's Suffrage Club	Dansville	Livingston	1907

Notes

Introduction

1. Katherine Devereux Blake and Margaret Louise Wallace, *Champion of Women: The Life of Lillie Devereux Blake* (New York: Fleming H. Revell Co., 1943), 75–76.

2. Grace Farrell, *Lillie Devereux Blake: Retracing a Life Erased* (Amherst: University of Massachusetts Press, 2002), 119.

3. Lori D. Ginzberg, *Untidy Origins: A Story of Woman's Rights in Antebellum New York* (Chapel Hill: University of North Carolina Press, 2005), 7–8.

4. "Mrs. Whitehouse is Renominated," *Rochester Democrat and Chronicle*, November 22, 1917, 3.

5. United States Census Bureau Statistical Reports, http://www.census.gov (accessed October 3, 2015); Robert F. Wesser, *Charles Evans Hughes: Politics and Reform in New York, 1905–1910* (Ithaca, NY: Cornell University Press, 1967), 4–5.

6. Carrie Chapman Catt and Nettie Rogers Shuler, *Woman Suffrage and Politics: The Inner Story of the Suffrage Movement* (New York: Charles Scribner's Sons, 1926), 281; National American Woman Suffrage Association, *Victory: How Women Won It, a Centennial Symposium, 1840–1940* (New York: H.W. Wilson Company, 1940), 107.

7. "Votes by State," 1916 Election for the Thirty-Third Term, Electoral Statistics, https://www.archives.gov/ (accessed December 5, 2015); Office of Clerks, US House of Representatives, "Congressional Apportionment," 64th Congress, http://www.census.gov/library/publications/1975/compendia/hist_stats_colonial-1970.html (accessed December 5, 2015); David Kevin McDonald, "Organizing Womanhood: Women's Culture and the Politics of Woman Suffrage in New York State, 1865–1917" (PhD diss., State University of New York at Stony Brook, 1987), 1.

8. Catt and Shuler, *Woman Suffrage and Politics*, 280–81; National American Woman Suffrage Association, *Victory*, 107; Alexander Keyssar, *The Right to Vote: The Contested History of Democracy in the United States* (New York: Basic Books, 2000), 214–15.

9. Some sources focused on the origin of the movement in New York State include Judith Wellman, *The Road to Seneca Falls: Elizabeth Cady Stanton and the First Woman's Rights Convention* (Urbana: University of Illinois Press, 2004); Lori D. Ginzberg, *Untidy Origins: A Story of Woman's Rights in Antebellum New York* (Chapel Hill: University of North Carolina Press, 2005); Sallie G. McMillen, *Seneca Falls and the Origins of the Women's Rights Movement* (New York: Oxford University Press, 2008); Faye E. Dudden, *Fighting Chance: The Struggle Over Woman Suffrage and Black Suffrage in Reconstruction America* (New York: Oxford University Press, 2011); Lisa Tetrault, *The Myth of Seneca Falls: Memory and the Women's Suffrage Movement, 1848–1898* (Chapel Hill: University of North Carolina, 2014); and Laura E. Free, *Suffrage Reconstructed: Gender, Race, and Voting Rights in the Civil Rights Era* (Ithaca: Cornell

University Press, 2015). Studies of the longer New York woman suffrage movement include McDonald, "Organizing Womanhood"; Ellen Carol Dubois, *Harriot Stanton Blatch and the Winning of Woman Suffrage* (New Haven: Yale University, 1997); and Susan Goodier, *No Votes for Women: The New York Anti-Suffrage Movement* (Urbana: University of Illinois, 2013).

10. The term "upstate" is used in its broadest sense, and includes all parts of the state outside of metropolitan New York City.

11. Newspaper accounts indicate that a Young Men's Woman Suffrage League to promote woman suffrage in the United States existed from July 1874 to April 1875. See "Woman Suffrage," *New York Times*, July 16, 1874; "City and Suburban News," *New York Times*, April 21, 1875.

1. Tenuous Ties

1. Elizabeth Cady Stanton, Matilda Joslyn Gage, and Susan B. Anthony, *History of Woman Suffrage*, vol. 1 (New York: Fowler & Wells, 1881), 528–30.

2. Sue Boland, "Matilda Joslyn Gage," in *American Radical and Reform Writers*, 2nd ser., ed. Hester Lee Furey (New York: Gale Cengage Learning, 2009), 147.

3. Faye E. Dudden, *Fighting Chance: The Struggle over Woman Suffrage and Black Suffrage in Reconstruction America* (New York: Oxford University Press, 2011), 32; Judith Wellman, *The Road to Seneca Falls: Elizabeth Cady Stanton and the First Woman's Rights Convention* (Urbana: University of Illinois Press, 2004), 146; Paula Doress-Worters, ed., *Mistress of Herself: Speeches and Letters of Ernestine L. Rose, Early Women's Rights Leader* (New York: Feminist Press, 2008); Judith Wellman, "Women's Rights, Republicanism, and Revolutionary Rhetoric in Antebellum New York State," *New York History* 69 (July 1988): 354–55; Jacob Katz Cogan and Lori D. Ginzberg, "1846 Petition for Woman's Suffrage, New York State Constitutional Convention," *Signs: Journal of Women in Culture and Society* 22, no. 2 (1997): 429.

4. Cogan and Ginzberg, "1846 Petition," 429–30; Wellman, *Road to Seneca Falls*, 150. The 1911 state capitol fire destroyed the original convention records from 1846.

5. A scan of the document can be found at the New York State Archives digital collection, http://digitalcollections.archives.nysed.gov/index.php/Detail/Object/Show/object_id/10821. This act is known more commonly as the "Married Women's Property Act." For the details of the debates see Lori D. Ginzberg, *Untidy Origins: A Story of Woman's Rights in Antebellum New York* (Chapel Hill: University of North Carolina Press, 2005), 144–50, 158. In 1860, the New York State Legislature passed a law granting married women full property rights, including the right for married women to bargain, sell, and transfer property, to carry on business and wages now considered her property, to sue or be sued, and to hold joint guardianship of her children. For legislation see Dudden, *Fighting Chance*, 28–29; Wellman, *Road to Seneca Falls*, 153–54; Sally G. McMillen, *Seneca Falls and the Origins of the Women's Rights Movement* (New York: Oxford University Press, 2008), 29.

6. Wellman, *Road to Seneca Falls*, 153.

7. Dennis Landis, "Samuel Joseph May," *The Dictionary of Unitarian and Universalist Biography*, May 30, 2003, http://uudb.org/articles/samueljmay.html.

8. Wellman, *Road to Seneca Falls*, 152.

9. McMillen, *Seneca Falls*, 89; Wellman, *Road to Seneca Falls*, 183–84.

10. McMillen, *Seneca Falls*, 89–91.

11. Stanton, Gage, and Anthony, *History of Woman Suffrage*, vol. 1, 70–71; McMillen, *Seneca Falls*, 92–93, 240.

12. McMillen, *Seneca Falls*, 93–95; Wellman, *Road to Seneca Falls*, 204–5. For a discussion regarding the significance of the Seneca Falls Convention, see Lisa Tetrault, *The Myth of Seneca Falls: Memory and the Women's Suffrage Movement, 1848–1898* (Chapel Hill: University of North Carolina, 2014).

13. Ann D. Gordon, ed., *The Selected Papers of Elizabeth Cady Stanton and Susan B. Anthony*, vol. 1, *In the School of Anti-Slavery, 1840–1866* (New Brunswick, NJ: Rutgers University Press, 1997), 123.

14. Karlyn Cohrs Campbell, *Man Cannot Speak for Her: Key Texts of the Early Feminists*, vol. 2 (New York: Greenwood Press, 1989), 145–46.

15. Natasha Kirsten Kraus, *A New Type of Womanhood: Discursive Politics and Social Change in Antebellum America* (Durham, NC: Duke University, 2008), 206.

16. Wendy Hamand Venet, *Neither Ballots Nor Bullets: Women Abolitionists and the Civil War* (Charlottesville, VA: University of Virginia, 1991), 146.

17. Jeanie Attie, *Patriotic Toil: Northern Women and the American Civil War* (Ithaca, NY: Cornell University Press, 1998), 270.

18. Elizabeth Cady Stanton, Matilda Joslyn Gage, and Susan B. Anthony, *History of Woman Suffrage*, vol. 2 (New York: Fowler & Wells, 1882), 50–89; Gordon, *Selected Papers*, vol. 1, 518–22; Laura E. Free, *Suffrage Reconstructed: Gender, Race, and Voting Rights in the Civil Rights Era* (Ithaca, NY: Cornell University Press, 2015), 51–52.

19. Gordon, *Selected Papers*, vol. 1, 569.

20. While Phillips worked for women's rights for the rest of his life, he was always reluctant to discuss women's rights and black civil rights together. Dudden, *Fighting Chance*, 63.

21. Hugh Davis, *"We Will Be Satisfied With Nothing Less": The African American Struggle for Equal Rights in the North during Reconstruction* (Ithaca, NY: Cornell University Press, 2011), 2–3.

22. Stanton, Gage, and Anthony, *History of Woman Suffrage*, vol. 2, 168, 171–72; Ellen Carol DuBois, *Feminism and Suffrage: The Emergence of an Independent Women's Movement in America, 1848–1869* (Ithaca, NY: Cornell University Press, 1978), 63–64.

23. Stanton, Gage, and Anthony, *History of Woman Suffrage*, vol. 2, 172. George F. Longenhelt, a prosperous farmer and Republican legislator from Otsego County, had unexpectedly presented a resolution to the New York State Assembly in 1859 to strike the word "male" from the state constitution's voting requirements. The Assembly's adverse response to Longenhelt's proposal to extend "to females the right to vote and hold office" attracted attention in the *Troy Daily Times* but few took him seriously. "News," *Troy Daily Times*, February 7, 1859.

24. Ellen Carol Dubois, *Feminism and Suffrage*, 63; Free, *Suffrage Reconstructed*, 6; Stanton, Gage, and Anthony, *History of Woman Suffrage*, vol. 2, 170.

25. Jane Rhodes, *Mary Ann Shadd Cary: The Black Press and Protest in the Nineteenth Century* (Bloomington, IN: Indiana University Press, 1998); Free, *Suffrage Reconstructed*.

26. Libby Garland, "'Irrespective of Race, Color, or Sex': Susan B. Anthony and the New York State Constitutional Convention of 1867," *Magazine of History* 19, no. 2 (2005): 61.

27. DuBois, *Feminism and Suffrage*, 65–67.

28. Stanton, Gage, and Anthony, *History of Woman Suffrage*, vol. 2, 183.

29. Garland, "Irrespective of Race, Color, or Sex," 64.

30. "Constitution of the United States of America: Analysis and Interpretation," https://www.congress.gov/constitution-annotated/ (accessed November 13, 2015).

31. DuBois, *Feminism and Suffrage*, 163–64.

32. Ibid., 54.

33. Sally Roesch Wagner, *Sisters in Spirit: Haudenosaunee Influence on Early American Feminists* (Summertown, TN: Native Voices Book Publishing Company, 2001), 42.

34. Wagner, *Sisters in Spirit*, 42–44, 88.

35. For details of the last American Equal Rights Association convention see DuBois, *Feminism and Suffrage*, 186–91.

36. Ida Husted Harper, *The Life and Work of Susan B. Anthony*, vol. 1 (Indianapolis: Hollenbeck Press, 1898), 324.

37. Stanton, Gage, and Anthony, *History of Woman Suffrage*, vol. 2, 400; Ann D. Gordon, ed. *The Selected Papers of Elizabeth Cady Stanton and Susan B. Anthony*, vol. 2, *Against an Aristocracy of Sex, 1866–1873* (New Brunswick, NJ: Rutgers University Press, 2000), 357.

38. Gordon, *Selected Papers*, vol. 2, 242–43.

39. Harper, *Life and Work*, vol. 1, 326–27; Sherry H. Penney and James D. Livingston, *A Very Dangerous Woman: Martha Wright and Women's Rights* (Amherst, MA: University of Massachusetts Press, 2004), 182–83.

40. Dubois, *Feminism and Suffrage*, 53–78.

41. Allison Sneider, "Woman Suffrage in Congress: American Expansion and the Politics of Federalism," in Jean Baker, ed., *Votes for Women: The Struggle for Suffrage Revisited* (New York: Oxford University Press, 2002), 77–87.

42. Penney and Livingston, "Getting to the Source: Hints for Wives—and Husbands," *Journal of Women's History* 15, no. 2 (Summer 2003): 183.

43. Paula Baker, *The Moral Frameworks of Public Life: Gender, Politics, and the State in Rural New York, 1870–1930* (New York: Oxford University, 1991), 74, 117.

44. "Officers and Members of the New York State Woman Suffrage Association," Minutes Book, vol. 1, pp. 1–8, box 1, MS 1369, Woman Suffrage Association of New York State and Woman Suffrage Party of New York City Records, 1869–1919, Rare Book and Manuscript Library, Butler Library, Columbia University, New York, NY.

45. Susan B. Anthony wrote many letters inviting prominent women around the country to attend the founding meeting of the New York association. Mary Rice Livermore, for example, responded to Anthony from Chicago, telling her that she could not attend the meeting in Saratoga. Gordon, *Selected Papers*, vol. 2, 251.

46. New York State Woman Suffrage Association Minutes Book, vol. 1, p. 1, box 1, MS 1369, Woman Suffrage Association of New York State and Woman Suffrage Party of New York City Records, 1869–1919, Rare Book and Manuscript Library, Butler Library, Columbia University.

47. Ten women served the New York State Woman Suffrage Association as presidents between 1869 and 1917: Martha Coffin Wright (1869–75), Matilda Joslyn Gage (1875–76, 1878), Susan B. Anthony (1876–77), Lillie Devereux Blake (1879–90), Jean Brooks Greenleaf (1890–96), Mariana Wright Chapman (1896–1902), Ella Hawley

Crossett (1902–10), Harriet May Mills (1910–13), Gertrude Foster Brown (1913–15), and Vira Boarman Whitehouse (1915–17). New York State Woman Suffrage Association Minutes Book, vol. 1, 2–8, MS 1369, Woman Suffrage Association of New York State and Woman Suffrage Party of New York City Records, 1869–1919, Rare Book and Manuscript Library, Butler Library, Columbia University, New York, NY. Ann D. Gordon, ed., *The Selected Papers of Elizabeth Cady Stanton and Susan B. Anthony*, vol. 4, *When Clowns Make Laws for Queens, 1880–1887* (New Brunswick, NJ: Rutgers University Press, 2006), 156–57.

48. It is not clear how many women founded formal suffrage or women's rights clubs as a result of Gage's tour. There is limited evidence that representatives of some of these county groups attended the New York State Woman Suffrage Association conferences. For example, Calista Andrews from McLean, near Groton, New York, in her role as suffrage representative of Tompkins County, attended the May 1878 convention in New York City. Lucy Hawley Calkins from Ithaca in Tompkins County attended the Buffalo Convention at Castle Inn in 1902 as a delegate. Convention Minutes, New York State Woman Suffrage Association, vol. 1 and vol. 5, box 1, box 1, Woman Suffrage Association of New York State and Woman Suffrage Party of New York City Records, 1869–1919, Rare Book and Manuscript Library, Butler Library, Columbia University.

49. "New York State Woman Suffrage Society," Lillie Devereux Blake Collection, Missouri History Museum Archives, St. Louis, MO.

50. Ibid.

51. President Blake did not call a convention in 1880. According to Ronald Yanosky, that year Blake lobbied at major party conventions that year, which likely interfered with her calling a suffrage convention. Yanosky, "Blake, Lillie Devereux," *American National Biography Online*, http://www.anb.org/articles/15/15-00067.html (accessed December 10, 2013).

52. Martha Coffin Wright to Susan B. Anthony, letter dated Auburn, June 25, 1874. Ann D. Gordon, ed., *The Selected Papers of Elizabeth Cady Stanton and Susan B. Anthony*, vol. 3, *National Protection for National Citizens, 1873 to 1880* (New Brunswick, NJ: Rutgers University Press, 2003), 90.

53. New York State Woman Suffrage Association Minutes Book, vol. 1, pp. 1–8, box 1, MS 1369, Woman Suffrage Association of New York State and Woman Suffrage Party of New York City Records, 1869–1919, Rare Book and Manuscript Library, Butler Library, Columbia University.

54. Dennis Landis, "Samuel Joseph May," *Dictionary of Unitarian and Universalist Biography*, http://uudb.org/articles/samueljmay.html, May 30, 2003.

55. Penney and Livingston, *A Very Dangerous Woman*, 186, 227; Penney and Livingston, "Getting to the Source: Hints for Wives—and Husbands," 184; *Revolution 3* (February 4, 1869), 66.

56. Wright complained of exhaustion and feeling unwell. Martha Coffin Wright, diaries, box 271, Garrison Family Papers, Sophia Smith Collection, Smith College, Northampton, MA.

57. Penney and Livingston, *A Very Dangerous Woman* 186.

58. "Woman Suffrage," hand dated May 11, 1876. Unattributed newspaper clipping attached to New York State Woman Suffrage Association Minutes Book, vol. 1,

p. 12, box 1, MS 1369, Woman Suffrage Association of New York State and Woman Suffrage Party of New York City Records, 1869–1919, Rare Book and Manuscript Library, Butler Library, Columbia University.

59. Eleanor Flexner and Ellen Fitzpatrick, *Century of Struggle: The Woman's Rights Movement in the United States* (Cambridge: Belknap Press, 1996 [1959]), 163–64; Boland, "Matilda Joslyn Gage," 144–48.

60. "Annual Convention of the State Woman Suffrage Association at Masonic Hall Yesterday—A Plea for Woman's Enfranchisement—Governor Robinson Denounced," unattributed newspaper clipping attached to New York State Woman Suffrage Association Minutes Book, vol. 1, box 1, p. 16, MS 1369, Woman Suffrage Association of New York State and Woman Suffrage Party of New York City Records, 1869–1919, Rare Book and Manuscript Library, Butler Library, Columbia University.

61. Boland, "Matilda Joslyn Gage," 147.

62. Stanton, Gage, and Anthony, *History of Woman Suffrage*, vol. 3, 4–6.

63. Gordon, *Selected Papers*, vol. 4, 444–45.

64. *New York World*, May 23, 1868.

65. Gordon, *Selected Papers*, vol. 2, 650.

66. Matilda Joslyn Gage, "Women Taxpayer," *Weekly Recorder* (Manlius), August 3, 1871, copy in collection of Sally Roesch Wagner.

67. *Woman's Journal*, November 15, 1873; Gordon, *Selected Papers*, vol. 2, 610.

68. Boland, "Matilda Joslyn Gage," 147–48.

69. Farrell, *Lillie Devereux Blake*, 152.

70. Elizabeth Cady Stanton, Susan B. Anthony, and Matilda Joslyn Gage, eds., *History of Woman Suffrage*, vol. 3 (Rochester: Susan B. Anthony, 1886), 417, 422–23; Grace Farrell, *Lillie Devereux Blake: Retracing a Life Erased* (Amherst, MA: University of Massachusetts Press, 2002), 152.

71. Farrell, *Lillie Devereux Blake*, 152; Matilda Joslyn Gage, "To the People of the State of New York," *National Citizen and Ballot Box* 4, no. 5 (September 1879), 4.

72. Farrell, *Lillie Devereux Blake*, 153. Cornell did not fully support women's rights, however, and was "found wanting in courage and conscience" when it came to signing the bill providing for the hiring of police matrons, another of Blake's causes. *Who's Who in New York City and State* (New York: L. R. Hamersly, 1904), 64; Stanton, Anthony, and Gage, *History of Woman Suffrage*, vol. 3, 432–33.

73. Lillie Devereux Blake, "The School Elections," unattributed newspaper clipping (August 18, 1880), copy in the collection of Sally Roesch Wagner; "City and Suburban News," *New York Times*, February 24, 1880, 8.

74. Barbara Rivette, *Fayetteville's First Woman Voter* (Fayetteville, NY: Matilda Joslyn Gage Foundation, 2006).

75. Stanton, Gage, and Anthony, *History of Woman Suffrage*, vol. 3 429–30.

76. "Clemence S. Lozier," *Woman's Words* (n.d.), box 2, Woman Suffrage Association of New York State and Woman Suffrage Party of New York City Records, 1869–1919, Rare Book and Manuscript Library, Butler Library, Columbia University.

77. Gordon, *Selected Papers*, vol. 4, 467; New York State Woman Suffrage Association Minutes Book, vol. 1, p. 23, box 1, MS 1369, Woman Suffrage Association of New York State and Woman Suffrage Party of New York City Records, 1869–1919, Rare Book and Manuscript Library, Butler Library, Columbia University.

78. The full text of Gage's *Woman, Church, and State* may be found at http://www.sacred-texts.com/wmn/wcs/index.htm (accessed December 15, 2013).

79. Jean H. Baker, *Sisters: The Lives of America's Suffragists* (New York: Hill and Wang, 2005), 132.

80. "Friends of Woman Suffrage," *New York Times*, October 28, 1886, 8.

81. "Woman Suffrage," unattributed newspaper clipping attached to New York State Woman Suffrage Association Minutes Book, vol. 1, p. 15, pp. 61–62, box 1, MS 1369, Woman Suffrage Association of New York State and Woman Suffrage Party of New York City Records, 1869–1919, Rare Book and Manuscript Library, Butler Library, Columbia University.

82. Farrell, *Lillie Devereux Blake*, 155; Sally Roesch Wagner, *A Time of Protest: Suffragists Challenge the Republic: 1870–1887* (Aberdeen: Sky Carrier Press, 1992), 111–14.

83. Unattributed broadside in the collection of Sally Roesch Wagner.

84. "The Exact Legal Status of Women in New-York," *New York Tribune*, December 18, 1869.

85. Stanton, Anthony, and Gage, *History of Woman Suffrage*, vol. 3, 418–19.

86. Gerda Lerner, "Forward," in Ellen Carol DuBois, *The Elizabeth Cady Stanton-Susan B. Anthony Reader: Correspondence, Writings, Speeches* (Boston, MA: Northeastern University, 1992), x–xi.

87. Gage strongly upheld the separation of church and state and perceived the suffrage movement as secular rather than embodying a religious component. Ann D. Gordon, ed., *The Selected Papers of Elizabeth Cady Stanton and Susan B. Anthony*, vol. 5, *The Place inside the Body-Politic, 1887 to 1895* (New Brunswick, NJ: Rutgers University, 2009), 68, 223.

88. Ibid., 219; Ruth Ellen Williamson Drish, "Susan B. Anthony De-Radicalizes, Re-Organizes, and Re-Unites the American Woman Suffrage Movement: 1880–1890" (PhD diss., University of Iowa, 1985), 88–95.

89. "Constitution of the New York State Woman Suffrage Association" (1890), New York State Woman Suffrage Association Minutes Book, vol. 1, p. 103, box 1, MS 1369, Woman Suffrage Association of New York State and Woman Suffrage Party of New York City Records, 1869–1919, Rare Book and Manuscript Library, Butler Library, Columbia University.

90. New York State Woman Suffrage Association Minutes Book, vol. 1, p. 93–94, box 1, MS 1369, Woman Suffrage Association of New York State and Woman Suffrage Party of New York City Records, 1869–1919, Rare Book and Manuscript Library, Butler Library, Columbia University.

91. Flexner and Fitzpatrick, *Century of Struggle*, 221-22.

92. New York State Woman Suffrage Association Minutes Book, vol. 3, p. 151, box 1, MS 1369, Woman Suffrage Association of New York State and Woman Suffrage Party of New York City Records, 1869–1919, Rare Book and Manuscript Library, Butler Library, Columbia University.

93. Yanosky, "Blake, Lillie Devereux."

94. Letter, Susan B. Anthony to Mariana W. Chapman, dated March 8, 1897, Mariana Wright Chapman Family Papers, http://www.swarthmore.edu/Library/friends/ead/MWC/MWCselections3.htm (accessed Apr. 9, 2012).

95. Alan P. Grimes, *The Puritan Ethic and Woman Suffrage* (New York: Oxford University Press, 1967), 11.

96. "The Women of New York and the Ballot," *Harper's Weekly* 6, no. 11 (1881), 374. Both suffragists and anti-suffragists suggested that women be polled, but it did not happen until 1895 when women were polled in Massachusetts.

2. "Ruffling the Somewhat Calm Domain"

1. Jennie O. Curtis [Mrs. H. W.] Cannon, "Report (1914)," box 1, p. 5, New York Woman Suffrage Collection, Collection 8041, 1914–1915, Division of Rare and Manuscript Collections, Carl A. Kroch Library, Cornell University.

2. Paula Baker, "The Domestication of Politics: Women and American Political Society, 1780–1920," in *Women, the State, and Welfare*, ed. Linda Gordon (Madison: University of Wisconsin Press, 1990), 620–64; Carroll Smith-Rosenberg, *Disorderly Conduct: Visions of Gender in Victorian America* (New York: Oxford University Press, 1985), 1–29; David Kevin McDonald, "Organizing Womanhood: Women's Culture and the Politics of Woman Suffrage in New York State, 1865–1917" (PhD diss., State University of New York at Stony Brook, 1987), 62.

3. Donald H. Parkerson, *The Agricultural Transition in New York State: Markets and Migration in Mid-Nineteenth Century America* (Ames: Iowa State University Press, 1995), 64; Thomas J. Schlereth, *Victorian America: Transformations in Everyday Life, 1876–1915* (New York: Harper Perennial, 1991), 233; Susan Strasser, *Never Done: A History of American Housework* (New York: Henry Holt and Company, 1982), 18.

4. Grey Osterud, *Putting the Barn before the House: Women and Family Farming in Early Twentieth-Century New York* (Ithaca, NY: Cornell University Press, 2012), 91–92, 106–7.

5. Walter A. Friedman, *Birth of a Salesman: The Transformation of Selling in America* (Cambridge, MA: Harvard University Press, 2004), 95–96. See also Grace PerLee Howe, *Gone Are the Days* (Ithaca, NY: Cayuga Press, 1952).

6. Karen Pastorello, *The Progressives: Activism and Reform in American Society, 1893–1917* (Boston: Wiley Blackwell, 2014), 29.

7. In 1910, roughly 21 percent of the state's population lived in rural areas, down from 42 percent in 1880, reflecting in part the high rate of migration to urban areas. United States Census Bureau, *Historical Abstracts of the United States: Colonial Times to 1957* (Washington, DC: Government Printing Office, 1960), 12; Richard L. McCormick, *From Realignment to Reform: Political Change in New York State, 1893–1910* (Ithaca, NY: Cornell University Press, 1979), 27–28; Elmer Fippin, *Rural New York* (Port Washington, NY: Kennikat Press, 1921), 40.

8. Paul E. Johnson, *A Shopkeeper's Millennium: Society and Revivals in Rochester, New York, 1815–1837* (New York: Hill and Wang, 1978), 108; Nancy A. Hewitt, *Women's Activism and Social Change: Rochester, New York, 1822–1872* (Ithaca, NY: Cornell University Press, 1984), 205; McDonald, "Organizing Womanhood," 160–68, 554, 560, 562. See also Whitney Cross, *The Burned-over District: The Social and Intellectual History of Enthusiastic Religion in Western New York, 1800–1850* (Ithaca, NY: Cornell University Press, 1950); Judith Wellman, *Grassroots Reform in the Burned-over District of Upstate New York* (New York: Garland, 2000).

9. Hewitt, *Women's Activism*, 201–2, 206–7. Women often traveled into urban areas from neighboring towns and villages and were exposed to urban activism. Much has been chronicled by Kathryn Kish Sklar, "The Historical Foundations of Women's Power in the Creation of the American Welfare State, 1830–1930," in *Mothers of a New World: Maternalist Politics and the Origins of Welfare States*, ed. Seth Koven and Sonya Michel (New York: Routledge, 1993), 163. See also Teri Gay, *Strength without Compromise: Womanly Influence and Political Identity in Turn-of-the-Twentieth Century*

Rural Upstate New York (New York: Ballston Lake, 2009); and John Burdick, "Political Equality Club of Clinton: An Analysis of the Intellectual, Professional, Religious, and Social Influences of their Fifty-Six Members circa 1911," June 14, 2013, unpublished paper, Clinton Political Equality Club Papers, Clinton Historical Society, Clinton, NY; Lucy (Mrs. H.) Calkins, "Political Study Club: Development of Woman Suffrage in Ithaca, 1899–1917," vol. 2, Minutes Book, Records of the Ithaca Women's Political Study Club, History Center, Ithaca, New York.

10. John Phillips and Fenwick Y. Hedley Downs, eds. *History of Chautauqua County New York, and Its People,* vol. 1 (New York: American Historical Society, 1921), 72, 219.

11. Caroline Cowles Richards, *Village Life in America, 1852–1872, Including the Period of the American Civil War as Told in the Diary of a School-Girl* (New York: Henry Holt and Company, 1913), 50.

12. Lisa Tetrault, "The Incorporation of American Feminism: Suffragists and the Postbellum Lyceum," *Journal of American History* 96, no. 4 (March 2010): 1032.

13. Elizabeth Cady Stanton, *Eighty Years and More: Reminiscences 1815–1897* (Boston: Northeastern University Press, 1993), 259–82; Elisabeth Griffith, *In Her Own Right: The Life of Elizabeth Cady Stanton* (New York: Oxford University Press, 1984), 161–62, 165.

14. Lisa Shawn Hogan, "Elizabeth Cady Stanton, 'Our Girls' (Winter 1880)," http://archive.vod.umd.edu/justice/stanton1880int.htm#_edn39 (accessed January 3, 2016); Stanton, *Reminiscences,* 252.

15. Joseph E. Gould, *The Chautauqua Movement: An Episode in the Continuing Revolution* (Albany: University of New York Press, 1961), 73–81, 83.

16. Carolyn Ostrander, informal interview by authors, January 5, 2016. Ostrander asserts that Kelley also saw the organization as a way to bridge the North and the South.

17. Andrew Baugnet, "Picturing the Grange: 130 Years," *Voices: The Journal of New York Folklore* 28 (Spring–Summer 2002): 1.

18. For dates of grange inceptions in New York, see Leonard L. Allen, *History of the New York State Grange* (Watertown, NY: Hungerford-Holbrook Co., 1934), appendix.

19. Mrs. H. W. Cannon, "Report (1914)," box 1, p. 5, New York Woman Suffrage Collection, Collection 8041, 1914–1915, Division of Rare and Manuscript Collections, Carl A. Kroch Library, Cornell University.

20. Paula Baker, *The Moral Frameworks of Public Life: Gender, Politics, and the State in Rural New York, 1870–1930* (New York: Oxford University Press, 1991), 145.

21. Donald B. Marti, *Women of the Grange: Mutuality and Sisterhood in Rural America, 1866–1920* (Westport, CT: Greenwood Press, 1991), 1–2, 108–9; Marilyn P. Watkins, *Rural Democracy: Family Farmers and Politics in Western Washington* (Ithaca, NY: Cornell University Press, 1995), 97–98.

22. Gay, *Strength without Compromise,* 48–49, 72; Marti, *Women of the Grange,* 8, 147.

23. Osterud, *Putting the Barn,* 78–79.

24. Marti, *Women of the Grange,* 7.

25. Ibid., 9; Allen, *History,* 187; Esther L. Ormsby Historical Sketch, February 1913, #4035, Division of Rare and Manuscript Collections, Carl A. Kroch Library, Cornell University, Ithaca, NY.

26. Marti, *Women of the Grange,* 111–14.

27. Mary A. Livermore, "A Word to Women," unidentified newspaper article, August 7, 1884, Suffrage Folder, Cortland County Historical Society, Cortland, New York; ibid., 111–13.

28. Allen, *History*, 63.

29. According to Carolyn Ostrander, a Subordinate Grange is a local grange with at least thirteen charter members, at least four to six of whom should be women. Pomona Grange is at the county level.

30. "Eliza Cornelia (Robertson) Gifford," in *Genealogical and Family History of Western New York: A Record of the Achievement of Her People in the Making of a Commonwealth and the Building of a Nation* vol. 3, ed. William Richard Cutter (New York: Lewis Publishing Company, 1912), 1127.

31. The New York State Grange of the Patrons of Husbandry and the Constitutional Convention, Twenty-Sixth Annual New York State Woman Suffrage Association Convention Report, Ithaca, New York, November 12–15, 1894, Jon A. Lindseth Woman Suffrage Collection, Collection 8002, Division of Rare and Manuscript Collections, Carl A. Kroch Library, Cornell University; Nancy Osterud, *Bonds of Community: The Lives of Farm Women in Nineteenth-Century New York* (Ithaca, NY: Cornell University Press, 1991), 260.

32. Donald Marti, "Sisters of the Grange: Rural Feminism in the Late Nineteenth Century," *Agricultural History* 58 (July 1984): 247–61; Baker, *Moral Frameworks*, 286.

33. Susan B. Anthony to Mrs. Eliza C. Gifford, May 22, 1900, Chautauqua County Historical Society, Westfield, New York.

34. "Report of Mrs. H. W. Cannon 1914," Jon A. Lindseth Woman Suffrage Collection, Collection 8002, Division of Rare and Manuscript Collections, Carl A. Kroch Library, Cornell University.

35. "Few Seats for Men on Suffrage Day," *New York Times*, February 22, 1911, 3.

36. Barbara Leslie Epstein, *Politics of Domesticity: Women, Evangelicalism, and Temperance in Nineteenth-Century America* (Middletown, CT: Wesleyan University Press, 1981), 109–10.

37. Baker, *Moral Frameworks*, 63.

38. Inez Haynes Irwin, *Angels and Amazons: One Hundred Years of American Women* (New York: Doubleday, Doran and Co., 1933), 70–73; Jack S. Blocker, Jr., *American Temperance Movements: Cycles of Reform* (Boston: Twayne Publishers, 1989), 50–51.

39. Irwin, *Angels and Amazons*, 70–73; Elizabeth Cady Stanton, Matilda Joslyn Gage, and Susan B. Anthony, *History of Woman Suffrage*, vol. 1 (New York: Fowler & Wells, 1881), 449, 490.

40. Stanton, Gage, and Anthony, *History of Woman Suffrage*, vol. 1, 500–515; Hewitt, *Women's Activism*, 163–65.

41. N. H. Daniels, *The Temperance Reform and Its Great Reformers* (New York: Nelson and Phillips, 1878), 252–53; Georgeanna M. Gardenier and Frances W. Graham, *Two Decades: A History of the First Twenty Years' Work of the Women's Christian Temperance Union of the State of New York, 1874–1894* (Oswego: R. J. Oliphant, 1894), 15; Elizabeth Putnam Gordon, *Women Torch-Bearers: The Story of the Woman's Christian Temperance Union* (Evanston, IL: National Woman's Christian Temperance Union, 1924), 11–12, 246; Blocker, *American Temperance Movements*, 79–80.

42. Gardenier and Graham, *Two Decades*, 16.

43. Baker, *Moral Frameworks*, 64–65; Epstein, *Politics of Domesticity*, 118–19.

44. Carolyn De Swarte Gifford and Amy R. Slagell, eds., *Let Something Good Be Said: Speeches and Writings of Frances E. Willard* (Urbana: University of Illinois Press, 2007), 24.

45. Biography, Frances Willard House Museum and Archives, https://franceswillard house.org/frances-willard/biography/ (accessed January 4, 2016). Genesee College eventually closed and became part of Syracuse University. See http://archives.syr. edu/collections/org_non_su/sua_gnc.htm (accessed January 4, 2016). For additional biographical information on Frances Willard, see Anna Adams Gordon, *The Life of Frances Willard* (Evanston, IL: National Woman's Christian Temperance Union, 1912).

46. Susan B. Anthony to Frances Willard, September 18, 1876, Woman's Christian Temperance and Prohibition Papers Series III, *Union Signal* Series XXI, roll 1, Subseries II, Frances E. Willard Memorial Library and Archives, Chicago, IL; Ruth Bordin, *Frances Willard: A Biography* (Chapel Hill: University of North Carolina Press, 1986), 98–99.

47. Gifford and Slagell, *Let Something Good*, 17–25.

48. Bordin, *Frances Willard*, 100.

49. Willard had clashed openly with Wittenmyer over policy including the publication of pro-suffrage articles in the *Union Signal*. Epstein, *Politics of Domesticity*, 119; Blocker, *American Temperance Movements*, 80–81; Robert J. Dinkin, *Before Equal Suffrage: Women in Partisan Politics from Colonial Times to 1920* (Westport, CT: Greenwood Press, 1995), 84–85.

50. Epstein, *Politics of Domesticity*, 120, 128–29.

51. Frances Elizabeth Willard, *Home Protection Manual* (New York: The Independent Office, 1879), 5, 8, 13–14. Women Working, 1800–1930, Harvard University Open Collections Program, https://iiif.lib.harvard.edu/manifests/view/drs:2574374$1i (accessed October 16, 2015).

52. Donald C. Swift, *Religion and the American Experience: A Social and Cultural History, 1765–1997* (Armonk, NY: M. E. Sharpe, 1998), 114.

53. Since the earliest leaders of the state Woman's Christian Temperance Union were not necessarily supportive of women's right to vote, they did not officially endorse suffrage until 1885 during Mary Towne Burt's presidency. Epstein, *Politics of Domesticity*, 124–25; Frances W. Graham, *Sixty Years of Action: A History of Sixty Years' Work of the Women's Christian Temperance Union of the State of New York, 1874–1894* (New York: Women's Christian Temperance Union, 1934), 130.

54. Dinkin, *Before Equal Suffrage*, 84–85; Blocker, *American Temperance Movements*, 87–88.

55. Ruth Ellen Williamson Drise, "Susan B. Anthony De-Radicalizes, De-Organizes, and Re-Unites the American Woman Suffrage Movement, 1880–1890" (PhD diss., University of Iowa, 1985), 121–22.

56. Dinkin, *Before Equal Suffrage*, 83–88; Baker, "Domestication of Politics," 620–47.

57. Baker, *Moral Frameworks*, 64–72.

58. William Travers Jerome, *The Liquor Tax Law in New York: A Plea for the Opening of Saloons on Sunday* (New York: G. P. Putnam's Sons, 1905), 52.

59. Susan Dye Lee, "Ella Boole," in *Notable American Women: The Modern Period*, ed. Barbara Sicherman and Carol Hurd Green (Cambridge, MA: Belknap Press of Harvard University, 1980), 91–92; Bordin, *Frances Willard*, 148–49.

60. New York Woman Suffrage Association Minutes Book, vol. 1, p. 112, box 1, and vol. 2, p. 68, box 2, MS 1369, Woman Suffrage Association of New York State and Woman Suffrage Party of New York City Records, 1869–1919, Rare Book and Manuscript Library, Butler Library, Columbia University.

61. Joseph Rowntree and Arthur Sherwell, *The Temperance Problem and Social Reform* (London: Hodder and Stoughton, 1901), 374–85; Gardenier and Graham, *Two Decades*, 87.

62. Charlotte A. Baldridge, "Woman's Work in the Christian Temperance Union," Scrapbook 3, p. 22, Miller National American Woman Suffrage Association Suffrage Scrapbooks, 1897–1911, Library of Congress, Rare Book and Special Collections Division, Washington, DC. Epstein, *Politics of Domesticity*, 120.

63. Baker, "Domestication of Politics," 637–38; McDonald, "Organizing Womanhood," 127.

64. "Suffrage Shock for Governor Hughes at Hearing," Albany, New York, December 22, 1909, Scrapbook 8, p. 38, Miller National American Woman Suffrage Association Suffrage Scrapbooks, 1897–1911, Library of Congress, Rare Book and Special Collections Division, Washington, DC; Gordon, *Women Torch-Bearers*, 260. Members of the New York women's clubs began to concentrate on suffrage goals well before the New York State Federation of Women's Clubs officially endorsed it. After years of association with the suffragists, the New York State Federation of Women's Clubs finally passed a suffrage resolution in 1912. Mary Garrett Hay was president of the New York State Federation of Women's Clubs (1910–12), director of the General Federation of Women's Clubs (1914–18) and president of the New York State Equal Suffrage League. Karen J. Blair, *The Clubwoman as Feminist: True Womanhood Redefined, 1868–1914* (New York: Holmes & Meier Publishers, 1980), 156.

65. Epstein, *Politics of Domesticity*, 147.

66. Although New York City contained 50 percent of the state's population, only 15 percent of New York State Woman Suffrage Association members resided in New York City. The movement there remained relatively weak and isolated until after 1909, when Alva Belmont paid for the move of national suffrage headquarters to New York City. McDonald, "Organizing Womanhood," 60–62, 71.

67. McDonald, "Organizing Womanhood," 60–71.

68. Baker, *Moral Frameworks*, 73.

69. McDonald, "Organizing Womanhood," 60–62, 71.

70. Martha Fuller Prather, "Equal Suffrage," p. 3, 1919 lecture for the Chautauqua County Historical Society, McClurg Museum, Westfield, New York.

71. According to Martha Prather, the suffrage groups that comprised the county organization were Carroll, Charlotte, Cherry Creek, Ellery, Gerry, Harmony, Kiantone, Kennedy, Mayville, Stockton, Sinclairville, Randolph, and the Pomona (county) and Ross Grange. Prather, "Equal Suffrage," 4. See also John Phillips Downs and Fenwick Y. Hedley, eds., *History of Chautauqua County New York, and Its People*, vol. 1 (New York: American Historical Society, 1921), 351.

72. "Women on the Platform: Mrs. Wallace and Others Speak for Woman Suffrage," *New York Times*, July 26, 1891, 8. Ithaca History Center, Ithaca, New York.

73. Ibid.

74. Prather, "Equal Rights," 7. See also "Political Equality Day," *Dunkirk Evening Observer*, April 7, 1892; "Political Equality Day at Chautauqua," *Westfield Republican*, July 19, 1893, 8; "Political Equality Day at Chautauqua," *Westfield Republican*,

July 19, 1899, 8; and "Political Equality Day," *Dunkirk Evening Observer*, February 9, 1908. Downs and Henley, *History of Chautauqua County*, vol. 1, 352. Political Equality Day has been on the program of the Chautauqua Institute from 1891 to the present.

75. New York State Woman Suffrage Association, "1894 Constitutional-Amendment Campaign Year," report of the New York State Woman Suffrage Association, Twenty-Sixth Annual Convention, Ithaca, New York, November 12–15 (Rochester, NY: Charles Mann Printer, 1895), 188; Marti, *Women of the Grange*, 114.

76. New York State Woman Suffrage Association, "1894 Constitutional-Amendment Campaign Year," 222.

77. Ida Husted Harper, *The Life and Work of Susan B. Anthony*, vol. 2 (Indianapolis: Hollenbeck Press, 1898), 760–61.

78. "Western New York Suffragists: Winning the Vote," www.winningthevote. org (accessed October 15, 2015); Susan B. Anthony and Ida Husted Harper, eds., *History of Woman Suffrage*, vol. 4 (Indianapolis: Hollenbeck Press, 1902), 247–48.

79. McDonald, "Organizing Womanhood," 42–43, 151.

80. Frances Maule and Annie Gertrude Webb, *Woman Suffrage: History, Arguments, and Results* (Utica: New York State Legislature, 1894), 228; Anthony and Harper, *History of Woman Suffrage*, vol. 4, 848–50; New York State Woman Suffrage, "1894 Constitutional-Amendment Campaign Year," 138–44; "Western New York Suffragists," www.winningthevote.org.

81. Susan B. Anthony to Mariana W. Chapman, December 27, 1896, Mariana Wright Chapman Family Papers, Friends Historical Library, Swarthmore College Archives, Swarthmore, PA.

82. Anthony and Harper, *History of Woman Suffrage*, vol. 4, 848–49.

83. Ida Husted Harper, *Life and Work of Susan B. Anthony*, vol. 2, 767–68; "Western New York Suffragists," www.winningthevote.org.

84. New York State Woman Suffrage Association, "1894 Constitutional-Amendment Campaign Year," 193.

85. "Address Delivered by the Hon. Elihu Root before the New York State Constitutional Convention on August 15, 1894," box 5, folder 6, S-446, Jon A. Lindseth Suffrage Collection, Collection 8002, Division of Rare and Manuscript Collections, Carl A. Kroch Library, Cornell University; Ellen Carol DuBois, *Harriot Stanton Blatch and the Winning of Woman Suffrage* (New Haven: Yale University Press, 1997), 167.

86. "Western New York Suffragists," www.winningthevote.org.

87. New York State Woman Suffrage Association, "1894 Constitutional-Amendment Campaign Year," 166–67; Anthony and Harper, *History of Woman Suffrage*, vol. 4, 247–48.

88. "Political Equality Day," *Wyoming County Times* (Warsaw, New York), September 20, 1894, 4.

89. Susan Goodier, "Anti-Suffragists at the 1894 New York State Constitutional Convention," chap. 1 in Goodier, *No Votes for Women: The New York State Anti-Suffrage Movement* (Urbana: University of Illinois Press, 2013).

90. During the 1894 state campaign approximately 15 percent of the state's voters signed the woman suffrage petitions. A closer examination reveals that in the cities of New York, Brooklyn, and Buffalo the number of signatures was approximately 5 percent compared to the 25 percent upstate. McDonald, "Organizing Womanhood," 151.

91. McDonald, "Organizing Womanhood," 61.

92. "Western New York Suffragists," www.winningthevote.org.

93. McDonald, "Organizing Womanhood," 62.

94. Rosemary Fry Plakas, "Catch the Suffragists' Spirit: The Millers' Suffrage Scrapbooks," introduction to the Miller National American Woman Suffrage Association Suffrage Scrapbooks, 1897–1911, Library of Congress, Rare Book and Special Collections Division, Washington, DC; St. Lawrence Branch of the American Association of University Women, "Marion Sanger Frank: Ogdensburg Suffragist," http://stlawrence.aauw-nys.org/frank.htm (accessed February 17, 2016).

95. McDonald, "Organizing Womanhood," 329.

96. McDonald notes that when New York City leaders blocked the submission of suffrage groups to the state federation, small town leaders formed the Western New York Federation of Women's Clubs. Ibid., 56.

97. McDonald, "Organizing Womanhood," 56.

98. Prather, "Equal Suffrage," 7. Ann Gordon calls Chautauqua County the best organized county in the nation, according to Judy Wellman, "Buildings, Hideaways, Papers, and Dreams: Evidence and Inference in Women's History," presentation, Upstate New York Women's History Organization Conference, Seneca Falls, September 19, 2015.

99. New York State Woman Suffrage Association Minutes Book, vol. 3, p. 85, box 1, MS 1369, Woman Suffrage Association of New York State and Woman Suffrage Party of New York City Records, 1869–1919, Rare Book and Manuscript Library, Butler Library, Columbia University.; "Anne Fitzhugh Miller," Western New York Suffragists: Winning the Vote, https://rrlc.org/winningthevote/biographies/anne-fitzhugh-miller (accessed February 17, 2016).

100. New York Woman Suffrage Association, "Women are Interested and So Are Men," (flyer) 1910, Scrapbook 8, p. 162, Miller National American Woman Suffrage Association Scrapbooks, 1897–1911, Library of Congress, Rare Book and Special Collections Division, Washington, DC.

101. Harriet May Mills, "New York State Woman Suffrage Association Newsletter," March 1901, Scrapbook 3, p. 73, Miller National American Woman Suffrage Association Scrapbooks, 1897–1911, Library of Congress, Rare Book and Special Collections Division, Washington, DC.

102. Hilda R. Watrous, *Harriet May Mills (1857–1935): A Biography* (Syracuse: New York State Fair, 1984), 8.

103. Mills, "Newsletter," March 1901, Scrapbook 3, p. 73, Miller National American Woman Suffrage Association Scrapbooks, 1897–1911, Library of Congress, Rare Book and Special Collections Division, Washington, DC.

104. Lyman Ward, "Emily Howland, Litt. D," *The Industrial Student* 26, no.10 (November 1926), 1, referenced in United States Department of the Interior, National Park Service, National Register of Historic Places, "Sherwood Equal Rights Historic District: National Register Significance Sheet," 26. "Financial Report of the Seventh Campaign District, Being the Counties of Livingston, Monroe, Ontario, Seneca, Steuben, Wayne, and Yates," February 1, 1914–December 31, 1915, Emma Biddlecom Sweet Papers, box 3, folder 3, Manuscript and Special Collections, Rush Rhees Library, University of Rochester, Rochester, New York.

105. Prather, "Equal Suffrage," 8.

106. New York State Woman Suffrage Association Minutes Book, vol. 3, p. 55, box 1, MS 1369, Woman Suffrage Association of New York State and Woman Suffrage Party of New York City Records, 1869–1919, Rare Book and Manuscript Library, Butler Library, Columbia University.

107. Harriet May Mills, "To the Political Equality Clubs of New York," *Newsletter*, February 7, 1900, and Harriet May Mills, "To the Political Equality Clubs of New York," *Newsletter*, April 1901, Scrapbook 3, p. 74, Miller National American Woman Suffrage Association Scrapbooks, 1897–1911, Library of Congress, Rare Book and Special Collections Division, Washington, DC. Baker, *Moral Frameworks*, 74; Gay, *Strength without Compromise*, 56. For details on women's voting efforts from 1868 to 1873, see "Women Who Voted, 1868 to 1873—Sorted by State," The Elizabeth Cady Stanton and Susan B. Anthony Papers Project, http://ecssba.rutgers.edu/resources/votersst.html (accessed August 17, 2015).

108. "Woman Suffrage Bill Passed," Albany, April 19, 1901, Scrapbook 3, p. 74, Miller National American Woman Suffrage Association Scrapbooks, 1897–1911, Library of Congress, Rare Book and Special Collections Division, Washington, DC.

109. Mary Hillard Loines to Mariana Chapman, January 14, 1902 and Mary H. Loines to Madame President, April 6, 1904, Scrapbook 3, p. 83, Miller National American Woman Suffrage Association Scrapbooks, 1897–1911, Library of Congress, Rare Book and Special Collections Division, Washington, DC; "New York Women Now Citizens!" *Friends' Intelligencer* 74, December 8, 1917, 177.

110. Workers in Tompkins County collected approximately 4,000 signatures before the 1894 Constitutional Convention. Twenty-Sixth Annual New York State Woman Suffrage Association Convention Report, Ithaca, November 12–15, 1894, 209, Jon A. Lindseth Woman Suffrage Collection, Collection 8002, Division of Rare and Manuscript Collections, Carl A. Kroch Library, Cornell University, Ithaca, NY.

111. This idea originated in the Rochester Political Equality Club. Grangers sent over 50,000 signatures to their legislators. "Twenty-Sixth Annual New York State Woman Suffrage Association Convention Report," Ithaca, November 12–15, 1894, 176, Jon A. Lindseth Woman Suffrage Collection, Collection 8002, Division of Rare and Manuscript Collections, Carl A. Kroch Library, Cornell University, Ithaca, NY.

112. Ruth Barrett Lacy, "A History of Women in Ithaca," September 1969, p. 2, Dewitt Historical Society [now the History Center in Tompkins County], Ithaca, New York.

113. Women's Club of Ithaca, "Topics for 1895–1896," 1896, Records of the Ithaca Women's Club, History Center, Ithaca, NY.

114. Mrs. H. Calkins, "Political Study Club: Development of Woman Suffrage in Ithaca, 1899–1917," vol. 2, Minutes Book, Records of the Ithaca Women's Political Study Club, History Center, Ithaca, NY.

115. Mrs. H. Calkins, "Political Study Club: Development of Woman Suffrage in Ithaca, 1899–1917," vol. 2, Records of the Ithaca Women's Political Study Club, Minutes Book, History Center, Ithaca, NY. When Harriet May Mills visited nearby Cortland and spoke of woman suffrage work, "a gentleman in the audience" suggested the formation of a Women's Political Club. Dr. Lydia Strawbridge organized the club in 1898, and Ithacan Helen Brewster Owens lent support for the new club.

See "Political Equality Club," "Grip's Historical Souvenir of Cortland," n.d., p. 78, Suffrage Folder, Cortland County Historical Society, Cortland, NY.

116. See Carol Kammen, "Ithaca's Suffragists Showed Strong Support," *Ithaca Journal*, May 20, 2000.

117. Between 1904 and 1913, the Ithaca Political Study Club leased meeting space from the Woman's Christian Temperance Union and received invitations to attend its meetings. Mrs. H. Calkins, "Political Study Club: Development of Woman Suffrage in Ithaca, 1899–1917," vol. 2, Minutes Book, Records of the Ithaca Women's Political Study Club, History Center, Ithaca, New York; Allen, *History*, 203.

118. *Cortland Democrat*, March 30, 1917, Suffrage Folder, Cortland County Historical Society, Cortland, NY.

119. Harriet May Mills and Isabel Howland compiled a *Manual for Political Equality Clubs* (New York: National American Woman Suffrage Publishing Co., 1896) for the use of organizers. New York State Woman Suffrage Association, "Report of 32nd Annual Convention [Glens Falls, October] 1900," box 1, Woman Suffrage Association of New York State and Woman Suffrage Party of New York City Records, 1869–1919, Rare Book and Manuscript Library, Butler Library, Columbia University; Watrous, *Harriet May Mills*, 5.

120. Watrous, *Harriet May Mills*, 5.

121. "Society Outside the Capital," *Washington Post*, September 21, 1911, 7.

122. New York State Woman Suffrage Association, "Organization Report," [Buffalo] 1902, New York State Woman Suffrage Association Minutes Book, vol. 5, box 1, MS 1369, Woman Suffrage Association of New York State and Woman Suffrage Party of New York City Records, 1869–1919, Rare Book and Manuscript Library, Butler Library, Columbia University; Watrous, *Harriet May Mills*, 6.

123. Watrous, *Harriet May Mills*, 6–7.

124. Ibid., 8.

125. Minutes, September 18, 1910, and September 22, 1911, Clinton Political Equality Club Papers, Clinton Historical Society, Clinton, NY.

126. John Burdick, "Political Equality Club of Clinton," 1–5, Clinton Political Equality Club Papers, Clinton Historical Society, Clinton, NY.

127. "A Flourishing Club," *Clinton Courier*, September 27, 1911.

128. Minutes, December 7, 1911, and January 4, 1912, Clinton Political Equality Club Papers, Clinton Historical Society, Clinton, NY; *Clinton Courier*, October 2, 1912.

129. Mrs. H. W. Cannon, "Report (1914)," box 1, p. 5, New York Woman Suffrage Collection, 1914–1915, Collection 8041, Division of Rare and Manuscript Collections, Carl A. Kroch Library, Cornell University, Ithaca, NY.

130. Mrs. H. W. Cannon, "Report (1913)," box 1, p. 3–5, New York Woman Suffrage Collection, 1914–1915, Collection 8041, Division of Rare and Manuscript Collections, Carl A. Kroch Library, Cornell University, Ithaca, NY.

131. Watrous, *Harriet May Mills*, 5, 7–8.

3. Suffrage, Immigrant Women Garment Workers, and the Quest for Industrial Citizenship

1. Harriet B. Dow, "Minutes of the First Meeting of the Women's Educational and Industrial Union," April 10, 1893, p. 1, Women's Educational and Industrial Union Papers, Rochester Public Library, Rochester, New York; Katherine Talbot Hodge, *History of the Women's Educational and Industrial Union, 1893–1943* (Rochester, 1943), 1,

Women's Educational and Industrial Union Papers, Rochester Public Library, Rochester, NY; Blake McKelvey, "Historic Origins of Rochester's Social Welfare Agencies," *Rochester History* 9, no. 2–3 (April 1947), 3.

2. McKelvey, "Historic Origins," 30.

3. Untitled newspaper article, *Rochester Daily American*, papers of Elizabeth Cady Stanton and Susan B. Anthony, Microfilm reel 7, frames 190–193C, Library of Congress, Washington, DC.

4. Gladys Boone, *The Women's Trade Union Leagues in Great Britain and the United States of America* (New York: Columbia University Press, 1942), 15–16, 50, 66–67.

5. Lynn Sherr, *Failure Is Impossible: Susan B. Anthony in Her Own Words* (New York: Times Books, division of Random House, 1995), 306.

6. Helen Barrett Montgomery, "Equal Suffrage," *Harper's Bazar* 27, no. 18 (May 5, 1894): 354–55.

7. "1894 Constitutional-Amendment Campaign Year," report of New York State Woman Suffrage Association, Twenty-Sixth Annual Convention, Ithaca, New York, November 12–15, (Rochester, NY: Charles Mann Printer, 1895), 197.

8. Rochester Political Equality Club, Programs for 1893–94, 1898–99, 1903–4, Women's Suffrage Collection, Rare Books, Special Collections and Preservation, Rush Rhees Library, University of Rochester, Rochester, New York.

9. New York State Woman Suffrage Minutes Book, vol. 7, p. 77, box 3, MS 1369, Rare Book and Manuscript Library, Butler Library, Columbia University.

10. Blake McKelvey, "Woman's Rights in Rochester: A Century of Progress," *Rochester History* 10, no. 2–3 (July 1948): 17–18.

11. McKelvey, "Woman's Rights," 6-7; Nancy A. Hewitt, *Women's Activism and Social Change: Rochester, New York, 1822–1872* (Ithaca, NY: Cornell University Press, 1984), 136–37.

12. "Susan B. Anthony Biography," http://susanbanthonyhouse.org/her-story/biography.php (accessed September 9, 2009).

13. "Workingwomen's Association, No. 2," *Revolution* 2, no. 13, October 1, 1868, p. 198, Lewis & Clark Digital Collections, Aubrey R. Watzek Library, Lewis & Clark College, Portland, OR; Israel I. Kruger, "The Trade Union Career of Susan B. Anthony," *Labor History* (Winter 1961): 97.

14. "What with Washing, Cooking and Sewing at Home After Factory Hours, Working Women Have No Time to Think of Suffrage, their Labor Leaders Explain," *New York Tribune*, March 3, 1915, 7.

15. Dow, "Minutes," p. 1–2.

16. Correspondence between Griesheimer and Leonora O'Reilly of the Women's Trade Union League suggests that Griesheimer may have explored the possibility of starting a branch of the Women's Trade Union League in Rochester. David Kevin McDonald, "Organizing Womanhood: Women's Culture and the Politics of Woman Suffrage in New York State, 1865–1917" (PhD diss., State University of New York at Stony Brook, 1987), 182–83; Karen J. Blair, *The Clubwoman as Feminist: True Womanhood Redefined, 1868–1914* (New York: Holmes & Meier Publishers, 1980), 104, 110.

17. Harriet B. Dow, "Minutes," p. 1.

18. Montgomery won reelection in 1901.

19. Although the Women's Educational and Industrial Union never took an official stance on suffrage, most of its members also belonged to the Rochester Political Equality Club. McDonald, "Organizing Womanhood," 183.

20. Several members belonged to both the Rochester Political Equality Club and the Women's Educational and Industrial Union. "Financial Report of the Seventh Campaign District," donor list, February 1, 1914–December 31, 1915, box 3, folder 3, Emma Biddlecom Sweet Papers, Rare Books, Special Collections and Preservation, Rush Rhees Library, University of Rochester, Rochester, NY.

21. George Eastman apparently made a one-time $1,000 donation to the Women's Opportunity Shop. Jeanette W. Huntington, "History and Literature of the Women's Educational and Industrial Union, 1893–1943," p. 8, Women's Educational and Industrial Union Papers, Rochester Public Library, Rochester, NY. See also Hodge, "History of the Women's Educational and Industrial Union, 1893–1943."

22. "Cayuga Suffragists," *Democrat and Chronicle*, May 20, 1912, 4.

23. After conferring with union leaders in 1911, city officials appointed women to the police force and to the public health department. McDonald, "Organizing Womanhood," 52.

24. Blake McKelvey, "Rochester's Ethnic Transformations," *Rochester History* 25, no. 3 (July 1963): 4–16.

25. According to Brayer, although Eastman donated large sums of money to political causes and even to the city school board, he had "no use for partisan politics." Elizabeth Brayer, *George Eastman: A Biography* (Baltimore: Johns Hopkins, 1996), 337, 378–83.

26. McKelvey, "Rochester's Ethnic Transformations," 12; Sanford M. Jacoby, *Modern Manors: Welfare Capitalism Since the New Deal* (Princeton: Princeton University Press, 1997), 57–65.

27. Edwin Rumball, "Rochester Factories and the Social Spirit," *Common Good* 4, no. 6 (March 1911): 10–12.

28. For detailed historical background on Adler Brothers see "Historical Material Scrapbook," box 2, Adler Brothers & Company Papers, Department of Rare Books, Special Collections and Preservation, Rush Rhees Library, University of Rochester, Rochester, NY. See also Blake McKelvey, "The Men's Clothing Industry in Rochester History," *Rochester History* 22, no. 3 (July 1960): 5.

29. The Clothiers' Exchange was formed in 1890 with a stated goal of self-protection but its activities, including blacklisting, were clearly anti-union. McKelvey, "The Men's Clothing Industry," 8–11. *Socialist Scrapbook* vol. 3 (October 2, 1911): 69–71, 126, Rochester Socialist Scrapbook Collection, Rare Books, Special Collections and Preservation, Rush Rhees Library, University of Rochester, Rochester, New York. See also McDonald, "Organizing Womanhood," 167–68. For a history of the Rochester garment industry see *Tailor Made: The Story of Rochester's Garment Industry*, television program, aired February 29, 2016, WXXI Public Broadcasting Station, Rochester, NY.

30. McKelvey refers to the early 1900s as the "low ebb" of suffrage agitation in Rochester. McKelvey, "Woman's Rights," 2, 19; "Suffrage Made Gains Up-State," *New York Times*, November 7, 1917, 1. For more on the Republican machine control of city politics and anti-suffrage activity see McDonald, "Organizing Womanhood," 203–6.

31. "Votes for Women Strongly Urged," unidentified newspaper clipping, Albany, NY (February 24, 1909), Scrapbook 7, pp. 77–79, Miller National American Woman Suffrage Association Suffrage Scrapbooks, 1897–1911, Library of Congress, Rare Book and Special Collections Division, Washington, DC.

32. "My Work in Rochester: By a Factory Girl," *Common Good* 6, no. 3 (December 1912): 71–74; "Analysis of the Chamber of Commerce Investigation of the Clothing Factories," *Common Good* 6, no. 4 (January 1913): 108–11; Edwin and Catherine Rumball, "The Working Girls and Women of Rochester," *Common Good* 6, no. 5 (February 1913): 132–57; Eileen Boris, *Home to Work: Motherhood and the Politics of Industrial Homework in the United States* (New York: Cambridge University Press, 1994), 56.

33. "Strikers Won't Return to Work, Says Organizer," *Democrat and Chronicle*, January 26, 1913, 31.

34. "The News Article That Aroused the Indignation of the Rochester Chamber of Commerce," *Common Good* 5, no. 11 (August 1912): 7; "Analysis of the Chamber of Commerce Investigation of the Clothing Factories," 108.

35. Edwin and Catherine Rumball, "The Working Girls and Women of Rochester," 132–58.

36. The league had a separate organizing committee, called the Italian Committee, from at least 1908. Italian women had a reputation among league members for being controlled by their husbands and fathers and for being used as strikebreakers. Jennifer Guglielmo, *Living the Revolution: Italian Women's Resistance and Radicalism in New York City, 1880–1945* (Chapel Hill: University of North Carolina Press, 2010), 32–40; Annelise Orleck, *Common Sense and a Little Fire: Women and Working-Class Politics in the United States, 1900–1965* (Chapel Hill: University of North Carolina Press, 1995), 17–18; Karen Pastorello, *A Power among Them: Bessie Abramowitz Hillman and the Making of Amalgamated Clothing Workers of America* (Urbana: University of Illinois Press, 2008), 5–6. See also Women's Trade Union of New York, "Annual Report, 1908–1909" (New York: Women's Trade Union League, 1909), 2; Women's Trade Union League of New York, "Annual Report, 1910–1911" (New York: Women's Trade Union League, 1911), 2–6; Women's Trade Union League of New York, "Annual Report, 1912–1913," (New York: Women's Trade Union League, 1913), 6.

37. Excerpts from "Address Delivered by Miss Rose Schneiderman before the Women's Industrial Conference," January 20, 1926, Papers of the United States Women's Bureau, Sophia Smith Collection, Smith College, Northampton, MA; Orleck, *Common Sense*, 30, 88.

38. Excerpts from "Address Delivered by Miss Rose Schneiderman before the Women's Industrial Conference"; Orleck, *Common Sense*, 30, 88.

39. Anna Goldstein, typescript in box 2, folder 11, Series 3: Edwin Alfred Rumball Papers, First Unitarian Church Collection, Rare Books, Special Collections and Preservation, Rush Rhees Library, University of Rochester, Rochester, NY.

40. Guglielmo takes issue with historians who tend to characterize Italian women as victims of patriarchal fathers and husbands who proved difficult to organize. She suggests that Italian women frequently engaged in resistance to oppression that originated in their homeland. Guglielmo, *Living the Revolution*, 77–78. Jewish women's labor and political activism is chronicled in Orleck, *Common Sense*. "Suffrage Demanded by Working Women," *New York Times*, April 23, 1912, 24; "Hinchey, Margaret," American National Biography Online, http://www.anb.org/articles/15/15-01325.html (accessed March 23, 2016); McDonald, "Organizing Womanhood," 208.

41. Lilian Lazurus, typescript in box 2, folder 11, Series 3: Edwin Alfred Rumball Papers, First Unitarian Church Collection, Rare Books, Special Collections and Preservation, Rush Rhees Library, University of Rochester, Rochester, NY.

42. Hodge, "History," 34.

43. "Baden Street Settlement Records—Summary Information," University of Minnesota Libraries, http://special.lib.umn.edu/findaid/xml/sw0003.xml (accessed August 19, 2009).

44. Hodge, "History," 28–29.

45. McDonald, "Organizing Womanhood," 196–97.

46. Lewis Street Center Papers, box 1, folder 4, p. 1, Rare Books, Special Collections and Preservation, Rush Rhees Library, University of Rochester, Rochester, NY.

47. "Useful Work for City's Italians," *Democrat and Chronicle*, September 25, 1907, 13; Florence Cross, "Italians in Rochester," *Post Express*, January 17, 1908, 4; Florence Cross, "What Shall We Do?" *Post Express*, January 30, 1908, 4.

48. Robert Woods and Albert Kennedy, *Handbook of Settlements* (New York: Charities and Publication Committee, 1911), 245–46.

49. "Mission Study Class," "Italy Topic for Meeting," "Talks on Patriots of Italy," clippings from unidentified newspapers, Fall 1911–1912, vol. 5, Good Housekeeping/Suffrage, Florence Ledyard Cross Kitchelt Papers, Arthur and Elizabeth Schlesinger Library on the History of Women in America, Radcliffe Institute, Harvard University, Cambridge, MA.

50. "Social Workers' Simple Wedding," *Rochester Herald*, June 25, 1911; "Couple Compose Ritual for Their Own Wedding," *World*, July 2, 1911; "Novel Rites as Girl Reformer Weds Socialist," *New York Evening Journal*, June 26, 1911, newspaper clippings, vol. 5, Good Housekeeping/Suffrage, Florence Ledyard Cross Kitchelt Papers, Arthur and Elizabeth Schlesinger Library on the History of Women in America, Radcliffe Institute, Harvard University, Cambridge, MA.

51. "Immigrant Women Neighbors," *Rochester Herald*, December 1911; "Our Candidate for Secretary of State," *New York Call*, July 26, 1914; "Talks to Federation on Immigrant Education"; "The Bureau of Information and Protection for Foreigners"; newspaper and unidentified clippings, vol. 5, Good Housekeeping/Suffrage, Florence Ledyard Cross Kitchelt Papers, Arthur and Elizabeth Schlesinger Library on the History of Women in America, Radcliffe Institute, Harvard University, Cambridge, MA.

52. "Financial Report of the Seventh Campaign District," February 1, 1914–December 31, 1915, box 3, folder 3; "Financial Report of the Rochester Political Equality Club," May 1, 1915 to May 10, 1916, box 3, folder 4; "Annual Report," Woman's Suffrage Party of Monroe County, May 12, 1917, box 3, folder 4, Emma Biddlecom Sweet Papers, Rare Books, Special Collections and Preservation, Rush Rhees Library, University of Rochester, Rochester, NY.

53. Nancy Schrom Dye, *As Equals and as Sisters; Feminism, the Labor Movement, and the Women's Trade Union League of New York* (Columbia: University of Missouri Press, 1980), 58–59; Orleck, *Common Sense*, 87–88.

54. Nancy F. Cott, *The Grounding of Modern Feminism* (New Haven: Yale University Press, 1987), 34–35.

55. "Rochester Political Equality Program, 1906–1907," Women's Rights Series 8, box 2, folder 4, First Unitarian Church Collection, Rare Books, Special Collections and Preservation, Rush Rhees Library, University of Rochester, Rochester, NY.

56. "To Address Joint Meeting," *Syracuse Post Standard*, February 15, 1910, 5; Carrie Chapman Catt and Nettie Rogers Shuler, *Woman Suffrage and Politics: The Inner Story of the Suffrage Movement* (New York: Charles Scribner's Sons, 1926), 288.

57. "Foes of Suffrage Confident in Utica," *New York Times*, October 31, 1915, 5.

58. For details of a suffrage talk by Rochester Political Equality Club member Clara B. Abbott at Labor Lyceum, see "Talk on Votes for Women," *Democrat and Chronicle*, March 31, 1913, 8.

59. Dye, *As Equals*, 125–26.

60. Orleck, *Common Sense*, 95–96.

61. Joshua Freeman, "Remembering the Triangle Fire," *Nation*, April 4, 2011, 23.

62. "Will Speak in Street," *Democrat and Chronicle*, July 3, 1911, 13; "Club Addressed by Campaigners," *Democrat and Chronicle*, September 20, 1911, 14.

63. Factory Girl, "My Work in Rochester," *Common Good* 7, no. 3 (December 1912), 74; "New York State Factory Investigating Commission," *Preliminary Report* vol. 1 (Albany: Argus, 1912): 295. The report stated that workers worked longer days in upstate factories than in New York City.

64. "New York State Factory Investigating Commission," 294–95.

65. Rose Schneiderman, "The Woman Movement and the Working Woman," *Woman Voter* 7, no. 6 (June 1915): 11.

66. Rumball and Rumball, "Working Girls," 146.

67. The women spoke to the Labor Lyceum, at the Socialist Sunday School, and to the Socialist Branch. Women's Trade Union League of New York, "Annual Report, 1912–1913" (New York: Women's Trade Union League, 1913), 22.

68. Emma Goldman, *Living My Life*, ed. Richard and Anna Maria Drinnon (New York: New American Library, 1977), 121.

69. "Lillian Wald," Women of Valor, Jewish Women's Archives, https://jwa.org/womenofvalor/wald (accessed April 8, 2016).

70. Joan Jensen, "The Great Uprising in Rochester," in *A Needle, a Bobbin, a Strike: Women Needleworkers in America*, ed. Joan Jensen and Sue Davidson (Philadelphia: Temple University Press, 1984), 98–101.

71. The total number of women in Rochester unions numbered fewer than 400 in 1909. Ibid., 112n13.

72. Leonard W. Hatch, ed., New York State Department of Labor, "Garment Workers' Strike, Rochester," *Bulletin 1913* vol. 15, no. 54–56 (Albany: J. B. Lyon and Company, 1914), 164; "First Definite Steps by State to End Strike," *Democrat and Chronicle*, February 6, 1913, 19.

73. Christopher Martin, "New Unionism at the Grassroots: the Amalgamated Clothing Workers of America in Rochester, New York, 1914–1929," *Labor History* 42, no. 3 (August 2001): 237–53.

74. Jensen, "The Great Uprising," 94–95.

75. "Following are the Conditions Under Which We Are Willing to Return to Work"; William Lippelt, "The Cause of the Garment Workers," box 2, folder 11, Series 3: Edwin Alfred Rumball Papers, First Unitarian Church Collection, Rare Books, Special Collections and Preservation, Rush Rhees Library, University of Rochester, Rochester, NY.

76. Jensen, "The Great Uprising," 101.

77. Rochester Museum and Science Center, Photographs of the 1913 Rochester Garment Workers' Strike, Albert Stone Negatives Collection (accessed April 9, 2016).

78. Rose Schneiderman first used the phrase "bread and roses" in a 1912 speech. It became a very popular slogan for striking workers. Sarah Eisenstein, *Give Us Bread*

But Give Us Roses: Working Women's Consciousness in the United States, 1890 to the First World War (New York: Routledge, 1983), 32.

79. Orleck, *Common Sense*, 88.

80. "The Strikers and the Kitchens," Socialist Scrapbook vol. 1 (1913), 47, Rochester Socialist Scrapbook Collection, Rare Books, Special Collections and Preservation, Rush Rhees Library, University of Rochester, Rochester, NY.

81. "Report," Lewis Street Center Papers, box 4, folder 4 (February 1913), p. 12, Rare Books, Special Collections and Preservation, Rush Rhees Library, University of Rochester, Rochester, NY; Hatch, "Garment Workers Strike," 165.

82. Both Etz and O'Reilly also addressed the Rochester Political Equality Club in early 1913. Jensen, "The Great Uprising," 104. See "Recent Activities of the Political Equality Club," box 2, folder 4 (January–April 1913), Women's Rights Papers, Rare Books, Special Collections and Preservation, Rush Rhees Library, University of Rochester, Rochester, NY.

83. Jensen, "The Great Uprising, 104–5.

84. In February 1919, the workweek was reduced to forty-four hours. "No General Advance in Pay or Shortening of Hours of Duty for Garment Workers," *Democrat and Chronicle*, February 11, 1913, 17; Hatch, "Garment Workers' Strike," 169. See also "Rochester Labor Council History: Organizing," www.rochesterlabor.org (accessed April 9, 2016); Max Holtz, "Review of the Accomplishments of the Rochester Clothing Industry for the Year 1919," Twenty-Ninth Annual Meeting of the Clothiers' Exchange, December 20, 1919.

85. "Hinchey, Margaret," American National Biography Online; McDonald, "Organizing Womanhood," 208.

86. Mena Brown advised against rabid suffrage tactics, and Anna Howard Shaw and Ella Hawley Crossett viewed parades as counterproductive. Successful working women's suffrage groups outside of New York City existed at least for a short time in Buffalo and Hornell. "How the Vote was Won," *Women's Political World* (June 1, 1914), 3. Harriot Stanton Blatch and Alma Lutz, *Challenging Years: The Memoirs of Harriot Stanton Blatch* (New York: G.P. Putnam's Sons, 1940), 129; McDonald, "Organizing Womanhood," 122, 142.

87. Susan B. Anthony died in 1906 and her sister Mary S. Anthony died in 1907.

88. With the 1915 defeat, though, the old school suffragists reasserted their authority and Clement retreated, urging suffragists to promote the cause by joining the boards of women's organizations. Although they tried to follow the directives of the Empire State Campaign, suffragists had little success. Clement cautioned the organizers against over-exerting themselves. Oreola Haskell, "Canvassing in the Flower City," *Woman Voter* 6, no. 5 (May 1915): 12–13; McDonald, "Organizing Womanhood," 214–16.

89. "Effective Plea for the Ballot," *Democrat and Chronicle*, March 16, 1913, 28.

90. Ibid.

91. "City and Guests Marvel Together at Water Carnival," *Democrat and Chronicle*, July 11, 1913, 19; McKelvey, "Woman's Rights," 20.

92. "Winning Votes," *Women's Political World* 2, no. 14 (July 15, 1914): 6.

93. "Procession of Sixty Domino Clad Women Heralds Suffrage Speech," *Rochester Herald*, August 16, 1914.

94. Isabelle K. Savell, *Ladies' Lib: How Rockland Women Got the Vote* (New York: Historical Society of Rockland County, 1979), photograph caption between pp. 29 and 30.

95. Ibid., 25.

96. Virginia Scharff, *Taking the Wheel: Women and the Coming of the Motor Age* (New York: Free Press, 1991), 85–86.

97. "Suffrage Autoists have Casualties," *Sun* (October 11, 1914): 13.

98. "Suffragists in Convention Swing," *New-York Tribune*, October 14, 1914, 7.

99. "Votes for Women, 46th Annual Convention of the New York State Woman Suffrage Association and General Conference of New York State Suffragists, October 12, 13, 14, and 15"; "Proposed Main Routes, State-Wide Pilgrimage"; "Equal Suffrage State Wide Pilgrimage," box 1, New York Woman Suffrage Collection, 1914–1915, Collection 8041, Division of Rare and Manuscript Collections, Carl A. Kroch Library, Cornell University, Ithaca, NY.

100. National Women's Trade Union League of America, "Fifth Biennial Convention, June 7–12, 1915," (New York: National Women's Trade Union League, 1915), 28; "Suffragists in Convention in the City of Rochester," *Scarsdale Inquirer*, October 17, 1914, 2.

101. Mrs. H. W. Cannon, "Report (1914)," no. 2, box 1, New York Woman Suffrage Collection, 1914–1915, Collection 8041, Division of Rare and Manuscript Collections, Carl A. Kroch Library, Cornell University, Ithaca, NY.

102. "Black-Robed Suffragists Enter Court," *Post Express*, March 30, 1915.

103. Carrie Chapman Catt to Suffrage Worker, March 15, 1915, Helen Brewster Owens Papers, Arthur and Elizabeth Schlesinger Library on the History of Women in America, Radcliffe Institute, Harvard University. When Maggie Hinchey, organizer for the Women's Trade Union League and the Woman Suffrage Party, went to Rochester in 1915, she spoke to Irish societies and Catholic clergy. See "Hinchey, Margaret."

104. "Reverend John H. O'Rourke, S. J., Says," *Catholic Journal* (October 29, 1915): 3. The Rochester Political Equality Club sponsored the statement.

105. "Foes of Suffrage Confident in Utica," *New York Times*, October 31, 1915, 5.

106. "How and Why Vote No on Woman's Suffrage Amendment," *Democrat and Chronicle*, October 30, 1915, 23.

107. "Vote Yes," *Democrat and Chronicle*, October 17, 1915, 33; "Ten Reasons Why Women Should Vote," *Democrat and Chronicle*, November 1, 1915, 20.

108. Kendall Mobley, *Helen Barrett Montgomery: The Global Mission of Domestic Feminism* (Waco, TX: Baylor University, 2009), 199–200.

109. Ibid., 195–200.

110. "Will Speak in Street," *Democrat and Chronicle*, July 3, 1911, 13; "Satisfied with Results," *Democrat and Chronicle*, July 8, 1911, 10.

111. McDonald notes that after 1914 at least thirty-nine Women's Educational and Industrial Union members participated in anti-suffrage activities. McDonald, "Organizing Womanhood," 167, 179, 182–83.

112. "Death of Frances B. Allan," *Democrat and Chronicle*, October 15, 1911, 19. Frances Allen voted with the group who accompanied Susan B. Anthony to the polls in 1872.

113. Caroline Bartlett Crane, "A Sanitary Survey," (1911), https://catalog.hathitrust.org/Record/002081764 (accessed April 9, 2016).

114. Edwin Rumball, "Fourth Ward Survey," *Common Good* (1912), box 2, folder 8, Series 3: Edwin Alfred Rumball Papers, First Unitarian Church Collection, Rare Books, Special Collections and Preservation, Rush Rhees Library, University of Rochester, Rochester, NY.

115. "Actress Speaks for Suffragists," *Democrat and Chronicle*, November 6, 1912, 11; "Suffragists to Convene To-day," *Democrat and Chronicle*, February 3, 1914, 11. Clement enthusiastically reported an increase to 436 members in the Rochester Political Equality Club by the end of the first year of her presidency.

116. "Talk on Votes for Women," *Democrat and Chronicle*, March 31, 1913, 8.

117. McDonald, "Organizing Womanhood," 206–7.

118. Ibid., 164, 172–75.

119. Rochester had twenty-two wards total. In an otherwise anti-suffrage stronghold, only seven wards, six of them comprised of predominately native-born voters, passed the amendment in 1915. McDonald, "Organizing Womanhood," 193.

120. Orleck, *Common Sense*, 55–56.

4. A Fundamental Component

1. Newspapers widely reported this meeting. See for example, "Mrs. Belmont Crosses Line," *Iowa City Press-Citizen*, February 7, 1910, 2; "Suffrage for All," *Washington Bee*, February 12, 1910, 1; "What Women are Doing," *Oakland* [California] *Tribune*, February 22, 1910, 8; "Suffrage for Negresses," *New York Times*, January 19, 1910, 5. Contemporaries often referred to the Equal Suffrage League of Brooklyn as the Colored Women's (or Woman's) Equal Suffrage League. Fanny Garrison Villard was the only daughter of renowned abolitionist William Lloyd Garrison.

2. Sylvia D. Hoffert, *Alva Vanderbilt Belmont: Unlikely Champion of Women's Rights* (Bloomington: Indiana University Press, 2012), 80.

3. "Negroes Join Mrs. Belmont," *Brooklyn Daily Eagle*, February 4, 1910, 22.

4. "Ask Negro Women to be Suffragists," *New York Age*, February 10, 1910, 1.

5. Ibid.

6. The significance historians have assigned to Belmont's event in 1910, documented in the literature of black women's activism in New York State, tends to overlook the strength of the black woman suffrage movement that already existed. Rosalyn Terborg-Penn, *African American Women in the Struggle for the Vote, 1850–1920* (Bloomington: Indiana University Press, 1998), 99–101; Julie Gallagher, *Black Women and Politics in New York City* (Urbana: University of Illinois Press, 2014), 22.

7. Jane E. Dabel, *A Respectable Woman: The Public Roles of African American Women in 19th-Century New York* (New York: New York University Press, 2008), 156.

8. Beverly Guy-Sheftall, *Daughters of Sorrow: Attitudes toward Black Women, 1880–1920* (Brooklyn: Carlson Publishing, 1990), 129.

9. Karlyn Kohrs Campbell, *Man Cannot Speak for Her: A Critical Study of Early Feminist Rhetoric* (New York: Greenwood Press, 1989), 145–46.

10. Guy-Sheftall, *Daughters of Sorrow*, 129.

11. Tetrault argues convincingly that the authors of the *History of Woman Suffrage* tended to cut material related to black women's involvement in suffrage and women's rights activism out of the official history of the movement. Lisa Tetrault, *The Myth of Seneca Falls: Memory and the Women's Suffrage Movement, 1848–1898* (Chapel Hill: University of North Carolina, 2014), 134–35.

12. Michele Mitchell, *Righteous Propagation: African Americans and the Politics of Racial Destiny after Reconstruction* (Chapel Hill: University of North Carolina Press, 2004), 136; Guy-Sheftall, *Daughters of Sorrow*, 114.

13. Paula Giddings, *When and Where I Enter: The Impact of Black Women on Race and Sex in America* (New York: Bantam Books, 1984), 129.

14. The Empire State Federation of Women's Clubs is sometimes called the New York State Federation of Colored Women's Clubs. See, for example, "Meetings," *Crisis* 10, no. 4 (August 1915): 165. The Empire State Federation of Women's Clubs continues its activism in the present day.

15. Rosalyn Terborg-Penn, "Discontented Black Feminists: Prelude and Postscript to the Passage of the Nineteenth Amendment," in *Black Studies Reader*, ed. Cynthia Hudley, Jacqueline Bobo, and Claudine Michel (New York: Routledge, 2004), 66.

16. Evelyn Brooks Higginbotham, *Righteous Discontent: The Women's Movement in the Black Baptist Church, 1880–1920* (Cambridge, MA: Harvard University Press, 1993), 185; Terborg-Penn, "Discontented Black Feminists," 66.

17. Terborg-Penn, "Discontented Black Feminists," 68.

18. Dorothy Sterling, ed. *We Are Your Sisters: Black Women in the Nineteenth Century* (New York: W. W. Norton, 1984), 410–11.

19. Giddings claims that "one would be hard pressed to find any Black women who did not advocate getting the vote." Giddings, *When and Where*, 119–20.

20. Fannie Barrier Williams, "Club Movement among Negro Women," in *The Colored American: From Slavery to Honorable Citizenship*, ed. J. W. Gibson and W. H. Crogman (Atlanta: Hertel, Jenkins & Company, 1905), 197.

21. Tetrault, *Myth of Seneca Falls*, 22.

22. Dabel, *Respectable Woman*, 155.

23. Jean Fagan Yellin, ed. *The Harriet Jacobs Family Papers*, vol. 2 (Chapel Hill, University of North Carolina Press, 2008), 673, 682.

24. Terborg-Penn shows that black women were divided as to which of the two organizations to join. Rosalyn Terborg-Penn, *African American Women in the Struggle for the Vote, 1850–1920* (Bloomington: Indiana University Press, 1998), 42.

25. Guy-Sheftall, *Daughters of Sorrow*, 104; Tetrault, *Myth of Seneca Falls*, 21.

26. Hallie Q. Brown, *Homespun Heroines and Other Women of Distinction* (New York: Oxford University Press, 1988), 16; Sterling, *We Are Your Sisters*, 413.

27. Tetrault, *Myth of Seneca Falls*, 107.

28. Catherine Clinton, *Harriet Tubman: The Road to Freedom* (New York: Back Bay Books, 2004), 191.

29. Ibid., 212.

30. Emma P. Telford, "Harriet: The Modern Moses of Her People," unpublished article, Cayuga County Historian's Office, Auburn, NY; Clinton, *Harriet Tubman*, 192.

31. Clinton, *Harriet Tubman*, 211–12.

32. Sterling, *We Are Your Sisters*, 411. The List of Life Members of the Geneva Political Equality Club, Scrapbook 9, p. 46, Miller National American Woman Suffrage Association Suffrage Scrapbooks, 1897–1911, Library of Congress, Rare Book and Special Collections Division, Washington, DC.

33. The District of Columbia bar also admitted Ray in 1872. She tried her first case, a divorce, in 1875: *Godling v. Godling*, Case No. 4278, Supreme Court of the District of Columbia. She belonged to the National Association of Colored Women. J. Clay Smith Jr., ed., *Rebels in Law: Voices in History of Black Women Lawyers* (Ann Arbor: University of Michigan Press, 1998), 6, 9, 24, 283. "Ray, Charles Bennett" and

"Ray, Charlotte E.," *American National Biography* 18, ed. John A. Garraty and Mark C. Carnes (New York: Oxford University Press, 1999), 201–3.

34. Elizabeth Cady Stanton, Susan B. Anthony, and Matilda Joslyn Gage, *History of Woman Suffrage*, vol. 3 (Rochester: Susan B. Anthony, 1886), 18–19; Terborg-Penn, *African American Women*, 42.

35. Sterling, *We Are Your Sisters*, 411.

36. Gallagher, *Black Women and Politics*, 22–23.

37. "Wanted—Work," *Brooklyn Daily Eagle*, September 25, 1888, 2.

38. "Female Smokers are Criticised," *New York Age*, July 10, 1913, 1.

39. "Finding Aid for the Empire State Federation of Women's Clubs, Inc., Records, 1938–1991," M. E. Grenander Department of Special Collections and Archives, University at Albany, State University of New York, Albany, NY. Any records of the federation from its first thirty years seem to no longer exist.

40. "Female Smokers are Criticised," 1; "Women Wanted to Boycott Age," *New York Age*, July 9, 1914, 1–2; "Empire State Federation," *New York Age*, July 20, 1916, 5; "Ask Wilson to Stop Acts of Lawlessness," *New York Age*, July 12, 1917, 7; "Women Meet in New York," *New York Age*, July 13, 1918, 5; "Eleventh Annual Convention of the Empire State Federation . . . Mrs. Lawton is Re-elected," *New York Age*, July 19, 1919, 1.

41. Mitchell, *Righteous Propagation*, 7.

42. Giddings, *When and Where*, 123–24.

43. Terborg-Penn, "Discontented Black Feminists," 68.

44. Craig Steven Wilder, *In the Company of Black Men: The African Influence on African American Culture in New York City* (New York: New York Univeristy Press, 2001), 216.

45. Higginbotham, *Righteous Discontent*, 16–17.

46. Ibid., 18.

47. Letter from Mabel E. Brown to W. E. B. Du Bois, July 27, 1917, Credo, Special Collections and University Archives, University Libraries, University of Massachusetts Amherst, Amherst, MA, http://credo.library.umass.edu/view/full/mums312-b010-i014 (accessed June 7, 2015).

48. Giddings, *When and Where*, 120.

49. N[annie] H[elen] Burroughs, "Black Women and Reform," in "Votes for Women: A Symposium by Leading Thinkers of Colored America," *Crisis* 10, no. 4 (August 1915): 187; "Burroughs, Nannie Helen (1883–1961)," entry at BlackPast. org, an online reference site dedicated to understanding African American history, http://www.blackpast.org/aah/burroughs-nannie-helen-1883-1961 (accessed February 7, 2016).

50. Floris Barnett Cash, *African American Women and Social Action: The Clubwomen and Volunteerism from Jim Crow to the New Deal, 1896–1936* (Westport, CT: Greenwood Press, 2001), 32.

51. Report of the "1910 Convention of the National Association of Colored Women," p. 29, Microfilm, Burke Library, Hamilton College, Clinton, NY.

52. Giddings, *When and Where*, 121.

53. Ibid.

54. Nancy Cott, *The Grounding of Modern Feminism* (New Haven: Yale University Press, 1987), 32.

55. Cash, *African American Women*, 5–6.

56. Terborg-Penn, *African American Women*, 41; Stanton, Anthony, and Gage, *History of Woman Suffrage*, vol. 3, 31, 72–73, 95.

57. Giddings, *When and Where*, 75; Jane Rhodes, *Mary Ann Shadd Cary: The Black Press and Protest in the Nineteenth Century* (Bloomington: Indiana University Press, 1998), 191.

58. Giddings, *When and Where*, 75.

59. Carla L. Peterson, *Black Gotham: A Family History of African Americans in Nineteenth-Century New York City* (New Haven: Yale University Press, 2011), 355.

60. Victoria Earle Matthews, "New York Letter," *Woman's Era* 1, no. 1 (March 24, 1894), 2.

61. Cash, *African American Women*, 40.

62. "Address of Josephine St. P. Ruffin, President of Conference," *Woman's Era* 2, no. 5 (August 1895): 13–15; Elizabeth Lindsay Davis, *Lifting as They Climb*, ed. Henry Louis Gates Jr. and Jennifer Burton (New York: G. K. Hall, 1996), 16; Higginbotham, *Righteous Discontent*, 152.

63. Lillian Serece Williams, *Strangers in the Land of Paradise: The Creation of an African American Community, Buffalo, New York, 1900–1940* (Bloomington: Indiana University Press, 1999), 20–21.

64. Cash, *African American Women*, 8.

65. "Jeffrey, Hester C. (1842–1934)," entry at BlackPast.org, http://www.black past.org/aah/jeffrey-hester-c-1842-1934 (accessed June 5, 2015).

66. Report of the "Fourth Convention of the National Association of Colored Women," p. 29, Microfilm, Burke Library, Hamilton College, Clinton, NY.

67. "Minutes of the Eighth Biennial Convention of the National Association of Colored Women (1912)," n.p., Microfilm, Burke Library, Hamilton College, Clinton, NY.

68. Cash, *African American Women*, 6; Judith Wellman, *The Road to Seneca Falls: Elizabeth Cady Stanton and the First Woman's Rights Convention* (Urbana: University of Illinois Press, 2004), 229–30; "Suffragists to Be Busy," *New York Times*, May 17, 1908, 7; "Commemorates First Suffrage Convention," *Press and Sun-Bulletin*, May 28, 1908, 1; "Elmiran Attends Suffrage Meeting," *Star-Gazette*, May 28, 1908, 9.

69. Judith Wellman, *Brooklyn's Promised Land: The Free Black Community of Weeksville, New York* (New York: New York University, 2014), 128.

70. Karen Garner, "Equal Suffrage League," in *Organizing Black America: An Encyclopedia of African American Associations*, ed. Nina Mjagkij (New York: Garland, 2001), 224; Peterson, *Black Gotham*, 355–56.

71. Garner, "Equal Suffrage League," 224.

72. Ibid.

73. Brooklyn and Queens YMCA Carlton Avenue Branch, the first branch in Brooklyn for African Americans, opened in 1902 and closed in 1955. "Brooklyn and Queens YMCA Carlton Avenue Branch: An Inventory of Its Records," Kautz Family YMCA Archives, Elmer L. Anderson Library, University of Minnesota, http://special.lib.umn.edu/findaid/html/ymca/ygny0025.phtml (accessed April 2, 2015).

74. Garnet, the first black woman to secure a position as a principal in the New York City public school system, worked in education for a total of fifty-six years. Brown, *Homespun Heroines*, 112.

75. Brown's *Homespun Heroines* claims there were eleven children. Ibid., 111.

76. Sylvain Cazalet, "History of the New York Medical College and Hospital for Women," http://www.homeoint.org/cazalet/histo/newyork.htm (accessed June 7, 2015); Brown, *Homespun Heroines*, 163.

77. Wilder, *In the Company*, 215.

78. Cash, *African American Women*, 9–10. Morton-Jones was also vice-president of the Mothers' Day Nursery, founded in 1905. "Mothers Day Nursery," *Brooklyn Daily Eagle*, April 10, 1906, 6.

79. Cash, *African American Women*, 102.

80. The Lincoln Settlement House struggled to keep up with the needs of a burgeoning black population, and eventually turned its operation over to the Urban League, forming the Brooklyn Urban League-Lincoln Settlement Association. In 1927 Morton-Jones established the Harriet Tubman Community Center in Hempstead, NY, resuming her medical practice around the same time. Cash, *African American Women*, 102, 104.

81. Cash, *African American Women*, 104.

82. "Honor Susan B. Anthony," *Brooklyn Daily Eagle*, April 2, 1906, 13; "Afro-American Notes," *Brooklyn Daily Eagle*, January 23, 1908, 10.

83. "Afro-American Notes," *Brooklyn Daily Eagle*, March 30, 1908, 5.

84. Verina Morton-Jones, M.D., worked as the matron in Warren Hall according to the listing of faculty and instructors for 1909–1910, "Clark University Register: Catalogue Edition, 1909–1910," available via Atlanta University Center Digital Commons @ Robert W. Woodruff Library, Atlanta University Center, http://digitalcommons.auctr.edu/cgi/viewcontent.cgi?article=1015&context=cccatalogs (accessed June 7, 2015).

85. "Suffragettes of Brooklyn," *New York Age*, June 24, 1909, 1.

86. "Afro-American Notes," *Brooklyn Daily Eagle*, February 13, 1910, 60; Brown, *Homespun Heroines*, 114. Eato also helped establish and run the Hope Day Nursery for Colored Children.

87. "Negroes Honor Lincoln," *Brooklyn Daily Eagle*, February 17, 1910, 10.

88. "Miss Craft Talks Suffrage," *Brooklyn Daily Eagle*, March 17, 1910, 2.

89. "Afro-American Notes," *Brooklyn Daily Eagle*, June 12, 1910, 22.

90. "Advancement of the Negro," *Brooklyn Daily Eagle*, April 29, 1911, 22.

91. Tonya Bolden, *Maritcha: A Nineteenth Century American Girl* (New York: Harry N. Abrams, 2005), 14–15, 20–21, 22, 42. St. Philip's Protestant Episcopal Church was an all-black church founded because parishioners resented the segregation of Trinity, the oldest Episcopal Church in New York. With a long career as an educator, Lyons ultimately became an assistant principal of Brooklyn's Public School No. 83.

92. Cash, *African American Women*, 20.

93. Brown, *Homespun Heroines*, 210.

94. Cash, *African American Women*, 92.

95. Brown, *Homespun Heroines*, 210–11; Jeffrey B. Perry, *Hubert Harrison: The Voice of Harlem Radicalism, 1883–1918* (New York: Columbia University, 2009), 94.

96. Her concern was the district lying between 59th and 127th Streets, from Park to First Avenue. African Americans had apparently been driven from Bleecker Street by the "influx of Italians." Brown, *Homespun Heroines*, 211.

97. Guichard Parris and Lester Brooks, *Blacks in the City: A History of the National Urban League* (Boston: Little, Brown and Company, 1971), 6–7; Steve Kramer, "Uplifting Our 'Downtrodden Sisterhood': Victoria Earle Matthews and New York City's White Rose Mission, 1897–1907," *Journal of African American History* 91, no. 3 (Summer 2006): 243.

98. Ingrid Overacker, *The African American Church Community in Rochester, New York, 1900–1940* (Rochester, NY: University of Rochester Press, 1998), 28.

99. "Afro-American Notes," *Brooklyn Daily Eagle*, July 26, 1907, 6; "Afro-American Notes," *Brooklyn Daily Eagle*, August 6, 1907, 7; and "Business Women's Clubs," *New York Age*, December 12, 1907, 2.

100. "In Memory of John Brown," *Brooklyn Daily Eagle*, December 12, 1907, 9.

101. "Women Visit Mercantile and Realty Company," *New York Age*, September 17, 1908, 10.

102. "Afro-American Notes," *Brooklyn Daily Eagle*, November 15, 1908, 41; "Past Week in Brooklyn," *New York Age*, December 24, 1908, 5; and "Colored Women Convene," *Brooklyn Daily Eagle*, July 8, 1909, 5.

103. "Minutes of the New York State Woman Suffrage Association, 1907–1910," vol. 7, p. 316, box 3, Woman Suffrage Association of New York State and Woman Suffrage Party of New York City Records, 1869–1919, Rare Book and Manuscript Library, Butler Library, Columbia University; "The Political Settlement," *Survey* 24, May 14, 1910, 279; "Mrs. Belmont's Club Opens," *New York Times*, January 13, 1910, 4; "What Mrs. Belmont Has Done for Women," *New York Times*, March 9, 1910, 1.

104. "New Equality League," *New York Age*, July 13, 1910, 5.

105. "New Rochelle, N.Y." *New York Age*, April 29, 1915, 3.

106. "St. Mark's Lyceum Opening," *New York Age*, September 24, 1908, 3. Keyser served as the first president of the Empire State Federation of Women's Clubs, affiliated with the National Association of Colored Women's Clubs, and she was active on the board of the Young Women's Christian Association. In 1909 and 1910 Keyser helped with the founding of the National Association for the Advancement of Colored People (NAACP), attending its first organizational meeting and serving on the first Board of Directors, the Executive Committee, and the Program Committee. In 1912, Mary McLeod Bethune met Keyser when Bethune stayed at the White Rose Home. She begged Keyser to help her at the Daytona Educational and Industrial School for Negro Girls (which became Bethune-Cookman University) in Florida. Perry, *Hubert Harrison*, 73, 77, 95; *A Hubert Harrison Reader*, ed. Jeffrey Babcock Perry (Middletown: Wesleyan University Press, 2001), 36; Charles Flint Kellogg, *NAACP: A History of the National Association for the Advancement of Colored People*, vol. 1 (Baltimore: Johns Hopkins Press, 1967), 47–48, 61.

107. "The Brooklyn Literary Union," *Brooklyn Daily Eagle*, September 8, 1886, 4.

108. Wellman, *Brooklyn's Promised Land*, 165–66.

109. St. Mark's African Methodist Episcopal Church was the largest A.M.E. church in New York. Founded in 1883, lyceum participants included journalists and community activists and held special events and discussions on subjects ranging from "Race Loyalty" to woman suffrage. "Easter at St. Mark's Lyceum," *New York Age*, April 15, 1909, 3.

110. "Afro-American Notes," *Brooklyn Daily Eagle*, March 30, 1909, 9.

111. "Metropolitan U.A.M.E. Church," *New York Age*, May 6, 1909, 8.

112. J. W. Thompson, *An Authentic History of the Douglass Monument: Biographical Facts and Incidents in the Life of Frederick Douglass* (Rochester, NY: Rochester Herald Press, 1903), 19. Susan B. Anthony, who spoke at the birthday celebration, and May Wright Sewall had also attended his funeral in Washington, DC.

113. Ibid., 28, 77. Jerome Jeffrey was a member of the "Douglass League" and an "active" casket bearer at Douglass's funeral in Rochester. Douglass and his family attended Plymouth Church. Ann Gordon, ed., *The Selected Papers of Elizabeth Cady Stanton and Susan B. Anthony*, vol. 6, *An Awful Hush, 1895 to 1906* (New Brunswick: Rutgers University Press, 2013), 215.

114. Stanton similarly criticized monuments to white men, such as the tomb to commemorate Ulysses S. Grant. Elizabeth Cady Stanton, *Eighty Years and More: Reminiscences, 1815–1897* (Boston: Northeastern University Press, 1993), 388; Thompson, *Authentic History*, 77-79; Gordon, *Selected Papers*, vol. 6, 124–25.

115. Brown, *Homespun Heroines*, 186. Matthews contracted tuberculosis but kept up with her busy activist schedule until the end of her life. After Matthews's death, in 1907, Keyser continued for some six years as superintendent of the White Rose Mission.

116. Adelaide M. Cromwell, *The Other Brahmins: Boston's Black Upper Class 1750–1950* (Fayetteville: University of Arkansas Press, 1994), 53; Vicki S. Welch, *And They Were Related, Too: A Study of Eleven Generations of One American Family!* (Bloomington, IN: Xlibris Corporation, 2006), 110–12.

117. The Jeffreys had four children, none of whom survived childhood. Welch, *And They Were Related*, 113; "Mrs. 'Hester C.' R. Jerome Jeffrey," http://www.math.buffalo.edu/~sww/0history/jeffrey_hester.html (accessed February 1, 2015).

118. Jeffrey knew Harriet Tubman, Mary Talbert, and Mary Church Terrell. Welch, *And They Were Related*, 111, 114.

119. Overacker, *African American Church Community*, 28, 182.

120. Ibid., 28.

121. Ibid., 125, 131.

122. "New Union Organized," *Democrat and Chronicle*, August 8, 1901, 9.

123. "Minutes of the Eighth Biennial Convention of the National Association (1912)," p. 48, Microfilm, Burke Library, Hamilton College, Clinton, NY; Davis, *Lifting as they Climb*, 33.

124. Overacker, *African American Church Community*, 182.

125. Giddings, *When and Where*, 125.

126. Welch, *And They Were Related*, 111; Gordon, *Selected Papers*, vol. 6, 477.

127. "To Interest All American Women," *Democrat and Chronicle*, June 9, 1906, 15; "Class in Parliamentary Law," *Democrat and Chronicle*, November 21, 1905, 13.

128. "Congratulations for the Grand Old Woman," *Democrat and Chronicle*, February 17, 1903, 13.

129. "Mrs. Lucy J. Sprague," *Democrat and Chronicle*, October 1, 1903, 12.

130. Blake McKelvey, "Lights and Shadows in Local Negro History," *Rochester History* 21, no. 4 (October 1959): 18; Welch, *And They Were Related*, 111.

131. "Woman Suffragists Meet," *Democrat and Chronicle*, November 2, 1905, 7.

132. Overacker, *African American Church Community*, 183.

133. Quoted in Welch, *And They Were Related*, 113.

134. "Miss Anthony in Rochester," *New York Age*, December 14, 1905, 4.

135. "Dedication to Occupy a Week," *Democrat and Chronicle*, August 19, 1907, 9.

136. Mary Jo Deegan, ed. *The New Woman of Color: The Collected Writings of Fannie Barrier Williams, 1893–1918* (DeKalb: Northern Illinois University Press, 2002), 137.

137. Clinton, *Harriet Tubman*, 212; Williams, *Strangers*, 155.

138. Judith Wellman, "Historic Structure Report, Michigan Street Baptist Church, Buffalo, New York" (March 27, 2013), 63.

139. See for example, "Buffalo Briefs," *New York Age*, May 13, 1914, 3.

140. "Woman's Suffrage Debate in Buffalo," *New York Age*, June 16, 1910, 8.

141. "Branch of Political Equality Association," *Afro-American*, October 15, 1910, 7.

142. "Literary League Meets," *New York Age*, December 15, 1910, 1.

143. "News of Greater New York," *New York Age*, September 14, 1911, 7; Brown, *Homespun Heroines*, 116.

144. "Women Will Nominate Dana," *Sun*, October 19, 1911, 1.

145. Ibid. Mulrooney married Gus Ruhlin, the heavyweight boxing champion.

146. May Martel, "Women's Department: Colored Women in Demonstration," *New York Age*, March 13, 1913, 5.

147. Irma Watkins-Owens, *Blood Relations: Caribbean Immigrants and the Harlem Community, 1900–1930* (Bloomington: Indiana University Press, 1996), 79.

148. "Englewood, N.J." *New York Age*, April 22, 1915, 5.

149. "News of Greater New York," *New York Age*, July 9, 1914, 8. Lawton held her presidency in the Empire State Federation of Women's Clubs from 1916 to 1926, during which time the club grew from a few clubs nestled around New York City to one with 103 clubs across the state. She would join the Colored Women's Department of the Republican National Committee after women won the right to vote nationwide in 1920. Louise A. Tilly and Patricia Gurin, eds., *Women, Politics, and Change* (New York: Russell Sage Foundation, 1990), 206.

150. Gallagher, *Black Women*, 24.

151. "Suffrage, Pro and Con," *Brooklyn Daily Eagle*, February 28, 1914, 20.

152. Terborg-Penn, "Discontented Black Feminists," 65.

153. Cash, *African American Women*, 110.

154. Gallagher, *Black Women*, 25.

155. Williams, *Strangers*, 231.

5. Persuading the "Male Preserve"

1. Will Irwin, quoted in Michael McGerr, "Political Style and Women's Power, 1830–1930," *Journal of American History* 77, no. 3 (December 1990): 878.

2. George Middleton, "Snapshot," *La Follette's Weekly Magazine* 20 (May 18, 1912): 6; "The Heroic Men," *New York Times*, May 3, 1912, 10.

3. "Suffragists in Brooklyn," *New York Tribune*, July 10, 1913, 6.

4. "Mary Lewis Gannett," Western New York Suffragists, https://rrlc.org/winningthevote/biographies/mary-lewis-gannett/ (accessed September 7, 2015); "Report of the New York State Woman Suffrage Association," p. 67, "Twenty-Sixth

Annual New York State Woman Suffrage Association Convention Report, Ithaca, November 12–15, 1894, Jon A. Lindseth Woman Suffrage Collection, Collection 8002, Division of Rare and Manuscript Collections, Carl A. Kroch Library, Cornell University; New York Woman Suffrage Association, "Newsletter" (March 1901), Scrapbook 3, p. 73, Miller National American Woman Suffrage Association Scrapbooks, 1897–1911, Library of Congress, Rare Book and Special Collections Division, Washington, DC.

5. A Young Men's Woman Suffrage League did exist in New York, 1874–1875, under the leadership of J. K. Hamilton Willcox, and was headquartered at Plimpton Hall on Stuyvesant Street in New York City. Sally Roesch Wagner, *A Time of Protest: Suffragists Challenge the Republic, 1870–1887* (Aberdeen, SD: Sky Carrier Press, 1992), 85; Kenneth Florey, *American Woman Suffrage Postcards: A Study and Catalog* (Jefferson, NC: McFarland and Company, 2015), 93.

6. Kevin F. White, "Men Supporting Women: A Study of Men Associated with the Women's Suffrage Movement in Britain and America, 1909–1920," *Maryland Historian* 18, no. 1 (Spring 1987): 50–52.

7. Michael S. Kimmel and Thomas E. Mosmiller, eds., *Against the Tide: Pro-Feminist Men in the United States, 1776–1990* (Boston: Beacon Press, 1992), 205–9.

8. Harriot Stanton Blatch, "How the Suffrage Referendum was Won in New York State," *Women's Political World* 2, no. 3 (June 1, 1914): 3; Ellen Carol DuBois, *Harriot Stanton Blatch and the Winning of Woman Suffrage* (New Haven: Yale University Press, 1997), 128–29. See also Susan Goodier, *No Votes for Women: The New York State Anti-Suffrage Movement* (Urbana: University of Illinois Press, 2013); Trisha Franzen, *Anna Howard Shaw: The Work of Woman Suffrage* (Urbana: University of Illinois Press, 2014).

9. "Few Seats for Men on Suffrage Day," *New York Times*, February 23, 1911, 3.

10. For more on demographic trends related to politics see Richard McCormick, *From Realignment to Reform: Political Change in New York State, 1893–1910* (Ithaca, NY: Cornell University Press, 1979), 27–28. For an account of grange support of woman suffrage, see "Hand in History: 145 Years of Grange in America," www.national grange.org (accessed December 27, 2014). For an interesting discussion of feminism in rural organizations, see Grey Osterud, *Putting the Barn before the House: Women and Family Farming in Early Twentieth-Century New York* (Ithaca, NY: Cornell University Press, 2012), 258–59, 286–87.

11. National American Woman Suffrage Association Press Release, January 22, 1909, box 65, National American Woman Suffrage Association Papers, Library of Congress, Rare Book and Special Collections Division, Washington, DC; Linda J. Lumsden, *Rampant Women: Suffragists and the Right of Assembly* (Knoxville: University of Tennessee Press, 1997), 69–71. For reference to the suffrage renaissance see Franzen, *Anna Howard Shaw*, 10.

12. Max Eastman, "Early History of the Men's League," *Woman Voter* 3, no. 9 (October 1912): 17; Max Eastman, *Enjoyment of Living* (New York: Harper, 1948), 306.

13. Oswald Garrison Villard to Anna Howard Shaw, January 7, 1908, Oswald Garrison Villard papers, bMS Am 1323, item number 3494, Houghton Library, Harvard University, Cambridge, MA; Franzen, *Anna Howard Shaw*, 110.

14. Oswald Garrison Villard to Anna Howard Shaw, January 7, 1908, Oswald Garrison Villard papers, bMS Am 1323, item number 3494, Houghton Library, Harvard University, Cambridge, MA. Villard had long recognized the contributions that women made on behalf of reform politicians at the local level in New York City. Robert J. Dinkin, *Before Equal Suffrage: Women in Partisan Politics from Colonial Times to 1920* (Westport, CT: Greenwood Press, 1995), 114–16.

15. Raymond Matthew Ortiz, "Ladies and Gentle Men: The Men's League for Woman Suffrage and its Liberation of the Male Identity" (MA Thesis, California State University at Fullerton, 2014), 32.

16. Anna Howard Shaw to Oswald Garrison Villard, February 6, 1908, Oswald Garrison Villard papers, bMS Am 1323, item number 3494, Houghton Library, Harvard University, Cambridge, MA; Ortiz, "Ladies and Gentle Men," 31–32.

17. Oswald Garrison Villard to Anna Howard Shaw, February 13, 1908, Oswald Garrison Villard papers, bMS Am 1323, item number 3494, Houghton Library, Harvard University, Cambridge, MA.

18. Stephen Wise to Oswald Garrison Villard, July 26, 1908, Oswald Garrison Villard papers, 1856–1949, bMS Am 1323, item number 4256, Houghton Library, Harvard University, Cambridge, MA; Harriet Taylor Upton, ed., "Fortieth Annual Report of the National-American Woman Suffrage Association, held at Buffalo, October 15th to 21st, inclusive 1908" (Warren, OH: Headquarters, 1908), 96.

19. Upton, "Fortieth Annual Report," 96.

20. Eastman, "Early History," 17; William L. O'Neill, *The Last Romantic: A Life of Max Eastman* (New York: Oxford University Press, 1978), 19.

21. Eastman, "Early History," 17.

22. Ibid.; Susan B. Anthony and Ida Husted Harper, *History of Woman Suffrage*, vol. 4 (Indianapolis: Hollenbeck Press, 1902), 484–85.

23. Letter from Annis Ford Eastman to Anne Fitzhugh Miller, July 1909, Scrapbook 7, p. 106, Miller National American Woman Suffrage Association Scrapbooks, 1897–1911, Library of Congress, Rare Book and Special Collections Division, Washington, DC; Eastman, *Enjoyment of Living*, 291, 297.

24. Eastman, *Enjoyment of Living*, 305–6.

25. Ibid., 265, 267, 282–83, 297.

26. Ibid., 268.

27. Ibid., 282–85.

28. Ibid., 306; O'Neill, *Last Romantic*, 19.

29. Eastman, *Enjoyment of Living*, 307.

30. Letter from Annis Ford Eastman to Anne Fitzhugh Miller, July 1909, Scrapbook 7, p. 106, Miller National American Woman Suffrage Association Scrapbooks, 1897–1911, Library of Congress, Rare Book and Special Collections Division, Washington, DC; Eastman, *Enjoyment of Living*, 307–8, 317.

31. "Men's League for Woman Suffrage," Scrapbook 9, pp. 82–83, Miller National American Woman Suffrage Association Scrapbooks, 1897–1911, Library of Congress, Rare Book and Special Collections Division, Washington, DC.

32. Eastman, "Early History," 17.

33. "Male Suffragettes Now in the Field," *New York Times*, May 21, 1909, 1; Eastman, *Enjoyment of Living*, 308.

34. Initial discussions suggested that the league would be an exclusively New York City league.

35. "Suffrage Statement," 1915, signed by Men's League for Woman Suffrage officers, Helen Brewster Owens Papers, Arthur and Elizabeth Schlesinger Library on the History of Women in America, Radcliffe Institute, Harvard University.

36. "A New 100 to Help Women," *Sun*, November 30, 1909, 6; "Men Cry 'Votes for Women,'" *Brooklyn Daily Eagle*, November 30, 1909, 20; Eastman, "Early History," 18; Eastman, *Enjoyment of Living*, 350. Eastman incorrectly states that the first meeting occurred in November 1910.

37. "Constitution and Charter Members of the Men's League for Woman Suffrage of the State of New York," Men's League for Woman Suffrage, Scrapbook 9, p. 82, Miller National American Woman Suffrage Association Scrapbooks, 1897–1911, Library of Congress, Rare Book and Special Collections Division, Washington, DC. Oswald Villard, Stephen Wise, and John Dewey all held official positions in the National Association for the Advancement of Colored People. See NAACP, *Freeing America: Seventh Annual Report of the National Association for the Advancement of Colored People* (New York: NAACP, 1917), front matter.

38. Eastman, "Early History," 17; Eastman, *Enjoyment of Living*, 308; Anthony and Harper, *History of Woman Suffrage*, vol. 4, 485.

39. "A New 100 to Help Women," *Sun*, November 30, 1909, 6.

40. Goodier, *No Votes*, 57–58.

41. "Working for Suffrage Bill," *New York Times*, December 2, 1909, 3. Fanny Garrison Villard chaired the State Legislative Committee.

42. "Suffrage Shock for Governor Hughes at Hearings," *New York World*, December 22, 1909, Scrapbook 8, p. 38, Miller National American Woman Suffrage Association Scrapbooks, 1897–1911, Library of Congress, Rare Book and Special Collections Division, Washington, DC; "Governor Hughes Silent on Woman Suffrage," *New York Times*, December 23, 1909, 18.

43. "Constitution and Charter Members of the Men's League for Woman Suffrage of the State of New York," Men's League for Woman Suffrage, Scrapbook 9, p. 82, Miller National American Woman Suffrage Association Scrapbooks, 1897–1911, Library of Congress, Rare Book and Special Collections Division, Washington, DC.

44. "Men's League for Woman Suffrage Invitation," Scrapbook 9, p. 83, Miller National American Woman Suffrage Association Scrapbooks, 1897–1911, Library of Congress, Rare Book and Special Collections Division, Washington, DC; "Suffragists Sing New Marching Song," *New York Times*, May 1, 1911, 5; Eastman, "Early History," 18; Eastman, *Enjoyment of Living*, 350–51; Men's League for Woman Suffrage of the State of New York, "Amended Constitution" (1912), box 13, p. 4, League of Woman Voters of New York State Records, 1912–1981, Rare Book and Manuscript Library, Butler Library, Columbia University.

45. "Women Using Hands, Feet, and Brains to Carry on Aggressive Campaign Everywhere," *Sun*, March 2, 1913, 14. See also Lumsden, *Rampant Women*, 112.

46. Lumsden, *Rampant Women*, 112–13.

47. Anthony and Harper, *History of Woman Suffrage*, vol. 4, 485; *Cornell University Theater Magazine* (May 2, 1913), cover, Woman's Suffrage Parade, May 3, 1913, box 5, folder 1, S-377, Jon A. Lindseth Woman Suffrage Collection, Collection 8002,

Division of Rare and Manuscript Collections, Carl A. Kroch Library, Cornell University, Ithaca, NY. Billed as "Woman Suffrage Addresses and Pageant Tableau," held at Metropolitan Opera House in New York City.

48. Amy Shore, *Suffrage and the Silver Screen* (New York: Peter Lang, 2014), 46.

49. Lumsden, *Rampant Women*, 37.

50. Eastman, "Early History," 18, including material contributed by the Men's League of New York through Thomas Hotchkiss.

51. "Kings County Plans Club and Flying Squads," *New York Tribune*, October 27, 1913, 9; Sara Hunter Graham, *Woman Suffrage and the New Democracy* (New Haven: Yale University Press, 1996), 61.

52. "Mrs. Julius Frank, Civic Leader Dies," unidentified newspaper clipping (1960), box 1, folder 14, series 3, Marion Sanger Frank and A. A. Brill Papers, 1844–1960, Rare Book and Manuscript Library, Butler Library, Columbia University.

53. "A Most Distinguished Citizen for More Than 60 Years," *Ogdensburg Journal*, March 3, 2015.

54. Mrs. Henry Cannon White, Chair of the Woman Suffrage Party in Delaware County makes this suggestion. See "Speeches 1913," New York Woman Suffrage Collection, 1914–1915, Collection 8041, Division of Rare and Manuscript Collections, Carl A. Kroch Library, Cornell University, Ithaca, NY.

55. Anne Fitzhugh Miller, "Greetings," Typescript, Thirty-Ninth Annual Convention, New York State Woman Suffrage Association, October 15, 1907, Scrapbook 6, p. 5, Miller National American Woman Suffrage Association Scrapbooks, 1897–1911, Library of Congress, Rare Book and Special Collections Division, Washington, DC.

56. Thirty-Ninth Annual Convention of New York State Woman Suffrage Association Program, October 15, 16, 17, 18, 1907, Scrapbook 5, p. 136, Miller National American Woman Suffrage Association Scrapbooks, 1897–1911, Library of Congress, Rare Book and Special Collections Division, Washington, DC.

57. "Western New York Suffragists," www.winningthevote.org (accessed February 14, 2016); "Suffrage Protest Meeting in Union Square," unidentified newspaper clipping, May 21, 1910, Scrapbook 8, p. 112, Miller National American Woman Suffrage Association Scrapbooks, Library of Congress, Rare Book and Special Collections Division, Washington, DC.

58. Rosemary Fry Plakas, "Catch the Suffragists' Spirit: The Miller Suffrage Scrapbooks," *Journeys and Crossings*, Library of Congress, https://www.loc.gov/rr/program/journey/millers.html (accessed February 13, 2016).

59. Eastman, *Enjoyment of Living*, 315; O'Neill, *Last Romantic*, 3–4, 19. $50 in 1910 is the equivalent of $1215.43 in 2016.

60. Eastman, *Enjoyment of Living*, 315, 319.

61. Graham, *Woman Suffrage*, 65–69; White, "Men Supporting Women," 54.

62. "The Suffrage Question," *Cambridge Tribune* 38, no. 24, August 14, 1915. One of Eastman's earliest pieces, "Woman's Suffrage and Sentiment," was published by the Equal Franchise Society of New York City in 1909. Published by H-Net, 1998, http://www.expo98.msu.edu/people/Eastman.htm (accessed April 11, 2015).

63. "Max Eastman on Woman Suffrage" n.d., box 53/reel 36, National American Woman Suffrage Association Records, Library of Congress, Rare Book and Special

Collections Division, Washington, DC; Max Eastman, "Confession of a Suffrage Orator," *Masses* (November 1915); O'Neill, *Last Romantic*, 21.

64. "Suffragettes and Antis Plead with Legislators," *Brooklyn Daily Eagle*, February 22, 1911, 16; Max Eastman, "Is Woman Suffrage Important?" *North American Review* 193 (January 1911), 65.

65. Eva Boice, "Woman Suffrage, Vassar College, and Laura Johnson Wylie," *Hudson River Valley Review* 20, no. 2 (Spring 2004): 36–49.

66. For a discussion of justice versus expediency arguments, see Aileen S. Kraditor, *The Ideas of the Woman Suffrage Movement/1890–1920* (New York: W.W. Norton, 1981), 38–63.

67. O'Neill, *Last Romantic*, 21; Eastman, "Is Woman Suffrage Important?," 67–68; Ida Husted Harper, *History of Woman Suffrage*, vol. 5 (New York: J.J. Little and Ives, 1922), 285.

68. Harriot Stanton Blatch, "How the Suffrage Referendum was Won in New York State," *Women's Political World* 2, no. 3 (June 1, 1914): 3.

69. DuBois, *Harriot Stanton Blatch*, 129.

70. Franzen, *Anna Howard Shaw*, 118.

71. DuBois, *Harriot Stanton Blatch*, 124–32.

72. "A New 100 to Help Women," *Sun*.

73. "Suffragists and Antis Storm State Capitol," *Brooklyn Daily Eagle*, March 9, 1910, 1–2.

74. Forty-Second National American Woman Suffrage Association Report, 1910, 48, Woman's Suffrage Pamphlets, box 2, folder 4, Onondaga County Library, Syracuse, NY.

75. Harriot Stanton Blatch and Alma Lutz, *Challenging Years: The Memoirs of Harriot Stanton Blatch* (New York: G.P. Putnam's Sons, 1940), 130–31.

76. "Suffragists in Storm Scold Lawmakers," unidentified New York newspaper clipping, Scrapbook 8, pp. 114–15, Miller National American Woman Suffrage Association Scrapbooks, 1897–1911, Library of Congress, Rare Book and Special Collections Division, Washington, DC.

77. Men's League for Woman Suffrage of the State of New York, "Amended Constitution" (1912), box 13, League of Woman Voters of New York State Records, 1912–1981, Rare Book and Manuscript Library, Butler Library, Columbia University; "Few Seats for Men on Suffrage Day," *New York Times*, February 23, 1911, 3; "2400 Women Jam State Capitol at Suffrage Hearing," unidentified newspaper clipping, February 22, 1911, Scrapbook 9, p. 51, Miller National American Woman Suffrage Association Scrapbooks, 1897–1911, Library of Congress, Rare Book and Special Collections Division, Washington, DC.

78. For examples see Max Eastman, "Is Woman's Suffrage Important?" *North American Review* 193 (January 1911): 65; "Suffragettes and Antis Plead with Legislators," *Brooklyn Daily Eagle*, February 22, 1911, 16; "Max Eastman on Woman Suffrage," box 53, National American Woman Suffrage Association Records, Library of Congress, Rare Book and Special Collections Division, Washington, DC; "Woman's Suffrage as Man Sees it," n.d., Scrapbook 9, p. 100, Miller National American Woman Suffrage Association Scrapbooks, Library of Congress, Rare Book and Special Collections Division, Washington, DC.

79. Men's League for Woman Suffrage of the State of New York, "Amended Constitution," (1912), box 13, League of Woman Voters of New York State Records, 1912–1981,

Rare Book and Manuscript Library, Butler Library, Columbia University; New York Woman Suffrage Association, "Forty-Sixth Annual Convention of the New York State Woman Suffrage Association, October 12 to 15, 1914," program, box 7, Woman Suffrage Association of New York State and Woman Suffrage Party of New York City Records, 1869–1919, Rare Book and Manuscript Library, Butler Library, Columbia University.

80. "The Women's Parade," unidentified newspaper clipping, Scrapbook 9, p. 79, Miller National American Woman Suffrage Association Scrapbooks, 1897–1911, Library of Congress, Rare Book and Special Collections Division, Washington, DC; Lumsden, *Rampant Women*, 92.

81. "Mayor Fails to Review Parade and So Misses the Enthusiasm," unidentified New York newspaper clipping, May 6, 1911, Scrapbook 9, p. 79, Miller National American Woman Suffrage Association Scrapbooks, 1897–1911, Library of Congress, Rare Book and Special Collections Division, Washington, DC.

82. George Middleton, "Snapshot," *La Follette's Weekly Magazine* 20 (May 18, 1912): 6; Charles Strong quoted in Harriet Burton Laidlaw, *James Lees Laidlaw* (Privately published, 1932), 20–21; Blatch and Lutz, *Challenging Years*, 132–33.

83. *How it Feels to be the Husband of a Suffragette,* by Him [probably Arthur Brown, husband of Gertrude Foster Brown] (New York: George Doran and Company, 1915); Mary Chapman and Angela Mills, eds. *Treacherous Texts: U.S. Suffrage Literature, 1846–1946* (New Brunswick, NJ: Rutgers University Press, 2012), 231. See also "My Wife's Joined the Suffrage Movement (I've Suffered Ever Since)," box 10, Jon A. Lindseth Woman Suffrage Collection, Collection 8002, Division of Rare and Manuscript Collections, Carl A. Kroch Library, Cornell University, Ithaca, NY.

84. Will Irwin, *The Making of a Reporter* (New York: G.P. Putnam and Sons, 1942), 198–99.

85. Frances Perkins, quoted in Harriet Burton Laidlaw, *James Lees Laidlaw*, 37–38.

86. "Mayor Fails to Review Parade and so Misses the Enthusiasm," unidentified New York newspaper clipping (May 6, 1911), Scrapbook 9, p. 79, Miller National American Woman Suffrage Association Scrapbooks, 1897–1911, Library of Congress, Rare Book and Special Collections Division, Washington, DC.

87. "Work for Women's Cause," *New York Tribune*, May 24, 1912, 3; "All Now Set for the Big Suffrage Parade," *Sun*, May 4, 1912, 18. Theodore Roosevelt was invited but declined, citing an engagement in Maryland. William Sulzer agreed to march in the November torchlight parade. See "Sulzer in Suffrage Parade," *Sun*, October 26, 1912, 1. See also Matthew L. Lifflander, *The Impeachment of Governor Sulzer: A Story of American Politics* (Albany: State University of New York Press, 2012), 73; Blatch and Lutz, *Challenging Years*, 222.

88. Men's League for Woman Suffrage of the State of New York, "Amended Constitution," (1912), box 13, League of Woman Voters of New York State Records, 1912–1981, Rare Book and Manuscript Library, Butler Library, Columbia University; Harper, *History of Woman Suffrage*, vol. 5, 674; George Foster Peabody, quoted in Harriet Burton Laidlaw, *James Lees Laidlaw*, 27–28. James Laidlaw remained president of the organization until 1920.

89. "Work for Women's Cause," *New York Tribune*, May 24, 1912, 3.

90. Ibid.

91. Men's League for Woman Suffrage of the State of New York, "Amended Constitution," (1912), box 13, League of Woman Voters of New York State Records,

1912–1981, Rare Book and Manuscript Library, Butler Library, Columbia University; Anthony and Harper, *History of Woman Suffrage*, vol. 4, 484–85; Harriet Burton Laidlaw, *James Lees Laidlaw*, 85.

92. Anthony and Harper, *History of Woman Suffrage*, vol. 4, 16, 21, 35, 106, 112, 133.

93. "All Now Ready for the Big Suffrage Parade," *Sun*, May 4, 1912, 18.

94. Irwin, *Making of a Reporter*, 198–99; Eastman, "Early History," 18; Middleton, "Snapshot," 6; "The Heroic Men," *New York Times*, May 3, 1912, 6.

95. Fannie Hurst, *Anatomy of Me: A Wanderer in Search of Herself* (New York: Doubleday and Company, 1958), 248.

96. "All Now Ready for the Big Suffrage Parade," *Sun*, May 4, 1912, 18.

97. Gertrude Foster Brown, "On Account of Sex: A Manuscript About the Fight for Woman Suffrage," chapters 2, 5; typescript, Suffrage Collection, Sophia Smith Collection, Smith College, Northampton, MA; "Why We March: A Symposium," *Woman Voter* 3, no. 4 (May 1912), quoted in David Kevin McDonald, "Organizing Womanhood: Women's Culture and the Politics of Woman Suffrage in New York State, 1865–1917" (PhD diss., State University of New York at Stony Brook, 1987), 68. Charles Strong, quoted in Harriet Burton Laidlaw, *James Lees Laidlaw*, 20–21; "8,000 in Great Suffrage March," *New York Tribune*, May 5, 1912, 1.

98. Men's League for Woman Suffrage of the State of New York, "Amended Constitution," (1912), box 13, League of Woman Voters of New York State Records, 1912–1981, Rare Book and Manuscript Department, Butler Library, Columbia University; "All Now Ready for the Big Suffrage Parade," *Sun*, May 4, 1912, 18.

99. "All Now Ready for the Big Suffrage Parade," *Sun*, May 4, 1912, 18.

100. Ibid.

101. Franzen, *Anna Howard Shaw*, 138.

102. "5,000 Women March, Beset by Crowds," *New York Times*, March 4, 1913, 5; Eastman, "Early History," 17; "Suffragettes and Antis Plead with Legislators," *Brooklyn Daily Eagle*, February 22, 1911, 16; U.S. House of Representatives, 63rd Congress, *Hearing Before the Committee on Rules Resolution on Establishing a Committee on Woman Suffrage*, December 3, 4, 5, 1913 (Washington: DC: GPO, 1914), 188.

103. Goodier, *No Votes*, 80–81.

104. "Suffragists Hiss Opposing Debaters," *New York Times*, January 27, 1914, 1.

105. Melanie Susan Gustafson, *Women and the Republican Party, 1854–1924* (Urbana: University of Illinois Press, 2001), 108–12; "T.R. is with Hughes on Vote Amendment," *New York Times*, August 9, 1916, 4; Max Eastman, "Is Woman Suffrage Important?," 60.

106. Harriot Stanton Blatch, "Secretary Brown Declares for Suffrage," *Women's Political World* 2, no. 15 (August 1, 1914): 5.

107. "Governor's Message," New York State Legislature, Documents of the Assembly of the State of New York One Hundred and Thirty-Sixth Session, no. 2, January 1, 1913, 8.

108. DuBois, *Harriot Stanton Blatch*, 146.

109. "Suffrage Hikers Come to Albany led by General Rosalie Jones," *Albany Journal*, January 7, 1914, 1; "Suffrage Hikers Weary; Storm Capitol To-day," *Syracuse Post Standard*, January 4, 1914, 3.

110. DuBois, *Harriot Stanton Blatch*, 168–70.

111. Blatch and Lutz, *Challenging Years*, 222.

112. "Governor Whitman Will Vote for Suffrage," *Woman Voter* 6, no. 1 (January 1915): 6–7. In three monthly issues in 1915 the *Woman Voter* devoted space to reprinting addresses from individual voters and organizations as well as from prominent state judges and politicians.

113. "Public Officials and Woman Suffrage," *Woman Voter* 6, no. 1 (January 1915), 7.

114. "Work for Women's Cause," *New York Tribune*, May 24, 1912, 3.

115. "An Elaborate Spectacular Pageant by the Men's League for Woman Suffrage," *Evening World*, April 13, 1914, 9; "The Suffrage Movement," *Woman Voter* 5, no. 5 (May 1914): 24–25.

116. "Suffrage Day in New York," and "The Suffrage Pageant," *Woman Voter* 5, no. 5 (May 1914), 24–25; "Men's League for Woman Suffrage," *Woman Voter* 5, no. 2 (February 1914): 31–32.

117. Graham, *Woman Suffrage*, 67. Late in the campaign women members of the Woman Suffrage Party in New York City suggested speaking to all working men, asking them to vote for the amendment. New York City Woman Suffrage Party, "City Committee Meeting," Minutes of the Woman Suffrage Party, p. 6 (August 30, 1915), box 9, Woman Suffrage Association of New York State and Woman Suffrage Party of New York City Records, 1869–1919, Rare Book and Manuscript Library, Butler Library, Columbia University.

118. "The Campaign Convention," *Woman Voter* 5, no. 11 (November 1914), 16–17; "Expects 10,000 Men in Suffrage March," *New York Times*, October 20, 1917, 2.

119. "The Campaign Convention," *Woman Voter* 5, no. 11 (November 1914), 16–17; Frederic C. Howe, "Why I Want Equal Suffrage," *Woman Voter* 6, no. 2 (February 1915), 18.

120. "Public Officials and Woman Suffrage," *Woman Voter* 6, no. 1 (January 1915), 7–10.

121. George Elliot Howard, "A Suffrage Creed," *Woman Voter* 5, no. 5, (May 1914): 32.

122. Howe, "Why I Want Equal Suffrage," 18.

123. Omar E. Garwood, quoted in Ida Husted Harper, *History of Woman Suffrage*, vol. 6 (New York: J.J. Little and Ives, 1922), 62–63.

6. Radicalism and Spectacle

1. The term "old time 'war horse'" probably refers to Susan B. Anthony, often derided by the press for her appearance. In fact, many observers perceived all women who supported women's rights in the nineteenth century to be masculine or unwomanly. "Women at Odds over Suffrage Question," *New York Times*, March 17, 1907, SM2.

2. Harriot Stanton Blatch and Alma Lutz, *Challenging Years: The Memoirs of Harriot Stanton Blatch* (New York: G.P. Putnam's Sons, 1940), 91; Isabelle K. Savell, *Ladies' Lib: How Rockland Women Got the Vote* (New York: Historical Society of Rockland County, 1979), 31; Margaret Finnegan, *Selling Suffrage: Consumer Culture & Votes for Women* (New York: Columbia University Press, 1999), 57.

3. Finnegan, *Selling Suffrage*, 81.

4. Sherna Gluck, *From Parlor to Prison* (New York: Vintage Books, 1976), 206, 208–9.

5. Ellen Carol DuBois, *Harriot Stanton Blatch and the Winning of Woman Suffrage* (New Haven: Yale University Press, 1997), 108; Gertrude Foster Brown, "On Account of Sex: A Manuscript about the Fight for Woman Suffrage," n.d., chapter 2, p. 2, box 7, folders 7–9, typescript in Suffrage Collection, Sophia Smith Collection, Smith College, Northampton, MA.

6. Finnegan, *Selling Suffrage*, 61.

7. Alice Sheppard, *Cartooning for Suffrage* (Albuquerque: University of New Mexico Press, 1994), 201.

8. Sarah Grand, "The New Aspect of the Woman Question," *North American Review* 158, no. 448 (1894): 276.

9. Lois W. Banner, *American Beauty* (New York: Alfred A. Knopf, 1983), 154.

10. Marilyn and Ann Jones Holscher, *Casting Off the Corset: Changes in Women's Clothing, 1880–1930*, ed. The 1890 House Museum (Cortland, NY: Graphics Plus, 1980), n. p.

11. Finnegan, *Selling Suffrage*, 80.

12. Paula Baker, *The Moral Frameworks of Public Life: Gender, Politics, and the State in Rural New York, 1870–1930* (New York: Oxford University Press, 1991), 18–20.

13. Kathy Peiss, *Cheap Amusements: Working Women and Leisure in Turn-of-the-Century New York* (Philadelphia: Temple University Press, 1986), 53–55.

14. Sara M. Evans, *Born for Liberty: A History of Women in America* (New York: Simon & Schuster, 1989), 161, 175–76.

15. Linda J. Lumsden, *Inez: The Life and Times of Inez Milholland* (Bloomington: Indiana University Press, 2004), 29.

16. Evans, *Born for Liberty*, 161.

17. Nancy F. Cott, *The Grounding of Modern Feminism* (New Haven: Yale University Press, 1987), 39.

18. Finnegan, *Selling Suffrage*, 95.

19. Carrie Chapman Catt, " 'Free Love' Charge Held Ridiculous," *New York Times*, February 15, 1914, SM4; Cott, *Grounding of Modern Feminism*, 14.

20. Rheta Childe Dorr, *A Woman of Fifty* (New York: Funk & Wagnalls, 1924), 268.

21. Edna Kenton, "Edna Kenton Says Feminism Will Give—Men More Fun, Women Greater Scope, Children Better Parents, Life More Charm," *Delineator* (July 1914), 17.

22. Cott, *Grounding of Modern Feminism*, 14, 15.

23. Ibid., 35.

24. Jacqueline Van Voris, *Carrie Chapman Catt: A Public Life* (New York: Feminist Press at the City University of New York, 1987), 30, 33.

25. "Mrs. Belmont Home for Suffrage War," *New York Times*, September 16, 1910, 9; "Gabrielle Stewart Mulliner," *Modern World and Business Woman's Magazine* 9 (September 1908): 197.

26. Finnegan, *Selling Suffrage*, 81.

27. Susan B. Anthony, handwritten notes (dated 1905), box 1, folder 11, "Women's Rights Material," First Unitarian Church Collection, Rare Books, Special Collections and Preservation, Rush Rhees Library, University of Rochester, Rochester, NY.

28. Holscher and Holscher, *Casting off the Corset*, n.p.

29. Hobble skirts had a very narrow circumference at the ankles, some requiring straps around the ankles to keep the wearer from making long strides and tearing the skirt. Ibid.

30. Finnegan, *Selling Suffrage*, 127.

31. See "Suffrage Colors," National Women's History Museum, https://www.nwhm.org/online-exhibits/votesforwomen/tour_02-02l.html, for an explanation of the suffrage colors (accessed August 31, 2016).

32. S. Josephine Baker, *Fighting for Life* (New York: MacMillan, 1939), 192.

33. Barbara Miller Solomon, *In the Company of Educated Women: A History of Women and Higher Education in America* (New Haven: Yale University Press, 1985), 111.

34. Anthony raised $100,000 to ensure that the University of Rochester would admit women. Lynn D. Gordon, *Gender and Higher Education* (New Haven, CT: Yale University Press, 1990), 194–95.

35. Nancy F. Cott, *No Small Courage: A History of Women in the United States* (New York: Oxford University Press, 2000), 312–13.

36. Solomon, *In the Company*, 58.

37. Susan Goodier, *No Votes for Women: The New York State Anti-Suffrage Movement* (Urbana: University of Illinois Press, 2013), 61–62.

38. Lumsden, *Inez*, 34; "To Pester Candidates," *New-York Tribune*, May 13, 1908, 5.

39. Ibid., 1–2; Ellen Carol DuBois, "Working Women, Class Relations, and Suffrage Militance: Harriot Stanton Blatch and the New York Woman Suffrage Movement, 1894–1909," *Journal of American History* 74, no. 1 (June 1987): 54–55.

40. Lumsden, *Inez*, 22.

41. Solomon, *In the Company*, 26.

42. "Reception for Miss Points," *Post-Standard*, February 5, 1910, 10.

43. Blatch and Lutz, *Challenging Years*, 136.

44. The club seems to have existed from 1912 to 1915 and to have been relatively inactive. Approximately nine students stated their affiliation with the club during its existence. No mention of suffrage accompanies Laura Ellsworth Cook's senior photograph. *Cornell University Class Book* (Ithaca, NY: Cornell University, 1913), 294; *Cornellian* 42 (Ithaca, NY: Cornell University, 1911), 578; Gluck, *From Parlor to Prison*, 188, 195.

45. "Owens, Helen Brewster, 1881–1968. Biography," Papers of Helen Brewster Owens, 1867–1948: A Finding Aid, Arthur and Elizabeth Schlesinger Library on the History of Women in America, Radcliffe Institute for Advanced Study, Harvard University, Cambridge, MA, 1988, http://oasis.lib.harvard.edu/oasis/deliver/~sch00069.

46. Gluck, *From Parlor to Prison*, 190.

47. "Anti-Suffragist to Talk in Barnes Hall," *Cornell Daily Sun* 35, no. 99, February 10, 1915, 2.

48. Suffragists also referred to the Collegiate Equal Suffrage League. Savell, *Ladies' Lib*, 18–19.

49. "Mrs. C. L. Tiffany, Civic Worker, Dead," *New York Times*, March 12, 1927, 15.

50. "Miss Jessie Ashley Dead," *New York Times*, January 22, 1919, 11; Sara Hunter Graham, *Woman Suffrage and the New Democracy* (New Haven: Yale University Press, 1996), 45; Savell, *Ladies' Lib*, 36.

51. "In the Women's Clubs," *Brooklyn Daily Eagle*, February 5, 1910, 11.

52. Ethel Pupper Howes, "College Equal Suffrage League Described by an Authority," *Columbia* [University] *Daily Spectator* 59, no. 30, November 1915.

53. Gordon, *Gender and Higher Education*, 157.

54. Mary Elizabeth Pidgeon to Folks, February 25, 1917, box 1, folder 6, Mary Elizabeth Pidgeon Papers, Friends Historical Library, Swarthmore College Archives, Swarthmore, PA.

55. Kenneth A. Yellis, "Prosperity's Child: Some Thoughts on the Flapper," *American Quarterly* 21, no. 1 (1969): 51.

56. Mary Elizabeth Pidgeon to Folks, August 28, 1917, box 1 folder 6, Mary Elizabeth Pidgeon Papers, Friends Historical Library, Swarthmore College Archives, Swarthmore, PA.

57. June Sochen, *Movers and Shakers: American Women Thinkers and Activists, 1900–1970* (New York: Quadrangle/New York Times, 1973), 10–11.

58. Kate E. Wittenstein, "The Heterodoxy Club and American Feminism, 1912–1930" (PhD, diss., Boston University, 1989), 23–24.

59. Christine Stansell, *American Moderns: Bohemian New York and the Creation of a New Century* (New York: Henry Holt, 2000), 229.

60. Wittenstein, "Heterodoxy Club," 7, 23, 25, 85.

61. Frederic C. Howe, *The Confessions of a Reformer* (New York: Quadrangle Books, 1967), 233.

62. "With the Members Sworn to Secrecy, Forty of New York's Prominent 'Advanced' Women Band into 'The Heterodoxy' and Meet to Eat and Decide Their Position on Problems of the Day," *New-York Tribune*, November 24, 1914, 7.

63. Evans, *Born for Liberty*, 167–68.

64. Mari Jo Buhle, *Women and American Socialism, 1870–1920* (Urbana: University of Illinois Press, 1981), 291–96.

65. Lumsden, *Inez*, 76; Mariea Caudill Dennison, "Babies for Suffrage: The Exhibition of Painting and Sculpture by Women Artists for the Benefit of the Woman Suffrage Campaign," *Woman's Art Journal* 24, no. 2 (2004): 24; Judith Schwarz, *Radical Feminists of Heterodoxy: Greenwich Village, 1912–1940* (Norwich, VT: New Victoria Publishers, 1986), 116–28.

66. Baker, *Fighting for Life*, 182–83.

67. Wittenstein, "Heterodoxy Club," 32.

68. Dorr, *Woman of Fifty*, 271.

69. Wittenstein, "Heterodoxy Club," 49.

70. $1,200 in 1894 is the equivalent of about $35,000 in today's money. Judith Wellman, "The Sherwood Equal Rights Historic District: 'A Storm Center of Reformers'" (Sherwood: Howland Stone Store Museum, 2008), 63.

71. Judith Wellman, "The Sherwood Equal Rights Historic District: National Register Significance Statement," United States Department of the Interior, National Parks Service, n.d., 26.

72. "Woman Gives $35,000 at Suffrage Meeting," *Sun*, October 31, 1914, 1.

73. Cathleen Nista Rauterkus, *Go Get Mother's Picket Sign: Crossing Spheres with the Material Culture of Suffrage* (Lanham, MD: University Press of America, 2010), 1.

74. Finnegan, *Selling Suffrage*, 69, 124.

75. Rauterkus, *Go Get Mother's Picket Sign*, 2.

76. "Recital to Aid Woman Suffrage," *New York Times*, April 29, 1912, 11.

77. Lumsden, *Inez*, 2; DuBois, *Harriot Stanton Blatch*, 60, 86.

78. Savell, *Ladies' Lib*, 20.

79. Ibid., 28–29.

80. Antonia Petrash, *Long Island and the Woman Suffrage Movement* (Charleston, SC: The History Press, 2013), 99.

81. Ibid., 100.

82. Savell, *Ladies' Lib*, 20.

83. Gluck, *From Parlor to Prison*, 209.

84. Blatch and Lutz, *Challenging Years*, 130.

85. "Harvey Scoffs at Anti-Suffragists," *New York Times*, March 25, 1910, 5; Petrash, *Long Island*, 101.

86. Membership grew from 20,000 in 1910 to 500,000 by 1917. Ida Husted Harper, *History of Woman Suffrage*, vol. 6 (New York: J.J. Little and Ives, 1922), 459–60.

87. "The Equal Franchise Society," Scrapbook 9, p. 56, Miller National American Woman Suffrage Association Scrapbooks, 1897–1911, Library of Congress, Rare Book and Special Collections Division, Washington, DC.

88. Finnegan, *Selling Suffrage*, 88.

89. She apparently had an affair with her husband's physician, whom Mackay married in Paris in 1914. That marriage also ended in divorce and Katherine died of cancer in 1930; Petrash, *Long Island*, 103–4.

90. Blatch and Lutz, *Challenging Years*, 156.

91. "A Day's Weddings," *New York Times*, May 1, 1898, 7; "Boarman," *Daily Picayune* [New Orleans], August 15, 1875, 4.

92. DuBois, *Harriot Stanton Blatch*, 119.

93. Blatch and Lutz, *Challenging Years*, 217–18.

94. DuBois, *Harriot Stanton Blatch*, 165.

95. Ibid., 154.

96. National American Woman Suffrage Association, *Victory: How Women Won It, a Centennial Symposium, 1840–1940* (New York: H.W. Wilson Company, 1940), 115.

97. "Mrs. Edna Buckman Kearns," *Broad Ax* (Salt Lake City, Utah), September 18, 1915, 2.

98. "Suffragists Active," *Oswego Daily Palladium*, August 31, 1915, 4.

99. Virginia Scharff, *Taking the Wheel: Women and the Coming of the Motor Age* (New York: Free Press, 1991), 81.

100. Finnegan, *Selling Suffrage*, 106.

101. Moderate suffragists frequently used the color yellow, but more radical societies employed green, purple, and white, similar to the colors radical British "suffragettes" wore to represent themselves. The National Woman's Party used purple, white, and gold.

102. Finnegan, *Selling Suffrage*, 125–6.

103. Scharff, *Taking the Wheel*, 81, 192n45.

104. Ibid., 87.

105. Quoted in ibid., 82.

106. Ibid., 83.

107. Ibid., 83–84.

108. "Suffragists to Fly at Aviation Meet," *Brooklyn Daily Eagle*, July 31, 1913, 4.

109. "Suffrage Aerial Party," *New York Times*, September 7, 1913, 21; "Suffrage Aviator to Scatter Flowers," unidentified newspaper clipping, Portia Willis Berg Articles, 1913–58, and Biographical Materials, Memorabilia, box 1, folder 4, Portia Willis Fitzgerald Papers, 1913–1958, Sophia Smith Collection, Smith College, Northampton, MA.

110. "Anti-Suffrage Notes," *Skaneateles Free Press*, September 7, 1915, clipping in collection of the Skaneateles Historical Society, Skaneateles, NY.

111. Savell, *Ladies' Lib*, 26.

112. "Declaration of Rights and Sentiments," http://www.loc.gov/teachers/ classroommaterials/presentationsandactivities/presentations/timeline/expref/ crusader/seneca.html (accessed December 1, 2015); Finnegan, *Selling Suffrage*, 63.

113. Lumsden, *Inez*, 13, 15, 18.

114. Ibid., 25, 28; Ann Marie Nicolosi, "'The Most Beautiful Suffragette': Inez Milholland and the Political Currency of Beauty," *Journal of the Gilded Age and Progressive Era* 6, no. 3 (2007): 292.

115. Nicolosi, "'The Most Beautiful Suffragette,'" 288. Quotation is from Lumsden, *Inez*, 183.

116. Lumsden, *Inez*, 4.

117. Gluck, *From Parlor to Prison*, 200.

118. Ibid., 203.

119. Dorr, *Woman of Fifty*, 154.

120. Gluck, *From Parlor to Prison*, 204–5.

121. Ibid., 206.

122. Savell, *Ladies' Lib*, 22; DuBois, *Harriot Stanton Blatch*, 153.

123. Finnegan, *Selling Suffrage*, 46, 138.

124. "Yellow Rallies is the Latest Suffrage Idea," *Sun*, August 16, 1915, 6.

125. Italics in the original. Dorr, *Woman of Fifty*, 273–74; "Women Parade and Rejoice at the End," *New York Times*, May 7, 1911, 1.

126. "Women Parade and Rejoice at the End," *New York Times*, May 7, 1911, 1.

127. Finnegan, *Selling Suffrage*, 92–93.

128. "8,000 in Great Suffrage March," *Sun*, May 5, 1912, 1.

129. Lumsden, *Inez*, 71.

130. Finnegan, *Selling Suffrage*, 52.

131. "Anti-Suffragism Gets a Hard Blow," *New York Times*, March 5, 1913, 16; Savell, *Ladies' Lib*, 38–39.

132. Lumsden, *Inez*, 87.

133. "Suffrage Pilgrims on First Day of Albany Hike," *Brooklyn Daily Eagle*, December 17, 1912, 19; "Onward Strolled the Noble 26," *Dunkirk Evening Observer*, December 17, 1912, 3; "Pilgrims' Sentries Watch for Sulzer," *Brooklyn Daily Eagle*, December 30, 1912, 4.

134. Linda Lumsden, *Rampant Women: Suffragists and the Right of Assembly* (Knoxville: University of Tennessee Press, 1997), 60–61, 78.

135. Donna Harrington-Lueker, "Finding a Market for Suffrage: Advertising and *The Revolution*, 1868–70," *Journalism History* 33, no. 3 (2007): 130, 131.

136. Ibid., 131, 138.

137. Lumsden, *Rampant Women*, 149; Miller National American Woman Suffrage Association Scrapbooks, 1897–1911, Library of Congress, Rare Book and Special Collections Division, Washington, DC.

138. Carrie Chapman Catt to Dear Friend, March 29, 1915, Helen Brewster Owens Papers, Arthur and Elizabeth Schlesinger Library on the History of Women in America, Radcliffe Institute for Advanced Study, Harvard University.

139. Theodore Peterson, *Magazines in the Twentieth Century* (Urbana: University of Illinois Press, 1956), 144.

140. "Pictorial Review," *Dry Goods Economist* 69, Issue 3700–3707, June 19, 1915; Linda Scott, *Fresh Lipstick: Redressing Fashion and Feminism* (New York: Palgrave, 2005), 144; Kathleen L. Endres and Therese L. Lueck, *Women's Periodicals in the United States: Consumer Magazines* (Westport, CT: Greenwood Press, 1995), 275.

141. Finnegan, *Selling Suffrage*, 47.

142. Broadside, *Mr. Edson R. Miles and a Cast of Amateurs in the Comedy, How the Vote was Won Saturday, August 26, 1911*. Oversize Box, Clinton Political Equality Club Papers, Clinton Historical Society, Clinton, NY.

143. "Suffrage Matinee for Elliot Theatre," *New York Times*, March 25, 1910, 5.

144. "Shaw's Play for Benefit," *New York Times*, March 27, 1912, 13.

145. "Suffragist Cigarettes," *New York Times*, September 15, 1912, 14; "Cigarettes Start a Suffrage Row," *New York Times*, September 17, 1912, 6.

146. Finnegan, *Selling Suffrage*, 101.

147. There is a series of letters from World Film Corporation to Helen Brewster Owens regarding *Your Girl and Mine*, a popular suffrage play scheduled to be shown in ten to thirty towns in the upper state territory. H. J. Sheporwich to Helen Brewster Owens, March 26, 1915, Helen Brewster Owens Papers, Arthur and Elizabeth Schlesinger Library on the History of Women in America, Radcliffe Institute for Advanced Study, Harvard University, Cambridge, MA.

148. "Dr. Shaw and Miss Addams in Suffrage Photoplay," *Brooklyn Daily Eagle*, May 30, 1912, 16; Finnegan, *Selling Suffrage*, 90.

149. Laura Prieto, *At Home in the Studio: The Professionalization of Women Artists in America* (Cambridge, MA: Harvard University Press, 2001), 167.

150. Ibid., 10.

151. Ibid., 186.

152. Elisabeth Israels Perry, "Introduction: Image, Rhetoric, and the Historical Memory of Women," in Sheppard, *Cartooning for Suffrage*, 6.

153. Jane Grant, "Preston, May Wilson," *Notable American Women, 1607–1950*, vol. 3, ed. Edward T. James, Janet Wilson James, and Paul S. Boyer (Cambridge, MA: Harvard University Press, 1971), 99–100; Mary Chapman and Angela Mills, eds., *Treacherous Texts: U.S. Suffrage Literature, 1846–1946* (New Brunswick, NJ: Rutgers University Press, 2012), 231. Catt writes "Give my love (May I) to the Suffragette's husband." Carrie Chapman Catt to Gertrude Foster Brown, December 30, 1916, series 2, Correspondence, box 1, folder 2, Carrie Chapman Catt Papers, Sophia Smith Collection, Smith College, Northampton, MA. Personal email correspondence with Mary Chapman regarding her sense that the newspaperman Arthur Brown authored the book illustrated by Preston (dated March 4, 2016).

154. Charlotte Streifer Rubinstein, *American Women Artists from Early Indian Times to the Present* (Boston, MA: G.K. Hall, 1982), 165–66, 171.

155. "Exhibition for Cause of Woman Suffrage," *New York Times Magazine*, September 26, 1915, 21; Dennison, "Babies for Suffrage," 25–26.

156. Quoted in Dennison, 25.

157. Ibid., 28.

158. Ibid., 27.

159. Some sources claim that membership probably came near the one million mark, but that it is virtually impossible to obtain an accurate count of suffragists. "Adding Up," and "A Million Appeal to the Voters of New York for Justice" Cornell Broadside, Empire State Campaign Committee (1915), box 1, New York Woman Suffrage Collection, 1914–1915, Collection 8041, Division of Rare and Manuscript Collections, Carl A. Kroch Library, Cornell University, Ithaca, NY.

160. Carrie Chapman Catt and Nettie Rogers Shuler, *Woman Suffrage and Politics: The Inner Story of the Suffrage Movement* (New York: Charles Scribner's Sons, 1926), 284. See also Endres and Lueck, *Women's Periodicals*, 456–57.

161. Catt served the National American Woman Suffrage Association as president from 1900 to 1904 and again from 1915 to 1920. Anna Howard Shaw assumed the presidency in the interim. Trisha Franzen, *Anna Howard Shaw: The Work of Woman Suffrage* (Urbana: University of Illinois Press, 2014), 162, 167–70.

162. McDonald points out that the idea to use a hierarchal structure to organize suffrage supporters originated with Matilda Joslyn Gage in 1869 but it did not find support in her lifetime. David Kevin McDonald, "Organizing Womanhood: Women's Culture and the Politics of Woman Suffrage in New York State, 1865–1917" (PhD diss., State University of New York at Stony Brook, 1987), 127.

163. Moats discusses a number of reasons for Blatch opting out of the Empire State Campaign Committee. DuBois, *Harriot Stanton Blatch*, 161–64, 168; McDonald, "Organizing Womanhood," 147; Sandra Ann Moats, "The New York Suffrage Campaign of 1915" (MA Thesis, Smith College, 1994), 33–35.

164. Savell, *Ladies' Lib*, 42, 52.

7. The Great Interruption

1. Rheta Childe Dorr, *A Woman of Fifty* (New York: Funk & Wagnalls, 1924), 306.

2. Ibid., 307–8.

3. Ibid., 308.

4. Nell Irvin Painter, *Standing at Armageddon: The United States, 1877–1919* (New York: W.W. Norton, 1987), 299.

5. Barbara J. Steinson, *American Women's Activism in World War I* (New York: Garland Publishing, 1982), 14.

6. "Women and War," *Woman Voter* 5, no. 9 (September 1914): 7.

7. Margaret Finnegan, *Selling Suffrage: Consumer Culture & Votes for Women* (New York: Columbia University Press, 1999), 170–71.

8. National American Woman Suffrage Association, *Victory: How Women Won It, a Centennial Symposium, 1840–1940* (New York: H.W. Wilson Company, 1940), 118.

9. See, for example, Thomas J. Jablonsky, "Duty, Nature, and Stability: Female Anti-Suffragists in the United States, 1894–1920" (PhD diss., University of Southern California, 1978), 93; Jacqueline Van Voris, *Carrie Chapman Catt: A Public Life* (New York: Feminist Press at the City University of New York, 1987), 145; Susan E. Marshall, *Splintered Sisterhood: Gender and Class in the Campaign against Woman Suffrage* (Madison: University of Wisconsin Press, 1997), 199.

10. Sara Hunter Graham, *Woman Suffrage and the New Democracy* (New Haven: Yale University Press, 1996), 105; "Two Studies in Patriotism," *Woman's Protest* 5, no. 1 (May 1914): 20.

11. Painter, *Standing at Armageddon*, 282.

12. Ibid., 283.

13. Ibid., 289.

14. Ibid., 285, 287, 291.

15. "Women Denounce War with Mexico," *New York Times*, April 24, 1914, 6.

16. "Find Suffrage Tour of Cheer to Cause," *New York Times*, February 16, 1914, 6; "Will and Won't Pledge," *New York Times*, February 23, 1914, 8.

17. "Two Studies in Patriotism," 20.

18. Dorr, *Woman of Fifty*, 306.

19. National American Woman Suffrage Association, *Victory*, 118.

20. Ibid.

21. Erik Larson, *Dead Wake: The Last Crossing of the Lusitania* (New York: Crown Publishers, 2015), 330–31; S. L. A. Marshall, *World War I* (Boston: Houghton Mifflin Company, 2001), 166.

22. "Women and War," *Woman Voter* 5, no. 9 (September 1914): 7.

23. Gertrude Foster Brown, "On to Rochester," *Woman Voter* 5, no. 9 (September 1914): 15.

24. "Annual Report of the New York State Woman Suffrage Association, Forty-Sixth Annual Convention," Rochester, NY, October 12 to 16, 1914, 5; "Women and War," *Woman Voter* 5, no. 11 (November 1914): 17.

25. Marshall, *World War I*, 61.

26. Steinson, *American Women's Activism*, 165.

27. "Suffragists Jubilant Over Western Victories," *Brooklyn Daily Eagle*, November 8, 1914, 18; "$1,222,522 in Eight Relief Funds Here," *Sun*, November 21, 1914, 5.

28. Alice Hill Chittenden, "Woman's Service or Woman Suffrage," *Woman's Protest* 11, no. 1 (May 1917): 5; Sara M. Evans, *Born for Liberty: A History of Women in America* (New York: Simon & Schuster, 1989), 170; Graham, *Woman Suffrage*, 107; Steinson, *American Women's Activism*, 317–18.

29. Spencer C. Tucker, *The Great War, 1914–1918* (Bloomington: Indiana University Press, 1998), 6, 9; "Antis and the Red Cross," *New York Times*, September 4, 1914, 6.

30. "Antis Aid the Red Cross," 6; "Theatrical Notes," *New York Times*, October 15, 1914, 13.

31. See, for example, "Will You Help Save the United States Seventy Thousand Dollars a Day?" *Woman Patriot* 2, no. 13 (March 29, 1919): 8.

32. "Anti-Suffrage Response to Red Cross Appeal," *Woman's Protest* 5, no. 6 (October 1914): 9; "How Anti-Suffrage Red Cross Work Progresses," *Woman's Protest* 6, no. 1 (November 1914): 11; "Notes and Comment," *Woman's Protest* 6, no. 2 (December 1914): 15; "Directions for Red-Cross Shipments," *Woman's Protest* 6, no. 5 (March 1915): 14.

33. "An Appeal for Red Cross Funds," *Woman's Protest* 5, no. 5 (September 1914): 7–8; National American Woman Suffrage Association, *Victory*, 118; Jablonsky, "Duty, Nature, and Stability," 93; Van Voris, *Carrie Chapman Catt*, 145; Marshall, *Splintered Sisterhood*, 199; Steinson, *American Women's Activism*, 163.

34. "Call Cavell Killing a Crowning Atrocity," *New York Times*, October 23, 1915, 3.

35. Mrs. O. H. P. Belmont, "Women of Today: Are Making Their Mark as World Builders," *New York Times*, November 22, 1914, SM10.

36. "An Army of Peace," *Woman Voter* 5, no. 10 (October 1914): 5.

37. "Guard Companies that Will Lead Preparedness Parade Will Arrive in City Today," *Democrat and Chronicle*, June 9, 1916, 23; "At Preparedness Parade in Albany,"

Middletown Times-Press, June 15, 1916, 10; "Preparedness Parade Badges Had Flag with 47 Stars," *Brooklyn Daily Eagle*, June 18, 1916, 23; "50,000 in Buffalo March in Preparedness Parade," *Brooklyn Daily Eagle*, June 25, 1916, 5.

38. Grace Isabel Colbron, "Women and the Military Spirit," *Woman Voter* 5, no. 11 (November 1914): 9.

39. Susan Goodier, *No Votes for Women: The New York State Anti-Suffrage Movement* (Urbana: University of Illinois Press, 2013), 94–95.

40. Dorothy Schneider and Carl J. Schneider, *American Women in the Progressive Era, 1900–1920* (New York: Anchor Books, 1994), 213–16.

41. Unidentified newspaper clipping [Fall 1916], Annie Nathan Meyer Papers, Jacob Rader Marcus Center, American Jewish Archives, Hebrew Union College, Cincinnati, OH.

42. "Conference at the Home Economics Library," [1916?] American Home Economics Association, box 4, folder 4, Annie Nathan Meyer Papers, Jacob Rader Marcus Center, American Jewish Archives, Hebrew Union College, Cincinnati, OH.

43. "Home Economic Conference of College and Settlement Workers," March 29, 1917, Annie Nathan Meyer Papers, Jacob Rader Marcus Center, American Jewish Archives, Hebrew Union College, Cincinnati, OH.

44. Isabel Ely Lord to the Members of the Emergency Committee, May 4, 1917, Annie Nathan Meyer Papers, Jacob Rader Marcus Center, American Jewish Archives, Hebrew Union College, Cincinnati, OH.

45. Elaine F. Weiss, *Fruits of Victory: The Woman's Land Army of America in the Great War* (Washington, DC: Potomac Books, 2008), 48.

46. "Women to Organize Army of Farmerettes," *New York Tribune*, March 18, 1917, 11; Weiss, *Fruits of Victory*, 44–45.

47. Weiss, *Fruits of Victory*, 39–40, 53–55.

48. Helen Rogers Reid, as treasurer of the New York State Woman Suffrage Association, paid Louis Wien, Jr., a private detective, to investigate the Men's League Opposed to Woman Suffrage, in February and March of 1917, so both sides were suspicious of each other. Part I: container D282, box 1, folder 13492, Reid Family Papers, Manuscript Division, Library of Congress, Washington, DC; Graham, *Woman Suffrage*, 102.

49. Isabelle K. Savell, *Ladies' Lib: How Rockland Women Got the Vote* (New York: Historical Society of Rockland County, 1979), 44.

50. Richard Hofstadter, *The Paranoid Style in American Politics, and Other Essays* (New York: Alfred A. Knopf, 1965), 3; Kristy Maddux, "When Patriots Protest: The Anti-Suffrage Discursive Transformation of 1917," *Rhetoric & Public Affairs* 7, no. 3 (2004): 292.

51. Dee Garrison, *Mary Heaton Vorse: The Life of an American Insurgent* (Philadelphia, PA: Temple University Press, 1989), 87.

52. "Plan Parade for Nation's Women," *New York Tribune*, August 9, 1914, 9; "Women, in Mourning Parade, New York, As Protest Against War," *Democrat and Chronicle*, August 30, 1914, 1.

53. Frances H. Early, *A World without War: How U.S. Feminists and Pacifists Resisted World War I* (Syracuse: Syracuse University Press, 1997), xvii.

54. "Articles About," box 1, folder 6, Portia Willis Fitzgerald Papers, 1913–1958, Sophia Smith Collection, Smith College, Northampton, MA; "Women Vote for Big Peace Parade," *New York Tribune*, August 13, 1914, 9; "Sombre Parade for Peace,"

Brooklyn Daily Eagle, August 29, 1914, 2; "Women, in Mourning Parade, New York, As Protest Against War," 1; "Protesting Women March in Mourning," *New York Times*, August 30, 1914, 11.

55. Steinson, *American Women's Activism*, 13.

56. Garrison, *Mary Heaton Vorse*, 87.

57. Linda J. Lumsden, *Inez: The Life and Times of Inez Milholland* (Bloomington: Indiana University Press, 2004), 118.

58. "Antis Again Attack Suffrage Leaders," *New York Times*, October 21, 1917, 3; "Preparedness or Pacifism," *Woman's Protest* 9, no. 6 (October 1916): 19; Steinson, *American Women's Activism*, 40.

59. "Peace or Politics," *Woman's Protest* 6, no. 5 (March 1914): 4; "Notes and Comment," *Woman's Protest* 7, no. 2 (June 1915): 23; Annie Nathan Meyer, "To the Editor," *Detroit Free Press*, April 25, 1915, clipping in Scrapbook, box 20, folder 1, Annie Nathan Meyer Collection, Jacob Rader Marcus Center, American Jewish Archives, Hebrew Union College, Cincinnati, OH; Steinson, *American Women's Activism*, 40.

60. S. Josephine Baker, *Fighting for Life* (New York: MacMillan, 1939), 182; Garrison, *Mary Heaton Vorse*, 70.

61. Christine Stansell, *American Moderns: Bohemian New York and the Creation of a New Century* (New York: Henry Holt, 2000), 315.

62. Garrison, *Mary Heaton Vorse*, 70.

63. Norman Angell won the Nobel Peace Prize in 1934 for his book *The Great Illusion*, first published in 1910. Translated into twenty-five languages, the book sold over two million copies. https://www.nobelprize.org/nobel_prizes/peace/laureates/1933/angell-facts.html (accessed February 4, 2017).

64. Dorr, *Woman of Fifty*, 309.

65. Garrison, *Mary Heaton Vorse*, 88.

66. Jane Addams, Emily G. Balch, Alice Hamilton, *Women at The Hague: The International Congress of Women and Its Results* (Urbana: University of Illinois Press, 2003), xviii.

67. Garrison, *Mary Heaton Vorse*, 91.

68. The congress ultimately resulted in the formation of the Women's International League for Peace and Freedom in 1919, an organization still striving for world peace today. Addams, Balch, Hamilton, *Women at The Hague*, xxv, xxxii.

69. Born Rebecca Shelly, she changed the spelling of her surname to "Shelley" to protect her parents from embarrassment when she sought repatriation in the 1920s and 1930s. Susan Goodier, "The Price of Pacifism: Rebecca Shelley and Her Struggle for Citizenship," *Michigan Historical Review* 36, no. 1 (2010): 71–72, 81–82.

70. Steinson, *American Women's Activism*, 78–81.

71. *Henry Ford's Peace Expedition Who's Who*, December 1915 (Copenhagen: J. Cohens, Printing House, n.d.), passim.

72. "Ford Peace Mission," Katherine Devereux Blake Papers, Swarthmore Peace Collection, Swarthmore College, Swarthmore, PA.

73. "Ford Peace Mission," Katherine Devereux Blake Papers, Swarthmore Peace Collection, Swarthmore College, Swarthmore, PA.

74. Lumsden, *Inez*, 139.

75. "Conscription and the 'Conscientious Objector' to War: Facts Regarding Exemptions from Military Service under the Conscription Act," *American Union*

Against Militarism (Washington, DC, 1917); Doris Groshen Daniels, *Always a Sister: The Feminism of Lillian D. Wald* (New York: The Feminist Press, 1989), 127.

76. "Plans for Taking Military Census," *Oneonta Star*, April 12, 1917, 1; "Party Committee Men Drafted to Colors," *Kingston Daily Freeman*, April 21, 1917, 1; "Westchester's Count Entrusted to Women Volunteers," *Sun*, April 29, 1917, 49.

77. Minutes of the New York State Woman Suffrage Party, April 17, 1917, Victory Volume, box 7, n. p., Woman Suffrage Association of New York State, 1869–1919, Rare Book and Manuscript Library, Butler Library, Columbia University, New York, NY; Graham, *Woman Suffrage*, 103.

78. Finnegan, *Selling Suffrage*, 42.

79. "Federal Bill Reported," *Woman Voter* 7, no. 2 (February 1916): 8.

80. "Convention Week in Albany," *Woman Voter* 7, no. 12 (December 1916): 12.

81. "A League of Nations vs. the League of Nations," *Woman Patriot* 2, no. 14 (April 5, 1919): 4.

82. Henry A. Wise Wood, "Government A Man's Job," "Anti-Suffrage—For Positive Patriotism," Alice Hill Chittenden, "Woman's Service or Woman Suffrage," and "An Address by Hon. George W. Wickersham," *Woman's Protest* 11, no. 1 (May 1917): 4-6; Rabbi Joseph Silverman, "The Patriotism America Needs," *Woman's Protest* 11, no. 2 (June 1917): 3; Alice Hill Chittenden, "Our Duty to the State," *Woman's Protest* 10, no. 6 (April 1917): 3.

83. "Antis Again Attack Suffrage Leaders," *New York Times*, October 21, 1917, 3; "Peace or Politics," *Woman's Protest* 6, no. 5 (March 1914): 4; "Preparedness or Pacifism," *Woman's Protest* 9, no. 6 (October 1916): 19; Graham, *Woman Suffrage*, 102; Steinson, *American Women's Activitism*, 40, 175, 181–82.

84. "Pilgrims for Peace to Visit Congress," *New York Times*, February 9, 1917, 11; Evans, *Born for Liberty*, 171–72; Graham, *Woman Suffrage*, 105.

85. Quoted in Steinson, *American Women's Activitism*, 236–37.

86. Crystal Eastman to Mrs. Leigh French, February 28, 1917, Correspondence, Woman's Peace Party Collection, Swarthmore Peace Collection, Swarthmore, PA.

87. "Resolutions Passed at Meeting of the Woman's Peace Party of New York City, March 13, 1917," Series A: Historical Records, microfilm reel 12:4, box 5, Records of the Women's International League for Peace and Freedom, Woman's Peace Party Collection, Swarthmore Peace Collection, Swarthmore, PA.

88. Carrie Chapman Catt and Nettie Rogers Shuler, *Woman Suffrage and Politics: The Inner Story of the Suffrage Movement* (New York: Charles Scribner's Sons, 1926), 294; Graham, *Woman Suffrage*, 100; Van Voris, *Carrie Chapman Catt*, 138–39; Steinson, *American Women's Activitism*, 237–38. Harriot Stanton Blatch remarked that Wilson held anti-suffrage sentiments, "but [was] sufficient of a politician to wish to hide the fact." Harriot Stanton Blatch and Alma Lutz, *Challenging Years: The Memoirs of Harriot Stanton Blatch* (New York: G.P. Putnam's Sons, 1940), 249–50.

89. Evans, *Born for Liberty*, 171.

90. Ibid., 171–72; Graham, *Woman Suffrage*, 105.

91. Wilson also campaigned as the candidate of "Peace, Prosperity, and Progress." Blatch and Lutz, *Challenging Years*, 270; Ellen Carol DuBois, *Harriot Stanton Blatch and the Winning of Woman Suffrage* (New Haven: Yale University Press, 1997), 198.

92. Painter, *Standing at Armageddon*, 322–23.

93. "Women Organize Canteen," *New York Times*, March 31, 1917, 9; "The National League for Woman's Service," *Woman's Protest* 10, no. 4 (February 1917): 3.

94. "The National League for Woman's Service," *Woman's Protest* 10, no. 4 (February 1917): 3; Newspaper clippings in Scrapbook, Annie Nathan Meyer Collection, box 20, folder 1 (1913–1918), Jacob Rader Marcus Center, American Jewish Archives, Hebrew Union College, Cincinnati, OH.

95. "The National League for Woman's Service," *Woman's Protest* 10, no. 6 (April 1917), 3.

96. Steinson, *American Women's Activism*, 310–11.

97. Some members of this league trained with machine guns, organized a cavalry troop, and were, for a short time, "ready to join the Russian Women's Battalion of Death." Schneider and Schneider, *American Women in the Progressive Era*, 213–16, 220, 243; David M. Kennedy, *Over Here: The First World War and American Society* (New York: Oxford University Press, 2004), 286; William L. O'Neill, *Everyone Was Brave: A History of Feminism in America* (Chicago: Quadrangle Books, 1971), 186; Steinson, *American Women's Activitism*, 309.

98. Quoted in Graham, *Woman Suffrage*, 103.

99. National American Woman Suffrage Association, *Victory*, 118.

100. Carrie Chapman Catt, "Suffragists Oppose Twelve Hour Day," *Woman Voter* 8, no. 5 (May 1917): 18.

101. "The Woman Suffrage Party of New York City," *Woman Voter* 8, no. 5 (May 1917): 23–26.

102. "While Waiting to Fall In," *Woman Voter* 8, no. 5 (May 1917), 16.

103. "Suffragists Give $10,000 to Colored Troopers," *New York Age*, October 18, 1917, 1. $10,000 in 1917 is worth approximately $208,130 today.

104. Harriot Stanton Blatch, *Mobilizing Woman-Power* (New York: The Womans Press, 1918), 174–75.

105. Lillian Serece Williams, "Mary Morris Burnett Talbert," *Black Women in America: An Historical Encyclopedia*, ed. Darlene Clark Hine (New York: Oxford University Press, 2005), 210.

106. Carl J. Schneider and Dorothy Schneider, *Into the Breach: American Women Overseas in World War I* (New York: Viking, 1991), 214.

107. Lumsden, *Inez*, 120, 125.

108. Sandra Adickes, *To Be Young Was Very Heaven: Women in New York before the First World War* (New York: St. Martin's Press, 1997), 73.

109. Lumsden, *Inez*, 153.

110. Ibid., 150–52, 157.

111. Ibid., 163, 165, 168, 173.

112. "Woman's Peace Party Public Meeting," Broadside, Madeleine Zabriskie Doty Papers, Sophia Smith Collection, Smith College, Northampton, MA.

113. "Voteless Women in Warring Europe," 1917, Series 4, Writings, Madeleine Zabriskie Doty Papers, Sophia Smith Collection, Smith College, Northampton, MA.

114. Garrison, *Mary Heaton Vorse*, 87, 115; Mary Heaton Vorse, *A Footnote to Folly: Reminiscences of Mary Heaton Vorse* (New York: Farrar & Rinehart, 1935), 80.

115. Dorr, *Woman of Fifty*, 320, 332–43.

116. Ibid., 375–80.

117. Ibid., 395, 416–17.

118. $46,000 in 1917 is worth $957,402.76 in today's money. "Notes From the States," *Woman's Protest* 11, no. 3 (July-August 1917): 12.

119. "President Wilson Conferred at the White House" [1917], MC 356, folder 15f+, Vira Boarman Whitehouse Papers, 1889–1957, Arthur and Elizabeth Schlesinger Library on the History of Women in America, Radcliffe Institute, Harvard University, Cambridge, MA.

120. National American Woman Suffrage Association, *Victory*, 118–19.

121. Ibid., 119.

122. Graham, *Woman Suffrage*, 111; David Morgan, *Suffragists and Democrats: The Politics of Woman Suffrage in America* (East Lansing: Michigan State University Press, 1972), 112–14; Steinson, *American Women's Activitism*, 315–16.

123. Alice Hill Chittenden, "Woman's Service or Woman Suffrage," *Woman's Protest* 11, no. 1 (May 1917): 5; Mrs. Barclay Hazard, "Penalizing Patriotism," *Woman's Protest* 11, no. 2 (June 1917): 5; "Anti-Suffragist in War Relief Work," *Woman's Protest* 11, no. 2 (June 1917): 8; "A Letter to the Governor of New York," *Woman's Protest* 11, no. 4 (September 1917): 17; Graham, *Woman Suffrage*, 111; Morgan, *Suffragists and Democrats*, 112–14; Steinson, *American Women's Activitism*, 315–16.

124. National American Woman Suffrage Association, *Victory*, 118.

125. "Opposes Suffrage Parade," *New York Times*, October 4, 1917, 13.

126. "President Wilson conferred at the White House" [1917], Vira Boarman Whitehouse Collection, Arthur and Elizabeth Schlesinger Library on the History of Women in America, Radcliffe Institute, Harvard University, Cambridge, MA.

127. Christine Lunardini, *From Equal Suffrage to Equal Rights: Alice Paul and the National Woman's Party, 1910–1928* (San Jose: toExcel Press, 2000), 106–7; Doris Stevens, *Jailed For Freedom* (New York: Boni and Liveright, 1920), 59–72. See also the website "Women and Social Movements in the United States, 1600-2000" (http://womhist. alexanderstreet.com/) for biographies of many of these women, as well as for more information on picketing the White House.

128. Harriot Stanton Blatch and Alma Lutz, *Challenging Years: The Memoirs of Harriot Stanton Blatch* (New York: G. P. Putnam's Sons, 1940), 279; Graham, *Woman Suffrage*, 109.

129. "The Futile Theatricals at Washington," *Woman's Protest* 8, no. 2 (December 1915): 5; "Suffragists Traitors to Democracy," *Woman's Protest* 8, no. 2 (December 1915): 6; *Brooklyn Daily Eagle*, September 28, 1917, Ida Harper Scrapbook, folder 4, Ida Husted Harper Papers, 1898–1926, Manuscripts and Archives Division, New York Public Library, New York, NY; Jablonsky, "Duty, Nature, and Stability," 93; Van Voris, *Carrie Chapman Catt*, 145.

130. National American Woman Suffrage Association, *Victory*, 119–20.

131. Van Voris, *Carrie Chapman Catt*, 146–47; Jane Jerome Camhi, *Woman against Woman: American Anti-Suffragism, 1880–1920* (Brooklyn: Carlson Publishing, 1994), 182.

132. Alexander Keyssar, *The Right to Vote: The Contested History of Democracy in the United States* (New York: Basic Books, 2000), 216; Robert F. Wesser, *A Response to Progressivism: The Democratic Party and New York Politics, 1902–1918* (New York: New York University Press, 1986), 210.

8. Rising from the Ashes of Defeat

1. Mary Elizabeth Pidgeon to Folks, August 6, 1917, box 1, folder 6, Mary Elizabeth Pidgeon Papers, Friends Library, Swarthmore College, Swarthmore, PA.

2. Mary Elizabeth Pidgeon to Folks, Woman's Union, Auburn, New York, August 6, 1917, box 1, folder 6, Mary Elizabeth Pidgeon Papers, Friends Library, Swarthmore College, Swarthmore, PA.

3. Ibid.

4. "The Suffrage Referendum," *Brooklyn Daily Eagle*, February 24, 1916, 6.

5. Jacqueline Van Voris, *Carrie Chapman Catt: A Public Life* (New York: Feminist Press at the City University of New York, 1987), 118.

6. John Phillips Downs and Fenwick Y. Hedley, eds., *History of Chautauqua County New York, and Its People*, vol. 1 (New York: American Historical Society, 1921), 355.

7. New York State Woman Suffrage Party, Minutes of the City Committee, April 5, 1915, box 2, New York State Woman Suffrage Association, Minutes of the Woman Suffrage Party, August 30, 1915, vol. 6, box 9, Woman Suffrage Association of New York State and Woman Suffrage Party of New York City Records, 1869–1919, Rare Book and Manuscript Library, Butler Library, Columbia University, New York, NY.

8. Suffrage workers had a history of traveling to every county in New York State, as they had since the campaign before the 1894 New York State Constitutional Convention. Minutes Book, vol. 3, box 1, pp. 142–43 and Minutes Book, vol. 8, box 7, p. 366, Woman Suffrage Association of New York State and Woman Suffrage Party of New York City Records, 1869–1919, Rare Book and Manuscript Library, Butler Library, Columbia University; "Antis Happy Today," *Utica Observer*, November 3, 1915, 4.

9. "Fine Address of Dr. Anna Howard Shaw," *Ogdensburg Advance and St. Lawrence Weekly Democrat*, July 1, 1915, 2.

10. Biographies, box 17, folder S, League of Women Voters of New York State Records, 1912–1981, Rare Book and Manuscript Library, Butler Library, Columbia University.

11. "Teachers to Campaign," *New York Times*, June 23, 1915, 11;National American Woman Suffrage Association, *Victory: How Women Won It, a Centennial Symposium, 1840–1940* (New York: H.W. Wilson Company, 1940), 112.

12. Carrie Chapman Catt to District Chairs, April 13, 1915, box 3, folder 46, Helen Brewster Owens Papers, Arthur and Elizabeth Schlesinger Library on the History of Women in America, Radcliffe Institute, Harvard University.

13. Carrie Chapman Catt to Helen Brewster Owens, April 6, 1915, box 3, folder 46, Helen Brewster Owens Papers, Arthur and Elizabeth Schlesinger Library on the History of Women in America, Radcliffe Institute, Harvard University; Paula Baker, *The Moral Frameworks of Public Life: Gender, Politics, and the State in Rural New York, 1870–1930* (New York: Oxford University Press, 1991), 80–81.

14. Carrie Chapman Catt to Suffrage Worker, March 15, 1915, box 3, folder 45, Helen Brewster Owens Papers, 1867–1948, Arthur and Elizabeth Schlesinger Library on the History of Women in America, Radcliffe Institute, Harvard University.

15. Carrie Chapman Catt to Helen Brewster Owens, March 25, 1915, box 3, folder 45, p. 5, Helen Brewster Owens Papers, 1867-1948, Arthur and Elizabeth

Schlesinger Library on the History of Women in America, Radcliff Institute, Harvard University.

16. "Suffrage Indorsed by 9,000 Policemen," *New York Times*, September 19, 1915, 7; "Expects 10,000 Men in Suffrage March," *New York Times*, October 20, 1915, 2.

17. "Mrs. Catt Answers Antis for Mitchel," *New York Times*, November 1, 1915, 6.

18. "A Matter of Record," *Woman Voter* 7, no. 2 (February 1916): 23; Linda J. Lumsden, *Inez: The Life and Times of Inez Milholland* (Bloomington: Indiana University Press, 2004), 132.

19. There seems to be some discrepancy regarding the vote in Cortland County. Reports initially showed suffrage passing by a margin of nine votes. "The Defeat of Equal Suffrage," *Cortland Standard*, November 8, 1915, clipping file, Cortland County Historical Society, Cortland, NY. Later accounts showed it failed to pass. Baker, *Moral Frameworks*, 144.

20. New York State Dept. of State, Manual for the Use of the Legislature of the State of New York (Albany: Department of State, 1916): 854–55; "Notes and Comment," *Woman's Protest* 7, no. 1 (May 1915): 23; Thomas J. Jablonsky, "Duty, Nature, and Stability: Female Anti-Suffragists in the United States, 1894–1920" (PhD diss., University of Southern California, 1978), 79, 92; Baker, *Moral Frameworks*, 142–43, 145.

21. "New York Turns Down Suffrage," *Boston Daily Globe*, November 3, 1915, 4.

22. National American Woman Suffrage Association, *Victory*, 114–15.

23. "$100,000 Pledged as Suffrage Fund," *New York Times*, November 5, 1915, 1.

24. "Mrs. Blatch Pours Out Wrath on Root," *New York Times*, November 4, 1915, 3; National American Woman Suffrage Association, *Victory*, 114–15.

25. Both major parties in New York State remained officially neutral on suffrage in the 1915 campaign. Sandra Ann Moats, "The New York State Suffrage Campaign of 1915" (MA Thesis, Smith College, 1994), 37; Inez Haynes Irwin, *Angels and Amazons: One Hundred Years of American Women* (New York: Doubleday, Doran and Co., 1933), 349.

26. Carrie Chapman Catt to Chairmen, November 4, 1915 and Carrie Chapman Catt to Chairmen, November 5, 1915, Carrie Chapman Catt Papers, New York Public Library, Manuscripts and Archives Division, New York, NY; "Suffragists Fight Antis with Silence," *New York Times*, December 3, 1915, 7. Catt explained the actual pledge did not amount to $100,000; Van Voris, *Carrie Chapman Catt*, 129; "Riddle How to Use Suffrage $100,000," *Sun*, November 9, 1915, 9.

27. "Annual Report of the New York State Woman Suffrage Association: Reorganization Convention," Suffrage Collection, Series I, United States, States, New York: Organizations: New York State Woman Suffrage Party: Annual Reports, 1915–17. Sophia Smith Collection, Smith College, Northampton, MA.

28. "Women Lobbyists Won Albany Over," *New York Times*, April 24, 1916, 4.

29. "New York to Greet Suffrage Envoys," *New York Times*, November 9, 1915, 9.

30. National American Woman Suffrage Association, *Victory*, 115–17.

31. "A Matter of Record," *Woman Voter* 7, no. 2 (February 1916): 9–10; New York State Woman Suffrage Association, "Victory Campaign, 1916–1917," box 7, Woman Suffrage Association of New York State and Woman Suffrage Party of New York City Records, 1869–1919, Rare Book and Manuscript Library, Butler Library, Columbia University.

32. "Victory and Setback for Suffragists," *Poughkeepsie Eagle-News*, February 23, 1916, 1; "Suffragists Win in Assembly, But Lose in Senate," *Democrat and Chronicle*, February 23, 1916, 1; "Temporary Setback for the Suffragists," *Atlanta Constitution*, February 23, 1916, 4; "The Suffrage Referendum," *Brooklyn Daily Eagle*, February 24, 1916, 6.

33. "The Legislature and 1917," *Woman Voter* 7, no. 4 (April 1916): 7–9.

34. National American Woman Suffrage Association, *Victory*, 116–17.

35. "Women Lobbyists Won Albany Over," *New York Times*, April 24, 1916, 4.

36. New York State Government, Constitutional Convention Committee Reports 1938, V-2 Amendments Proposed to the New York State Constitution 1895–1937, VP-1, p. 64, available digitally through New York State Library, www.nysl.nysed. gov/scandocs/nysgovernment.htm (accessed July 21, 2016); "Legislature and 1917," *Woman Voter* 7, no. 4 (April 1916): 1.

37. "The New Officers," *Woman Voter* 7, no. 1 (January 1916): 9–11; Moats, "New York Suffrage Campaign of 1915," 52.

38. Evidence that Catt or her colleagues reached out to African American woman suffrage organizations is scant, although some black women joined the New York State Woman Suffrage Party. "Suffragists Give $10,000 to Colored Troopers," *New York Age*, October 18, 1917, 1.

39. David Kevin McDonald, "Organizing Womanhood: Women's Culture and the Politics of Woman Suffrage in New York State, 1865–1917" (PhD diss., State University of New York at Stony Brook, 1987), 366–69; Eleanor Flexner and Ellen Fitzpatrick, *Century of Struggle: The Woman's Rights Movement in the United States* (Cambridge: Belknap Press, 1996 [1959]), 273.

40. National American Woman Suffrage Association, *Victory*, 115.

41. The March 1916 edition of the *Woman Voter* listed Vira Boarman Whitehouse as the chair. Apparently Carrie Chapman Catt closed the door of her hotel room and wept following her acceptance of the national level presidency. Van Voris, *Carrie Chapman Catt*, 130.

42. "Mrs. Whitehouse, Suffrage Leader," *New York Times*, April 12, 1957, 25; National American Woman Suffrage Association, *Victory*, 115.

43. Finding Aid, Vira Boarman Whitehouse Papers, Arthur and Elizabeth Schlesinger Library on the History of Women in America, Radcliffe Institute, Harvard University; "Vira B. Whitehouse, 81: Woman Suffrage Leader," *Washington Post and Times Herald*, April 13, 1957, B2; Vira B. Whitehouse, *A Year as a Government Agent* (New York: Harper & Brothers Publishers, 1920), 5; Ellen Carol DuBois, *Harriot Stanton Blatch and the Winning of Woman Suffrage* (New Haven: Yale University Press, 1997), 178.

44. Helen Rogers Reid's papers are at the Library of Congress. National American Woman Suffrage Association, *Victory*, 115.

45. Carrie Chapman Catt Papers, Library of Congress, Manuscript Division, Washington, DC, quoted in Moats, "New York State Suffrage Campaign of 1915," 56.

46. "A Call to Campaign," *Woman Voter* 7, no. 5 (May 1916): 10–11.

47. "New York 1917," *Woman Voter* 7, no. 10 (October 1916): 8.

48. Jennette Howell Deal Diary, 1916, box 2, Collection 3881, Jennette Howell Deal Diaries, 1892–1941, Division of Rare and Manuscript Collections, Carl A. Kroch Library, Cornell University, Ithaca, NY.

49. "List of Enrolled Women," Series I: United States, Suffrage Collection, 1851–2009, Sophia Smith Collection, Smith College, Northampton, MA.

50. "Votes by State," 1916 Election for the Thirty-Third Term, Electoral Statistics, https://www.archives.gov/ (accessed December 5, 2015); Office of Clerks, U.S. House of Representatives, "Congressional Apportionment," 64th Congress http://www.census.gov/library/publications/1975/compendia/hist_stats_colonial-1970.html (accessed December 5, 2015).

51. McDonald, "Organizing Womanhood," 147–48, 155.

52. Mary Elizabeth Pidgeon to Folks, August 28, 1917, box 1, folder 6, Mary Elizabeth Pidgeon Papers, Friends Library, Swarthmore College, Swarthmore, PA. See letterhead designating positions for New York State Woman Suffrage Party, Eighth Campaign District, New York 1917, box 3, folder 32, Mary Elizabeth Pidgeon Papers, Friends Library, Swarthmore College, Swarthmore, PA; Fowler and Jones, "Carrie Chapman Catt," 135–37.

53. Lawrence Abbott, "How I Became Converted to Woman Suffrage," *Woman Voter* 7, no. 11 (November 1916): 14–16.

54. Abby Hamlin Abbott, Lawrence Abbott's mother, had convinced his father during the early years of their marriage that women did not need the vote. Susan Goodier, *No Votes for Women: The New York State Anti-Suffrage Movement* (Urbana: University of Illinois Press, 2013), 24.

55. Abbott, "How I Became Converted to Woman Suffrage," 14–16.

56. Suffrage Correspondence School Lessons I–XII with exam, Suffrage Collection, Series I, United States, New York: Organizations: New York State Woman Suffrage Party: Suffrage Correspondence School, 1916, Sophia Smith Collection, Smith College, Northampton, MA.

57. "The Mail-Order Suffragist," *Independent* 86, no. 3516 (April 24, 1916), 143.

58. Ibid.

59. National American Woman Suffrage Association, *Newsletter* 2, no. 2 (May 15, 1916): 4–5.

60. For examples see "25th Election District Total," and "Canvas Report, May 1915," Dorothy Hubert to Mrs. Oppenheimer, August 1917, Series I: United States, Sophia Smith Collection, Smith College, Northampton, MA.

61. Moats, "The New York Suffrage Campaign of 1915," 37–38.

62. "Woman Gives $35,000 at Suffrage Meeting," *Sun*, October 31, 1914, 1.

63. United States Department of the Interior National Park Service, "Sherwood Equal Rights Historic District: National Register of Historic Places Significance Statement," 26.

64. Rose Young, *The Record of the Leslie Woman Suffrage Commission, Inc., 1917–1929* (New York: The Leslie Woman Suffrage Commission, Inc., 1929), 59–62, 91.

65. National American Woman Suffrage Association, *Victory*, 109.

66. Moats, "The New York State Suffrage Campaign of 1915," 38.

67. Moats, "The New York State Suffrage Campaign of 1915," 38; Helen Brewster Owens Papers, Arthur and Elizabeth Schlesinger Library on the History of Women in America, Radcliffe Institute, Harvard University; Mrs. H. W. Cannon, "Report (1914)," box 1, folder 3, New York Woman Suffrage Collection, 1914–1915, Collection 8041, Division of Rare and Manuscript Collections, Carl A. Kroch Library,

Cornell University; "A Million Appeal to the Voters of New York for Justice" Cornell Broadside, Empire State Campaign Committee (1915), Jon A. Lindseth Collection of Woman Suffrage, Collection 8002, Division of Rare and Manuscript Collections, Carl A. Kroch Library, Cornell University, Ithaca, NY.

68. Violet Morawetz to Mrs. Oppenheimer, September 18, 1917, Series I: United States, Sophia Smith Collection, Smith College, Northampton, MA.

69. Sara Hunter Graham, "The Suffrage Renaissance: A New Image for a New Century, 1896–1910," in *One Woman, One Vote: Rediscovering the Woman Suffrage Movement*, ed. Marjorie Spruill Wheeler (Troutdale, OR: NewSage Press, 1995), 170–71. For more on mentoring relationships between older women and younger movement recruits see Adele Clark interview, February 28, 1964, Southern Oral History Program Collection, 4007, http://docsouth.unc.edu/sohp/G-0014-2/menu.html.

70. Carrie Chapman Catt and Nettie Rogers Shuler, *Woman Suffrage and Politics: The Inner Story of the Suffrage Movement* (New York: Charles Scribner's Sons, 1926), 263.

71. Mary Elizabeth Pidgeon to Folks, August 6, 1917, box 1, folder 6, Mary Elizabeth Pidgeon Papers, Friends Library, Swarthmore College, Swarthmore, PA.

72. Interview with Mary Elizabeth Pidgeon by Sherna Berger Gluck, Feminist History Research Project, Virtual Oral History Archive, California State University at Long Beach, 1973 (hereafter, Interview, 1973).

73. Interview, 1973.

74. "Annual Report of New York State Woman Suffrage Association, Forty-Seventh Annual Convention, November 30-December 2, 1915," box 3, folder 32, Mary Elizabeth Pidgeon Papers, Friends Library, Swarthmore College, Swarthmore, PA.

75. Interview, 1973.

76. Ibid.

77. Mary Elizabeth Pidgeon to Mother, February 25, 1917, box 1, folder 6, Mary Elizabeth Pidgeon Papers, Friends Library, Swarthmore College, Swarthmore, PA.

78. "Guests of Suffragists," *Washington Times*, February 16, 1917, 9; "Women Prepare," *Washington Herald*, February 26, 1917, 1, 3.

79. Mary Elizabeth Pidgeon to Folks, February 25, 1917, box 1, folder 6, Mary Elizabeth Pidgeon Papers, Friends Library, Swarthmore College, Swarthmore, PA; "Suffrage," *Washington Times*, January 4, 1917, 10.

80. Mary Elizabeth Pidgeon to Mother, February 20, 1917, box 1, folder 6, Mary Elizabeth Pidgeon Papers, Friends Library, Swarthmore College, Swarthmore, PA.

81. Gertrude Foster Brown to "My dear Organizer," February 23, 1917, box 3, folder 32, Mary Elizabeth Pidgeon Papers, Friends Library, Swarthmore College, Swarthmore, PA.

82. Interview, 1973. Pidgeon's parents supplemented her income in the early days of her work. See Mary Elizabeth Pidgeon to Mother, February 25, 1917, box 1, folder 6, Mary Elizabeth Pidgeon Papers, Friends Library, Swarthmore College, Swarthmore, PA.

83. McDonald, "Organizing Womanhood," 353, 423; "The Campaign in the Country," *Woman Voter* 7, no. 8 (August 1916). According to the 1910 Buffalo Census, 63% of the city's population listed as non-British immigrants.

84. New York State Woman Suffrage Association, Minutes of the Woman Suffrage Party, August 30, 1915, vol. 6, box 9, Woman Suffrage Association of New York State and Woman Suffrage Party of New York City Records, 1869–1919, Rare Book and Manuscript Library, Butler Library, Columbia University.

85. "Biographic Note," Helen Zaidee Marie Rogers Papers, 1890–1960, University Archives, State University of New York at Buffalo, Buffalo, New York; Virginia Yans-McLaughlin, *Family and Community: Italian Immigrants in Buffalo, 1880–1930* (Ithaca, NY: Cornell University Press, 1977); "Membership is Growing," *New York Age*, July 10, 1913, 1; McDonald, "Organizing Womanhood," 362.

86. "Home Gardening League Organizes to Aid U.S. in Meeting War Demand," *Buffalo Courier*, April 17, 1917, box 1, folder 6, Mary Elizabeth Pidgeon Papers, Friends Library, Swarthmore College, Swarthmore, PA.

87. Ethel Hall, New York State Woman Suffrage Party Sales Manager to Suffragists, May 2, 1917, box 3, folder 32, Mary Elizabeth Pidgeon Papers, Friends Library, Swarthmore College, Swarthmore, PA; Margaret Finnegan, *Selling Suffrage: Consumer Culture & Votes for Women* (New York: Columbia University Press, 1999), 121–28.

88. Mary Elizabeth Pidgeon to Folks, August 6, 1917, box 1, folder 6, Mary Elizabeth Pidgeon Papers, Friends Library, Swarthmore College, Swarthmore, PA.

89. Interview, 1973.

90. Violet Morawetz, Chairman of Speakers' Bureau for the New York State Woman Suffrage Party to Leaders, July 20, 1917, box 3, folder 32, Mary Elizabeth Pidgeon Papers, Friends Library, Swarthmore College, Swarthmore, PA.

91. Mary Elizabeth Pidgeon to Folks, August 6, 1917, box 1, folder 6, Mary Elizabeth Pidgeon Papers, Friends Library, Swarthmore College, Swarthmore, PA.

92. Interview, 1973; Jean H. Baker, ed. *Votes for Women: The Struggle for Suffrage Revisited* (New York: Oxford University Press, 2002), 7.

93. "Suffragists Launch Offensive This Week to Open Biggest Battle in 'Votes' War," *New York Tribune*, August 26, 1917, 9.

94. Mrs. Carrie Chapman Catt, "Text of Speech delivered at the State Suffrage Convention in Saratoga," August 30, 1917, box 3, folder 33; Mary Elizabeth Pidgeon to Folks, August 26, 1917, box 1, folder 6, Mary Elizabeth Pidgeon Papers, Friends Library, Swarthmore College, Swarthmore, PA.

95. "933,152 New York Women Ask for Ballot," *Sun*, August 30, 1917, 5; "Suffragists Launch Offensive This Week to Open Biggest Battle in 'Votes' War," 9.

96. "Colored Women Attend Suffragette Meeting," *New York Age*, September 6, 1917, 2.

97. "Suffragists Drew No Line," *New York Age*, September 20, 1917, 1–2.

98. "Colored Women Attend Suffragette Meeting," *New York Age*, September 6, 1917, 2.

99. Executive Committee of the New York State Woman Suffrage Party, "Plan to be Submitted to the State Committee," August 1917, box 3, folder 32. Mary Elizabeth Pidgeon Papers, Friends Library, Swarthmore College, Swarthmore, PA.

100. Ibid.

101. Finnegan, *Selling Suffrage*, 69, 92. "Announcement of Women's Parade, Saturday, October 27, 1917, box 3, folder 32, Mary Elizabeth Pidgeon Papers, Friends Library, Swarthmore College, Swarthmore, PA.

102. "Tammany Neutral in Suffrage Fight," *New York Times*, October 27, 1915, 6; "Tammany Hall," *City Encyclopedia of New York* (accessed March 30, 2015); Van Voris, *Carrie Chapman Catt*, 147.

103. National American Woman Suffrage Association, *Victory*, 120.

104. Baker, *Moral Frameworks*, 145; Elmer Fippin, *Rural New York* (Port Washington, NY: Kennikat Press, 1921), 348.

105. Irma Mae Griffin, *History of the Town of Roxbury* (Roxbury, New York: 1975), 135.

106. "Attention!," box 1, New York Woman Suffrage Collection, 1914–1915, Collection 8041, Division of Rare and Manuscript Collections, Carl A. Kroch Library, Cornell University, Ithaca, NY.

107. Jennie Curtis Cannon, "Report 4," box 1, New York Woman Suffrage Collection, 1914–1915, Collection 8041, Division of Rare and Manuscript Collections, Carl A. Kroch Library, Cornell University, Ithaca, NY.

108. "Catholic Opinions," (New York: National American Woman Suffrage Association, 1915), leaflet, box 5, folder 13, Jon A. Lindseth Woman Suffrage Collection, Collection 8002, Division of Rare and Manuscript Collections, Carl A. Kroch Library, Cornell University; National American Woman Suffrage Association, *Victory*, 117.

109. "Female Suffrage Notes," *New York Age*, September 27, 1917, 8.

110. Suffragists raised $90,000 between 1913 and 1915 for the Empire State Campaign. Helen Rogers Reid to Mrs. Oppenheimer, April 29, 1918, Series I, United States, Sophia Smith Collection, Smith College, Northampton, MA; National American Woman Suffrage Association, *Victory*, 117–18.

111. Sara Hunter Graham, *Woman Suffrage and the New Democracy* (New Haven: Yale University Press, 1996), 111.

112. "War Work of Women in Suffrage Movie," unidentified newspaper clipping [Summer 1917], Oversize Folder, Mary Elizabeth Pidgeon Papers, Swarthmore College Library, Swarthmore, PA.

113. "State Suffragists Denounce Pickets," *Sun*, August 31, 1917, 5.

114. The Referendum to the New York State Constitution, Art. II, Section 1, Amendment to 1894, Text Submitted to People but rejected, 1913, 1915. 1. Woman Suffrage. Amendment to 1894 Text Submitted to People and Adopted. 1917 Text Section 1. Every [male] citizen of the age of twenty-one years, who shall have been a citizen for ninety days, and an inhabitant of this state one year next preceding an election, and for the last four months a resident of the county and for the last thirty days a resident of the election district in which he *or she* may offer his *or her* vote, shall be entitled to vote at such election in the election district of which he *or she* shall at the time be a resident and not elsewhere for all officer that now or hereafter may be elective by the people, and upon all questions which may be submitted to the vote of the people, *provided however that a citizen by marriage shall have been an inhabitant of the United States for five years; and* provided that in the time of war no elector in the actual military service of the state, or of the United States, in the army or navy thereof, shall be deprived of his *or her* vote by reason of his *or her* absence from such election district; and the legislature shall have power to provide the manner in which and the time and place at which such absent electors may vote, and for the return and canvass of their votes in the election districts in which

they respectively reside. Adopted Nov. 6, 1917. Votes: for 703,129, against 600,776. *New York State Constitutional Convention*, vol. 2, *Amendments Adopted and Proposed*, 1895–1937 (1938), p. 64. Digitized by New York State Library from the Library's Collection, Albany, NY.

115. National American Woman Suffrage Association, *Victory*, 120.

116. Florence Woolston, "On With the Campaign," *Woman Voter* 7, no. 12 (December 1916).

117. Susan B. Anthony and Ida Husted Harper, eds., *History of Woman Suffrage*, vol. 4 (Indianapolis: Hollenbeck Press, 1902), 133.

118. Baker, *Moral Frameworks*, 145–46.

119. Isabelle K. Savell, *Ladies' Lib: How Rockland Women Got the Vote* (New York: Historical Society of Rockland County, 1979), 47.

Conclusion

1. Jacqueline Van Voris, *Carrie Chapman Catt: A Public Life* (New York: The Feminist Press, 1987), 142.

2. At current value, the wreath would cost over $20,000. Newspaper Clippings, Vira Boarman Whitehouse Papers, Schlesinger Library, Radcliffe Institute, Harvard University. See also "French Connection: Paul Gillot, Marcus and Company, and Gustav Manz," Carving and Casting, http://gustavmanz.blogspot.com/2012/05/french-connection-paul-gillot.html, May 7, 2012; Judith Price, *Masterpieces of American Jewelry* (Running Press: Philadelphia, PA, 2004), 31. The wreath was in a private collection in 2004 but was sold sometime after the 2004 exhibit at the American Folk Art Museum, New York, NY. The current location of the wreath is unknown. Personal email correspondence with Judith Price, dated February 8, 2017.

3. "Suffragists Dine, Put Men in Gallery," *New York Times*, November 22, 1917, 15; "Mrs. Whitehouse Will Take Emblem," *New York Times*, December 1, 1917, 13.

4. Sara Hunter Graham, *Woman Suffrage and the New Democracy* (New Haven, Yale University Press, 1996), 113–14.

5. "Online Biographical Dictionary of the Woman Suffrage Movement in the United States," *Women and Social Movements, 1600–2000*, ed. Kathryn Kish Sklar and Thomas Dublin (co-published by the Center for the Historical Study of Women and Gender, Binghamton University, and Alexander Street Press, 1917–1920), accessible online through subscribing academic libraries; Linda G. Ford, "Alice Paul and the Triumph of Militancy," in *One Woman, One Vote: Rediscovering the Woman Suffrage Movement in the Southern States*, ed. Marjorie Spruill Wheeler (Troutdale: New Sage Press, 1995), 290.

6. Personal email correspondence with Marguerite Kearns, the granddaughter of Edna Buckman Kearns and niece of Serena (dated September 14, 2016).

7. Ford, "Alice Paul," 282.

8. Doris Stevens, *Jailed for Freedom: American Women Win the Vote*, ed. Carol O'Hare (Troutdale, OR: NewSage Press: 1995 [1920]), 205-11; Jo Freeman, *A Room at a Time: How Women Entered Party Politics* (Lanham, MD: Rowman & Littlefield Publishers, 2000), 53.

9. Stevens, *Jailed for Freedom*, 98–99.

10. Ibid., 97–98.

11. Ibid., 193.

12. "Talk of Dropping Capital Pickets," *New York Times*, November 9, 1917, 13.

13. "Woodrow Wilson," White House History and Grounds, https://www.whitehouse.gov/1600/presidents/woodrowwilson (accessed September 16, 2016).

14. Kathy Peiss, *Hope in a Jar: The Making of America's Beauty Culture* (New York: Metropolitan Books, 1998), 137.

15. Vira B. Whitehouse, *A Year as a Government Agent* (New York: Harper & Brothers Publishers, 1920), 3–4.

16. In addition to disseminating war news and stories about the American cause, the film division of the Domestic Section expanded its reach to distribute war films to South America, China, Russia, and European countries. Altogether, 6,200 reels of American movies were sent to twenty-four countries to spread America's war message. Cedric Larson and James R. Mock, "The Lost Files of the Creel Committee of 1917–19," *The Public Opinion Quarterly* 3, no. 1 (January 1939): 16, 17.

17. Whitehouse, *A Year as a Government Agent*, 6.

18. Finding Aid, Helen Zaidee Rodgers Papers, 1895–1959, University Archives, State University of New York at Buffalo, Buffalo, NY; Finding Aid, Harriet Burton Laidlaw Papers, Arthur and Elizabeth Schlesinger Library on the History of Women in America, Radcliffe Institute, Harvard University; Finding Aid, Gertrude Foster Brown Papers, Arthur and Elizabeth Schlesinger Library on the History of Women in America, Radcliffe Institute, Harvard University; Vivien E. Rose, "After Suffrage: What Upstate Women Did with the Vote," unpublished paper, U.S. Department of the Interior, National Park Service, Women's Rights National Historical Park, March 27, 2010, 18.

19. Addie W. Hunton and Kathryn M. Johnson, *Two Colored Women with the American Expeditionary Forces* (Brooklyn: Brooklyn Eagle Press, n. d.); LaQuantae Davis, "Mary B. Talbert," http://www.blackpast.org/aah/talbert-mary-b-1866-1923 (accessed September 9, 2016).

20. Biography, Madeleine Zabriskie Doty Papers, 1880–1984, Sophia Smith Collection, Smith College, Northampton, MA, https://asteria.fivecolleges.edu/findaids/sophiasmith/mnsss13.html (accessed September 16, 2016).

21. Susan Goodier, *No Votes for Women: The New York State Anti-Suffrage Movement* (Urbana: University of Illinois Press, 2013), 158–59.

22. "District Organization Committee," New York State Woman Suffrage Association, 1918, box 2, Woman Suffrage Association of New York State and Woman Suffrage Party of New York City Records, 1869–1919, Rare Book and Manuscript Library, Butler Library, Columbia University.

23. "Women Voters Council of the Woman Suffrage Party of the State and the City of New York," February 1917, and "The Committee on Education for Citizenship of the Woman Suffrage Party," December 1917, box 2, Woman Suffrage Association of New York State and Woman Suffrage Party of New York City Records, 1869–1919, Rare Book and Manuscript Library, Butler Library, Columbia University.

24. "Simple Course in Citizenship at Central Jewish Institute," box 2, Woman Suffrage Association of New York State and Woman Suffrage Party of New York City Records, 1869–1919, Rare Book and Manuscript Library, Butler Library, Columbia University.

25. "Harlem Women Form Non-Partisan League," *New York Age*, March 23, 1918, 1; "Women Voters Hold First Mass Meeting," *New York Age*, April 27, 1918, 1; "Women Voters Invite Leaders to Debate, *New York Age*, May 4, 1918, 5; "Manhattan and the Bronx," *New York Age*, August 31, 1918, 8; "Negro Women in Politics," *Negro Year Book: An Annual Encyclopedia of the Negro 1918–1919*, vol. 5, ed. Monroe N. Work (Tuskegee, AL: Negro Year Book, 1919), 56.

26. "Loyal League Election," *Brooklyn Daily Eagle*, May 28, 1913, 31; "Charity Ball Held at Manhattan Casino," *New York Age*, May 2, 1912, 1; "News of Greater New York," *New York Age*, March 26, 1914, 8.

27. "Negro Women in Politics," 56; Bessye B. Bearden Papers, Manuscripts, Archives and Rare Books Division, Schomburg Center for Research in Black Culture, New York Public Library, New York, NY.

28. New York State Woman Suffrage Association, "Minutes of the Twenty-Fifth Assembly District New York City and League of Women Voters," book 2, January 20, 1916–March 5, 1917, box 11, Woman Suffrage Association of New York State and Woman Suffrage Party of New York City Records, 1869–1919, Rare Book and Manuscript Library, Butler Library, Columbia University; Nancy Schoonmaker, "League of Women Voters—New York State," box 17, League of Women Voters of New York State Records, 1912–1981, Rare Book and Manuscript Library, Butler Library, Columbia University.

29. "Woman Suffrage Party of New York City: Work Accomplished in 1918," vol. 10, box 11, Woman Suffrage Association of New York State and Woman Suffrage Party of New York City Records, 1869–1919, Rare Book and Manuscript Library, Butler Library, Columbia University.

30. "Constitution of National American Woman Suffrage Association," Article X, March 26, 1919, box 2, Woman Suffrage Association of New York State and Woman Suffrage Party of New York City Records, 1869–1919, Rare Book and Manuscript Library, Butler Library, Columbia University.

31. Louise M. Young, *In the Public Interest: The League of Women Voters, 1920–1970* (New York: Greenwood Press, 1989), 1–2, 36.

32. Anna L. Harvey, *Votes without Leverage: Women in American Electoral Politics, 1920–1970* (New York: Cambridge University Press, 1998), 98.

33. "1917: When Women Won the Right to Vote," *New York Times*, November 1, 1987, WC8.

34. Kristi Andersen, *After Suffrage: Women in Partisan and Electoral Politics before the New Deal* (Chicago: University of Chicago Press, 1996), 2.

35. Harvey, *Votes without Leverage*, 99.

36. Freeman, *A Room at a Time*, 81–82.

37. Melanie Gustafson, Kristie Miller, and Elisabeth I. Perry, *We Have Come to Stay: American Women and Political Parties, 1880–1960* (Albuquerque: University of New Mexico Press, 1999), 97.

38. Alexander Keyssar, *The Right to Vote: The Contested History of Democracy in the United States* (New York: Basic Books, 2000), 220.

39. Anna L. Harvey, "Culture or Strategy? Women in New York State Parties, 1917–1930," in Gustafson, Miller, and Perry, *We Have Come to Stay*, 88.

40. Keyssar, *Right to Vote*, 220.

41. "Dry Resolution Introduction in Legislature," *Times Herald* (Olean), January 15, 1919, 2.

42. Susan Dye Lee, "Ella Boole," *Notable American Women: The Modern Period*, Barbara Sicherman and Carol Hurd Green, eds. (Cambridge, MA: Belknap Press of Harvard University, 1980), 91–92.

43. Andersen, *After Suffrage*, 17.

44. "Ida Sammis," *Her Hat Was In the Ring! US Women Who Ran for Political Office before 1923*, http://www.herhatwasinthering.org/biography.php?id=5147 (accessed July 21, 2016).

45. "Women in Politics," *Woman Citizen* 4, no. 15 (September 13, 1919): 364; "Mary M. Lily," *Her Hat Was In the Ring! US Women Who Ran for Political Office before 1923*, http://www.herhatwasinthering.org/biography.php?id=5520 (accessed July 21, 2016).

46. Hilda R. Watrous, *Harriet May Mills (1857–1935): A Biography* (Syracuse: New York State Fair, 1984), 12–13.

47. Schneiderman found a much more welcoming political climate two decades later, when the Franklin Delano Roosevelt administration appointed her New York State secretary of labor. Annelise Orleck, *Common Sense and a Little Fire: Women and Working-Class Politics in the United States, 1900–1965* (Chapel Hill: University of North Carolina Press, 1995), 138–40, 164.

48. Finding Aid, Mary Elizabeth Pidgeon Papers, Friends Historical Library, Swarthmore College, Swarthmore, PA.

49. Young, *In the Public Interest*, 1.

50. Harvey, "Culture or Strategy?," 90.

51. Keyssar, *Right to Vote*, 218.

52. Ibid.

53. Gustafson, Miller, and Perry, *We Have Come to Stay*, 9.

54. Stevens, *Jailed for Freedom*, 198.

55. "New York Women Now Citizens!" *Friends' Intelligencer* 74 (December 8, 1917), 777.

56. New York State Woman Suffrage Association, Minutes of the Twenty-Fifth Assembly District and League of Women Voters Minutes, box 2, book 2, January 20, 1916–March 5, 1917, Woman Suffrage Association of New York State and Woman Suffrage Party of New York City Records, 1869–1919, Rare Books and Manuscript Library, Butler Library, Columbia University.

57. Jacqueline Van Voris, "Catt, Carrie Chapman," *American National Biography* online http://www.anb.org/articles/15/15-00118.html (accessed August 26, 2016).

58. Carrie Chapman Catt and Nettie Rogers Shuler, *Woman Suffrage and Politics: The Inner Story of the Suffrage Movement* (New York: Charles Scribner's Sons, 1926), 316.

59. Martha G. Stapler, "Woman Suffrage Yearbook" (New York: National Woman Suffrage Publishing Company, 1917), 22; National American Woman Suffrage Association, *Victory: How Women Won It, a Centennial Symposium, 1840–1940* (New York: H.W. Wilson Company, 1940), 124.

60. Graham, *Woman Suffrage*, 127.

61. National American Woman Suffrage Association, *Victory*, 123–54; Van Voris, *Carrie Chapman Catt*, 153–55.

62. "Voting Rights for Native Americans: Elections . . . the American Way," Library of Congress, https://www.loc.gov/teachers/classroommaterials/presentations andactivities/presentations/elections/voting-rights-native-americans.html (accessed September 18, 2016); Willard Hughes Rollings, "Citizenship and Suffrage: The Native American Struggle for Civil Rights in the American West, 1830–1965," *Nevada Law Journal* 5, no. 1, 139.

63. "S. 112, Native American Voting Rights Act of 2015," https://www.congress.gov/bill/114th-congress/senate-bill/1912 (accessed September 18, 2016).

64. See Holly J. McCammon, *The U.S. Women's Jury Movements and Strategic Adaptation: A More Just Verdict* (New York: Cambridge University Press, 2012), 38.

65. Kathryn Kish Sklar, "The Historical Foundations of Women's Power in the Creation of the American Welfare State, 1830–1930," in *Mothers of a New World: Maternalist Politics and the Origins of Welfare States*, ed. Seth Koven and Sonya Michel (New York: Routledge, 1993), 78.

 BIBLIOGRAPHY

Primary Sources

Suffrage Periodicals:
National Citizen and Ballot Box
New York State Woman Suffrage Association Newsletter (also known as the
New York Political Equality Club's Newsletter)
Revolution
Woman Citizen
Woman Voter
Woman's Journal
Women's Political World

Newspapers

Albany Times
Brooklyn Daily Eagle
Democrat and Chronicle
New York Age
New York Times
New York Tribune
New York *Sun*
Rochester Express
Syracuse Herald

Manuscript Collections

Arthur and Elizabeth Schlesinger Library on the History of Women in
America, Radcliffe Institute, Harvard University, Cambridge, MA

Anna Howard Shaw Papers
Carrie Chapman Catt Papers
Florence Ledyard Cross Kitchelt Papers
Helen Brewster Owens Papers

Mary Putnam Jacobi Papers
Matilda Joslyn Gage Papers
Maud Wood Park Papers
Vira Boarman Whitehouse Papers
Woman Suffrage Study Club Papers
Woman's Rights Collection

Canaday Library, Rare Books, Manuscripts, and Archives, Bryn Mawr College, Bryn Mawr, PA

Carrie Chapman Catt Collection
Gertrude Foster Brown, Portfolio of Advertisements
Susan Walker Fitzgerald Papers
Women's Suffrage Ephemera Collection

Clinton Historical Society, Clinton, NY

Clinton Political Equality Club Papers

Cortland County Historical Society, Cortland, NY

Suffrage Folder

Delaware Historical Society, Delhi, NY

Cannon Collection

Division of Rare and Manuscript Collections, Carl A. Kroch Library, Cornell University, Ithaca, NY

Jon A. Lindseth Woman Suffrage Collection
New York State Grange Collection
New York Woman Suffrage Collection, 1914–1915

Friends Historical Library, Swarthmore College Archives, Swarthmore, PA

Friends Equal Rights Association, 1900–1917
Emily Howland Family Papers and Photographs
Mariana Wright Chapman Family Papers
Mary Elizabeth Pidgeon Papers
New York Yearly Meeting Papers

History Center, Ithaca, NY

Records of the Political Equality Club
Records of the Ithaca Women's Club
Records of the Ithaca Woman's Christian Temperance Union
Records of the Tompkins County Grange

Library of Congress, Washington, DC

　　Manuscript Division

　　　　Carrie Chapman Catt Papers
　　　　Reid Family Papers

　　Rare Book and Special Collections Division

　　　　Leonora O'Reilly Papers
　　　　Miller National American Woman Suffrage Association Suffrage
　　　　　　Scrapbooks, 1897–1911
　　　　National American Woman Suffrage Association Papers
　　　　National Women's Trade Union League Papers

New York Public Library, New York, NY

　　Manuscripts and Archives Division

　　　　Carrie Chapman Catt Papers
　　　　New York State Woman Suffrage Party Records, 1915–1919

　　Woman Suffrage Collections

Rare Book and Manuscript Library, Butler Library, Columbia University,
　　New York, NY

　　　　East Side House Records, 1851–1992
　　　　Marion Sanger Frank and A.A. Brill Papers, 1844–1960
　　　　Lillian D. Wald Papers, 1895–1936
　　　　Woman Suffrage Association of New York State and Woman Suffrage
　　　　　　Party of New York City Records, 1869–1919
　　　　League of Women Voters of New York State Records, 1912–1981

Rare Books, Special Collections and Preservation, University of Rochester
　　Library, Rochester, NY

　　　　Emma Biddlecom Sweet Papers
　　　　First Unitarian Church Collection
　　　　Lewis Street Center Papers
　　　　Rachel Foster Avery Collection
　　　　Rochester Socialist Scrapbook Collection
　　　　Susan B. Anthony Memorial Collection
　　　　Woman's Suffrage Collection

Sally Roesch Wagner collection, Matilda Joslyn Gage Center, Fayetteville, NY

Schomburg Center for Research in Black Culture, New York Public
　　Library, New York, NY

　　　　Bessye B. Bearden Papers

Harriet Tubman Research Material, 1939–1940
Maritcha Rémond Lyons, 1848–1929, and Pauline Lyons, Harry A.
    Williamson papers, 1831–1965, microfilm

Sophia Smith Collection, Smith College, Northampton, MA

Alice Morgan Wright Papers
Blake Family Papers
Carrie Chapman Catt Papers
Ethel Eyre Valentine Dreier Papers
Garrison Family Papers
Madeleine Zabriskie Doty Papers
Papers of the United States Women's Bureau
Peace Collection
Portia Willis Fitzgerald Papers, 1913–1958
Woman Suffrage Collection

Stone Store Museum, Sherwood, NY

Woman Suffrage Poster and Memorabilia Collection

Swarthmore Peace Collection, Swarthmore College, Swarthmore, PA

Katherine Devereux Blake Papers
Woman's Peace Party Collection

Vassar College Special Collections, Poughkeepsie, NY

Alma Lutz Papers
Harriot Stanton Blatch Papers
Lucy M. Salmon Papers
Susan B. Anthony Papers

Select Secondary Sources

Adams, Betty Livingston. *Black Women's Christian Activism: Seeking Social Justice in a Northern Suburb*. New York: New York University Press, 2016.
Addams, Jane, Emily G. Balch, and Alice Hamilton. *Women at The Hague: The International Congress of Women and Its Results*. 1915. Urbana: University of Illinois Press, 2003.
Adickes, Sandra. *To Be Young Was Very Heaven: Women in New York before the First World War*. New York: St. Martin's Press, 1997.
Allen, Leonard L. *History of the New York State Grange*. Watertown, NY: Hungerford-Holbrook Co., 1934.
Andersen, Kristi. *After Suffrage: Women in Partisan and Electoral Politics before the New Deal*. Chicago: University of Chicago Press, 1996.

Anthony, Susan B., and Ida Husted Harper, eds. *History of Woman Suffrage*. Vol. 4. Indianapolis: Hollenbeck Press, 1902.

Attie, Jeanie. *Patriotic Toil: Northern Women and the American Civil War*. Ithaca, NY: Cornell University Press, 1998.

Baker, Jean H. *Sisters: The Lives of America's Suffragists*. New York: Hill and Wang, 2005.

———, ed. *Votes for Women: The Struggle for Suffrage Revisited*. New York: Oxford University Press, 2002.

Baker, Paula. "The Domestication of Politics: Women and American Political Society, 1780–1920." In *Women, the State, and Welfare*, edited by Linda Gordon. Madison: University of Wisconsin Press, 1990.

———. *The Moral Frameworks of Public Life: Gender, Politics, and the State in Rural New York, 1870–1930*. New York: Oxford University Press, 1991.

Baker, S. Josephine. *Fighting for Life*. New York: MacMillan, 1939.

Banner, Lois W. *American Beauty*. New York: Alfred A. Knopf, 1983.

Basch, Norma. *In the Eyes of the Law: Woman, Marriage, and Property in Nineteenth Century New York*. Ithaca, NY: Cornell University Press, 1982.

Blair, Karen J. *The Clubwoman as Feminist: True Womanhood Redefined, 1868–1914*. New York: Holmes & Meier Publishers, 1980.

Blake, Katherine Devereux, and Margaret Louise Wallace. *Champion of Women: The Life of Lillie Devereux Blake*. New York: Fleming H. Revell Co., 1943.

Blatch, Harriot Stanton. *Mobilizing Woman-Power*. New York: The Womans Press, 1918.

Blatch, Harriot Stanton, and Alma Lutz. *Challenging Years: The Memoirs of Harriot Stanton Blatch*. New York: G.P. Putnam's Sons, 1940.

Blocker, Jack S., Jr. *American Temperance Movements: Cycles of Reform*. Boston: Twayne Publishers, 1989.

Boland, Sue. "Matilda Joslyn Gage." In *American Radical and Reform Writers*, 2nd ser., edited by Hester Lee Furey. New York: Gale Cengage Learning, 2009.

Bolden, Tonya. *Maritcha: A Nineteenth Century American Girl*. New York: Harry N. Abrams, 2005.

Bordin, Ruth. *Frances Willard: A Biography*. Chapel Hill: University of North Carolina Press, 1986.

Boris, Eileen. *Home to Work: Motherhood and the Politics of Industrial Homework in the United States*. New York: Cambridge University Press, 1994.

Brown, Hallie Q. *Homespun Heroines and Other Women of Distinction*. 1926. New York: Oxford University Press, 1988.

Buhle, Mari Jo. *Women and American Socialism, 1870–1920*. Urbana: University of Illinois Press, 1981.

Campbell, Karlyn Cohrs. *Man Cannot Speak for Her: Key Texts of the Early Feminists*, vol. 2. Westport, CT: Greenwood Press, 1989.

Camhi, Jane Jerome. *Woman against Woman: American Anti-Suffragism, 1880–1920*. Brooklyn: Carlson Publishing, 1994.

Cash, Floris Barnett. *African American Women and Social Action: The Clubwomen and Volunteerism from Jim Crow to the New Deal, 1896–1936*. Westport, CT: Greenwood Press, 2001.

Catt, Carrie Chapman, and Nettie Rogers Shuler. *Woman Suffrage and Politics: The Inner Story of the Suffrage Movement*. New York: Charles Scribner's Sons, 1926.

Chapman, Mary. *Making Noise, Making News: Suffrage Print Culture and U.S. Modernism*. New York: Oxford University Press, 2014.

Chapman, Mary, and Angela Mills, eds. *Treacherous Texts: U.S. Suffrage Literature, 1846–1946*. New Brunswick, NJ: Rutgers University Press, 2012.

Clinton, Catherine. *Harriet Tubman: The Road to Freedom*. New York: Back Bay Books, 2004.

Cogan, Jacob Katz, and Lori D. Ginzberg. "1846 Petition for Woman's Suffrage, New York State Constitutional Convention." *Signs: Journal of Women in Culture and Society* 22, no. 2 (Winter 1997): 427–39.

Cooney, Robert P. J., Jr. *Winning the Vote: The Triumph of the American Woman Suffrage Movement*. Santa Cruz, CA: American Graphic Press, 2005.

Cott, Nancy F. *The Grounding of Modern Feminism*. New Haven: Yale University Press, 1987.

——, ed. *No Small Courage: A History of Women in the United States*. New York: Oxford University Press, 2000.

Cromwell, Adelaide M. *The Other Brahmins: Boston's Black Upper Class, 1750–1950*. Fayetteville: University of Arkansas Press, 1994.

Cross, Whitney. *The Burned-over District: The Social and Intellectual History of Enthusiastic Religion in Western New York, 1800–1850*. Ithaca, NY: Cornell University Press, 1950.

Dabel, Jane E. *A Respectable Woman: The Public Roles of African American Women in 19th-Century New York*. New York: New York University Press, 2008.

Daniels, Doris Groshen. *Always a Sister: The Feminism of Lillian D. Wald*. New York: The Feminist Press, 1989.

Daniels, N. H. *The Temperance Reform and Its Great Reformers*. New York: Nelson and Phillips, 1878.

Davis, Elizabeth Lindsay. *Lifting as They Climb*. Edited by Henry Louis Gates, Jr. and Jennifer Burton. New York: G.K. Hall, 1996.

Davis, Hugh. *"We Will Be Satisfied With Nothing Less": The African American Struggle for Equal Rights in the North during Reconstruction* (Ithaca, NY: Cornell University Press, 2011).

Deegan, Mary Jo, ed. *The New Woman of Color: The Collected Writings of Fannie Barrier Williams, 1893–1918*. DeKalb: Northern Illinois University Press, 2002.

Dennison, Mariea Caudill. "Babies for Suffrage: The Exhibition of Painting and Sculpture by Women Artists for the Benefit of the Woman Suffrage Campaign." *Woman's Art Journal* 24, no. 2 (Autumn 2003–Winter 2004): 24–30.

Dinkin, Robert J. *Before Equal Suffrage: Women in Partisan Politics from Colonial Times to 1920*. Westport, CT: Greenwood Press, 1995.

Doress-Worters, Paula, ed. *Mistress of Herself: Speeches and Letters of Ernestine L. Rose, Early Women's Rights Leader*. New York: Feminist Press, 2008.

Dorr, Rheta Childe. *A Woman of Fifty*. New York: Funk & Wagnalls, 1924.

Downs, John Phillips, and Fenwick Y. Hedley, eds. *History of Chautauqua County New York and Its People*, vol. 1. New York: American Historical Society, 1921.

Drish, Ruth Ellen Williamson. "Susan B. Anthony De-Radicalizes, Re-Organizes, and Re-Unites the American Woman Suffrage Movement: 1880–1890." PhD diss., University of Iowa, 1985.

DuBois, Ellen Carol. *Feminism and Suffrage: The Emergence of an Independent Women's Movement in America, 1848–1869.* Ithaca, NY: Cornell University Press, 1978.

——, ed. *The Elizabeth Cady Stanton-Susan B. Anthony Reader: Correspondence, Writings, Speeches.* Boston: Northeastern University Press, 1992.

——. *Harriot Stanton Blatch and the Winning of Woman Suffrage.* New Haven: Yale University Press, 1997.

——. "Working Women, Class Relations, and Suffrage Militance: Harriot Stanton Blatch and the New York Woman Suffrage Movement, 1894–1909." *Journal of American History* 74, no. 1 (June 1987): 35–58.

Dudden, Faye E. *Fighting Chance: The Struggle over Woman Suffrage and Black Suffrage in Reconstruction America.* New York: Oxford University Press, 2011.

Dye, Nancy Schrom. *As Equals and as Sisters: Feminism, the Labor Movement, and the Women's Trade Union League of New York.* Columbia: University of Missouri Press, 1980.

Early, Frances H. *A World without War: How U.S. Feminists and Pacifists Resisted World War I.* Syracuse, NY: Syracuse University Press, 1997.

Eastman, Max. *Enjoyment of Living.* New York: Harper, 1948.

Eisenstein, Sarah. *Give Us Bread But Give Us Roses: Working Women's Consciousness in the United States, 1890 to the First World War.* New York: Routledge and K. Paul, 1983.

Endres, Kathleen L., and Therese L. Lueck. *Women's Periodicals in the United States: Consumer Magazines.* Westport, CT: Greenwood Press, 1995.

——. *Women's Periodicals in the United States: Social and Political Issues.* Westport, CT: Greenwood, 1996.

Epstein, Barbara Leslie. *Politics of Domesticity: Women, Evangelicalism, and Temperance in Nineteenth-Century America.* Middletown, CT: Wesleyan University Press, 1981.

Evans, Sara M. *Born for Liberty: A History of Women in America.* New York: Simon & Schuster, 1989.

Farrell, Grace. *Lillie Devereux Blake: Retracing a Life Erased.* Amherst: University of Massachusetts Press, 2002.

Finnegan, Margaret. *Selling Suffrage: Consumer Culture & Votes for Women.* New York: Columbia University Press, 1999.

Fippin, Elmer. *Rural New York.* Port Washington, NY: Kennikat Press, 1921.

Flexner, Eleanor, and Ellen Fitzpatrick. *Century of Struggle: The Woman's Rights Movement in the United States.* 1959. Cambridge, MA: Belknap Press, 1996.

Florey, Kenneth. *American Woman Suffrage Postcards: A Study and Catalog.* Jefferson, NC: McFarland and Company, 2015.

——. *Women's Suffrage Memorabilia: An Illustrated Historical Study.* Jefferson, NC: McFarland and Company, 2013.

Fowler, Robert Booth, and Spencer Jones. "Carrie Chapman Catt and the Last Years of Struggle for Woman Suffrage: The Winning Plan." In *Votes for Women: The Struggle for Suffrage Revisited.* Edited by Jean H. Baker. New York: Oxford University Press, 2002.

Franzen, Trisha. *Anna Howard Shaw: The Work of Woman Suffrage.* Urbana: University of Illinois Press, 2014.

Free, Laura E. *Suffrage Reconstructed: Gender, Race, and Voting Rights in the Civil Rights Era*. Ithaca, NY: Cornell University Press, 2015.

Freeman, Jo. *A Room at a Time: How Women Entered Party Politics*. Lanham, MD: Rowman & Littlefield Publishers, 2000.

Friedman, Walter A. *Birth of a Salesman: The Transformation of Selling in America*. Cambridge, MA: Harvard University Press, 2004.

Gallagher, Julie. *Black Women and Politics in New York City*. Urbana: University of Illinois Press, 2014.

Gardenier, Georgeanna M., and Frances W. Graham. *Two Decades: A History of the First Twenty Years' Work of the Woman's Christian Temperance Union of the State of New York, 1874–1894*. Oswego, NY: R.J. Oliphant, 1894.

Garland, Libby. "'Irrespective of Race, Color, or Sex': Susan B. Anthony and the New York State Constitutional Convention of 1867." Organization of American Historians *Magazine of History* 19, no. 2 (March 2005): 61–64.

Garner, Karen. "Equal Suffrage League." In *Organizing Black America: An Encyclopedia of African American Associations*. Edited by Nina Mjagkij. New York: Garland, 2001.

Garrison, Dee. *Mary Heaton Vorse: The Life of an American Insurgent*. Philadelphia, PA: Temple University Press, 1989.

Gay, Teri. *Strength without Compromise: Womanly Influence and Political Identity in Turn-of-the-Twentieth Century Rural Upstate New York*. New York: Ballston Lake, 2009.

Giddings, Paula. *When and Where I Enter: The Impact of Black Women on Race and Sex in America*. New York: Bantam Books, 1984.

Gifford, Carolyn De Swarte, and Amy R. Slagell, eds. *Let Something Good Be Said: Speeches and Writings of Frances E. Willard*. Urbana: University of Illinois Press, 2007.

Ginzberg, Lori D. *Untidy Origins: A Story of Woman's Rights in Antebellum New York*. Chapel Hill: University of North Carolina Press, 2005.

Gluck, Sherna. *From Parlor to Prison*. New York: Vintage Books, 1976.

Goodier, Susan. *No Votes for Women: The New York State Anti-Suffrage Movement*. Urbana: University of Illinois Press, 2013.

——. "The Price of Pacifism: Rebecca Shelley and Her Struggle for Citizenship." *Michigan Historical Review* 36, no. 1 (Spring 2010): 71–101.

Gordon, Ann D., ed. *The Selected Papers of Elizabeth Cady Stanton and Susan B. Anthony*. Vol. 1, *In the School of Anti-Slavery, 1840–1866*. New Brunswick, NJ: Rutgers University Press, 1997.

——, ed. *The Selected Papers of Elizabeth Cady Stanton and Susan B. Anthony*. Vol. 2, *Against an Aristocracy of Sex, 1866–1873*. New Brunswick, NJ: Rutgers University Press, 2000.

——, ed. *The Selected Papers of Elizabeth Cady Stanton and Susan B. Anthony*. Vol. 3, *National Protection for National Citizens, 1873 to 1880*. New Brunswick: Rutgers University Press, 2003.

——, ed. *The Selected Papers of Elizabeth Cady Stanton and Susan B. Anthony*. Vol. 4, *When Clowns Make Laws for Queens, 1880–1887*. New Brunswick, NJ: Rutgers University Press, 2006.

——, ed. *The Selected Papers of Elizabeth Cady Stanton and Susan B. Anthony*. Vol. 5, *The Place inside the Body-Politic, 1887 to 1895*. New Brunswick: Rutgers University, 2009.

——, ed. *The Selected Papers of Elizabeth Cady Stanton and Susan B. Anthony.* Vol. 6, *An Awful Hush, 1895 to 1906.* New Brunswick: Rutgers University Press, 2013.

Gordon, Elizabeth Putnam. *Women Torch-Bearers: The Story of the Woman's Christian Temperance Union.* Evanston, IL: National Woman's Christian Temperance Union, 1924.

Gordon, Lynn D. *Gender and Higher Education.* New Haven, CT: Yale University Press, 1990.

Gould, Joseph E. *The Chautauqua Movement: An Episode in the Continuing Revolution.* Albany: State University of New York Press, 1961.

Graham, Frances W. *Sixty Years of Action: A History of Sixty Years' Work of the Woman's Christian Temperance Union of the State of New York, 1874–1894.* Lockport, NY: Woman's Christian Temperance Union, 1934.

Graham, Sara Hunter. "The Suffrage Renaissance: A New Image for a New Century, 1896–1910." In *One Woman, One Vote: Rediscovering the Woman Suffrage Movement.* Edited by Marjorie Spruill Wheeler. Troutdale, OR: NewSage Press, 1995.

——. *Woman Suffrage and the New Democracy.* New Haven, CT: Yale University Press, 1996.

Grand, Sarah. "The New Aspect of the Woman Question." *North American Review* 158, no. 448 (March 1894): 270–76.

Griffith, Elisabeth. *In Her Own Right: The Life of Elizabeth Cady Stanton.* New York: Oxford University Press, 1984.

Grimes, Alan P. *The Puritan Ethic and Woman Suffrage.* New York: Oxford University Press, 1967.

Guglielmo, Jennifer. *Living the Revolution: Italian Women's Resistance and Radicalism in New York City, 1880–1945.* Chapel Hill: University of North Carolina Press, 2010.

Gustafson, Melanie, Kristie Miller, and Elisabeth I. Perry, eds. *We Have Come to Stay: American Women and Political Parties, 1880–1960.* Albuquerque: University of New Mexico Press, 1999.

Gustafson, Melanie Susan. *Women and the Republican Party, 1854–1924.* Urbana: University of Illinois Press, 2001.

Guy-Sheftall, Beverly. *Daughters of Sorrow: Attitudes toward Black Women, 1880–1920.* Brooklyn: Carlson Publishing, 1990.

Harper, Ida Husted. *History of Woman Suffrage.* Vol. 5. New York: J.J. Little and Ives, 1922.

——. *History of Woman Suffrage.* Vol. 6. New York: J.J. Little and Ives, 1922.

——. *The Life and Work of Susan B. Anthony.* Vol. I. Indianapolis: Hollenbeck Press, 1898.

——. *The Life and Work of Susan B. Anthony.* Vol. 2. Indianapolis: Hollenbeck Press, 1898.

Harrington-Lueker, Donna. "Finding a Market for Suffrage: Advertising and the *Revolution,* 1868–70." *Journalism History* 33, no. 3 (Fall 2007): 130–39.

Harvey, Anna L. *Votes without Leverage: Women in American Electoral Politics, 1920–1970.* New York: Cambridge University Press, 1998.

Hewitt, Nancy A. *Women's Activism and Social Change: Rochester, New York, 1822–1872.* Ithaca, NY: Cornell University Press, 1984.

Higginbotham, Evelyn Brooks. *Righteous Discontent: The Women's Movement in the Black Baptist Church, 1880–1920.* Cambridge, MA: Harvard University Press, 1993.

Hoffert, Sylvia D. *Alva Vanderbilt Belmont: Unlikely Champion of Women's Rights*. Bloomington: Indiana University Press, 2012.

——. *When Hens Crow: The Woman's Rights Movement in Antebellum America*. Bloomington: Indiana University Press, 1995.

Hofstadter, Richard. *The Paranoid Style in American Politics and Other Essays*. New York: Alfred A. Knopf, 1965.

Holscher, Marilyn, and Ann Jones. "Casting Off the Corset: Changes in Women's Clothing, 1880–1930." Edited by The 1890 House Museum. Cortland, NY: Graphics Plus, 1980.

Howe, Frederic C. *The Confessions of a Reformer*. New York: Quadrangle Books, 1967.

Howe, Grace PerLee. *Gone Are the Days*. Ithaca, NY: Cayuga Press, 1952.

Huston, Reeve. *Land and Freedom: Rural Society, Popular Protest, and Party Politics in Antebellum New York*. New York: Oxford University Press, 2000.

Irwin, Inez Haynes. *Angels and Amazons: One Hundred Years of American Women*. New York: Doubleday, Doran and Co., 1933.

Isenberg, Nancy. *Sex and Citizenship in Antebellum America*. Chapel Hill: University of North Carolina Press, 1998.

Jablonsky, Thomas J. "Duty, Nature, and Stability: Female Anti-Suffragists in the United States, 1894–1920." PhD diss., University of Southern California, 1978.

Jensen, Joan. "The Great Uprising in Rochester." In *A Needle, a Bobbin, a Strike: Women Needleworkers in America*. Edited by Joan Jensen and Sue Davidson. Philadelphia: Temple University Press, 1984.

Johnson, Paul E. *A Shopkeeper's Millennium: Society and Revivals in Rochester, New York, 1815–1837*. New York: Hill and Wang, 1978.

Kellogg, Charles Flint. *NAACP: A History of the National Association for the Advancement of Colored People*. Vol. I, Baltimore: Johns Hopkins Press, 1967.

Kennedy, David M. *Over Here: The First World War and American Society*. New York: Oxford University Press, 2004.

Kessler-Harris, Alice. *In Pursuit of Equity: Women, Men, and the Quest for Economic Citizenship in 20th-Century America*. New York: Oxford University Press, 2001.

——. *Out to Work: A History of Wage-Earning Women in the United States*. New York: Oxford University Press, 1982.

Keyssar, Alexander. *The Right to Vote: The Contested History of Democracy in the United States*. New York: Basic Books, 2000.

Kimmel, Michael S., and Thomas E. Mosmiller, eds., *Against the Tide: Pro-Feminist Men in the United States, 1776–1990*. Boston: Beacon Press, 1992.

Kozakiewicz, Lauren. "Political Episodes 1890–1960: Three Republican Women in Twentieth Century New York State Politics." PhD diss., University at Albany, 2007.

Kraditor, Aileen S. *The Ideas of the Woman Suffrage Movement/1890–1920*. 1965. New York: W.W. Norton, 1981.

Kramer, Steve. "Uplifting Our 'Downtrodden Sisterhood': Victoria Earle Matthews and New York City's White Rose Mission, 1897–1907." *Journal of African American History* 91, no. 3 (Summer 2006): 243–66.

Kraus, Natasha Kirsten. *A New Type of Womanhood: Discursive Politics and Social Change in Antebellum America*. Durham, NC: Duke University, 2008.

Larson, Cedric, and James R. Mock. "The Lost Files of the Creel Committee of 1917–19." *The Public Opinion Quarterly* 3, no. 1 (January 1939): 5–29.

Larson, Erik. *Dead Wake: The Last Crossing of the Lusitania*. New York: Crown Publishers, 2015.

Lumsden, Linda J. *Inez: The Life and Times of Inez Milholland*. Bloomington: Indiana University Press, 2004.

——. *Rampant Women: Suffragists and the Right of Assembly*. Knoxville: University of Tennessee Press, 1997.

Lunardini, Christine. *From Equal Suffrage to Equal Rights: Alice Paul and the National Woman's Party, 1910–1928*. San Jose: toExcel Press, 2000.

Maddux, Kristy. "When Patriots Protest: The Anti-Suffrage Discursive Transformation of 1917." *Rhetoric & Public Affairs* 7, no. 3 (Fall 2004): 283–310.

Marshall, S. L. A. *World War I*. Boston: Houghton Mifflin Company, 2001.

Marshall, Susan E. *Splintered Sisterhood: Gender and Class in the Campaign against Woman Suffrage*. Madison: University of Wisconsin Press, 1997.

Marti, Donald B. *Women of the Grange: Mutuality and Sisterhood in Rural America, 1866–1920*. Westport, CT: Greenwood Press, 1991.

McCammon, Holly J. *The U.S. Women's Jury Movements and Strategic Adaptation: A More Just Verdict*. New York: Cambridge University Press, 2012.

McCormick, Richard L. *From Realignment to Reform: Political Change in New York State, 1893–1910*. Ithaca, NY: Cornell University Press, 1979.

McDonald, David Kevin. "Organizing Womanhood: Women's Culture and the Politics of Woman Suffrage in New York State, 1865–1917." PhD diss., State University of New York at Stony Brook, 1987.

McMillen, Sally G. *Seneca Falls and the Origins of the Women's Rights Movement*. New York: Oxford University Press, 2008.

Mitchell, Michele. *Righteous Propagation: African Americans and the Politics of Racial Destiny after Reconstruction*. Chapel Hill: University of North Carolina Press, 2004.

Moats, Sandra Ann. "The New York Suffrage Campaign of 1915." MA Thesis, Smith College, 1994.

Mobley, Kendall. *Helen Barrett Montgomery: The Global Mission of Domestic Feminism*. Waco, TX: Baylor University, 2009.

Morgan, David. *Suffragists and Democrats: The Politics of Woman Suffrage in America*. East Lansing: Michigan State University Press, 1972.

National American Woman Suffrage Association. *Victory: How Women Won It, a Centennial Symposium, 1840–1940*. New York: H.W. Wilson Company, 1940.

Nicolosi, Ann Marie. "'The Most Beautiful Suffragette': Inez Milholland and the Political Currency of Beauty." *Journal of the Gilded Age and Progressive Era* 6, no. 3 (July 2007): 286–309.

O'Neill, William L. *Everyone Was Brave: A History of Feminism in America*. Chicago: Quadrangle Books, 1971.

——. *The Last Romantic: A Life of Max Eastman*. New York: Oxford University Press, 1978.

Orleck, Annelise. *Common Sense and a Little Fire: Women and Working-Class Politics in the United States, 1900–1965*. Chapel Hill: University of North Carolina Press, 1995.

Ortiz, Raymond Matthew. "Ladies and Gentle Men: The Men's League for Woman Suffrage and its Liberation of the Male Identity." MA Thesis, California State University at Fullerton, 2014.

Osterud, Grey. *Putting the Barn before the House: Women and Family Farming in Early Twentieth-Century New York*. Ithaca, NY: Cornell University Press, 2012.

Osterud, Nancy Grey. *Bonds of Community: The Lives of Farm Women in Nineteenth-Century New York*. Ithaca, NY: Cornell University Press, 1991.

Overacker, Ingrid. *The African American Church Community in Rochester, New York, 1900–1940*. Rochester: University of Rochester Press, 1998.

Painter, Nell Irvin. *Standing at Armageddon: The United States, 1877–1919*. New York: W.W. Norton, 1987.

Parker, Alison M. *Purifying America: Women, Cultural Reform, and Pro-Censorship Activism, 1873–1933*. Urbana: University of Illinois Press, 1997.

Parkerson, Donald H. *The Agricultural Transition in New York State: Markets and Migration in Mid-Nineteenth Century America*. Ames: Iowa State University Press, 1995.

Parris, Guichard and Lester Brooks. *Blacks in the City: A History of the National Urban League*. Boston: Little, Brown and Company, 1971.

Pastorello, Karen. *A Power among Them: Bessie Abramowitz Hillman and the Making of Amalgamated Clothing Workers of America*. Urbana: University of Illinois Press, 2008.

——. *The Progressives: Activism and Reform in American Society, 1893–1917*. Boston: Wiley-Blackwell, 2014.

Peiss, Kathy. *Cheap Amusements: Working Women and Leisure in Turn-of-the-Century New York*. Philadelphia, PA: Temple University Press, 1986.

——. *Hope in a Jar: The Making of America's Beauty Culture*. New York: Metropolitan Books, 1998.

Penney, Sherry H. and James D. Livingston. *A Very Dangerous Woman: Martha Wright and Women's Rights*. Amherst: University of Massachusetts Press, 2004.

Perry, Jeffrey B., ed. *A Hubert Harrison Reader*. Middletown: Wesleyan University Press, 2001.

——. *Hubert Harrison: The Voice of Harlem Radicalism, 1883–1918*. New York: Columbia University, 2009.

Peterson, Carla L. *Black Gotham: A Family History of African Americans in Nineteenth-Century New York City*. New Haven, CT: Yale University Press, 2011.

Peterson, Theodore. *Magazines in the Twentieth Century*. Urbana: University of Illinois Press, 1956.

Petrash, Antonia. *Long Island and the Woman Suffrage Movement*. Charleston, SC: The History Press, 2013.

Price, Judith. *Masterpieces of American Jewelry*. Philadelphia, PA: Running Press, 2004.

Prieto, Laura. *At Home in the Studio: The Professionalization of Women Artists in America*. Cambridge, MA: Harvard University Press, 2001.

Rauterkus, Cathleen Nista. *Go Get Mother's Picket Sign: Crossing Spheres with the Material Culture of Suffrage*. Lanham, MD: University Press of America, 2010.

Rhodes, Jane. *Mary Ann Shadd Cary: The Black Press and Protest in the Nineteenth Century*. Bloomington: Indiana University Press, 1998.

Richards, Caroline Cowles. *Village Life in America, 1852–1872, Including the Period of the American Civil War as Told in the Diary of a School-Girl*. New York: Henry Holt and Company, 1913.

Ridarsky, Christine L., and Mary M. Huth, eds. *Susan B. Anthony and the Struggle for Equal Rights*. Rochester, NY: University of Rochester Press, 2012.

Rivette, Barbara. *Fayetteville's First Woman Voter*. 1969. Fayetteville, NY: Matilda Joslyn Gage Foundation, 2006.

Rowntree, Joseph, and Arthur Sherwell. *The Temperance Problem and Social Reform*. London: Hodder and Stoughton, 1901.

Rubinstein, Charlotte Streifer. *American Women Artists from Early Indian Times to the Present*. Boston: G. K. Hall, 1982.

Rupp, Leila J. *Worlds of Women: The Making of an International Woman's Movement*. Princeton: Princeton University Press, 1997.

Savell, Isabelle K. *Ladies' Lib: How Rockland Women Got the Vote*. New York: Historical Society of Rockland County, 1979.

Scharff, Virginia. *Taking the Wheel: Women and the Coming of the Motor Age*. New York: Free Press, 1991.

Schlereth, Thomas J. *Victorian America: Transformations in Everyday Life, 1876–1915*. New York: Harper Perennial, 1991.

Schneider, Carl J., and Dorothy Schneider. *Into the Breach: American Women Overseas in World War I*. New York: Viking, 1991.

Schneider, Dorothy, and Carl J. Schneider. *American Women in the Progressive Era, 1900–1920*. New York: Anchor Books, 1994.

Schwarz, Judith. *Radical Feminists of Heterodoxy: Greenwich Village, 1912–1940*. Norwich, VT: New Victoria Publishers, 1986.

Scott, Linda. *Fresh Lipstick: Redressing Fashion and Feminism*. New York: Palgrave, 2005.

Sheppard, Alice. *Cartooning for Suffrage*. Albuquerque: University of New Mexico Press, 1994.

Sherr, Lynn. *Failure Is Impossible: Susan B. Anthony in Her Own Words*. New York: Times Books, division of Random House, 1995.

Shore, Amy. *Suffrage and the Silver Screen*. New York: Peter Lang, 2014.

Sklar, Kathryn Kish. "The Historical Foundations of Women's Power in the Creation of the American Welfare State, 1830–1930." In *Mothers of a New World: Maternalist Politics and the Origins of Welfare States*. Edited by Seth Koven and Sonya Michel. New York: Routledge, 1993.

Smith-Rosenberg, Carroll. *Disorderly Conduct: Visions of Gender in Victorian America*. New York: Oxford University Press, 1985.

Smith, J. Clay, Jr., ed. *Rebels in Law: Voices in History of Black Women Lawyers*. Ann Arbor: University of Michigan Press, 1998.

Sochen, June. *Movers and Shakers: American Women Thinkers and Activists, 1900–1970*. New York: Quadrangle Book, 1973.

Solomon, Barbara Miller. *In the Company of Educated Women: A History of Women and Higher Education in America*. New Haven, CT: Yale University Press, 1985.

Stansell, Christine. *American Moderns: Bohemian New York and the Creation of a New Century*. New York: Henry Holt, 2000.

Stanton, Elizabeth Cady. *Eighty Years and More: Reminiscences 1815–1897*. 1897. Boston, MA: Northeastern University Press, 1993.

Stanton, Elizabeth Cady, Susan B. Anthony, and Matilda Joslyn Gage, eds. *History of Woman Suffrage*. Vol. 1. New York: Fowler & Wells, 1881.

——. *History of Woman Suffrage*. Vol. 2. New York: Fowler & Wells, 1882.

——. *History of Woman Suffrage*. Vol. 3. Rochester: Susan B. Anthony, 1886.

Steinson, Barbara J. *American Women's Activism in World War I*. New York: Garland Publishing, 1982.

Sterling, Dorothy, ed. *We Are Your Sisters: Black Women in the Nineteenth Century*. New York: W.W. Norton, 1984.

Stevens, Doris. *Jailed for Freedom: American Women Win the Vote*. 1920. Troutdale, OR: New Sage Press, 1995.

Strasser, Susan. *Never Done: A History of American Housework*. New York: Henry Holt and Company, 1982.

Swift, Donald C. *Religion and the American Experience: A Social and Cultural History, 1765–1997*. Armonk, NY: M.E. Sharpe, 1998.

Terborg-Penn, Rosalyn. *African American Women in the Struggle for the Vote, 1850–1920*. Bloomington: Indiana University Press, 1998.

——. "Discontented Black Feminists: Prelude and Postscript to the Passage of the Nineteenth Amendment." In *Black Studies Reader*. Edited by Cynthia Hudley, Jacqueline Bobo, and Claudine Michel. New York: Routledge, 2004.

Tetrault, Lisa. *The Myth of Seneca Falls: Memory and the Women's Suffrage Movement, 1848–1898*. Chapel Hill: University of North Carolina Press, 2014.

Thompson, J. W. *An Authentic History of the Douglass Monument: Biographical Facts and Incidents in the Life of Frederick Douglass*. Rochester, NY: Rochester Herald Press, 1903.

Tilly, Lousie A., and Patricia Gurin, eds. *Women, Politics, and Change*. New York: Russell Sage Foundation, 1990.

Tucker, Spencer C. *The Great War, 1914–1918*. Bloomington: Indiana University Press, 1998.

Vacca, Carolyn S. *A Reform against Nature: Woman Suffrage and the Rethinking of American Citizenship, 1840–1920*. New York: Peter Lang, 2004.

Van Voris, Jacqueline. *Carrie Chapman Catt: A Public Life*. New York: Feminist Press at the City University of New York, 1987.

Venet, Wendy Hamand. *Neither Ballots nor Bullets: Women Abolitionists and the Civil War*. Charlottesville: University of Virginia Press, 1991.

Vorse, Mary Heaton. *A Footnote to Folly: Reminiscences of Mary Heaton Vorse*. New York: Farrar & Rinehart, 1935.

Wagner, Sally Roesch. *Sisters in Spirit: Haudenosaunee Influence on Early American Feminists*. Summertown, TN: Native Voices Book Publishing Company, 2001.

——. *A Time of Protest: Suffragists Challenge the Republic: 1870–1887*. Aberdeen, SD: Sky Carrier Press, 1992.

Watkins-Owens, Irma. *Blood Relations: Caribbean Immigrants and the Harlem Community, 1900–1930*. Bloomington: Indiana University Press, 1996.

Watkins, Marilyn P. *Rural Democracy: Family Farmers and Politics in Western Washington* Ithaca, NY: Cornell University Press, 1995.

Watrous, Hilda R. *Harriet May Mills (1857–1935): A Biography*. Syracuse, NY: New York State Fair, 1984.

Weiss, Elaine F. *Fruits of Victory: The Woman's Land Army of America in the Great War*. Washington, DC: Potomac Books, 2008.

Welch, Vicki S. *And They Were Related, Too: A Study of Eleven Generations of One American Family!* Bloomington, IN: Xlibris Corporation, 2006.

Wellman, Judith. *Brooklyn's Promised Land: The Free Black Community of Weeksville, New York.* New York: New York University Press, 2014.

——. *Grassroots Reform in the Burned-over District of Upstate New York.* New York: Garland, 2000.

——. *The Road to Seneca Falls: Elizabeth Cady Stanton and the First Woman's Rights Convention.* Urbana: University of Illinois Press, 2004.

——. "The Sherwood Equal Rights Historic District: 'A Storm Center of Reformers'." Sherwood: Howland Stone Store Museum, 2008.

——. "Women's Rights, Republicanism, and Revolutionary Rhetoric in Antebellum New York State." *New York History* 69 (July 1988): 353–84.

Wesser, Robert F. *A Response to Progressivism: The Democratic Party and New York Politics, 1902–1918.* New York: New York University Press, 1986.

——. *Charles Evans Hughes: Politics and Reform in New York, 1905–1910.* Ithaca, NY: Cornell University Press, 1967.

Wheeler, Marjorie Spruill. *One Woman, One Vote: Rediscovering the Woman Suffrage Movement in the Southern States.* Troutdale: New Sage Press, 1995.

Whitehouse, Vira B. *A Year as a Government Agent.* New York: Harper & Brothers Publishers, 1920.

Wilder, Craig Steven. *In the Company of Black Men: The African Influence on African American Culture in New York City.* New York: New York Univeristy Press, 2001.

Williams, Fannie Barrier. "Club Movement among Negro Women." In *The Colored American: From Slavery to Honorable Citizenship.* Edited by J. W. Gibson and W. H. Crogman. Atlanta: Hertel, Jenkins & Company, 1905.

Williams, Lillian Serece. *Strangers in the Land of Paradise: The Creation of an African American Community, Buffalo, New York, 1900–1940.* Bloomington: Indiana University Press, 1999.

Wittenstein, Kate E. "The Heterodoxy Club and American Feminism, 1912–1930." PhD diss., Boston University, 1989.

Yellin, Jean Fagan, and John C. Van Horne, eds. *The Abolitionist Sisterhood: Women's Political Culture in Antebellum America.* Ithaca, NY: Cornell University Press, 1994.

Yellis, Kenneth A. "Prosperity's Child: Some Thoughts on the Flapper." *American Quarterly* 21, no. 1 (Spring 1969): 44–64.

Young, Louise M. *In the Public Interest: The League of Women Voters, 1920–1970.* New York: Greenwood Press, 1989.

Young, Rose. *The Record of the Leslie Woman Suffrage Commission, Inc., 1917–1929.* New York: The Leslie Woman Suffrage Commission, Inc., 1929.

Zaeske, Susan. *Signatures of Citizenship: Petitioning, Antislavery, and Women's Political Identity.* Chapel Hill: University of North Carolina Press, 2003.

INDEX